Bloomsbury
Family Travel Handbook 1991

Bloomsbury Family Travel Handbook

1991

How to choose, plan and enjoy travelling at
home and abroad with your children

BLOOMSBURY

Acknowledgements

In addition to the writers who contributed to Section 1, the publishers would like to thank the following for their help in the compilation and revision of this book.

Kate Bell, Trish Burgess, Candida Clark, Alastair Cording, Rachel Crasnow, Daniel Jewesbury, Helen Goalen, Boyd Hilton, Mike Hirst, Kate Newman, Anne-Lucie Norton, Kathy Rooney, Shaie Selzer, Blanche Sibbald, Tracey Smith, Matthew Whyman, Theresa Wright.

First published in 1991
by Bloomsbury Publishing Limited, 2 Soho Square, London W1V 5DE

Copyright © 1991 by Bloomsbury Publishing

British Library Cataloguing in Publication Data

A CIP record for this book is available from the British Library

ISBN 0 7475 0744 9

Designed by Geoff Green
Typeset by Florencetype Ltd, Kewstoke, Avon
Printed by Richard Clay Ltd, Bungay, Suffolk

IMPORTANT NOTICE
Every care has been taken to ensure the accuracy of the information contained in this publication but no liability can be accepted by Bloomsbury Publishing Limited for errors or omissions of any kind. To ensure that such errors are eliminated from future editions readers are kindly invited to notify the publishers.

Contents

Preface   xi
Abbreviations   xiii

Section 1: Choosing your destination

- Introduction   3
- Albania   4
- Australia   6
- Austria   8
- Belgium   10
- Brazil   12
- Britain   13
- Bulgaria   17
- Canada   19
- China   21
- Cyprus   24
- Denmark   25
- Egypt   27
- Eire and Northern Ireland   29
- France   31
- Germany   34
- Greece   36
- Hong Kong   38
- India   40
- Israel   42
- Italy   44
- Jamaica   48
- Japan   50
- Jordan   52
- Kenya   54
- Malaysia and Singapore   57
- Malta   58
- Mauritius   60
- Mexico   62
- Morocco   65

- Nepal   67
- The Netherlands   69
- New Zealand   71
- Norway   74
- The Philippines   75
- Portugal   77
- Saudi Arabia   79
- South Africa   81
- Spain   83
- Sweden   88
- Switzerland   90
- Thailand   91
- Tunisia   93
- Turkey   97
- United States   100
- USSR   104
- West Indies   106
- Yugoslavia   108
- Zimbabwe   110
- Contributors   112

Section 2: Choosing and planning your holiday

- Where should we go and what should we do?   117
- Camping, caravan sites and mobile homes   119
- Canal holidays   128
- Car rental   133
- Coach transport and coach tours   136
- Cottages, gîtes and farmhouses   140
- Cruises   158
- Cycling   162
- Fly-drive   165
- Holiday centres   170
- Home-swapping   180
- Hotel holidays   182
- Rail travel   211
- Safaris, treks and exotic tours   220
- Sailing   227
- Skiing   231
- Special interest and activity holidays   242
- Villas and apartments   248
- Walking holidays   262

Section 3: Holiday transport

- Airports 267
- Airlines 277
- Ferries 280

For information on car rental, coaches, fly-drive holidays and railways, see relevant entries in Section 2

Section 4: Getting there

- Keeping the Kids Amused . . . and keeping your sanity *Sheila Sang* 287
- Holiday reading for kids *Wayne Jackman* 295
- Renting somewhere to stay *Kathy Rooney* 301
- Holiday insurance *Ernest Jones* 306

Section 5: Family Travel know-how

- Air travel 313
- Airports 316
- Baby-sitting 317
- Boredom 318
- Breastfeeding 319
- Clothing 320
- Coach travel 321
- Coping in cold weather 321
- Coping in hot weather 322
- Ferries 323
- Getting lost 324
- Homoeopathic medicine 324
- Long-haul travel 325
- Medical emergencies 326
- Motorail 327
- Motoring 328
- Nappies 329
- Necessities 330
- Open spaces, parks and shopping 331
- Passports 332
- Preparation 332
- Rail travel 333

- Sightseeing   334
- Skiing   335
- Travel cots   335
- Walking   336

Section 6: Medical know-how
Richard Dawood MD

- Accidents   339
- Air travel   340
- Allergy   340
- Animal bites   340
- Antibiotics   341
- Antihistamines   341
- Bee stings   341
- Blisters   342
- Blood transfusion   342
- Breastfeeding   342
- Cold climates   343
- Colds   343
- Contraception   343
- Constipation   343
- Creeping eruption   344
- Dehydration   344
- Diarrhoea   344
- Dogs   345
- Drugs and medicines abroad   345
- Dysentery   346
- Earache   346
- Fever   346
- First-aid kits   346
- Food safety   347
- Heat stroke   347
- Hepatitis   348
- Ice   348
- Injections   348
- Insects   349
- Insurance   349
- Jellyfish   350
- Jet lag   350
- Malaria   350
- Prickly heat   351

- Rabies   351
- Return home   352
- Stitches   352
- Sun   352
- Sunburn   352
- Teeth   352
- Travel sickness   352
- Vaccinations   353
- Vomiting   353
- Water   353

Section 7: Useful addresses and phone numbers   355

Section 8: International SOS

- A five-language vocabulary of 90 useful words   367

Index   377

Preface

Based on the highly successful *Family Travel*, the Bloomsbury *Family Travel Handbook* is an essential manual for all those planning to travel with children. It is packed with down-to-earth advice and helpful tips for family travellers that may help to make the holiday journey a pleasure rather than a chore.

The book is split into eight sections, organized to guide the reader through the process of choosing the type and destination of their holiday, choosing a company to travel with, preparing for departure and coping with emergencies while away from home.

The countries featured in Section One are described evocatively by the personal experiences of travelling families. Each article is full of essential information for those holidaying with children. They may not tell you what a standard guide book will think important, but the authors have tried to describe exactly what it is like to travel in each country with children. We have also included a selection of recent guide books for further information.

Section Two helps you to choose the type of holiday you would like and describes the facilities provided by many hundreds of travel companies. This exclusive survey includes sample prices to help you gauge the character of the holidays offered by the company concerned.

In Section Three, 'Holiday Transport', we describe what you can expect during your journey. This section includes an exclusive survey of facilities at airports throughout Britain. You may find your local airport far more comfortable to travel from than that suggested by the holiday brochure!

We have commissioned a series of articles for Section Four that will help you to prepare for your holiday: Sheila Sang, a highly experienced journalist and travelling mother, advises you on how to cope with your children while you are travelling and gives many handy hints picked up on her travels; Wayne Jackman, a well-known personality on children's television and capable travelling father, has compiled an extensive holiday reading list of inexpensive paperbacks graded by age, that will eliminate boredom from your journey; Ernest Jones advises families on the type of holiday insurance available; and Kathy Rooney, having just returned from a highly-successful family holiday in a Norfolk windmill, tells you how to avoid disaster when booking self-catering accommodation.

Section Five is full of practical holiday know-how, which we have arranged alphabetically. This will prove invaluable during the holiday, when you want to know what to do to avoid travel sickness, boredom, and other nightmare situations.

The straightforward advice of Dr Richard Dawood is well known. For Section Six he has compiled an A–Z of the most common holiday problems encountered by families, including such headaches as diarrhoea, insect bites and sun-stroke.

The final two sections are equally essential. Section Seven, 'Useful Addresses and Phone Numbers', will help you to obtain expert advice and information on the destination you have chosen, the type of holiday you are planning and many other holiday topics. The final section, Section Eight, gives a five-language vocabulary of 90 words that will help you to deal with family emergencies. It is often difficult to find medical vocabulary in a standard phrase book – you will find everything you need here, from allergy to vomiting!

Finally, we would like to appeal to our readers to help us to keep this book as up-to-date as possible. Please write and tell us of your holiday experiences with children (both good and bad). If you disagree with any advice or information in this book, please tell us. We will endeavour to include your views in the next edition and in this way, you may help us to raise the standard of service we expect when embarking on a family holiday.

Bon voyage and, above all, enjoy travelling with your family!

Family Travel Handbook
Bloomsbury Publishing
2 Soho Square
London
W1V 5DE
Tel: 071 494 2111

Abbreviations

Af	Africa	Gam	Gambia
ala	Alaska	Ger	Germany
Alb	Albania	Gib	Gibraltar
And	Andorra	Go	Gozo
Au	Austria	Gr	Greece
Aus	Australia	Grn	Greenland
Az	Azores		
		Haw	Hawaiian Islands
Bal	Balkans	Him	Himalayas
Bar	Barbados	HK	Hong Kong
Bel	Belgium	Hol	Holland
Ber	Bermuda	Hun	Hungary
Bl.Sea	Black Sea		
Bor	Borneo	Ice	Iceland
Brz	Brazil	Ind	India
Bul	Bulgaria	Ind.Oc.	Indian Ocean
Bur	Burma	Indo	Indonesia
		Ire	Ireland
Can	Canada	Isr	Israel
Can.Is.	Canary Islands	It	Italy
Crb	Caribbean		
Ch	China	Jap	Japan
Ch.Is.	Channel Islands	Jor	Jordan
Corf	Corfu		
Cors	Corsica	Ken	Kenya
Cub	Cuba	Kor	Korea
Cyp	Cyprus		
Cze	Czechoslovakia	Lan	Lanzarote
		Lat.Am.	Latin America
Den	Denmark	Lie	Liechtenstein
		Lux	Luxembourg
Eur	Europe		
Egy	Egypt	Mad	Madeira
		Maj	Majorca
Fal	Falkland Islands	Mal	Malta
Far	Faroes	Mly	Malaysia
Fin	Finland	Mld	Maldives
Fr	France	Mau	Mauritius
		Med	Mediterranean

Mex	Mexico	Sng	Singapore
Mor	Morocco	SL	Sri Lanka
		Sp	Spain
Nep	Nepal	Swe	Sweden
Nor	Norway	Swi	Switzerland
NZ	New Zealand	Syr	Syria
Pac.Is.	Pacific Islands	Tnz	Tanzania
Phi	Philippines	Th	Thailand
PNG	Papua New Guinea	Tib	Tibet
Pol	Poland	Tun	Tunisia
Por	Portugal	Tur	Turkey
Rom	Romania	UAE	United Arab Emirates
		UK	United Kingdom
		US	United States
S.Am.	South America	USSR	Russia
S.Pac.	South Pacific		
Sar	Sardinia	Vie	Vietnam
Sca	Scandinavia		
Sco	Scotland	W.Ind.	West Indies
Sey	Seychelles	Yem	Yemen
Sic	Sicily	Yug	Yugoslavia

Section 1

Choosing your destination

Introduction

Is it to be Spain again this year or should you try Thailand? The travel industry can offer you boundless choices of hotels and villas in Spain and Greece, but they also go to somewhat more exotic parts of the world *and* offer child discounts – so why not step out of the familiar? We firmly believe that it is possible to travel far and wide with children, but understand that parents will want practical information which is aimed at their special needs. As in any reference book the selection of what goes in and what does not is a difficult one. At first glance the choice of countries featured in this section may appear idiosyncratic, but there was method in our madness!

We have made the assumption for the purposes of this book that people are setting out from the UK, and therefore some countries feature because they have a special relationship with Britain. Not many people go on holiday to Saudi Arabia, for instance, but there are thousands of people working there from this country whose families want to visit them.

You will find the familiar holiday destinations here – France, Spain, Greece – but your wanderlust may be stimulated by the entries on the more unusual spots of the world – Nepal, Jordan, Bulgaria and Zimbabwe. Also this year we have 'double' entries on several popular countries such as France, Turkey and Spain. A special feature for Spain are separate descriptions of the Canaries and Majorca, the latter being the story of one family's holiday in a charming port town.

Fact boxes
The fact boxes provide essential information about each country's major cities, climate, languages, currency and time difference. The following terms are among those which are used to describe climate:

Continental	Wide seasonal temperature range. Reasonably predictable.
Temperate	Relatively small annual and daily temperature range. Highly variable and often unsettled.

Mediterranean	Hot dry summer and mild cool winter. Summer reliable but winter more disturbed.
Tropical	Hot throughout the year; often high humidity.
Monsoonal	As tropical with alternate dry and (very) wet seasons.
Desert	Extreme continental, with wide daily temperature range; dry.

The information given in the boxes is intended only as a rough guide. The temperatures given are the daily average for the month.

Remember, weather varies between coast and inland, and in general temperatures fall 0.6°C for every 100m increase in altitude. If you are travelling to a climate very different from what you are used to, it is advisable to do more research into what you can expect and buy the appropriate clothing to cope with it.

Albania

Capital Tirana
Major cities Scutari, Durazzo, Valona, Koritza, Elbasan
Time GMT + 1
Currency Lek (LK) = 100 quintars
Language Albanian (dialects are Tosk, Gheg)

Climate Mediterranean
Annual weather range – Tirana:
Temperature Max 31°C (Jul–Aug) Min −2°C (Jan–Feb)
Rainfall Max 211mm (Nov) Min 32mm (Jul–Aug)

Albania is a small country about the size of Wales and three-quarters of it is mountainous. Along its coast lie some of the finest sandy beaches in Europe, mile after mile after mile of them. They are certainly the best in the Adriatic and rival even those of Burnham-on-Sea.

The odd thing is that few British people (perhaps about 400 per year) think of going to Albania, yet it is well suited to a family seaside holiday with small children.

In Albania (the natives' name for their country is Shqiperia which means 'Land of the Eagles'), you must not expect sophistication. Through no fault of its own it is a comparatively poor country but the basic needs of a visitor with small children are well provided for. The national cuisine (in which the influences of Greece, Turkey and Italy are easily discernible) is very pleasant. There is a good variety of well-prepared and well-cooked food of a kind which most children find appetizing and there is a good variety of soft drinks (especially pure fruit juices). Fruit is excellent; so is the water.

In summer it is hot (or even very hot) and you can be sure of week after week of almost cloudless skies. Inland tends to be even hotter than on the coast but it is a pity to confine your holiday to the seaside. All sightseeing tours are organized by the Albanian tourist authorities and journeys up into the grandiose mountain ranges with their great gorges and ravines and noble valleys are exciting. It is worth, too, visiting some of the old cities in the uplands.

The Albanians are naturally hospitable and courteous, and your children will be more than welcome anywhere – and, as foreign visitors are so few, they will be subject to intense curiosity.

One of the pleasantest features of Albania is the wonderfully clean air. The main reason for this is that there are practically no cars (only about 500 in the whole country), though there are a number of buses and lorries. Most people walk or use a bicycle, or ride a horse, mule or donkey. The whole tempo of life is much, much slower than in Britain – or anywhere else in Europe. The 'atmosphere' is completely different from anything a visitor may have experienced in any other European country. Intelligent and observant children of four and five would find much of interest because they will be exposed to a totally strange mode of life (especially in the rural areas; for example a 100 or more village women gathering a harvest with sickle and scythe).

Diversion and entertainment for children are in short supply. You make your own, as the locals do. Emergency medical treatment is very limited and you should take all the pharmaceutical goods you think you may need.

J.A.C.

Please Note
Recent political changes are such that it is difficult to know the effect they will have on holiday makers. We would advise you to contact the relevant National Tourist Office for further details before travelling.

Recommended reading:
Albania, A Travel Guide, P. Ward (Oleander, 1985, £6.95)
Albania, T & A Dawson (Bradt, 1989, £9.95)

Antigua *see West Indies*

Australia

Capital Canberra	*Temperature* Max 26°C
Major cities Sydney, Melbourne, Brisbane, Adelaide, Perth, Darwin	(Jan–Feb) Min 8°C (Jul)
	Rainfall Max 135mm (Apr) Min 71mm (Oct)
Time GMT + 8–10	**Annual weather range** –
Currency Australian dollar (A$) = 100 cents	Southwest (Perth): mediterranean
Language English	*Temperature* Max 29°C
Climate Wide regional variation from tropical monsoon to cool temperate and deserts	(Jan–Feb) Min 9°C (Jul–Aug)
	Rainfall Max 180mm (Jun) Min 8mm (Jan)
Annual weather range – North (Darwin): tropical	**Annual weather range** – Centre (Alice Springs): desert
Temperature Max 34°C (Oct–Nov) Min 19°C (Jul)	*Temperature* Max 36°C (Dec–Jan) Min −4°C (Jul)
Rainfall Max 386mm (Jan) Min 0mm (Jul)	*Rainfall* Max 43mm (Jan) Min 8mm (Jul– Sep)
Annual weather range – Southeast (Sydney): warm temperate	

Australia is a paradise for family holidays. Once recovered from the exhausting plane journey, it's plain sailing. However, for those who have not been before, it is best to consider your mode of travel carefully. Australia is a large country and distances between places are often very considerable. For local travel, a hire car (ask for air-conditioning and, if you want one, a baby seat) is leisurely, but for interstate travel, it is advisable to use the domestic airline. You can get substantial discounts (see your travel agent for details).

Accommodation is varied and similar to the US and Canada. Motels with large family rooms are common and cots are normally available on request. The better motels have swimming pools and some have playgrounds. An alternative is the campsite or caravan park. These usually have playgrounds and sometimes swimming pools and you will probably see Ova-nite caravans which are cabins and caravans to rent at larger sites.

You will find parks in most towns with free toilets, playgrounds and picnic tables. A swimming pool, often with toddler's pool attached, is common in most towns.

Remember that the seasons are reversed in the southern hemisphere and January is hot and dusty. If your accommodation is not air-conditioned you can request a fan. I have often asked for one, sometimes with favourable results.

Supermarkets are found in every large town with fresh food supplies, long opening hours and special baby sections. In general, the cost of living is less than in the UK.

There is no national health service that covers foreign travellers and you would be well advised to include medical insurance with your travel arrangements. For minor problems, I have found the local pharmacist in small towns most helpful.

Mother's rooms and baby changing rooms are more likely to be found in department stores attached to the ladies' cloakroom – as in the UK.

If you are out and about with small children you should be aware of the hazards peculiar to Australia. You should be wary of spiders. They can be lethal in Australia so 'hands off' all creepy crawlies is the best policy to follow. Playing around long grass or wood piles is also not wise because of the snakes – there are several deadly varieties. The sun in Australia is very intense and you must monitor your children very carefully. High-factor sun-protection creams and hats are essential for the whole family.

Eating *en famille* poses no problems. Australians eat their evening meal (often called tea) from 6.00 to 6.30 p.m. Certain chain restaurants actually advertise themselves as family restaurants. Fresh fruit, vegetables, salads, grilled meat and fish are reasonably priced and commonplace. We have found cafés in small country towns excellent value for family meals. They provide good plain food and serve informal meals at all hours. Often as not the owner will be happy to prepare simpler fare for your baby. Another source of good, cheap meals is the local club where you have to be signed in. The club generally relies on revenue from visitors so the Secretary, usually found in the office, will be happy to oblige.

M.B.

Recommended reading:
Australia: A Travel Survival Guide (Lonely Planet, 1989, £12.95)
Insight Guides – Australia (APA Publications, 1990, £10.95)
The Insider's Guide to Australia, Robert Wilson (MPC, 1989, £9.99)

For further information:
Australian High Commission, Australia House, Strand, London WC2B 4LU. Tel: (071) 379 4334

Austria

Capital Vienna	**Climate** Moderate climate
Major cities Graz, Linz, Salzburg, Innsbruck	**Annual weather range** – Vienna: *Temperature* Max 25°C (Jul)
Time GMT +1	Min −4°C (Jan)
Currency Schilling (Sch) = 100 groschen	*Rainfall* Max 84mm (Jul) Min 39mm (Jan)
Language German	

Austria is, I would say, a good place for a 'safe' family holiday. For all its mountain ranges, forests and rivers, Austria is tame, almost cosy. Everything (or nearly everything) works. Public transport is efficient; communications are excellent. The hotels and inns are well run, immaculate and comfortable, but then Austrian hoteliers have few equals in the world. The restaurants and cafes are impeccably clean and efficient and produce delicious food – naturally, because Austrian restaurateurs have no peers (unless they be the Swiss). The water is drinkable. Medical facilities are first rate and chemists sell anything you might need. If your child is stung in the gullet while eating a slice of scrumptious Viennese strawberry flan *mit Schlagsahne* (whipped cream) his chances of survival are much higher here than in most places. In short, there is an absence of hazard which may be very reassuring. Moreover, the people are prompt, industrious, well-organized and obliging. Children are very welcome.

If you are confined to the towns and cities (e.g. Graz, Vienna, Salzburg, Innsbruck – fascinating places all), then of course you will find the kind of entertainment available for children that you would find in any other large urban area in Europe, but if your children can be profitably lured into museums, you will find more.

Beach life is confined to the shores of the lakes where the resorts are very well equipped. Frankly, I would not take small children to Austria unless they enjoy rustic life, walking, hiking, scrambling in streams, catching butterflies and so on. Then, you could well base yourself in one of the excellent *Gasthofes* (inns) in a village where your benign host would fill your children with nourishing food. Day trips by mountain railway and cable cars will appeal to little ones.

Other possible diversions are the festivals, such as the Corpus Christi processions on boats in the Traunsee, Hallstättersee and Abersee. Another notable Corpus Christi celebration is the Samson Procession at Tamsweg in Salzburg province. A monstrous red-haired Samson (25ft tall) dances before the Town Hall. In other villages there are stage fights between Davids and Goliaths. In Carinthia, Whit Monday is the occasion for knight-like contests between boys on horses. In the Tyrol certain villages stage carnivals with traditional dances and mumming plays.

The Tyrol is well known to the English; less well known perhaps is the Vorarlberg region at the far western end of the country. The Austrians have been at some pains to develop this part for family holidays and there is a good deal of entertainment for children in delightful surroundings. It's nothing like on the scale that the Danes have devised (see description about Denmark) but the diversions are similar: playgrounds, amusement parks, 'adventure' grounds and so forth. Austria has a well-developed tourism industry and offers accommodation in private rooms, farms, campsites, inns, pensions and all types of hotel. Most of these places have special arrangements and prices for children. There is a lot of organized entertainment for little ones, including soapbox races, medieval pageants with fire-eaters, magicians and bear tamers, puppet theatres and torchlight processions.

J.A.C.

Recommended reading:
Baedeker's Austria (AA, £10.95)
Michelin Guide to Austria (Michelin, £5.95)
Fodor's 90 – Austria (Fodor, 1990, £9.99)

For further information:
Austrian National Tourist Office, 30 St George Street, London W1R 0AL. Tel: (071) 629 0461

Barbados *see* West Indies

Belgium

Capital Brussels	**Climate** Cool temperate
Major cities Antwerp, Bruges, Ghent, Mons, Liège	**Annual weather range** – Brussels: *Temperature* Max 23°C (Jul) Min −1°C (Jan)
Time GMT + 1	
Currency Belgian franc (Bfr) = 100 centimes	*Rainfall* Max 95mm (Jul) Min 31mm (Mar)
Languages French, Dutch, German	

One thing all Belgians have in common is a fondness for their food. Coming a close second is their emphasis on family unity. In this way Belgium is very similar to France, so British families can expect a holiday where children are well catered for.

The Belgian welcome for young children is most evident in the coastal resorts and Antwerp rather than the main city of Brussels – notorious for being a lively capital with an extensive but rather expensive shopping centre. Even the picture-book towns of Ghent and Bruges cannot match the facilities available for children and their parents that can be found along the north-western coast of Belgium from Ostende to Knokke, which also incorporates the most fashionable beach spot of Knokke-Le Zoute.

Along Knokke-Le Zoute's winding promenade that seems to be endless, a wide variety of beach, playground and indoor sports are available for the youngest of age groups. The promenade, known as the *digue* is a haven for the *cuistax* lover. Cuistax can best be described as pedal-driven open-topped carts; the largest ones hold twelve people and also provide baby chairs – although these do not have pedals. Alternatively, there are enclosed play areas situated between rows of outdoor coffee bars that provide special half-portions and high chairs for children. For those families who forgot to bring games for their children there are plenty of beach toy shops to be found along the *digue*.

Further into the countryside, restaurants invariably have large gardens with an assortment of slides and swings and make the celebrated *gaufres* or waffles that can appease any screaming child. The Belgians, like the Dutch, are also great eaters of *frites* – fried potato chips served only with home-made mayonnaise – and since there are stalls at many street corners all over Belgium they are a convenient between-meals snack.

Baby supplies are readily available in Belgium in pharmacies, drugstores and supermarkets, and many of the larger department stores and *galleries* (long covered arcades of shops) are very likely to contain their own baby section. For those who enjoy baby couture, 'Dujardin' – known to its clientele as 'DJ' – is the best-known children's clothes shop (for style as well as prices). Yet it is much patronized by benevolent grandparents, for the quality and design cannot be equalled anywhere else.

Larger shops are likely to provide a mother's room, rest areas and places to leave prams, while you will find that the smaller shop, often run by a family team, will be hospitable and accommodate your needs. Most hotels will be able to provide cots with little fuss.

As a member of the EEC, the usual reciprocal arrangements apply regarding medical care. Most doctors in Belgium are specialists and there are not many general practitioners like those in the UK.

On the whole, you will find Belgian outdoor culture and desire for respectability and comfort make the country attractive for travelling with young children.

S.G.

Belgium contains not only the bustling holiday resorts of the north coast and the old world towns of Ghent and Bruges, but also miles of unspoilt wooded countryside – in particular the forests and farms of the Ardennes. It's an area of hills and dramatic river gorges, where wild boar roam in endless tracts of forest criss-crossed by miles of beautiful and well sign-posted footpaths.

If you want a country holiday, where the children can help get the milk from the farm in the morning, try renting a gîte – addresses available from Federation Touristique de Luxembourg Belge, Quai de L'Ourthe 9, 6980 La Roche en Ardenne. These holiday homes, similar to those in France, can vary from small primitive farm cottages to grand chateaux with several acres of grounds.

Eating out *en famille* is common, both at midday and in the evening, with Sunday lunch particularly popular. Meals are relatively cheap; not so snacks in cafés. Jars of baby food are easy to buy and can be good, though you may consider some varieties too sweet.

M.H.

Recommended reading:
Fodor's 90 – Belgium and Luxembourg (Fodor, 1990, £9.99)

For further information:
Belgian Tourist Office, Premier House, 2 Gayton Road, Harrow, Middlesex, HA1 2XU. Tel: (081) 861 3300

Brazil

Capital Brasilia	**Climate** Tropical with wide regional variations
Major cities São Paulo, Rio de Janeiro, Salvador, Belo Horizonte, Recife	**Annual weather range** – Rio de Janeiro:
Time GMT −2−4	*Temperature* Max 29°C (Jan–Feb) Min 17°C (Jul)
Currency Cruzeiro (Cr) = 100 centavos	*Rainfall* Max 137mm (Dec) Min 41mm (Jul)
Language Portuguese	

Brazilian life is child orientated: family life revolves around them, consumer advertising is heavily directed at them, and as a traveller in Brazil you can't fail to notice that Brazilians do regard them as a very important part of life.

So no problems when it comes to people being friendly or helpful with your children – hotels and restaurants in the major cities will provide all the necessities like cots and high chairs, and hotels will always arrange for someone (usually one of the staff) to babysit if you warn them at the beginning of the day. In the major cities too, there is no problem finding everything you need for children at fairly normal prices. Shops are open until late; most restaurants or American-style snack-bars serve some international-type food; getting around by taxi or even by bus is relatively easy too, but if you hire a car, don't expect child seats to be provided.

Outside the affluent centres of the major cities, travelling with children is another matter. Take key necessities with you and stick to food which is thoroughly cooked except for the wonderful fruit like papaya, avocado, pineapple or oranges which you should open or peel yourself. Bottled drinks will always be on offer. Never drink tap water or use ice. Malaria tablets and a vaccination against yellow fever and cholera are strongly recommended.

Distances are enormous in Brazil, and although there are some good long-distance buses (and it is an excellent way to see the country), children have limited stamina for the heat and dust. The internal air network may prove a more attractive, if a more expensive, option. The amazing Iguaçu Falls in Paraná state are a must. In Rio children love the cable-car ride up the Sugar Loaf mountain. There is a playground half way up. In Flamengo park on the waterfront there are many activities for children. And don't forget Carnival!

Wherever you are, you are likely to spend time on the beach. Take note: the sun is very strong, even if it seems very hazy, and children unused to it need very good protection and only limited exposure to start with. You may also need a strong repellent against the little beach flies which bite, particularly at dawn and dusk. Be very careful of the sea – the current or undertow can often be quite strong, and children unused to this type of sea can be easily frightened if they are tumbled by the undertow. Beware of the pickpocket teams of small children that work the main beaches.

Brazil is a magical country. Its warmhearted people, all-pervasive music, marvellous beaches and tropical vegetation make it a very special place. Most people with small children are unlikely to feel up to seeing many of the wonderful areas of Brazil which involve travel over big distances, but living very simply, and with a bit of common sense you *can* travel with children to Brazil with a minimum of fuss and have a great amount of fun.

J.M.

Recommended reading:
1990 South American Handbook (Trade & Travel, 66th edition 1990, £19.95)
South America on a Shoestring (Lonely Planet, 1986, £7.95)

For further information:
Brazilian Embassy, Information Department, 32 Green Street, London W1Y 4AT. Tel: (071) 499 0877

Britain

Capital London	**Climate** Temperate
Major cities Birmingham, Manchester, Liverpool, Bristol, Edinburgh, Glasgow, Cardiff, Belfast	**Annual weather range** – London: *Temperature* Max 22°C (Jul) Min 2°C (Jan–Feb) *Rainfall* Max 64mm (Nov) Min 37mm (Apr)
Time GMT	
Currency Pound (£) = 100 pence	
Language English	

For such a small cluster of islands, the UK is surprisingly complex. For a start, it's four countries in one – and don't let anyone persuade you that England, Scotland, Wales and Northern Ireland are all the same. The variety of scenery, accent and welcome can be astonishingly different and the people who live in these principalities will not welcome being called English.

There are many enduring myths about Britain and no doubt you've heard them all: the bad weather, the terrible food and the frosty people. It's true that the country does not boast a predictable or especially enticing climate, but it's really not as bad as it's painted. Certain areas, like Scotland, the Lake District and Wales can be rather damp, but you'd have to go an awfully long way to beat the stunning scenery. The best months to holiday in the UK are often June and September when the sun seems to try harder than usual. If warm weather is really important to you, try the Channel Islands. Although much nearer to France they are, in fact, British territory and offer a warmer climate and a friendly welcome to families with children.

Like other capital cities, London is not really indicative of the rest of the UK. Expatriates and non-Londoners complain of the dirt and dishonesty, but foreign visitors often compare it favourably with their own cities. It is reasonably safe and compact, with excellent museums and art galleries (all free). Public transport is fast and frequent, although expensive by some standards. Buy a Travel Card pass for London Transport and you can hop on and off buses and tubes all day (after 9.30 a.m.).

Restaurants in London and other major cities offer every imaginable cuisine, but the variety can be somewhat severely restricted out in the 'sticks'. Chinese take-aways and McDonald's are in virtually every provincial town, but traditional English food can be very hard to find, and apart from fish and chips, often poorly cooked. Indian cuisine, however, has taken a grip and there are ample opportunities to sample cheap and exciting menus. Eating out is not a family tradition in Britain but it is gradually becoming a more popular habit. The pub often seems to be the social centre of British life, and even the tiniest village will have one. However, some town pubs are smoke-filled male enclaves that are not particularly inviting. In Britain pubs may now stay open all day, but in some parts of Wales they may still be closed all day Sunday. Nowadays, thank goodness, the wind of change is blowing and a lot more pubs have children's rooms and/or gardens with swings. Many landlords will allow children to eat in their pubs if they have a separate eating area – but if in doubt, ask. Pub food is often only available at lunchtime and the quality varies, but it is usually hot and sustaining, if nothing else. The *Good Beer Guide* (published by CAMRA), *Good Food Guide* and *Egon Ronay* will help you to choose good places to eat.

Wherever you eat – hotel, restaurant or pub – it's unwise to expect anything to be provided for children, so take your own high chair (preferably one that clamps to the table). British people are not overtly fond of children, but then they're not overtly fond of anyone! However, they are usually polite, and it's merely the famous British reserve which can make them seem frosty.

All major cities have big and well-kept parks. They are safe and often have special play areas designated and fenced off for children. Usually there are toilets nearby. London's major parks are especially good, and in summer there are often (free) puppet shows, concerts, plays and other entertainment. Look in local papers or listings magazines for details.

Increasingly shops and public places have rest areas for children, but they are still few and far between. On the other hand, public toilets are practically a national institution and it's rare to have difficulty in finding one. If the need is desperate, large department stores always have toilet facilities.

Hotels come in all shapes and sizes, but invariably charge per person. Note that there is no universally agreed system of classification for hotels or restaurants. Cots are available in most hotels, but do not rely on finding them in guest houses without making prior arrangements. Bed and breakfast in private houses (and sometimes pubs) is an excellent British institution. Ask at the local tourist information office for details.

Despite the sometimes off-hand service, shopping for and with children can be a pleasure. Look out in particular for Sainsbury (supermarket grocers with shops in many towns), Marks and Spencer (hundreds of large stores with food and excellent value clothes), and Mothercare (a specialist chain of clothing and equipment shops for children). All sell own-brand nappies at very competitive rates and have additional ranges of baby necessities. In a pinch, late-closing corner shops sell most essentials, if rather more expensively.

Car rental agencies are plentiful (see Yellow Pages), and taxis are easy to find on streets of major cities, but you can always call a 'mini cab' from a private firm if you get stuck. If you don't know the number, dial 192 and ask for details. British Rail offers an extensive and expensive network of trains which sometimes leaves a lot to be desired in terms of punctuality and comfort, though a Family Railcard or one of the frequent Awayday bargain tickets can save you a lot of money. Coaches offer a cleaner and cheaper alternative. Air travel within the UK is very expensive, and given the short distances involved, rarely worthwhile. However, international travel from the UK is the best in the world. Heathrow is London's main airport and one of the busiest. Gatwick is smaller and used by many charter companies and cheaper carriers, such as Virgin. Although the distances within the airport are not great, it is quite a long way to the direct link railway and there are very few porters. We found this extremely frustrating at the end of an overnight flight from the US.

Britain's often maligned National Health Service will provide free medical assistance, although not all hospitals have casualty departments. As the system is under severe strain, it would be prudent for overseas visitors to take out private insurance. Emergency calls (Fire, Police, Ambulance and Coastguard) are free. Simply dial 999.

It would be foolish to limit your holiday in Britain to a frantic week spent in the centre of London. By far the best places to spend a relaxing and enjoyable holiday are away from the traditional tourist attractions of the capital (which, during the holiday months are usually full of foreign tourists and may be considered overpriced).

It would be well worth your while to contact the various British tourist offices for leaflets and brochures – we have found them unceasingly helpful and eager to ply you with information on more out-of-the-way locations and unusual activities. England, Wales and Scotland are packed full of picture-postcard scenery and, with a little advance preparation, you will find it surprisingly easy to get away from the standard tourist tracks and spend time on your own in beautiful countryside.

There are many unspoilt places in Britain and a great way to enjoy these is by renting a cottage by the week. Many companies offer country cottages all year round and, if booked in advance, cots and bunk beds are often available (*see* 'Cottages, Gîtes and Farmhouses' p. 140 for some suggestions). The regional tourist boards also organize a grading scheme and award prizes to accommodation they consider to be of a particularly high standard (further information is available in tourist board publications).

To find details of the historic buildings, monuments and gardens that are open to the public, you can contact English Heritage, Cadw (Wales) and Historic Scotland [properties owned by the Department of the Environment]. The National Trust and the National Trust for Scotland are charities that own sites of historic or environmental interest and although you may have to pay a little more for entry, it is well worth contacting them for details of the buildings and gardens they administer in the area you are visiting. (The phone numbers are in 'Useful Addresses & Phone Numbers' p. 357).

Local tourist offices (situated in larger towns throughout Britain) will tell you of events and places of interest in the area. You may be pleasantly surprised at what you find – there is a popular jazz festival each August in Brecon for instance and the National Show at Stoneleigh provides a highly enjoyable family day out.

Britain's National Parks are specially designated areas of natural beauty and you won't go far wrong for scenery if you visit one. They each run an information service and you can find their addresses from the regional tourist offices.

All in all, the countryside of Britain provides an endless variety of activities and scenery and, with a little thought, you can have an enjoyable family holiday without meeting too many other tourists!

S.S.

Recommended reading:
Blue Guide: England, Ian Onsby (A&C Black, 1989, £20.00)
Insight Guides: Great Britain (APA Publications, 1985, £10.95)
Let's Go: Britain and Ireland (Pan, 1990, £10.99)

For further information:
English Tourist Board, Thames Tower, Black's Road, Hammersmith, London W6 9EL. Tel: (071) 846 9000
London Tourist Board, Tourist Information Service, Victoria Station Forecourt, London SW1. Tel: (071) 730 3488
Scottish Travel Centre, Scottish Tourist Board, 23 Ravelston Terrace, Edinburgh EH4 3EU. Tel: (031) 332 2433 *or* 17 Cockspur Street, London SW1Y. Tel: (071) 930 8661
Wales Tourist Board, Brunel House, Cardiff CF2 1UY. Tel: (0222) 499909 *or* 34 Piccadilly, London W1V. Tel: (071) 409 0969

Bulgaria

Capital Sofia	**Climate** Cool Mediterranean
Major cities Plovdiv, Varna, Ruse, Burgas	**Annual weather range** – Varna: *Temperature* Max 30°C (Jul) Min −1°C (Jan–Feb)
Time GMT + 2	
Currency Lev (Lv) = 100 stótinki	*Rainfall* Max 64mm (Jun) Min 26mm (Mar)
Languages Bulgarian, Turkish	

The Bulgarians are basically an orderly and tidy people so they are well organized for visitors and have made a great success of their tourist industry.

This is especially true of the Black Sea coast (no more than a long afternoon by air from Britain). Forty years ago this coast was untouched except at Varna, which between the wars developed into a resort for the members of the European middle and upper classes. Some regions were snake-infested, so the Bulgarians imported mongooses and then created a series of well-designed hotels, chalets, villas and campsites at Slanchev Briag and 'Golden Sands' and elsewhere along the many miles of superb sandy beaches. These are absolutely ideal for a family seaside holiday with small children. It is a stimulatingly cosmopolitan place. There are a lot of splendid open-air restaurants and much music and dancing in the evenings.

Most budgets and tastes are catered for and the hotel proprietors and staffs are very obliging and welcoming. Numerous diversions and entertainments are available for small children and there are folklore spectacles and camel rides.

Bulgarians eat well. They enjoy a fertile country and there are copious supplies of good meat, vegetables and fruit. Meals are well prepared and well cooked. Particularly appetizing are the soups, hors d'oeuvres, goulashes and various kinds of kebab. As you would expect, the main influences on the cuisine have been Russian and Turkish. There is a plentiful range of soft drinks, and the water is very good; but, as in all Balkan countries, I would be cautious about drinking tap water. Emergency medical treatment is adequate and so is the supply of pharmaceutical goods.

Most people go on a package tour, but individual travel is perfectly feasible on public transport and by car. Self-drive car hire is well organized. It's good country for camping and there are big regions of totally unspoilt and very beautiful countryside, especially in the ranges of the Rhodope mountains. Trips on the lower reaches of the Danube can be organized and I would recommend visits to such towns as Plovdiv and Assenovgrad, as well as to the capital Sofia which is quite a sophisticated place. Nor should one miss a visit to Nessebur, a small Byzantine settlement on a peninsula which juts into the blue and seductive waters of the Black Sea. There is much to divert small children in all these places – donkey rides, playgrounds and even organized entertainment like treasure hunts.

J.A.C.

Please Note
Recent political changes are such that it is difficult to know the effect they will have on holiday makers. We would advise you to contact the relevant National Tourist Office for further details before travelling.

Recommended reading:
Bulgaria – A Travel Guide, Philip Ward (Oleander, 1989, £9.95)
AA – Essential Bulgaria (AA, 1990, £3.95)

For further information:
Bulgarian Tourist Office, 18 Princes Street, London W1R. Tel: (071) 499 6988

Canada

Capital Ottawa	**Annual weather range** – West
Major cities Toronto, Montreal,	(Vancouver): temperate
Vancouver, Edmonton,	*Temperature* Max 23°C
Calgary, Winnipeg, Quebec	(Jul–Aug) Min 0°C (Jan)
Time GMT −3½ – 8	*Rainfall* Max 224mm (Dec) Min
Currency Canadian dollar (C$) =	31mm (Jul)
100 cents	**Annual weather range** – Prairies
Languages English, French	(Winnipeg): continental
Climate Polar to warm	*Temperature* Max 26°C (Jul)
Annual weather range – South	Min −25°C (Jan)
(Ottawa): cool continental	*Rainfall* Max 79mm (Jun–Jul)
Temperature Max 27°C (Jul)	Min 23mm (Dec–Feb)
Min −16°C (Jan–Feb)	
Rainfall Max 89mm (Jun) Min	
56mm (Feb)	

Most British people visit Canada to see or stay with friends or relatives, in which case they will be well provided for. The comparatively few who go as tourists will find highly developed and civilized amenities and there will be few problems for parents. The main centres such as Quebec, Toronto, Montreal, Ottawa, Vancouver – and many of the smaller urban settlements – cater for almost every need. Communications and public transport are excellent and fly/drive tours are easily arranged.

There are some obvious places and events which will appeal to small children. For example, there is the Wye Marsh Wildlife Centre near Midland, Ontario – a waterland sanctuary for muskrat, mink, beaver, frogs, turtles and numerous species of birds. This is a remarkable place to explore and possesses much of interest to little ones.

Niagara Falls are virtually an obligatory visit but should that awe-inspiring sight not have the hoped-for impact on your child's sensibility there are more mundane attractions at-hand such as Ripley's Believe it or Not Museum and Louis Tussaud's waxwork collection which, naturally, includes such notorious figures as Queen Victoria, Henry VIII and Mrs Thatcher.

For the technically minded 5-year-old there is a splendid aviation museum at Rockliffe Airport, Ottawa, which displays flying machines ranging from early balloons to jet fighters.

Toronto annually mounts the Canadian National Exhibition which combines water shows, air shows, bathtub races, horse shows, wilderness adventure rides, merry-go-rounds and pet zoos. It's a sort of vast amalgam of circus, fairground, tattoo, theatre and adventure play-ground. Also sited at Toronto is Canada's Wonderland where there are many entertainments for children.

Canada is wonderfully well suited to an adventurous open-air holiday but it has to be remembered that the country is so vast that the whole UK would fit into it over forty times.

Given a choice with small children in tow I would be tempted by the province of Alberta. In that huge area, several times the size of England, there lie the splendid Banff and Jasper national parks where there is a year-long range of outdoor activities. Calgary has its famous rodeo in July each year. This is every bit as good as a fine circus and the chuck-wagon races, steer roping and bronco busting are exciting events for children and adults alike. East of Calgary is the Dinosaur Provincial Park where the world's largest collection of dino-saurs has been preserved in rock buttes and spires. The existence of real-life Indians would appeal to small boys. There are marvellous trips possible on the Icefields Parkway between Lake Louise and Jasper.

From Alberta one could go into the 'outback' of the Northwest Territories and the Yukon. There is a good museum about Indians at Fort Smith. In the Nahanni National Park are the Virginia Falls (twice the height of Niagara).

Every year at Yellowknife the Caribou Carnival and the champion-ship Dog Derby take place and there is another weeklong carnival at Frobisher Bay in April. Dawson City and Watson Lake in August hold parades and raft and canoe races; and at Dawson City in September there is a bizarre event: the Klondike International Outhouse Race (outhouses on wheels!).

Newfoundland and Labrador have their fair share of spectacles. A daily tattoo is held at St John's in July and August. In the Avalon Wilderness Reserve area native animals can be seen. Two big annual festivals take place in Labrador each year: the Heritage Festival in July and the Bakeapple Festival in August. Some small children might also be diverted by the settlement at L'Anse aux Meadows which recreates Viking life around 1000 AD.

In Saskatchewan there are several things of interest, including good museums at North Battleford, Moose Jaw and Saskatoon. Entertain-ing events are Mosaic, a kind of festival at Regina in May, the Buffalo Days Exhibition in early August, and the Folkfest at Saskatoon in late August.

Manitoba is rich in diversions for little ones. Winnipeg has the splendid Assiniboine Park and Zoo, with playgrounds, picnic sites and a miniature railway. The Manitoba Museum of Man and Nature is of interest to children of all ages. At Steinbach, the Mennonite Village

Museum depicts the life of settlers from Russia in the nineteenth century. Each year, in Manitoba there is a whole series of festivals and events which provide any amount of entertainment.

The provinces of New Brunswick, Nova Scotia, Prince Edward Island, British Columbia, Quebec and Ontario also provide a wide range of diversions for the whole family.

J.A.C.

Recommended reading:
Canada – A Travel Survival Guide (Lonely Planet, 1989, £7.95)
Michelin Guide to Canada (Michelin, 1989, £5.95)
Fodor's 90 – Canada (Fodor, £10.99)
Insight Guides – Canada (APA Publications, 1990, £10.95)

For further information:
Tourism Canada, Canadian High Commission, Canada House, Trafalgar Square, London SW1Y 5BJ. Tel: (071) 629 9492

Canaries *see* Spain

China

Capital Beijing (Peking)	*Temperature* Max 31°C
Major cities Chongqing, Canton,	(Jun–Jul) Min −1°C (Jan)
Shenyang, Wuhan, Nanjing,	*Rainfall* Max 243mm (Jul) Min
Harbin, Shanghai	3mm (Dec)
Time GMT + 8	**Annual weather range** – Coast
Currency Ren min bi yuan	(Shanghai):
(RMB Y) = 100 yen	*Temperature* Max 37°C
Language Chinese	(Jul–Aug) Min −1°C
Climate Wide variation,	(Jan–Feb)
predominantly monsoonal	*Rainfall* Max 180mm (Jul) Min
Annual weather range – Northeast	36mm (Dec)
(Peking):	

China is a huge country, well over a million square miles larger than the US, and thus has wide variations in climate, language, custom, tradition, attitude and food. You may be surprised by how few children you see considering the fact that you are travelling in a nation of over 1000 million people. This is because of the rigorous birth-control laws that encourage the number of children to be kept to one per family.

This restriction is a severe hardship because the Chinese are deeply interested in children, *any* children. Babies are adored, coddled and spoiled in China. Their wardrobes are very fancy and varied, more so than any other family member. They get the choicest bits at meal-times, the best spot to sleep in and are the focus of most family outings and get-togethers. In no country have we seen children better cared for, healthier or happier.

Children from the West are especially fascinating to the Chinese. They are welcome everywhere and likely to receive a lot of attention. There is, anyway, *intense* curiosity in all 'Western' visitors.

Foreigners are likely to find themselves in the main urban centres (Beijing, Canton or Shanghai) where they will probably be accommodated in the increasing number of European and American style hotels, often of Hiltonesque proportions and similar style; for the most part extremely boring establishments. It is *much* more interesting to stay in the less ostentatious places (often well appointed and comfortable) which are actually used by the Chinese themselves.

China provides very little in the way of specialized baby equipment. Babies are usually carried by their mothers in simple cotton yokes (newborn are carried in front, toddlers at the back).

Outside the very large and sophisticated hotels entertainment for small children is somewhat limited. No child can be expected to appreciate Chinese opera or drama, but for a few pence (or *yen*) a Peoples' Theatre will provide an acrobatic and conjuring show of the highest international standards. The performers are droll, witty and marvellously skilful, which explains why they are in great demand world-wide (for example on the Paul Daniels' TV show in Britain). Nor should one fail to see the superb jugglers and puppet shows. Parks and zoos are other attractive diversions.

Toys and novelties are few, given that China exports toy products to many countries, but some homemade products such as dolls are beautiful and absurdly cheap. An hour or two in the Friendship Stores (there are several of these in most of the main towns) is time well spent. Small children will enjoy themselves in them and be surprised how different they are from those at home.

Children also enjoy the many different kinds of open markets, street markets and 'bazaars' which are common. The variety of goods is amazing, as is the variety of unfamiliar goods. Restaurant and hotel food should provide no problems for your children. Chinese food and cooking are excellent and differ from region to region. Most people in the West now know something of Chinese food, if only from the local take-away. Much of it in China will be easily recognizable except for, in some areas, delicacies such as cat, dog, watersnake, sea slugs, fish lips and some species of caterpillar. Parents with children who cannot cope with Chinese cuisine will have to confine themselves to the more sophisticated hotels and restaurants where Western-type food can be bought. On the whole staff are most helpful and obliging. You can get babysitters. Care is assured to be gentle and solicitous although few can be expected to speak anything but Chinese.

Travel by public transport is a hazardous business unless you speak some Chinese and is really to be avoided. Chauffeur-driven cars can be hired but self-drive hire is virtually unknown. However, most visitors will be involved in some kind of organized tour. If the tour includes train travel so much the better. Nearly all small children love train journeys and China is one of the places for this. It's a splendid adventure, comparable to the big rides on the transcontinental trains of North and South America, the USSR and India. The trains move at a thoroughly gentlemanly pace and afford an unfolding view of other ways of life, which any four- or five-year-old will be fascinated by.

Courtesies are as important in China as in any other country. Public displays of affection involving physical contact should be avoided and modesty in dress is desirable. Visitors are often welcomed by applause and the correct response is to applaud back. Patience is vital in the East and you should not lose your temper, for that is to lose face. The best passport is a big smile, and that applies to children.

Any parent taking children to China needs to remember that the great majority of the population survive at subsistence level. A few hundred metres from the luxurious 'Hilton' spreads the labyrinth of *yutongs* (alleyways) where, in drab and primitive hovels, without running water or sewage system, tens of millions live in congestion.

Remember, too, to take all the pharmaceutical goods you think you may need (including remedies for coughs, colds and grazes) and before going study the climate of the region(s) you are visiting. Many areas are stupefyingly hot (and humid) in summer, bitterly cold in winter. There are also monsoon regions. A carefully balanced wardrobe may be necessary.

J.A.C. & F.K.

Recommended reading:
China – A Travel Survival Guide (Lonely Planet, 1988, £11.95)
Inside Guides – China (APA Publications, 1990, £10.95)

For further information:
China National Tourist Office, 4 Glentworth Street, London NW1. Tel: (071) 935 9427

Cyprus

Capital Nicosia	**Climate** Mediterranean
Major cities Limassol, Famagusta, Larnaca	**Annual weather range** – Nicosia: *Temperature* Max 37°C (Jul–Aug)
Time GMT + 2	Min 9°C (Jan–Feb)
Currency Cyprus pound (C£) = 100 cents	*Rainfall* Max 76mm (Jan)
Languages Greek, Turkish, English	

In general, tourists are welcomed in the Greek part of Cyprus (for details of travel to Turkish Cyprus, see below). Many British people have settled there and there are still large RAF bases so wherever you go people speak English. Children are very much included and expected to join in at restaurants and tavernas. All along the coast the usual chips and fast foods Greek-style, are available at tourist restaurants. Most are very happy to give small portions or special combinations to suit children.

Living in a villa we found it easy to get a take-away from local restaurants in the evenings to feed the children – plenty of salad, chips and kebabs. Baby supplies and all modern commodities are easily available and inexpensive in the towns. Inland, however, away from the touristy and sometimes seedy coast, life has changed very little. The traditional hill farming communities remain as you imagine they have always been; and should you get off the beaten track you are always welcomed, particularly the children.

Public transport is easy in the towns but it is also easy and cheap to arrange a self-drive rental car – with child seats – to get about in. Like many of the villa packages, we had a car (in fact a mini-bus) thrown in. This meant we were able to take all six of our (combined) children to deserted beaches and villages. For all of us this was the best part of the holiday.

The spring and autumn climates are ideal for children, but you should be prepared for very hot summers. The beaches are lovely for children, sandy and relatively pollution-free but during our stay there were a few storms which produced heavy deposits of oil all round the coast and eventually all over the children and their clothes. I suppose, though, this could happen anywhere.

On the whole I would say that Cyprus is a very easy (if bland) place to holiday with children. One can combine a seaside holiday with visiting easily understood Greek mythological/archaeological features, such as the birthplace of Aphrodite on the south-west coast.

The castles are certainly a must especially if your children are the hanging-over-the-edge kind!

Food and supplies are no problem and at the right time of year, the climate is perfect. The people certainly are most friendly and usually keen to please. Medical facilities are similar to those you would find travelling in other eastern Mediterranean countries and you should take out insurance to cover emergencies. Accommodation is the usual range of resort hotels, self-catering flats and villas.

Several companies now offer holidays in the northern Turkish part of Cyprus. Scenically beautiful and much more old-fashioned than the Greek area, it is indisputably very attractive and families with children are undoubtedly welcome. However, travellers should be aware that there are no direct flights (all planes are routed via Turkey), that the self-declared Republic is not recognised by the British Government (so consular assistance is not available), and that a North Cyprus stamp in a passport may prevent further travel in Greece. The latter problem can be avoided by requesting that the North Cyprus stamp is marked on a separate sheet of paper folded into the passport.

E.K-H.

Please Note
Recent political changes are such that it is difficult to know the effect they will have on holiday makers. We would advise you to contact the relevant National Tourist Office for further details before travelling.

Recommended reading:
Landscapes of Cyprus (Sunflower Books, 1986, £5.95)
Days out in Cyprus, Robert Bulmer (Bulmer Publications, 1987, £5.50)

For further information:
Cyprus Tourism Organisation, 213 Regent Street, London W1R 8DA. Tel: (071) 734 2593 or (071) 737 9822

Denmark

Capital Copenhagen	**Climate** Temperate
Major cities Aarhus, Odense, Aalborg	**Annual weather range –** Copenhagen:
Time GMT + 1	*Temperature* Max 22°C (Jul)
Currency Danish krone (Dkr) = 100 öre	Min −3°C (Feb)
Languages Danish	*Rainfall* Max 71mm (Jul) Min 32mm (Mar)

You can hardly imagine that the native land of Hans Christian Andersen would be in any way allergic to children, or vice versa. Indeed, Danish children are happy, outgoing, and much is done for them. Much for the visitor, too.

For example, there is Sommerland West: a vast 'leisure paradise' or adventure playground which will keep little ones occupied for days. It includes a zoo and islands on lakes, cafés and picnicking grounds. For diversion there are sandpits, mini-trains, mini-go-carts, a giant air cushion, pedaloes, canoes, aqua bikes, pony riding, a climbing castle and mini-toboggans. All the activities are included in the admission fee.

There is also the Varde Sommerland in Varde Engpark whose entertainments include excursion boats, moon cars, air cushions, canoes, aviaries, pets and pony rides. Similar recreations are available at Farup Summerland, and at Dyrehavsbakken which lies in the middle of a forest ten kilometres from Copenhagen. There is a big water dipper plus tombolas, adventure playgrounds and performances by clowns. There is no admission charge.

Nor should you miss the famous Legoland Parken. Thirty million Lego bricks have gone into its creation. Each day there are Lego building competitions with prizes. The park boasts what is claimed to be the world's largest collection of dolls, plus Titania's miniature palace and a collection of antique mechanical toys. Should boredom appear then there are puppet theatres, 'activities' and the 'Wild West' of Legoredo Town.

I would also recommend Knuthenborg, which is a kind of safari park but includes a 'playland' – Smaland where attractions include a miniature steam train. There is a big zoo at Givskud, plus a large play area with a children's farm and you should not miss the Fisheries Museum and Sealarium at Esbjerg. There is a vast pool for the big seals, and a smaller one for baby seals, plus an aquarium. A visit includes a tour of a fishing vessel.

Another favourite place is Djurs Sommerland. As well as many of the diversions already mentioned, there is a cowboy land with gold mining and shooting rinks, a Red Indians' island and a waterland with spiral slides and paddling pools.

The capital Copenhagen boasts the famous Tivoli. Apart from the fairground there are performances in the children's theatre as well as a pantomime theatre. Four days a week, in the evening, there is a fireworks display.

The more precocious five-year-old will find the Viking Ship Hall at Roskilde interesting. There are five restored ships here.

Getting about in Denmark is very easy. Communications are excellent and every conceivable form of accommodation is available.

Danish inns are particularly attractive. Hoteliers are friendly and welcoming and children will find Danish food sustaining and appetizing. The water is safe.

Most Danes speak English fluently, but, like other peoples, they appreciate some attempt by visitors to say a few words in Danish. Besides, it's a language which is quite fun for children to learn a few words of. After all, we have common roots.

J.A.C.

Recommended reading:
Baedeker's Denmark (AA, 1987, £10.95)

For further information:
Danish Tourist Board, Sceptre House, 169 Regent Street, London W1R. Tel: (071) 734 2637

Egypt

Capital Cairo	**Annual weather range –**
Major cities Alexandria, Giza,	Alexandria:
Hurghudo, Luxor	*Temperature* Max 31°C (Aug)
Time GMT + 2	Min 11°C (Jan–Feb)
Currency Egyptian pound (E£) =	*Rainfall* Max 56mm (Dec) Min
100 piastres	0mm (May–Sep)
Languages Arabic, English	**Annual weather range –** Cairo:
Climate Dry and humid	*Temperature* Max 36°C (Jul)
	Min 8°C (Jan)
	Rainfall Max 5mm (Dec–Mar)
	Min 0mm (Jun–Oct)

Egyptians, like Arabs everywhere, adore children – including other people's. Whole families enjoy a promenade along the Nile on a hot summer evening, taking advantage of a cooling breeze off the river.

Public holidays and the Friday Sabbath are picnic days, and every available green patch in the capital, Cairo, is occupied by parents, assorted cousins, aunts and uncles, and children playing, eating, talking or listening to a blaring radio.

On these days, too, the zoological garden overflows with humanity, to the intense annoyance of its permanent residents. The foreign visitors may attempt these entertainments (on a Monday to Thursday basis), or else, with innocent boldness saunter through the grounds of a private 'sporting club' whose shaded park areas are a bequest of a bygone era of British imperialism. Tourists should not be put off, therefore, by the genuinely friendly stares and comments directed at their own children. Blond, blue-eyed youngsters are especially admired. The indulgence of Egyptians towards children in general should ensure a sympathetic response to your requests regarding your own. However, you must not expect the same facilities for children that you would find at home.

The tourists' short-term stay will centre around the major hotels, such as the Hilton and Sheraton, and smaller hotels which accept package tours. The 'package' is the only sensible way to see Egypt if you are a first-timer. European languages are spoken in some fashion by most employees in hotel receptions, while universally recognized hand signals work wonders with porters and maids. Special portions of food for children can be requested (even if they don't appear on the menu) and the waiter will warm a bottle of milk for your child. Sad to relate, McDonald's, Wimpy and Colonel Sanders all have outlets in Cairo; convenient they may be, but they are yet another obstacle between the tourist and nourishing, genuine Egyptian food. Nappies and some baby foods are available, at a price, from many pharmacies. Bottled mineral water (imported) is also available, but the intense summer heat can best be alleviated by a superb local beer (*Stella*), which even European children have enjoyed with no known ill-effect.

The best months to visit Egypt are November to March; July and August should be avoided. Public transport in urban areas is often difficult. Buses, trams and commuter trains are packed and taxis are the only way to travel about, apart from the new Metro system, which is very well organized and is the exception to ground-level transport facilities. Taxis can be found parked in convoys around the big hotels and daily rates can be negotiated (with the help of the hotel doorman – who will inevitably be a cousin of the cab-driver). Taxis are painted black and white in Cairo and the fare should always be agreed in advance as meters are not to be relied on.

For the less adventurous, or those with very young children, tours in luxury air-conditioned coaches can be arranged through the hotels. The Cairo–Alexandria road is well served this way as well, while train or plane is the usual way to visit the archeological sites of Upper Egypt at Luxor and Aswan. Shopping in the 'native' markets (*souk*) is crowded, noisy, stuffy and fascinating. Small babies are best carried in slings Indian-fashion; somewhat older youngsters should be put in a harness and led so you don't lose them.

Public toilet facilities are virtually non-existent, but in extremis any wall will do. No one will notice.

There are also main streets packed with small specialist shops selling shoes, cloth and souvenirs. All items except the last usually have fixed prices, but you never lose face by trying to bargain. And finally, remember the ancient Egyptian adage: once you have drunk from the Nile waters, you are destined to return to Egypt.

D.W.

Recommended reading:
Egypt & Sudan – A Travel Survival Guide (Lonely Planet, 1987, £6.95)

For further information:
Egyptian State Tourist Office, 168 Piccadilly, London W1. Tel: (071) 493 5282/3

Eire and Northern Ireland

Capital Dublin, Belfast	**Climate** Temperate
Major cities Cork, Galway, Limerick	**Annual weather range** – Dublin:
	Temperature Max 20°C (Jul)
Time GMT + 1	Min 1°C (Jan)
Currency Irish pound (I£) = 100 pence	*Rainfall* Max 74mm (Aug–Dec)
	Min 45mm (Apr)
Languages English, Irish	

The first thing you will notice about Eire is that being a parent is the norm; Eire has more children, in proportion to its population than any other European country and families will find babies and children welcomed, accepted and catered for everywhere they go. This doesn't mean that the Irish are, like the Italians or Chinese, a nation of child worshippers, just that children are seen everywhere and not regarded as noisy nuisances. Hotels and restaurants expect to provide small portions, early teas, high chairs, cots and single beds in parents' rooms as a matter of course. Standards of food and hygiene are similar to British ones, though health-conscious parents may be horrified at the cholesterol level of the Irish fry-up. Baby foods and disposable nappies are available in the smallest village – but be warned, Ireland is now an expensive country and you will probably pay more than you would at home.

The Irish pub is a national institution and, in the country, often doubles as the village shop; they're friendly places and no one banishes families to a chilly garden.

Most large shops have good facilities for feeding and changing babies – one large supermarket chain, Superquinn, even provides free crèches in some of its larger stores. A word of warning on breastfeeding – Ireland is a deeply conservative and religious country and women do not bare their breasts in public, so if you can find somewhere private to feed, do. Standard forms of contraception are available in Eire. Condoms and spermicides may legally be sold to anyone over the age of eighteen but IUDs, diaphragms, caps and the Pill are only available on prescription. In practice, however, all contraceptive devices may be difficult to obtain and travellers are advised to take their own supplies, though Family Planning Clinics in larger towns can usually be relied on.

On holiday, don't miss Dublin, the most cosmopolitan and intimate of capital cities, small enough to push a buggy round the centre, full of green spaces, good friendly, child-centred shops and watering holes. Phoenix Park is especially lovely – acres of parkland and a smashing zoo. The whole of the west coast is breathtakingly beautiful, with dreamlike, empty beaches; the only joker in this otherwise perfect pack is the weather – that well-known soft Irish day of fine misty rain – so pack your wellies and raincoats.

Most people would probably put Northern Ireland at the bottom of their holiday list – understandable, but a great pity; you're still in the UK, but also unmistakably in Ireland, and the North contains some of the most beautiful places in these islands – the Antrim Coast and Lough Erne. You can spend a holiday there without any sight of the troubles, but it's only fair to say that slightly older children can be both excited and frightened if they see armed soldiers and police, so some prior, simple explanation would probably be a good idea.

One final, heartfelt word of warning – if, like so many families, you decide to take your car, be warned that the ferry journey is, in my experience, a nightmare with children; maybe I've just been unlucky but I've always found it overcrowded and not very clean, with no facilities to entertain small children. The only thing that gets me through it is the certainty that the journey is worth it.

A.C.

Recommended reading:
Fodor's Ireland (Fodor's Travel Publications Inc., 1989, £9.99)
Holiday Ireland 1990, Katie Wood and George McDonald (£3.99)

For further information:
Irish Tourist Board, Ireland House, 150 New Bond Street, London
W1Y. Tel: (071) 493 3201

England *see* Britain

France

Capital Paris	**Annual weather range** – North (Paris):
Major cities Lyons, Marseilles, Lille, Bordeaux, Toulouse, Nantes, Strasbourg	*Temperature* Max 25°C (Jul) Min 1°C (Jan–Feb)
Time GMT + 1	*Rainfall* Max 64mm (Aug) Min 35mm (Mar)
Currency Franc (Fr) = 100 centimes	**Annual weather range** – South (Marseilles):
Language French	*Temperature* Max 29°C (Jul) Min 2°C (Jan)
Climate Temperate in north, mediterranean in south	*Rainfall* Max 76mm (Oct) Min 11mm (Jul)

France is probably the most civilized country in the world and therefore, for the potential traveller with very small children, it can provide virtually everything that might be needed. All French cities, major towns and most of the minor ones are equipped with every conceivable kind of resource. However, pharmaceutical goods are more expensive in France so it is wise to take the obvious basics such as analgesics, plasters and mosquito repellent.

The French are very family-minded, more so than most peoples and the family is a strong unit. Parental discipline tends to be somewhat stricter than we are used to in Britain and a good deal more so than in the US. Although expectations of children's behaviour are somewhat higher, they are usually given a great deal of attention. Your small children are likely to be welcomed and well looked after anywhere and everywhere.

The French eat out a lot (especially during the holidays). They do so *en famille* and children are allowed to stay up later than in other countries. It is very common to see large family parties in restaurants and cafes. They like everyone to be involved, from granny to the baby.

French cuisine is the best in the world and it is the best also in the sense that in any decent cafe, restaurant or hotel they will do their utmost to provide what their customers like. There is no need to go by the menu which, anyway, will often be varied and copious. Do not be afraid to ask for what you would like to eat. If you are staying in a place for a few days all the meals can be discussed and planned in advance. Proprietors and patrons are particularly good at providing the most desirable food for children. If you cannot get the kind of food you want and eat well, then you will never eat well anywhere. There is something for everyone. A *relais routier* – favourite stopping place of long-distance lorry drivers – will provide better food (and much more of it) than many a London restaurant and for a quarter of the price. My wife and I and our three children have been to France several times for several weeks each time in the last six years and the children have rejoiced over the food. As you can eat pretty well whenever you like in France there is little problem about mealtimes.

You can get almost any kind of hotel accommodation and hotel proprietors are flexible and helpful in making particular arrangements to suit your needs. It is still possible to get a comfortable room with a double bed for as little as £20 per night.

Plumbing has never been a strong point among the French, though they are improving. In some hotels lavatories and washing facilities are inferior to English standards, and sometimes they may seem a little squalid. Pay careful attention, therefore, to the hygiene in such installations – be careful about drinking water. I would not drink water from any old tap (especially in rural districts). Ask for fresh drinking water. Or better still, bottled. Tap water is considered perfectly safe in restaurants.

Do remember that in central and southern France it is very much hotter than it is in Britain during the summer. The sun may be fierce and the temperatures high. In June, July and August you should be very careful about exposing children to the sun. In an hour or less your child may be badly burned.

Medical facilities in any emergency are among the best in the world and French doctors are renowned for their skills. However, fees for private patients are high, so you must be sure that you have either taken out a comprehensive insurance policy or filled in the necessary forms (the E111) in Britain so you can benefit from the reciprocal National Health arrangements that exist.

Basically, you are most unlikely to encounter any inconvenience in any part of France when you travel with small children. One final point – no visitor should fail to take advantage of the clothes that are available for small children. They design and make excellent, inexpensive clothes that are original, colourful and stylish.

J.A.C.

France is deservedly popular with English families, for obvious reasons: a short ferry ride and you're there. Couples who have been there before having children will have discovered their own favourite part. However, it is worth considering that the holiday is going to be different with children, so don't try to cram in too much travel.

Many people drive to the south by car, camping or staying in hotels en route. Children usually love camping, and French hotels are certainly more accommodating to children and babies than English ones. Long car rides are more of a problem, particularly if your children keep you awake at night, leaving you too tired to concentrate on driving.

There are two ways of coping. Some people travel at night while the children sleep, and hope they can get there in one stretch. This can be quite an endurance test. Others take a more leisurely pace, and travel by day, stopping frequently and expecting to spend two or three nights en route. Arthur Eperon or Michelin guides can be helpful in finding hotels. If you have young children and a long journey you should consider using the motorail or arranging a fly-drive holiday (contact your travel agent for the best available deals).

If your baby is at the travel cot stage and sleeps badly if you are in the same room, try asking for a room with a bathroom; you may be able to squeeze the cot in there. Don't feel you *have* to go to the seaside with young children – it can be very busy in August. River bathing and paddling is common in France (Loire camp sites can be a splendid choice for stops en route). Bathing is also allowed in reservoirs like Lac de Salagou. Small towns and even villages have their own outdoor pools, and sandpits and play areas are quite common.

Food will play a large part in any holiday in France and children are welcome in cafes and restaurants. French children stay up late and eat with the adults, but seem to behave remarkably well; wild behaviour from children may be frowned on.

For those used to restrictive English pubs it is a boon to know you can always find a cafe where the children can get a drink or snack at any time of the day.

Jars of savoury baby food are excellent, with delicacies such as puréed artichokes and green beans. If you are trying to keep your baby off sweet things, however, you may find it difficult to find an unsweetened baby cereal.

Nappy changing and toilets can be a problem. Public toilets are difficult to find and often smelly, though toddlers seem to find this less of a problem than older children. Camp-site loos are particularly variable.

Ferry companies have recently started doing more to accommodate children, and you should enquire when booking whether there is a playroom on the boat. My children particularly liked the Sally Line *Sea of Balls*.

M.H.

Recommended reading:
Rough Guide – France, Baillie & Salmon (Harrap Columbus – Rough Guides, 1989, £6.95)
Let's Go – France 1990 (Pan, 1990, £10.99)
French Entrée 3: Normandy, P. Fenn (Quiller, 1985, £4.95)
American Express Guide – Paris (Mitchell Beazley, 1989, £5.95)
Paupers' Paris, M. Turner (Pan, 1990, £4.99)

For further information:
French Government Tourist Office, 178 Piccadilly, London W1V. Tel: (071) 499 6911 (24 hour recorded message)

Germany

Capital Bonn, Berlin	**Climate** Temperate continental
Major cities Berlin, Hamburg, Munich, Cologne, Essen, Frankfurt	**Annual weather range** – Munich: *Temperature* Max 23°C (Jul–Aug) Min −5°C (Jan–Feb)
Time GMT + 1	*Rainfall* Max 139mm (Jul) Min 47mm (Dec)
Currency Deutsch mark (DM) = 100 pfennig	
Language German, English widely spoken	

Germany is a country of great variety ranging from the sandy, wind-swept beaches of the North Sea to the industrial centre and the mountains of the Black Forest and Bavaria. The Germans are friendly and like children although travel in southern Germany with its relaxed, outgoing people is likely to be easier with young children than in northern Germany which is more formal.

Children are welcome in most hotels and cafeteria-style restaurants; the more formal restaurants may turn children away. There are plenty of cafes in Germany which sell hot and cold meals all day. In family-style restaurants children's portions and special children's meals are likely to be available and high chairs will not be a problem.

Shopping hours are restricted by law. The shops open early in the morning, often before 8 a.m. and stay open until 6 or 7 p.m. Late-night shopping now operates in most German towns on Thursdays, when shops are open until 8.30 p.m. The shops close on Saturday at midday, except on the first Saturday of the month when they will be open all day.

Nappies, baby food and all the other paraphernalia are readily available, either in the 'drugstores' or larger supermarkets. You can buy beautiful children's clothes in Germany. There are wonderful toys, including of course the famous 'Steiff' range of soft toys.

Germany in general is not a country with many parks in the major cities, although in the countryside there are many walks, amenities and picnic places. Playgrounds are generally well and imaginatively equipped with a variety of amusements.

Germany is a well-organized country and if you are organized, travel with children will be pleasurable and easy. Most major hotels will provide cots and high chairs, and baby seats in rented cars can be easily arranged – if booked well in advance. Hotels generally charge per person, but additional beds are usually available at a nominal charge.

The food in Germany in both restaurants and shops is usually very good. As in most countries travel with young children can be fun – if you organize it and are philosophical about the mishaps. In Germany this is as true as anywhere else, perhaps even more so.

Gute Reise!

L.S.

Please Note
Recent political changes are such that it is difficult to know the effect they will have on holiday makers. We would advise you to contact the relevant National Tourist Office for further details before travelling.

Recommended reading:
Frommer Dollarwise Guide: Germany (Simon & Schuster, 1990, £11.95)
Insight Guides – Germany (APA Publications, 1989, £10.95)

For further information:
German National Tourist Office, 65 Curzon Street, London W1Y 7PE. Tel: (071) 495 3990

Greece

Capital Athens	*Rainfall* Max 62mm (Jan) Min
Major cities Thessaloniki, Larissa	7mm (Aug)
Time GMT + 2	**Annual weather range** – Aegean
Currency Drachma (Dr)	Islands (Naxos):
Language Greek	*Temperature* Max 32°C
Climate mediterranean	(Jul–Aug) Min 10°C (Jan–Feb)
Annual weather range – Inland	*Rainfall* Max 91mm (Jan) Min
(Athens):	1mm (Aug)
Temperature Max 33°C	
(Jul–Aug) Min 6°C (Jan)	

The Greeks adore children and always make a fuss of them. They normally become the centre of attention and older people will often offer advice to what they consider an errant parent if a child is not protected against the sun or the chill of the evening.

Young children participate in all the family outings, so you are very welcome with them in restaurants, cafes and shops. It is a good idea to follow the Greek way and put your children to sleep at midday when it is usually very hot. During June, July and August it is best to take your children out (including swimming) in the mornings until noon and after 5 p.m. During this 'siesta' period (between 1 p.m. and 5 p.m.) quiet should be observed. Greek children will generally be up until 10 or 11 p.m., so feel free to enjoy your meal at restaurants if your little ones can stay up that late. You can order children's portions in most restaurants, but high chairs are uncommon. Restaurants stay open late, so they do not open before 7 p.m. in most places. The normal lunch opening hours are 12.30-3 p.m.

Shops open at 8.30 a.m., stay open unil 2 p.m. close for siesta time until 5.30 and open again 8.30 p.m. Monday, Wednesday and Saturday afternoons shops are closed, except those in tourist areas near the beach. There is always a pharmacy that opens late in every town and this is indicated on the shop itself.

Nappies can be found almost anywhere, even in the smallest village shop. Baby food, however, is found only in supermarkets and some chemists and it is more expensive than in the UK. Fresh milk is difficult to find in the villages, but tinned or long-life is available. Babies' formula milk can only be found in big supermarkets and is very expensive, so take your own.

It is important to boil water of any kind (even bottled) in most areas for making baby food in any form. It might be a good idea to take along sterilizing tablets.

Holiday equipment is plentiful and costs about the same as in the UK, however sun creams and toys are much more expensive.

Avoid travelling by public buses in summer, but if you must, catch the early morning ones. Hiring a car with a child seat should not prove difficult with a reputable firm. If you have booked a holiday through a UK tour operator ask them to arrange that the child seat be installed before the car is delivered. Some tour operators will arrange for high chairs and playpens to be available when you arrive at your hotel or villa.

Greek food is richer than English and often cooked in olive oil. Remember that you are welcome to visit the kitchen and can order something plain, without sauce. Restaurants will always cook chips for the children. Fruit and vegetables are excellent value and available anywhere in the summer months.

Greece is a member of the EEC so British citizens are entitled to emergency medical treatment. However, the DHSS advises that you take out private medical insurance. This advice is very sensible since you have to pay a doctor to call at your hotel or villa. You will be pleased to know there is no shortage of paediatricians in every town.

Greek shops carry a large variety of mosquito-repelling devices and the best is the small electrical appliance which you put tablets into and plug in the wall socket. (*See* 'Coping in Hot Weather', p. 322.)

Athens is not overblessed with parks, but there are a few for those who would like to see some of Greece's ancient glory. The best of these is the zoological gardens (National Gardens) near the Parliament buildings. Other useful parks are at Lykabettos, Philipapou and Areos. Travel within Athens is greatly eased by using the underground railway system (pronounced '*eelektriko*') and the double-decker express-bus service that links the airports with central Athens and Pireaus (details of this service can be obtained from Olympic Airways).

M.W.

Recommended reading:
Guide to Greece (Michael Haag, 1986, £7.95)
Let's Go – Greece (Pan, 1990, £10.99)
Rough Guide to Greece (Harrap Columbus, 1989, £6.95)

For further information:
The National Tourist Office of Greece, 4 Conduit Street, London W1R 0DJ. Tel: (071) 734 5997

Holland *see* **The Netherlands**

Hong Kong

Time   GMT + 8

Currency   Hong Kong dollar
   (HK$) = 100 cents

Languages   English, Chinese

Climate   Tropical monsoon

Annual weather range:

Temperature   Max 31°C (Jul–Aug)
   Min 13°C (Jan–Feb)

Rainfall   Max 394mm (Jul)   Min
   31mm (Dec)

Hong Kong is not well-suited to children: urban space is extremely dangerous and congested, both pedestrian and vehicular traffic are dense and frenetic at almost all hours. Most parks are tiny and playgrounds teem with children, even at night. Some calm and fresh air can be found at the colony's outer fringes and islands, usually a day's outing from the urban centres.

There are, of course, hundreds of thousands of children growing up happily in Hong Kong, it's just that you hardly notice them amidst the frenetic pace and commercial obsessions of the place. Children are left pretty much to fend for themselves (not altogether a bad thing) within a rather confined and structured domain (home, schools and parks).

Hong Kong is a largely Chinese place and Chinese culture, which developed quite independently of the West, so it has naturally developed its own unique theories and methods of child-rearing. However, the colony's 150-year-old history as a British possession provides a full array of British child-rearing customs and accoutrements. Disposable nappies are available cheaply, and you can get prepared baby foods even in small neighbourhood shops. There are cheap prams, Chinese-style cloth slings (for front and back), glorious clothing, good, fresh pasteurized milk (from the local 'Dairy Farm' brand, as well as a competitor from China), fresh biscuits in endless variety and sweets galore. Tap water is not drinkable (except at the major hotels) but cold, bottled beverages of every description are available everywhere.

Hong Kong must certainly rank with New York and Paris as one of the great places in the world for dining out. Virtually every major international cuisine is represented here, from northern Italian to kosher-style delicatessens including, of course, all the major regional

Chinese cuisines, many of which are arguably better prepared here than in their places of origin. All this to say that children visiting Hong Kong will never be far from the taste of something familiar. Local Chinese frequently take all their children out to dinner, so restaurants are well-equipped and reassuringly tolerant. The full panoply of fast-food emporia is here if you need them.

While not yet qualifying as one of the cleanest cities in the world, Hong Kong would rank pretty well within Asia. Public conveniences and changing places are relatively numerous and nicely kept up (most are attended). Public transport, especially the sparkling MTR underground system are well kept and have fine safety records. Children's fares apply throughout the system. Chemists are well-supplied and reliable (the big Western-style chain is Watson's).

Babysitters of Western nationality are available (or English-speaking Chinese) from the hotels or from agencies. Standards are quite high, with substantial fees charged. Chinese nannies called *amahs* can be hired on a longer term basis. They are certain to be stern and conscientious although their English may be wanting.

One final note: Hong Kong hotels in general now charge by the number of occupants, with nominal fees charged for extra beds or cots in the room.

F.K.

Recommended reading:
Hong Kong, Macau & Canton – A Travel Survival Kit (Lonely Planet, 1989, £11.95)
Insight Guides – Hong Kong (APA Publications, 1990, £10.95)

For further information:
Hong Kong Tourist Association, 125 Pall Mall, London SW1Y. Tel: (071) 930 4775

India

Capital New Delhi	**Annual weather range** – Northern plains (Delhi):
Major cities Bombay, Calcutta, Delhi, Madras, Hyderabad, Ahmenabad, Bangalore	*Temperature* Max 41°C (Mar) Min 7°C (Jan)
Time GMT + 5½	*Rainfall* Max 180mm (Jul) Min 3mm (Nov)
Currency Indian rupee (IR) = 100 paise	**Annual weather range** – West coast (Bombay):
Languages Hindi, English, local languages	*Temperature* Max 33°C (Mar) Min 19°C (Jan–Feb)
Climate Tropical; wide variation with region and altitude	*Rainfall* Max 617mm (Jul) Min 0mm (Apr)

'Please, you must go to the front of the queue; your children look tired,' insisted about twenty Indians in an early-morning, seething queue at Bombay Airport. Those were the first words we heard on Indian soil and continued to hear throughout our month's holiday there – in busy Bombay, on the overflowing buses in Goa, on rickshaws at Agra, on shikaras (small boats) in Kashmir.

We do tend to be the sort of family who hoist small children on backs and then take pot luck, but as India carries its fair share of health horror stories we were more careful for this trip. For a start we planned our itinerary in detail and I must admit in luxury: we had several nights at The Holiday Inn in Bombay though that did not stop us eating in very basic restaurants.

'Eat the cheapest food as long as it is cooked on the spot there and then,' advised a doctor friend of ours who knew India well. Why? Because that has the quickest turnover. Of course we avoided salads, fruit without peel, unsealed water and ice, and ice-cream (the children did not miss it).

Goa. Well, most people do not even see paradise once; it is a land of unspoilt beaches, unspoilt Portuguese architecture and archetypal paddy fields and was, childwise, plain-sailing. Even the water from the taps at the Taj Holiday Village was purified; for food we went lock, stock and child to various rustic restaurants where the fish was fantastic and so was the child-welcome. As I can remember, the children got more fun out of swinging on the basket chairs in one of the restaurant gardens than actually eating, but such was life in Goa.

Our plane journey to Delhi was rather late so we checked in hastily at the Imperial only to get up very early to take a booked train journey to Agra the next morning. But nobody starved; air snacks, even on short journeys, are quite good and safe. Breakfast on the train was novel – greasy omelettes cooked in a very black and even greasier galley did not do our lot any harm.

The Mogul Sheraton provided a cot, as did the Holiday Inn, the Taj Holiday Village and the Imperial but we were less excited by the food, so had a curry in one of the dusty locals – after all, most mini-travellers learn to like rice and vegetables even if the rest is lip-searing.

The Imperial in Delhi seems quite imperial – toast and tea was served on a trolley in our rooms by old retainers. We never actually learnt if they appreciated our amused relief at reading on a huge surgical strip stuck across the loos the message 'sterilized for your use'.

But it was at Mr Butt's Clermont Houseboats on the Dal Lake in Kashmir when the children really got their feet under the table or more pedantically, their feet in the drawer. Our youngest, aged one and a bit, had to sleep in a huge drawer, not that she cared. Solemnly, at very small people's bed time, the boy (aged about 60) entered the houseboat with hot water bottles and again later for the rest of us. The junior team also got into the habit of sauntering along to the cook-house to order what they thought fitting for an early supper – French toast, Kashmiri doughnuts and maple syrup.

For a child brought up on Saudi sand, making daisy chains in Mr Butt's Moghul Garden was what India was all about but we managed to drag her out with the rest and walk for hours round the lake and up the mountains. The village children insisted on teaching ours how to bowl rubber tubes; another family pulled us out of the pouring rain and would not let us go till we had warmed up under a pile of blankets and a gallon of tea. We could not understand each other's language except the common one that we all had to look after our own and each other's children.

I mentioned precautions. We always knew our destination though would prefer to be more happy-go-lucky next time. Healthwise we followed the school of thought which avoids any extra jabs except the usual triple for all British children but we took malaria pills and ate natural yoghurt daily for the month before our trip. (Our elder children's boarding school was asked by us to do likewise for them.) We carried a couple of emergency packets of Milupa and Farex for the one year-old but only used a few spoonfuls. For the same member we had 200 nappies; we cannot remember whether there were disposables in the shops, only that we had judged the right number by the skin of her bottom.

Oh yes, and the chicken pox. After four weeks of wishing for 20 eyes to catch the sights of Bombay life turned inside-out on the streets, of listening to echoes in the Taj Mahal, of bussing, carting, boating, training, flying and walking round a country, one rather forgets matters like spots. But on our return to Saudi we learnt that there had been an epidemic. The rash that our fourth child had suffered in Kashmir was not due to daisy chains after all – so much for the diagnosis of the local pharmacist-*cum*-quack.

You may be cautious about spending part of your holiday in Kashmir. For advice on the current situation it is advisable to ring either the High Commissioner of India on (071) 836 8484 or the Indian Tourist Office on (071) 437 3677.

A.H.

P.S. The jabs issue: we personally were advised that anti-hepatitis jabs can give a traveller a dangerously false sense of security. Add the fact that a jab appropriate for one bug in one area of India is not necessarily useful elsewhere – and we decided to be very careful instead about water, eating and so on. My advice is to talk to a doctor you really trust and decide on the situation as it stands at the time.

Recommended reading:
India: A Travel Survival Kit (Lonely Planet, 1989, £11.95)
Fodor's India (inc. Nepal), ed. Andrew E. Beresky (Fodor's Travel Publications Inc., 1988, £11.95)
India in Luxury, L. Nicolson (Century, 1989, £8.95)

For further information:
India Government Tourist Office, 7 Cork Street, London W1X 2AB. Tel: (071) 437 3677

Israel

Capital Jerusalem	**Climate** Mediterranean
Major cities Nazareth, Haifa, Tel Aviv, Beersheba, Eilat, Netanya	**Annual weather range** – Haifa:
Time GMT + 2	*Temperature* Max 32°C (Aug) Min 9°C (Jan)
Currency Israeli Shekel (IsS) = 100 agorot	*Rainfall* Max 185mm (Dec) Min 0mm (Jun–Aug)
Languages Hebrew, Arabic, English	

Israel is a country of striking contrasts, where you can ski on Mount Herman in winter and sunbathe on the sandy Mediterranean beaches and see many unique historical and religious sites. It is also a country where children are loved and cherished and no matter where you go there are facilities for them.

Summer lasts from April until October and is usually very hot. August is the hottest month. Winter is from November to March but it is still pleasantly sunny with occasional rain. Whichever time of year you go it is wise to make sure your children are well protected from the sun. Cotton clothing for day is best but remember to take something warmer for the evenings. Protective creams, sun lotions, nappies and all other items you might need for a baby are easily available from local pharmacies.

Israel is a small country and easy to get around. There are several reputable car hire firms and children's seats are available. Although the railway system is limited and slow it does have some unusual scenic routes which children enjoy. The buses are reasonably efficient and there is a good network of them throughout the country. *Sherut* is a taxi service which runs between the main cities. Individual seats can be purchased at reasonable prices and there are plenty of local taxis which have regulated fares. There are many places to visit in addition to Jerusalem, Tel Aviv and Haifa and there are special organized tours available which are suitable for children – and often they go free.

Shops are generally open Sunday to Thursday from 8 a.m. until 1 p.m. and then from 4 until 7 p.m. Fridays the shops are open from about 8.30 a.m. until 2 p.m. and close for Sabbath until sunset on Saturday.

Medical care is extremely good and available all the time. Most doctors speak English and there are hospitals and clinics throughout the country. First-aid and emergency care is provided by the Magen David Adom, similar to the Red Cross. The English daily newspaper, *The Jerusalem Post*, lists emergency hospitals and pharmacists. You should take out medical insurance before you go since treatment can be expensive.

Fruit and vegetables are plentiful and of good quality. Restaurants and cafés offer an incredible variety of international cuisines and Western tastes are catered for in most hotels, which are often kosher. Kosher food conforms to Jewish dietary laws. This means that dairy food (milk, cheese, butter) will not be served with meat; pork and shellfish are prohibited.

Israel is an outdoor paradise for children – there are sandy beaches, all kinds of sports facilities and opportunities for walking and birdwatching. There is also an excellent range of cultural activities in every city – concerts, theatre, dance and museums, many of which have special children's areas. Just a few are the Ramat Gan

Biblical Zoo, Jerusalem's Israel Museum, the Nature Museum in Haifa and the National Maritime Museum.

Finally, there are excellent hotels of every standard throughout the country as well as many kibbutz inns. You can also rent villas and flats and there are good campsites and youth hostels with family accommodation, or there is the option of staying in a Christian hospice. You will get a friendly welcome wherever you go.

Shalom, and enjoy.

A.R.

Please Note
Recent political events are such that it is difficult to know the effect they will have on holiday makers. We would advise you to contact the relevant National Tourist Office for further details before travelling.

Recommended reading:
Baedeker's Israel (AA, 1987, £9.95)
Rough Guide to Israel and the Occupied Territories (Harper Columbus, 1989, £5.95)
Israel − A Travel Survival Guide (Lonely Planet, 1989, £7.95)

For further information:
Israel Government Tourist Offices, 18 Great Marlborough Street, London W1V 1AF. Tel: (071) 434 3651

Italy

Capital Rome	**Annual weather range −**
Major cities Milan, Naples, Turin,	Peninsular Italy (Rome):
Genoa, Palermo, Bologna	*Temperature* Max 30°C
Time GMT + 1	(Jul–Aug) Min 5°C
Currency Lira (L) = 100	*Rainfall* Max 129mm (Nov)
centesimi	Min 21mm (Aug)
Language Italian	**Annual weather range** − Great
Climate Mediterranean	Northern Plain (Milan):
	Temperature Max 24°C (Jul)
	Min 2°C (Jan)
	Rainfall Max 125mm (Oct)
	Min 44mm (Jan)

Italy is the perfect holiday place for children, but it also has much to offer adults. Choose from mountains, lakes, seaside resorts or cities of great historical and artistic interest, all with endless sun and the warmest welcome in Europe. The scenery varies from dramatic mountain panoramas in the north to the fertile plains of the Po Valley, so temperatures vary enormously. In the mountains the heat is never overwhelming whereas it can be stifling on the plains at midday. Cities, of course, tend to trap the heat and Florence is notorious for this in summer.

Italians are naturally friendly, but become even more so if you have children with you since they play a central part in Italian life and are always a focus of attention.

There are many campsites, especially in the popular resorts, and hotels are plentiful and very welcoming. They charge by the room rather than by the person and are usually willing to put up an extra bed for a small child, if necessary. Cots are not always available, however, so if you have a baby it is a good idea to take a travelling cot. The staff are always willing to heat up baby's bottles and help in any way they can, even offering to dry baby clothes or babysit in some cases.

Eating out with children is easy and fun in Italy. Restaurants always have high chairs, and children are accepted without question – even quite late at night. Staff are generally willing to serve half portions or to supply extra plates so that children can share a parent's portion.

Italian food is very popular with most children. Pasta heads the menu in every restaurant and is one of the cheapest dishes. Fast food and convenience foods are available throughout Italy. Takeaway pizza and pasta are sold in larger towns and sandwiches are quite easy to get hold of. Otherwise look out for *tavola calda* – the Italian version of a self-service restaurant. The noise level in restaurants tends to be high, so there is no need to worry about your children causing disturbance. Eating places are always very relaxed and as Italy's climate allows you to eat outside, it is a common sight to see children playing together while their parents finish a leisurely meal.

Bars are not quite so well adapted to children's needs. They often have no seating, and when they do they charge much more for waiter service – although you can sit for a long time with just one drink.

Everything you might need for children is readily available, even in small towns, but prices vary considerably. For instance, nappies (*pannolini*) cost far more in a local shop than in a supermarket where the price would be much the same as in Britain. If your child needs typical British foods, it is probably a good idea to take them with you, as although foods such as breakfast cereals are becoming more popular they are still quite expensive. On the other hand, ice creams and

ice lollies are very cheap and very good. Shops tend to close for three
or four hours in the middle of the day, but stay open until 8 p.m.

Trains and buses are efficient and cheap in Italy, with reduced
fares for children. Travelling on a crowded bus in the heat of the day
with small children, however, is not to be recommended. The Italians
themselves complain of the heat and organize their lives accordingly.
If you decide to hire a car, it can be expensive and children's safety
seats are much less common than in Britain.

Most towns have a municipal park with a special play area for small
children. Sometimes they are supervised in the morning and late
afternoon, and charge a small fee for entry, but many are free and
open to children at all times. They are always shady and offer a
pleasant retreat from the heat of the day, particularly if your child
doesn't take to the idea of a siesta. Bicycles may be hired for a nominal
sum.

As a member of the EEC, Britain has a reciprocal health agreement
with Italy. On completion of the relevant form – E111 – (available
from the DHSS), British citizens are entitled to free medical treatment in Italy; but you may decide to take out private health insurance
as well.

M.C.

Sicily

It is easy to be evangelical about Sicily – it has so much to offer:
wonderful scenery, marvellous beaches, terrific food and wine (far
more varied than, say, Tuscany, thanks to the Greek, Arab, French
and Spanish influences from its chequered past), and some of the
finest archaeological remains in the world. Visit Agrigento, for
example, on the south coast and you will see the Valley of Temples
which surpasses anything you will find in Greece.

If you take a package trip to Sicily, chances are you will end up in
one of the two main resorts on the island. Cefalu, on the north coast,
is a small town with a lovely cathedral, numerous hotels, a stony beach
and a sprinkling of discos; Taormina, on the east coast, is a former
fishing village that has been rather self-consciously prettified. It has
too many souvenir shops and tourist buses for my taste and is packed
to the gills in summer, but it sits on a beautiful bay and it is easy to see
why D.H. Lawrence rented a villa overlooking it.

For more intrepid visitors, I strongly recommend hiring a car and
setting off in search of undiscovered Sicily. If you travel outside the
peak season (July and August, when mainland Italians flock in),
it is very easy to find accommodation without booking in advance,

although it is a good idea to get a list of hotels and pensione from the Italian Tourist Office so you can plan your route. Note that the south coast has the best sandy beaches; elsewhere they tend to be pebbly. Don't be frightened of driving in Sicily; the natives may be noisy and flamboyant road-users, but they are no worse, in my experience, than London taxi-drivers. If driving really is out of the question, buses and trains are cheap and efficient.

Family life is paramount in Sicily, so the welcome that all visitors receive is particularly warm if you have children. In fact, producing a baby can often gain you entrance to previously full hotels or restaurants, and hotel proprietors gladly offer to babysit.

If you and your children require little entertainment beyond uncrowded beaches and good food, try the southern coast. Selinunte is a delightful place to stay, the 'modern' fishing village next to the tumbled ruins of the ancient city creating a curious feeling of time warp.

Should the coasts prove too hot, head for the cooler air of the mountains inland. Mount Etna is snow-capped all year round and you will need warm clothing at the summit, no matter what temperature it is below. The medieval hill-town of Enna, bang in the middle of the island, is well worth a visit, but its isolation makes it rather expensive to stay in. The nearby village of Pergusa has a small, modern hotel which is much more affordable, although it does not boast the atmosphere or views of the Hotel Belvedere in Enna itself.

Families, particularly those with very young children, would be well advised to avoid holidaying during July and August when temperatures, inflated by the sirocco wind from North Africa, are often uncomfortably hot and make sleeping at night difficult. If you cannot avoid visiting during these months, make sure you ask for a room with a balcony. And do remember, whether you sleep indoors or out, to cover all exposed flesh with insect repellent.

While you are in Sicily, it is worth considering a visit to the islands. The Aeolians, reached by boat or hydrofoil from Messina, are extraordinarily varied, ranging from smelly Vulcano (full of sulphur springs which can be quite overpowering) to the desolate Stromboli (volcanic black beaches and a high cost of living as everything, including drinking water, has to be imported). The Egadi Islands, reached by boat from Trapani, are particularly splendid. They have dozens of beautiful, safe beaches, clear water, caves and grottoes. There are few tourist facilities, but rooms can be rented.

For those who think the Mediterranean has nothing left to reveal, Sicily will be a pleasurable surprise. See it before the rest of the world catches on.

P.M.B.

Recommended reading:
Baedeker's Italy (AA, 1987, £9.95)
Italy: A Phaidon Cultural Guide, ed. Franz N. Mehling (Phaidon, £10.50)
Italy: Off the Beaten Track (Moorland, 1988, £9.99)
Independent Traveller's Guide to Southern Italy, I. Thompson (Collins, 1989, £6.95)
Italy at its Best, R. Skane (Passport, 1989, £7.95)

For further information:
Italian Tourist Board, 1 Princes Street, London W1R. Tel: (071) 408 1254

Jamaica

Capital Kingston	**Annual weather range** – Kingston:
Time GMT −5	*Temperature* Max 32°C
Currency Jamaican dollar (J$) =	(Jul–Sep) Min 20°C (Jan–Feb)
100 cents	*Rainfall* Max 180mm (Oct) Min
Language English	15mm (Feb)
Climate Tropical	

Jamaica is twelve hours away by plane – something to be endured rather than enjoyed by parents and babies. But the warmth of the tropics smooths the kinks of the journey. Jamaica is everything the song says and the air has an effect on adults and children alike.

The northern winter is the best time to visit the island but it is also the busiest time. The summer is hot and humid, and though most places claim to have air-conditioning, this should not be taken too literally. There is always the odd power cut or water shortage and the islanders seem to have their own time and ways to do things.

Jamaica may be billed as a honeymooners' paradise but Jamaicans love to spoil children. To have a baby is positively an advantage. There are plenty of houses of all sizes to rent on or near the beach on Jamaica's north coast between Negril and Port Antonio. For a family they can be more economical than a hotel, and most come with a housekeeper or maid. It's worth checking, however, if cots are provided.

Nannies or childminders are available everywhere so parents can enjoy some time off too. The housekeeper will usually do the cooking (hot and spicy Jamaican food) but will go easy on the pepper for the children if requested. Let the housekeeper take you shopping in the local market and see the wonderful – and healthy – tropical fruit, vegetables and fresh seafood.

Baby food and care products are not always available and are expensive. Nappies are extremely expensive so it is preferable to bring your own. Since it is so hot there is also an opportunity for the children to wear very few clothes, which eases the packing. No nappies during the day is the rule because the odd accident is usually no disaster. Both our children were potty trained in Jamaica.

Eating out is expensive, high chairs are rare and the service is slow. Not much fun for impatient little ones who would rather be at their favourite playground, the beach with its clean, shallow water.

'Higglers', local mobile traders, are everywhere and some require friendly but firm handling. Bargaining (higgling) is a way of life because few prices are fixed. The best price guide is what it is worth to you. Sensible offers are seldom refused. Higglers can offer a worthwhile service when the next shop is a mile down the beach. Most have fresh-pressed orange juice and fruit. No child will miss sweets when offered pieces of sugarcane to chew or milk fresh from the coconut.

Since you will spend a lot of time on the beach the sun has to be taken seriously. Repeated application of sunblock is essential for children and grown-ups; so are sunhats or some kind of shade. A shower in the afternoon and an aloe vera rub at night should cool everybody down. If you want to watch the picture-postcard sunset you will need some effective mosquito repellent; for a good night's sleep local burning coils called 'fish' or good old mosquito nets (bring your own) are recommended.

A day's rest from the beach is usually provided by the odd tropical downpour, which is exciting in itself. A cloudy day should be used as a reason for a journey into the mountainous and cool interior of the island, only a short drive away. Car rental is expensive, as is petrol, and baby seats are unheard of. Local drivers know the beauty spots and the sometimes hazardous roads. Hidden waterfalls and old plantation Great Houses are interesting, but young children are usually bored by long hot car rides and viable alternatives are trips in glass-bottomed boats to view the varied underwater life; rafting down rivers keeps them still for a while too.

There is no free health service in Jamaica so adequate medical insurance is needed. Vaccinations are not required but general rules of hygiene should be observed.

Jamaica is a friendly place for children, even though established play areas are rare and facilities somewhat lacking, but by bringing a pushchair, folding babydiner and travel cot we've felt quite comfortable. When our children were safely sleeping next door we would relax and watch the fireflies illuminate the scenery.

Recommended reading:
Insight Guides: Caribbean (The Lesser Antilles), ed. David Schwab (APA Publications, 1989, £10.95)
Zellers 1990 Caribbean, Margaret Zellers (Fielding-Morrow, 1990, £10.95)
The Penguin Guide to the Caribbean 1990, ed. Alan Tucker (Penguin, 1990, £5.99)

For further information:
Jamaica Tourist Board, 111 Gloucester Place, London W1. (071) 224 0505

Japan

Capital Tokyo	**Climate** Temperate monsoon
Major cities Kyoto, Kobe, Nagoya, Osaka, Sapporo, Yokohama	**Annual weather range** – Tokyo: *Temperature* Max 30°C (Aug) Min −2°C (Jan)
Time GMT + 9	*Rainfall* Max 234mm (Sep) Min 48mm (Jan)
Currency Yen (Y) = 100 sen	
Language Japanese	

Japan must be one of the easiest countries to travel to with a child. It is safe, clean and efficient. Baby food, supplies and disposable nappies can be found everywhere. The Japanese, old and young, adore babies, and will come up to talk to yours. Don't worry about not understanding what is being said. Most probably it is only the word *kawaii* (cute) expressed over and over again.

If your first destination is Tokyo, be prepared for the commute into the city centre from the international airport at Narita. It takes a lot more than an hour by coach or rail and can be tedious after a long flight. If you are travelling around the country it is advisable to avoid travelling by air which is expensive and airports are usually some distance from the cities. The best way, especially with children, is to use the super-efficient rail system which may not be cheap (nothing in this country is cheap) but is fast and convenient. If you are using the bullet train *shinkansen* get ready for your station as it will stop for no more than one to two minutes. Japanese children take off their shoes if they want to stand on the seats of trains and adults give up their seats for children!

In Tokyo, avoid travelling by train between seven and nine in the morning unless you want your child to experience what it is like to be a sardine. It can be an unnerving experience. If you have a baby, come with sensible shoes and a pushchair as platforms are long and there are several flights of stairs to manage, often with no escalators. Travel by taxi is very expensive and please note that the taxi doors are controlled by the driver so make sure children are not standing too close to the passenger door which will swing open automatically.

If you are staying in an international hotel it will, of course, have all the international amenities. If you are not, there will be no space in the rooms for extra beds or cots, no babysitting service and little English will be spoken. It would be more interesting to experience staying at Japanese-style inns called *ryokan*. There will be no problem about extra beds as everyone will be sleeping on *futons* on the *tatami* floors. Breakfast and dinner will be covered in the cost of accommodation and served in your room when the *futons* are out of the way, cleverly hidden in the wall cupboards. The problem then is that there is no choice of menu. You eat what you get – which is usually good.

Eating out in local restaurants is easy as there are often plastic replicas of dishes on the menu displayed in the windows and you need only point. There may not be high chairs but there are tatami mat floors which may not be so comfortable for you but great for babies to lie on or toddlers to romp around. Of course the usual fast food outlets like McDonalds, Mr Donut, Pizza Hut and the whole range of Western family-style restaurants can be found in most of the cities. You can always get yoghurt and fruit juices at shops and supermarkets.

Local shops and big stores open only after ten o'clock in the morning but stay open till late. They are open on Sundays and public holidays but close one day in the middle of the week. There are many 24-hour supermarkets as well. The department stores are the best places to head for to take a rest, feed or change your baby, or entertain your child. Go to the floor for children's things. There is a nursing room with cots provided and a baby menu available. There is a small play area for toddlers and there are samples of the toys for the children to test. Also there is usually a large playground on the roof of the store. A city like Tokyo can be very tiring for parents and children and, surprisingly, the department store can be a refuge.

Of course there are parks, zoos and museums but they are hardly just round the corner. Then there is Tokyo Disneyland but it is away from the city centre so be prepared for the long queues to do or go on anything. It will be much worse if it is a Sunday, public holiday or school holiday. You might have to wait for an hour or more to get into anything. We took our toddler on an ordinary day and even so the entire outing was a torture for her and us.

If you are at your wit's end trying to keep your child entertained, an outing to the local public bath might prove to be the most interesting cultural experience for you and your child. It is a communal bath, the water is very hot and everything is extremely clean. Ask where the nearest public bath-house is (it's probably just round the corner), and stay in there as long as you like. Just observe what the Japanese do and follow them. Bath-houses are usually open from 4.00 to 11.00 pm.

The main problem you will encounter is language. You will just have to ask for help. There are police boxes called *kobans* outside major train stations and at big road intersections. The tourist information centres (TIC) at Narita, Tokyo and Kyoto are very helpful and the staff speak English. Use their 'Travel Phone' service which is ready to help you solve a language or travel problem.

S.O.

Recommended reading:
Baedeker's Japan (AA, 1987, £10.95)
Japan Handbook, J.D. Bisignani (Moon Publications, 1987, £12.95)

For further information:
National Japan Tourist Organization, 167 Regent Street, London W1R 7FD. Tel: (071) 734 9638

Jordan

Capital Amman	**Annual weather range** – Amman:
Major cities Zarka, Irbid	*Temperature* Max 32°C (Jul–Aug)
Time GMT + 2	Min −4°C (Jan–Feb)
Currency Jordanian dinar (JD) =	*Rainfall* Max 74mm (Feb) Min
1000 fils	0mm (Jun–Sep)
Language Arabic	
Climate Desert	

If you are not already in possession of a young child on entry into Jordan you might be well advised to hire one! Jordanians adore children who are the instant bond between tourist and the would-be host. Travelling in an Islamic country without my husband, as I was, my children were an essential passport to respectability.

We spent ten weeks there basing ourselves at Irbid, a town in the beautifully unspoilt countryside of northern Jordan. We bussed our way to historical sites, untouched villages, Amman and its surroundings and finally way south to Aqaba and Petra.

I am not qualified to comment on five-star hotels. Except in Irbid where we rented rooms, we had recourse to the cheapest hotels which featured along with the five-stars in the invaluable 'Classified Hotel Price List', courtesy of the Ministry of Tourism in Amman. (Staff there bent over backwards to help, apparently surprised, dare I say it, that they had visitors.) Bedsheets and bathrooms in no-star hostelries were tacky. The Ministry of Tourism Resthouses are excellent value – very clean, with good, cheap food.

Fast food has not yet hit Jordan unless you count the traditional *filafel* fried by the roadside. The place is still a haven for simple, wholesome cheap food. The children ate like kings in cheap restaurants or in friends' homes, on a diet of fresh vegetables, rice, a little meat, olives, sesame bread, yoghurt and honey. During the month of Ramadan, however, when most people fast between sunrise and sunset, midday eating was a problem if you were not self-catering. Children are not expected to fast, but in the towns there was nowhere private to consume food; in villages there was space but no food, unless you count stale biscuits and wrinkled oranges gathering dust in dubious looking village stores.

In the early days we were careful to drink bottled water but we soon had to lose our inhibitions about drinking well water; there was no alternative when we stayed with chance acquaintances in the middle of nowhere. The children survived it until our final two weeks, when we had to beetle off to a local government-run hospital. I do not know whether the water had upset them, but I mention the incident simply because we were impressed by the friendliness of the hospital staff and, incidentally, by the practical help we met in ordinary chemists in towns throughout Jordan.

Transport by bus or 'service taxi' is efficient, cheap and enchanting. The buses serving outlying villages are mobile gossip columns – everyone knew everyone else and insisted on knowing who we were too. Then, once our credentials had been established, we were invariably invited home, entertained, fed and watered. Service taxis were a boon in towns. They follow a prescribed route, picking up and dropping off passengers on the way for a minimal fare. Children on laps rode for free. We made the five-hour bus journey from Amman to Aqaba by Jett bus for 3 dinars (£6) for the lot of us. (Again the two-year-old rode free.) The bus was air-conditioned, with a loo, hostess service and video. The latter was welcome as the King's Highway route is dull, scrubby, grey desert with the odd dusty town thrown in.

Petra, which we reached by means of an overflowing mini-bus (a two-hour journey from Aqaba), was a test in ingenuity and infant stamina. Any normal human being would hire a horse for the day at a mere 2 dinars and enjoy wandering round the ancient city at leisure. However, my toddler refused to mount so we footed it into Petra, which was fine for the first few hours before the sun was really hot.

After rest and refreshments at the resthouse in the middle of the old city the children could not face the several kilometres walk back to new civilization. A boy on a donkey saved the day, but that was a close one.

Would our children recommend Jordan to their friends? I think so, with one special caveat: 'Don't get excited about swimming in the Dead Sea until you have grown out of falling over – the salt stings the wounds.' And what did they like best? Eating okra and having a go on Bassim's homemade swing.

A.H.

Please Note
Recent political events are such that it is difficult to know the effect they will have on holiday makers. We would advise you to contact the relevant National Tourist Office for further details before travelling.

Recommended reading:
Fodor's Jordan and the Holy Land – a Practical & Historical Guide, Kay Showker (Fodor's Travel Publications Inc., 1989, £9.99)
Jordan and Syria: A Travel Survival Kit, Hugh Finlay (Lonely Planet, 1987, £5.95)

For further information:
Jordanian Embassy, 6 Upper Phillimore Gardens, London W8. Tel: (071) 937 3685/9611

Kenya

Capital Nairobi	**Annual weather range** –
Major cities Mombasa, Kisumu	Mombasa:
Time GMT + 3	*Temperature* Max 31°C
Currency Kenya shilling (Ksh) =	(Jan–Mar) Min 22°C (Jul–Sep)
100 cents	*Rainfall* Max 320mm (May) Min
Languages Swahili, English	18mm (Feb)
Climate Subtropical; variation	**Annual weather range** – Nairobi:
between coast and higher	*Temperature* Max 26°C (Feb)
altitude inland	Min 11°C (Jun–Sep)
	Rainfall Max 211mm (Apr) Min
	15mm (Jul)

Not many British or American people take children to East Africa for the simple reason that it is a very expensive trip. Given the opportunity of a holiday in East Africa – or any form of trip which may include a holiday – I doubt whether it is worth taking children under four years old.

Most people go to these regions to visit the game reserves and look at the wildlife. For the most part the wildlife will mean little or nothing to small children because they have little sense of scale. It is a basic error on the part of adults to suppose that children will respond like adults, though of course adults very much want them to do so. I have taken my children (aged four and nine) to several splendid zoos and game parks. The smaller the animals the more they were interested in them. In short, they have no capacity for being awe-inspired when they behold a herd of 100 elephants, a pride of lions or a column of wildebeeste 5000 strong. On the other hand, a tame hyrax (they resemble large rabbits but are related to the elephant) or a tame mongoose (kept to deter snakes) pottering round a fixed camp or the grounds of a game lodge will be a source of great fascination.

If you do go to East Africa with little children various precautions are essential. They must have inoculations against tropical diseases and remember that apart from Nairobi and Mombasa no town has adequate supplies of anything you might take for granted in Britain and Europe. Remember, too, that in summer (November to March) the sun is very strong; no child should be exposed to it for long.

If you travel through or camp in game reserves the rules must be rigorously adhered to: after dusk you must not venture outside the designated camping area; in daylight stay in or very near your vehicle; avoid getting too close to wild animals. Lions and elephants often show complete indifference to vehicles, but rhinoceroses are dangerous. Their sight is poor but their hearing and smell are excellent. Moreover, they are as nimble as ballet dancers and will charge at high speed on very little pretext. Two-and-a-half tons of rhino travelling at 30 m.p.h. will make 'Whiskas' of you and your vehicle. The African buffalo is perhaps the most dangerous of all. Lastly, you must never attempt to approach any wild animal on foot however innocuous or tame it may appear to be.

Colonies of baboon are a common feature of campsites. They wander in when there are few people about and look for titbits. Never leave your tent unattended for any length of time. Baboons are extremely inquisitive and given the chance they will have the tent (however strong or secure it may be) down in a flash and will create total havoc among your belongings. Baboons often look friendly enough but they are wild animals. A male baboon may weigh 350lb and could have Muhammad Ali in his prime completely incapacitated in five seconds flat. Never leave your children unattended anywhere in a game reserve.

In the game reserves you must use the appointed camping sites and obey any local rules. These sites are supplied with fresh water and, in some cases, with brick-built installations which provide shower/washing/lavatory facilities.

The game lodges are extremely well run and very comfortable. The cuisine in all these places is absolutely first-class by any standards, including those that prevail in France. Children will lack for nothing in such establishments.

There are two places which would particularly appeal to children. The first is Governor's Camp in the Mara reserve. This is a tent 'hotel' in surroundings of magical beauty. Every conceivable amenity is provided and the food and wines are what you would expect in a three-star restaurant in Burgundy. Schools of hippo wallow in the brown river (I have seen as many as forty at a time) and at night a cloaked watchman with a spear guards the guests from intruders.

The second is Tree Tops, a hotel high in the Aberdare Mountains in Kenya. It is built on high wooden stilts and is literally in the tree tops. Stout stockades protect the precincts against wild animals. Its balconies afford a view of a big waterhole. At night this is artificially illuminated so that you may spend a whole night watching the animals when they come out of the forest to drink. This, too, is a site of magical enchantment and if you are very lucky you may see a leopard. But on the other hand something totally unexpected may steal the show. I once saw seven huge cow elephants completely routed by a rabbit no bigger than a teapot.

Finally, most important of all, the Africans. They love children and understand them. You may be sure that your children will receive VIP attention. They will lack for nothing here.

J.A.C.

Recommended reading:
The Insider's Guide to Kenya, Michael and Peggy Bond (M.P.C, 1989, £8.99)
Kenya: A Visitor's Guide, Arnold Curtis (Evans Brothers Ltd, 1988, £5.95)

For further information:
Kenya Tourist Office, 25 Brook's Mews, London W1. Tel: (071) 355 3144

Majorca *see* Spain

Malaysia and Singapore

Capital (Malaysia) Kuala Lumpur	**Climate** Equatorial
Time GMT + 8	**Annual weather range** – Kuala
Currency Malaysian dollar or	Lumpur:
ringgit (Ma$) = 100 cents	*Temperature* Max 33°C
Singapore dollar (S$) = 100 cents	(Feb–Jun) Min 22°C (Dec–Feb)
Languages Bahasa Malaysia	*Rainfall* Max 610mm (Jan) Min
English, Malay, Chinese, Tamil	180mm (Jun)

Children are seen, heard and taken everywhere in Malaysia and Singapore so it is very easy to travel with them there. The two national airlines – MAS and SIA – are well known for the attention and care they offer babies and children. Even domestic travel between the major towns is best done by air as it is both cheap and convenient. Of course the trains and buses are cheaper but can be very tiring and trying for children in hot and humid climates. Car rental is easily available but the highways can be rather hazardous. In the towns don't hesitate to use taxis. They are not expensive.

The big hotels have excellent facilities and offer very good rates. They usually provide cots at no extra charge and babysitters can be arranged. Baby food can also be requested without much trouble and tap water is safe for drinking.

All restaurants, even very small ones, provide high chairs and no one minds children being taken out to meals anywhere and at anytime. Children are allowed to stay up late and are included in most activities. Life happens a lot outdoors and people love eating out at the hawkers' centres where there is such variety of food, fruit and fresh drinks. Let your child experience all the different tastes of Chinese, Malay and Indian dishes and local fruits like papayas and mangoes are delicious and nutritious.

Shops and restaurants stay open till late. English is easily understood everywhere and is on all labels and menus. All doctors speak English well and most doctors' surgeries are open in the evenings.

Baby food and supplies, including disposable nappies, can be bought at most places. Don't confine yourself to the supermarkets. Venture into the little grocers' shops. As it is very hot and humid throughout the year, do take precautions against sunburn, nappy rash and mosquitoes.

Besides the time spent on the beaches in these two countries, which can easily fill up all your holiday, in Singapore you might consider a trip to the zoo (considered to be the best in southeast Asia), the Jurong Bird Park and a ride on the cable car to Sentosa. The Tiger Balm Gardens might not be such a good idea for sensitive children with vivid imaginations. In Malaysia, if you are in Penang, the butterfly farm is unique and a ride on the funicular railway up to Penang Hill could be interesting.

S.O.

Recommended reading:
Malaysia In Your Pocket (M.P.C, 1988, £5.95)
Malaysia, Singapore and Brunei; A Travel Survival Kit, Geoff Crowther and Tony Wheeler (Lonely Planet, 1988, £6.95)

For further information:
Malaysian Tourist Development Corporation, Malaysian House, 57 Trafalgar Square, London WC2. Tel: (071) 930 7932
Singapore Tourist Promotion Board, Carrington House, 126–130 Regent Street, London W1. Tel: (071) 437 0033

Malta

Capital Valletta	**Climate** Mediterranean
Time GMT + 1	**Annual weather range** – Valletta:
Currency Maltese lira (LM) = 100 cents	*Temperature* Max 29°C (Jul-Aug) Min 10°C (Jan-Feb)
Languages Maltese, English	*Rainfall* Max 110mm (Dec) Min 0mm (Jul)

Malta's long tradition of association with Britain makes it an ideal holiday destination for people with young children. The island is small enough to explore without spending too much time travelling and the Maltese are very pro-British; they also adore small children and babies which makes life far more relaxed for the potentially harassed parent of hot and bothered infants.

The climate is very hot and dry during the summer months and it would probably be advisable to avoid booking for July and August if at all possible. June and September are still hot enough for the most dedicated sunbather and even early October should be warm with the added benefit of the sea still beautifully warm. You should, however, be wary of tar patches which can spoil some of the beaches.

All the sandy beaches in Malta are concentrated towards the western tip; the rest of the coastline is rocky and swimming would have to be off the rocks. If your hotel has a good pool this is not a problem, although most small children enjoy playing in the sand. Many of the small hotels situated in Valletta and Sliema (unless you are heading for one of the more secluded luxury establishments) are likely to be in fairly crowded neighbourhoods and thus rather noisy. If you enjoy a more peaceful lifestyle, the fishing villages and the area around St Paul's Bay would perhaps be more suitable.

Another area worth considering is Gozo, Malta's sister island. Gozo is quieter and greener than Malta and also has several sandy beaches. It can be reached by ferry in about 30 minutes from Malta. Hand-made lace and knitted garments are a speciality and are good value. There are also good buys to be made in the way of jeans and baby clothes, many of which are manufactured on the mainland.

A self-catering holiday is easily organized as most English goods and supplies, disposable nappies and baby food are readily available and reasonably priced even in the local shops. Eating out is inexpensive although you might find the fare rather unexciting. Chicken, steak, chips and salad are standard but the fish, particularly swordfish in season, is excellent. Pasteurized milk is good but it is advisable to boil drinking water.

Children's portions are happily supplied. You may not find that many restaurants go in for high chairs but children are so welcome and readily accommodated that you won't feel guilty if they slip off their seats to explore.

Most Maltese children keep late hours so if your children aren't too tired after a day at the beach there is no reason for not eating out together in the evenings.

Car hire is well-priced and it is always convenient to have your own transport for visiting some of the more inaccessible areas of the island. Child seats are not common however. Buses run regularly and are cheap but crowded; don't be surprised if the local passengers offer to hold your child or even just plonk one on to their lap. My seven-month old son was happily nursed by countless ladies, but I was never offered a seat with him.

Most Maltese speak English, especially those in the shops. Shops close for a long lunch from 2 p.m. until around 4 p.m. but are then open until later in the evening. There is a pharmacy in every town. Beach umbrellas and chairs can be hired at many of the beach shops fairly inexpensively. Mosquito repellents and fly sprays are necessary for comfort, especially in the evenings.

Malta is a strongly Catholic country and there are many associated feast days in different towns and villages, especially throughout the summer months. The processions are colourful and great fun and are usually accompanied by fireworks.

C.D.

Recommended reading:
Blue Guide: Malta (A. & C. Black 1990) £9.95
The Travellers' Guide: Malta and Gozo, Christopher Kininmonth, revised by Robin Gordon-Walker (Jonathan Cape, 1987, £7.95)
Discover Malta, Terry Palmer (Heritage House, 1988, £4.95)

For further information:
Malta National Tourist Office, Mappin House, Suite 300, 4 Winsley Street, London W1N 7AR. Tel: (071) 323 0506

Mauritius

Capital Port Louis	**Climate** Tropical
Major cities Beau Bassin-Rose Hill, Curepipe	**Annual weather range** – Port Louis:
Time GMT + 4	*Temperature* Max 30°C (Jan)
Currency Mauritius rupee (MR) = 100 cents	Min 17°C (Jun- Sep)
Languages English, French	*Rainfall* Max 221mm (Mar) Min 36mm (Sep)

Getting to Mauritius is likely to be the worst part of your holiday: some flights involve over 24 hours' travelling time and that's no fun in a crowded aircraft, for adults or infants, so try to use the fastest route.

On the ground, however, Mauritius is delicious: an island in the middle of the Indian Ocean surrounded by warm blue seas and a subtropical climate that's best, I think, in the European summer months when Mauritius is hot and sunny with cool breezes and short freshening showers.

Tourists stay mainly at 'beach hotels' rather than inland local hotels; there are also self-catering apartments and a Club Med. The beaches are well-designed for small swimmers: mostly shallow, sandy lagoons inside coral reefs, barely deep enough for grown-ups to swim and safe for children – except for the ubiquitous sea urchins which make plastic swimming shoes (sold on the beach) obligatory. The hotel where I stayed employed people to sweep the beach and shallows clean of small spiky pieces of coral but this does not seem essential: on the public beach nearby, Mauritian children of all sizes were playing in and out of the water – which is bright and clear. Hotel beaches have pedaloes and glass-bottomed boats for viewing the corals and fish, as well as sailboarding, water-skiing and snorkelling facilities. Boat excursions for swimming, diving, fishing and visiting coves can also be arranged, but do make sure they provide lifejackets for younger passengers.

The people of Mauritius are welcoming and fond of children who, locally, are expected to behave well but join the extended family's outings, so the response of hotels and restaurants is relaxed. My hotel provided an open-air 'playschool' service in the mornings with games, songs and stories for children, and a babysitting service in the evenings. On Fridays, when local people came to the hotel casino, toddlers were playing in the foyer or snoozing on the sofa with granny (children aren't admitted to gambling areas).

Meals are formal or informal according to choice with both a restaurant and a buffet/barbecue service where everyone selects their own platefuls, sort of suit-yourself-servings which could contain only what you fancy, from oysters to shredded carrot. The food however is chiefly European, while the local cuisine is part-Indian, part-Creole. Fresh fruit and vegetables are splendid, especially the small, sweet pineapples.

Mauritius is a smallish island, and excursions and tours are available by mini-bus, taxi and hire car. No distances are great, so in my view the rough state of some roads isn't important although some people complain. Public transport – by bus – is cheap and frequent but they are short distance only and regarded locally as extremely uncomfortable. Self-drive cars may be hired, but it can be useful to have a local driver, who will also act as information source and negotiator when deciding where to go, shopping or searching for special services.

I didn't need to do much everyday shopping, but my impression is that most necessities are available and, if not immediately visible, can be obtained by asking. On the beach itinerant hawkers (who can be a nuisance) will undertake to supply various other items – at a price to be negotiated.

There are several European-style stores in the capital, Port Louis, and other main towns, including a Kentucky Fried Chicken if any rising-fives are feeling deprived. Don't miss the markets – for fruit, spices, knitwear and plastic toys.

The main public parks are gardens in and around Port Louis including the huge Pamplemousses botanical garden with pools and streams and palm-shaded avenues. The only public lavatories I saw were on the public beach, but if you need them elsewhere I'd try asking – everyone is sure to be helpful and sympathetic, as long as you surround your request with smiles and courtesy – Mauritians are not taken with arrogant, demanding behaviour. The local language is

Creole, but nearly everyone speaks and understands both English and French. Many Mauritians have visited Britain and have relatives living here – don't be surprised if they turn out to know London well – and professional people, such as the doctor or nurse on duty at your hotel, will probably have studied and trained in Britain, which could be useful in an emergency. No special immunization or health procedures are required for visitors coming from Europe since the island is free of tropical diseases, including malaria.

On the whole, children should enjoy Mauritius. At my conference delegates from Japan, Denmark and Madagascar had brought husbands and children with them, who appeared to spend the days very happily. So it should be possible to combine a business trip and family holiday on this beautiful tropical island.

J.M.

Recommended reading:
Guide to Mauritius: for Tourists, Business Visitors and Independent Travellers, Royston Ellis (Bradt, 1988, £7.95)
Mauritius, Reunion and Seychelles : A Travel Survival Kit, Robert Willcox (Lonely Planet, 1989, £6.95)

For further information:
Mauritius Government Tourist Office, 49 Conduit Street, London W1. Tel: (071) 437 7508

Mexico

Capital Mexico City
Major cities Guadalajara, Monterrey, Puebla de Zaragoza, Ciudad Juárez, Léon de los Aldamas, Tijuana
Time GMT −6–8
Currency Mexican peso (Mex$) = 100 centavos
Language Spanish
Climate Warm temperate/ tropical

Annual weather range – Centre (Mexico City 2275m):
Temperature Max 26°C (Mar) Min 6°C (Dec-Feb)
Rainfall Max 170mm (Jul) Min 5mm (Feb)
Annual weather range – Southeast (Mérida):
Temperature Max 41°C (Apr) Min 17°C (Jan-Feb)
Rainfall Max 173mm (Jul) Min 18mm (Feb)

The tourist road to Mexico is, by now, comparatively well-travelled – both because it is a physically beautiful and interesting land and, once you have got there, cheap to live and travel in. Whether you want to go to enjoy the ritzy west coast around Acapulco or to explore the Mayan ruins in the Yucatan, you can be confident of always being within reasonable reach of those things that make travelling with a baby comfortable, while not, at the same time, losing your awareness of being in a very foreign part of the world. Mexicans are warm and friendly and they like both visitors and babies.

Health is bound to be every parent's main concern when travelling and Mexico has as many hazards as most poor and hot countries. To start with Mexico City is at an altitude of 7000 feet which means thin air. Most children adapt well and quickly, but don't be surprised at a near total loss of appetite in the first few days. This, coupled with the loss of energy which comes while you adapt to the altitude and the fact that neither parents nor children sleep as deeply or as well, can make the first few days of arrival rather bad-tempered and fraught. Unfortunately there are no obvious remedies apart from taking it easy and waiting for bodies to adapt.

Whatever precautions you all take, and however stringent, you are bound to get tummy pains and diarrhoea at some time. The best stuff for everybody to take is a locally-made medicine called Kaopectate, although it's a good idea to carry some imported Lomotil with you (suitable for children). Don't forget also that the ubiquitous Coca-Cola is surprisingly good for unsettled tummies and is very effective against dehydration.

Mexico is well supplied with good chemists, and in the major towns and cities you can usually find someone in the shop who speaks some English. Chemists have a more active role in medicine than in many countries and, if you can describe symptoms accurately, they will usually either refer you to a doctor or prescribe a medicine themselves (if the illness is quite commonplace). In the towns that tourists are most likely to visit (and this excludes small country towns on the way to ruins or beaches well off the beaten track), chemists stock disposable nappies, powdered milk and baby food plus all the other obvious paraphernalia, so that there is no need to arrive in the country burdened down with endless amounts of babykit. The prices are much the same as at home. At certain times of the year parts of the Yucatan are potentially malarial so it is strongly advisable to start a course of anti-malaria pills before arriving.

Food and drink are the second item of major concern and Mexican food may not be universally popular in your travelling family. Restaurants are open at the usual times, and are very adaptable on the whole. They will try and provide you with the food your children will like. Eggs and chicken abound, though the latter may be stringy and sometimes expensive (by Mexican standards) and there are always potatoes and other vegetables. On the coast there is always lots of fish and in most parts of the country, beef. Don't ever risk drinking tap water, even in the poshest hotel; mineral water in sealed bottles is available everywhere. Similarly, don't risk eating fruit that has been peeled by someone else, however tempting; Montezuma will wreak formidable revenge! That apart, Mexican food and drink is spicy and delicious, and you are in the home of Tequila which means memorable margaritas.

Places to stay are no problem. Mexico has good hotels of almost every class and style. The deluxe are scarcely distinguishable from the Hiltons, Intercontinentals and Holiday Inns of the rest of the world, but good tourist hotels are clean and inexpensive and even the simplest are quite acceptable within their limitations. Loos are clean and the showers (usually) work and, unless you are travelling in the most popular season and are in the most popular places you should not have a problem finding a room. The better hotels will provide cots and all the receptionists will be able to put you in touch with someone who will come in and babysit – either in the day or evening.

Travel within Mexico is not a problem, and it is a wonderful country to explore. There is an extensive internal airline system and, if time is at a premium, it's best to use it. If you have time (and Mexico is fabled for losing it) there are good intercity bus services covering the entire country. At local level the buses are always full, colourful and fun . . . and having a baby with you will certainly make you part of things. Despite the Mexican reputation local buses do have schedules, so don't rely on their mañana attitude if you are visiting a faraway place late in the day! In the major centres you will find organized tourist buses, often air-conditioned, visiting the local places of interest – either just one or several during a half- or full-day trip. The hotels usually carry the information, as will the local tourist office. Alternatively, you can check with the hotel desk about hiring a car or taxi for the day; they will certainly find you either. If there are no printed tariffs consult with the hotel or other tourists about a reasonable price and then haggle with the driver before starting. Safety awareness is not high. Mexican driving leaves a lot to be desired and there may not be seatbelts or baby seats – but on the other hand, it is the best way to travel if you don't want to be tied in to other people's schedules.

As for places to go – well the tourist travel guides say it all. The Yucatan is special because it combines a wonderful coast with the evidence of an extraordinary past. Don't miss it.

D.K.

Recommended reading:
Fielding's 1990 Mexico, Lynn V. Foster & Lawrence Foster (Hodder & Stoughton, 1990, £10.95)
Let's Go 1990 – The Budget Guide to Mexico inc. Belize and Guatemala (PAN, 1990, £10.99)

For further information:
Mexican Tourist Office, 60 Trafalgar Square, London WC2. Tel: (071) 734 1058

Morocco

Capital Rabat	**Annual weather range** – Rabat:
Major cities Casablanca, Marrakesh, Fez, Meknes, Tangier	*Temperature* Max 28°C (Jul–Aug) Min 8°C (Jan–Feb)
Time GMT	*Rainfall* Max 86mm (Dec) Min 0mm (Jul–Aug)
Currency Dirham (Dh) = 100 centimes	**Annual weather range** – Marrakesh:
Languages Arabic, French, Spanish	*Temperature* Max 38°C (Jul–Aug) Min 4 °C (Jan)
Climate Mediterranean	*Rainfall* Max 33mm (Mar) Min 3mm (Jul–Aug)

Except for more intrepid travellers, it is probably best to stick to package holidays or international-style hotels when you visit Morocco with children since conditions out of the tourist resorts can still be primitive.

Morocco can get very hot in the summer, but it is a dry heat, so it is much easier to tolerate than the tropics. The Atlantic coast has the most superb long sandy beaches, ideal for a seaside holiday. However, if you visit in the winter or spring, despite the hot sun, the ocean can be freezing cold and there may be a strong wind. So choose a hotel or apartment complex with a pool.

Self-catering apartments are becoming very popular at the coastal resorts and most travel companies will provide detailed information on where to shop. French is spoken by most Moroccans you will come across and English is quite common in the tourist resorts. Most towns have supermarkets of sorts where baby foods and nappies can be bought, but shopping is most characteristic at the *souk*. Wandering round the *souk* is the high spot of the holiday, but keep an eye on your children – they can easily get lost in the winding narrow lanes and among the shops and stalls crowded with people and goods. (Some sights, especially whole sheeps' heads on butcher's stalls, can be gory, but a source of fascination for children!)

Haggling is, unfortunately, the norm. Bargains can undoubtedly be had, but it's an exhausting business. There is plenty to buy for the children, local musical instruments, leather slippers, cheap shirts and teeshirts and the flowing, embroidered Moroccan shifts.

Moroccan food is not very highly spiced, although children brought up on fish fingers and baked beans may not be keen. Most hotels, however, serve international menus, together with wonderful displays of Moroccan oranges, dried dates and figs – even at breakfast. Yoghurt is also popular. It is wise to stick to bottled water and be cautious when eating in small restaurants. It's best to arm yourselves with diarrhoea medicines and other drugs before you leave home.

Morocco has some wonderful sights, ancient walled cities and palaces as well as the desert. Most travel companies run tours which are quite feasible for young and old, with regular stops at good hotels or restaurants for food and loos. Outside these stops, loos can be very primitive indeed.

For older children, the beach resorts provide lots of sporting activities, from windsurfing and fishing, to tennis and volleyball and they can join the evening out to the local Bedouin-tent-disco to watch the belly dancers. Even the younger children can enjoy the amazing spectacle of a *Fantasia*. Here, while you sip mint tea in an enormous Bedouin tent, ancient, gnarled warriors brandishing muskets charge towards you through the dust on fiery Arab steeds, yelling blood-curdling war cries! Just as you imagine they are going to trample right through you, they wheel the horses and gallop back where they came from. In between each spectacle, you are entertained by troupes of jugglers, child acrobats and snake charmers. Just don't sit in the front row!

C.B.

Recommended reading:
Insight Guides: Morocco (APA Publications, 1989, £10.95)
Blue Guide: Morocco, Jane Holliday (A & C Black, 1990, £8.95)

For further information:
Moroccan Tourist Office, 174 Regent Street, London W1. Tel: (071) 437 0073

Nepal

Capital Kathmandu	**Climate** Monsoonal
Major cities Patan, Morang	**Annual weather range** –
Time GMT + 5½	Kathmandu:
Currency Nepalese rupee (NR) =	*Temperature* Max 30°C (May)
100 pice	Min 2°C (Jan)
Languages Nepali, Bihara	*Rainfall* Max 373mm (Jul) Min
	3mm (Dec)

Few travellers to the Far East plan their trip without being tempted by the numerous attractions of this beautiful and, as yet, largely unspoilt mountain kingdom. Kathmandu, its capital and the only city, is now an established tourist centre offering the inevitable five-star hotels, tour operators and luxuries for those who can afford them. Do not be fooled, however, by the apparent high standards of the few top hotels. Nepal opened to foreigners only in the mid-1950s and, although rapidly expanding, its tourist trade is relatively new and restricted only to the few major towns.

Kathmandu is constantly described as 'medieval' and, although this adds to its charm and fascination, it also reflects the sanitary standards or lack of them. The water supply is the main cause for concern.

If you do decide to visit Nepal, it is vital that you get all the necessary vaccinations before you leave home and start precautions against diseases like malaria. This said, there is no reason why you shouldn't take your healthy three-year-old along – providing you are careful. The golden rule is to avoid fresh fruits, salads and all water that has not been boiled for at least ten minutes. (Tourist restaurants do boil their water, but rarely for ten minutes.) Stick to tea, boiled milk, bottled soft drinks or mineral water.

Children are welcomed anywhere in Nepal and there are very few places that would not happily accommodate a child's special needs. Local food is not as hot or spicy as Indian, but if it is a problem for your youngster you can always request rice and vegetables. Thamel is a unique remnant of the hippy era. It has pizza houses, burger bars (made of buffalo meat, not beef), ice cream parlours and all kinds of international cuisines. The best indication as to which eating establishments are safest is whether or not they are frequented by other tourists.

Imported Indian food is available including powdered milk, baby cereal (Farex) and tinned foods. You can find them at the frozen food stores and shops along the New Road, the main shopping street in Kathmandu. This is where you will find the best stocked pharmacies and even imported children's clothes. One further word of warning:

pharmacists are not medically trained.

Metered taxis are available as well as rickshaws and you can hire a taxi or car for the whole day at a very reasonable price. Public transportation consists of buses which are very cheap but slow and crowded. There are no trains.

Kathmandu valley provides much to see and your children may particularly enjoy the Monkey Temple at Swayambhunath, a 20-minute walk from the centre of town. Although a steep climb, you can stop and watch the monkeys along the way. Do not feed the monkeys – or any other animals you see – they can be vicious and they do carry fleas and disease. Elephant rides are an attraction and there is a safari park at Gokarna. Although there are public conveniences available at most of the tourist attractions you will probably be safer to do as the locals and go behind bushes.

Although tour operators make trekking and climbing trips relatively safe and comfortable they discourage taking along young children. You can, however, take a leisurely trek around the Kathmandu Valley or Pokhara, which brings you nearer to the Himalayas and is a lake of outstanding beauty. Tour operators will provide all the necessary equipment including a porter to carry your child. You should take out insurance whenever you trek – and make sure it covers the cost of a helicopter. Do not take your children on longer treks even when the tour operators offer a doctor at extra cost. They are taxing and can be hazardous even for the strongest and healthiest person.

October, November, February, March and April are the best times to visit Nepal. Avoid the monsoons of June which continue through September. It is cold in Nepal from February until April so make sure you bring enough warm clothing – and note that only the top hotels have central heating.

If you decide to take the plunge and take your children to Nepal, be prepared to be restricted in your activities and pay for the best. It is foolish to travel with young children on a shoestring. This said, you can have a fascinating holiday among friendly and charming people if you plan your trip wisely.

J.C.

Recommended reading:
Insight Guide to Nepal (APA Publications, 1989, £10.95)
Trekking: The Nepal Himalayas (Lonely Planet, 1985, £4.95)
Hildebrand's Travel Guide to India and Nepal (Kartografik, 1988, £5.95)

For further information:
The Royal Nepalese Embassy, 12A Kensington Palace Gardens, London W8. Tel: (071) 229 1594/4536/6231

The Netherlands

Capital Amsterdam	**Climate** Temperate
Major cities Rotterdam,	**Annual weather range –**
The Hague, Utrecht, Endhoven,	Amsterdam:
Arnhem	*Temperature* Max 22°C
Time GMT + 1	(Jul–Aug) Min 1°C (Jan–Feb)
Currency Guilder (Gld) = 100	*Rainfall* Max 87mm (Aug) Min
cents	44mm (Mar)
Languages Dutch, English	

A fifth of the Netherlands is covered by water and about 25 per cent of the soil area of Holland comprises land reclaimed from the sea and marshes and bogs which have been drained, so the Dutch understand water. They live by it, on it and they are constantly contending with it. These facts alone make it one of the most remarkable places in the world.

It's a small country, extremely well connected by networks of roads and railways and by waterways. Distances are short so travel is very easy. Every conceivable kind of water transport is available and using it is an exciting way of seeing the country and such wonderful places as Delft and Amsterdam; and getting about by boat is something that appeals a good deal to the small child.

I could never work up much enthusiasm for the Dutch coast though it does have plenty of sandy beaches. It is well-equipped with resort facilities and does attract large numbers of holidaymakers from northern Europe. However, sunshine is often at as great a premium as it is on British shores.

There is a vast range of accommodation, from top-class international hotels down to simple inns. The small hotels are easily the best bet for a family holiday with small children. They are cosy and comfortable and the Dutch hoteliers are congenial and hospitable.

There are also some 500 bungalow parks in the country, often sited by woodland and lakes. These are well-equipped with modern comforts and make a useful base for an open-air holiday. The Dutch are also highly organized for campers; there are well over 2000 camping sites, some of which you need to book in advance. Another possibility is to take rooms in a private house or farm. This can be most enjoyable with small children.

One of the great advantages of Holland is that many Dutch people, at all social levels, are likely to speak English as well as (and, in many instances, better than) many English people. Their fluency and ease is astonishing since they have often never set foot in England.

Medical services are highly efficient. Chemists have everything you might need for small children in an emergency or in ordinary day-to-day events.

There are any number of facilities and diversions for children, including zoos, safari parks, recreation parks, fairytale parks, miniature towns, aquaria and dolphinaria.

The average child will find Dutch food appetizing. It is more or less international; everyone is catered for; variety is provided by Indonesian restaurants. Water is good and soft drinks are abundant.

Parents should not forget to take advantage of the 'Holland Leisure Card'. For a modest outlay you receive substantial discounts on public transport, cruises, in shops and museums and for entertainments.

J.A.C.

The flat countryside of Holland has a special beauty of its own, and there are two obvious ways to see it – by bike or by boat.

Bikes are everywhere in Holland, and children are naturally accommodated. You can hire sturdy bikes, with clip-on child seats so that even a child of six or so could go on the back. Babies go in a basket in front, and it is quite common to see two child passengers on one adult bike.

Holland is ideal for a cycling holiday with children with miles of cycle tracks passing through beautiful countryside, with woods and lakes for variety. The tracks continue in the big cities such as Amsterdam and there are special lights for cyclists at junctions and crossings.

Canal holidays are also popular, but could be difficult with toddlers. Older children usually love boats, and there are boat trips round the old parts of Amsterdam. For a more unusual holiday, try the islands on the Waddenzee, where English people are rarely seen. Passenger ferries go from the north coast of Holland, and there are very few cars on the smaller ones, which are criss-crossed by beautiful cycle tracks. All the holidaymakers hire cycles and child seats, children's bikes, pedal cars and trikes are often available.

Center Parcs are holiday centres of a standard far superior to our conceptions of traditional British holiday camps. A similar service is offered by a company called Gran Dorado and both provide a relatively sophisticated family holiday. These organizations are to be distinguished from bungalow parks, which are holiday chalets in quiet woodland or beside lakes.

Dutch people are usually nice to children; shopkeepers often give them a sweet (worries about dental cavities don't seem to exist here) or a slice of cheese or sausage.

There are high chairs everywhere, buggies can often be hired at zoos, and *kinder* menus are common. Children are free on public transport up to the age of four.

Breastfeeding is not usual after two to three months, so feeding older babies can produce odd looks.

Amsterdam is renowned for its dog fouling; but fortunately it does not spread to children's playgrounds, which are guarded by wardens who keep dogs out. There may sometimes be a fee, but these play areas – in most parks – are wonderful value. The water playground Gaasperplas, south of Amsterdam, is free.

There is a good variety of vegetable baby food, including more unusual varieties like brown beans, but the dental cavity warning applies to the sweet varieties.

Any kind of holiday accommodation (including self-catering bungalow parks, bed & breakfast, log cabins etc.) can be booked via the Netherlands Reservation Centre in Holland (tel: 010 31 70 3202 500).

M.H.

Recommended reading:
Blue Guide: Holland (Blue Guide, 1989, £11.95)
Fodor's Holland '90 (Fodor's Travel Publications, 1990, £9.99)
Holland at its best (Passport, 1990, £6.95)

For further information:
Netherlands Board of Tourism, Eggington House, 25-28 Buckingham Gate, London SW1E. Tel: (071) 630 0451

Nevis *see* West Indies

New Zealand

Capital Wellington	**Climate** Temperate
Major cities Auckland, Christchurch, Dunedin	**Annual weather range** – Wellington:
Time GMT + 12	*Temperature* Max 21°C
Currency New Zealand dollar (NZ$) = 100 cents	(Jan–Feb) Min 6°C (Jul–Aug)
Language English	*Rainfall* Max 137mm (Jul) Min 81mm (Jan–Mar)

New Zealand is a beautiful country, roughly the size of the UK, but with a population of only three million people. New Zealanders are justifiably proud of it, and enjoy showing it off to visitors. The feeling of space and room to breathe, pervades attitudes to travellers and their children, which makes for a generally relaxed time (except if you are in a hurry).

Air New Zealand are very welcoming and helpful on internal flights, carrying pushchairs and car seats in the hold, and if necessary allowing pushchairs out onto the tarmac. There are adequate facilities for changing babies at the international airports, although inevitably hit and miss at the smaller airports.

Renting cars at the main centres is straightforward. Child seats are generally available, and as most cars have rear seat belts, security is no problem. New Zealand driving is anarchic, and lane discipline on the few motorways is, to put it politely, erratic although there is a speed limit on all roads which is firmly enforced in the main urban areas. The New Zealand railway system is shrinking and not particularly comfortable, but there are good bus services. Coaches on the main tourist routes are reasonably modern.

New Zealand is said to have a greater proportion of its land area designated as National Parks than any other country in the world. Visitors are welcomed and there are often informative displays with good graphics in the visitor centres, which interest children – as well as clean loos. There are dozens of the most wonderful sandy beaches. In the summer the main ones have lifeguards on duty with warnings where there are potential hazards. Beaches are considered crowded if you can see other families. In addition, there are nature reserves along all the main roads where travellers can enjoy a picnic and children can stretch their legs in safety. Most towns and settlements have reasonable loos and very often a recreational area equipped with swings and other apparatus. Dairies are almost everywhere. These are the equivalent of an English corner shop, open long hours and selling a range of sandwiches, fast foods and soft drinks at reasonable prices.

There are well-placed campsites in most of the holiday areas, and it is possible to get into them without booking except at peak times in January. Most have adequate washing facilities although they vary in standard. Youth hostels will also take families, but it is worth booking in the peak holiday season and at holiday weekends. The main centres and tourist spots have first-class hotels, but many people prefer to stay in motels which are extremely good value especially for families with children. Facilities vary; some offer baby listening services, swimming pools and saunas; some have their own restaurants; others simply offer self-catering. Nearly all rooms have television and radio, and are generally very clean. Tea, coffee and milk are always provided for breakfast, and there are usually fast food take-aways or dairies nearby if the motel doesn't have its own restaurant. Most restaurants have high chairs and children's menus, but service although friendly can be very erratic. New Zealand pubs are not on the whole to be recommended when travelling with children. Most of them have take-away bottle stores for thirsty parents.

Disposable nappies are easily available at supermarkets and chemists, but along with cotton wool, wipes and suchlike, are comparatively expensive. The New Zealand National Health service has reciprocal arrangements with the UK, and it is usually efficient and friendly. There is a small charge for visiting a GP and a low prescription charge, although if you have an accident, treatment is free under the automatic accident compensation scheme.

J. and R.R.

Recommended reading:
New Zealand In Your Pocket Arnold Schuchter (Horizon, 1990, £6.95)
Fodor's 1990 New Zealand (Fodor, 1990, £6.99)
Berlitz Travel Guide; New Zealand (Macmillan, 1989, £3.95)
Hildebrand's Travel Guide; New Zealand, Sowman and Schultz-Tesmar (K&G Karto & Grafik, 1988, £5.95)

For further information:
New Zealand Tourism Office, New Zealand House, Haymarket, London SW1 4TQ. Tel: (071) 973 0360.

Northern Ireland *see* Eire & Northern Ireland

Norway

Capital Oslo	**Climate** Arctic/temperate
Major cities Bergen, Trondheim, Stavanger	**Annual weather range** – Oslo: *Temperature* Max 22°C (Jul)
Time GMT + 1	Min −7°C (Jan–Feb)
Currency Norweigan krone (Nkr) = 100 ore	*Rainfall* Max 95mm (Aug) Min 35mm (Feb)
Language Norwegian	

Norway is a country of spectacular natural beauty and, with a population half the size of London, most of it is completely unspoilt. It is not more than half an hour's tramride from any of the capital's cafés to a spot where you can pick wild berries. The coast itself is a marvel of nature with the famous ice-blue fjords and safe, sandy beaches where you can swim.

The Norwegians like children and there are many parks and open spaces for them to play in. The air is marvellously fresh and clean.

The summer is short, with June, July and August being the best months to visit the country. Autumn is also an attractive season when the mountainous terrain turns lovely shades of yellow and red. Winter starts early, at the end of October or early November. Some of the mountain roads are closed in the winter and will only open in the spring or even summer. There are few motorways but the road standard is good and well signposted. Compared with most European countries the traffic is very light, except at ferry crossing points at the weekends.

Camping and skiing are the national pastimes. There are hundreds of approved campsites around the country and they are all well-equipped, clean and welcoming. You can even rent cabins in them if you are tentless.

All public facilities in Norway can be expected to be clean and functional.

Eating out *en famille* is not a tradition in Norway and the cafeterias are more welcoming places to take children than restaurants. English people will find the food to their taste, but there will be a higher proportion of salted or preserved meats and fish. Indeed, fish of all sorts is a staple of the diet and you will find it boiled, salted, smoked, dried, cured, marinated, pickled and fried. Make sure you try *gravet laks*, a traditional Norwegian dish, which is salmon marinated in salt, sugar and spices.

Hotel chains have several discount schemes you should take advantage of if travelling with your family. In individual hotels you will find special offers covering everything from walking tours in the glacier fields and sightseeing to babysitting and windsurfing. Many double hotel rooms will have an extra sofabed in the room so you can accommodate one more person or two small children.

The Norwegian's own favourite holiday is going to a *hytta* – a wooden cottage in the mountains or by the sea. You can rent these cottages and although they vary in size, standard, location and price, most sleep four to six people and consist of a kitchen, sitting room, often with open fireplace and one or more bedrooms.

You can also expect to find every kind of item for your baby, including nappies and baby food, in the supermarkets which are well-stocked but, as with everything in Norway, expensive.

Recommended reading:
Drive Around Norway Robert Spark (Grafton, 1990, £5.95)

For further information:
Norwegian Tourist Board, Charles House, 5 Regent Street (Lower), London SW1 4LR. Tel: (071) 839 6255

The Philippines

Capital Manila	**Climate** Tropical
Major cities Quezon City, Davao, Cebu, Zamboanga	**Annual weather range** – Manila:
	Temperature Max 34°C
Time GMT + 8	(Apr–May) Min 21°C
Currency Philippine peso (PP1 =	(Dec–Feb)
100 centavos)	*Rainfall* Max 432mm (Jul) Min
Languages Tagalog, English	13mm (Feb)

Even though Filipinos dote on their own children, they are head over heels about foreign babies. 'They are gold', the saying goes. The Filipino cultural aesthetic is such that Western babies are regarded as exceptionally beautiful and are almost constant targets of affectionate curiosity and cooing.

Products and services specifically designed for children are difficult to obtain outside the capital. However, Western influences are powerful here and the upper middle classes import a wide range of baby-care products and foods from Europe and America. Manila, of course, is the best supplied. Shops such as Rustan's, ShoeMart or Robinson's sell disposable nappies, processed baby foods, formula, 'long-life' and powdered milks, cereals, inexpensive children's clothing and shoes (indeed, girls' fancy dresses, manufactured widely in the Philippines for export, are sold at bargain prices).

The climate is hot and humid during most of the year (heavy rains and typhoons occur, from June through October). Most hotels are well air-conditioned as some taxis. Skin rashes may occur, however, insect bites are common and parasites, such as ringworm, may lurk in hotel swimming pools. A good variety of Western preparations are readily available at chemists, particularly a national chain called Mercury.

Western-style food (McDonald's, pizza and so on) is liberally strewn around Manila which could rate as Asia's 'junk food' paradise. Most hotels and several restaurants serve good Western dishes, but many Filipino dishes are only moderately spiced and are palatable and wholesome: boiled rice, roast chicken, grilled fish and prawns, fresh fruits and vegetables. Restaurants as a rule do not provide high chairs. Meals are eaten 'family-style' with everyone sharing from dishes in the centre of the table.

Water is generally not drinkable in the Philippines, although some large hotels pump in safe water from private wells. Overall, hygiene conditions are poor and all reasonable precautions should be taken outside hotel confines.

The Philippines may be one of the easiest places in the world to find competent, inexpensive babysitters who speak English. Any hotel can make the contact for you with agencies also available in large cities.

Manila is a noisy, congested city and not very conducive to getting about with children. There are a few small urban pools and the occasional playground and most hotels have pools.

Most TV programming is in English including both middling fare imported from the US and some engaging children's programmes, including a local imitation of 'Sesame Street' called 'Batibot'.

F.C.K.

Recommended reading:
The Philippines in Your Pocket (MPC, 1988, £5.99)
Philippines, A Travel Survival Kit (Lonely Planet, 1987, £5.95)
Insight Guide: Philippines (APA Publications, 1988, £10.95)

For further information:
Philippines Department of Tourism, 199 Piccadilly, London W1V 9LE. Tel: (071) 734 6358

Portugal

Capital Lisbon	**Climate** Mediterranean
Major cities Porto, Amadora, Coimbra, Barreiro	**Annual weather range** – Lisbon: *Temperature* Max 28°C (Aug) Min 8°C (Jan–Feb)
Time GMT	
Currency Escudo (ESc) = 100 centavos	*Rainfall* Max 111mm (Jan) Min 3mm (Jul)
Language Portuguese	

As it happens Portugal is England's oldest ally. The 600th anniversary of the Treaty of Windsor was marked in 1986 and was celebrated on a grand scale with Anglo-Portuguese events and exchanges which can only have benefited the prospective visitor from Britain.

The Portuguese are a very charming, civilized and hospitable people. They like the English and many of them have some knowledge of our language. They live in a spectacularly beautiful country which is for the most part unspoilt by the ugly manifestations of twentieth century progress. The summers are hot and the winters mild; in fact, you can take a family holiday there at almost any time. Pretty well every conceivable need is catered for and small children are very welcome everywhere.

I particularly recommend the state-owned *pousadas*, comfortable inns (sometimes in converted monasteries, castles and palaces) which are reminiscent of the convivial *gostilne* of Slovenia. There are privately run inns (*estalgens*) and private enterprise also provides excellent holiday accommodation in manor houses and farmhouses. All these provide rural environments in splendid countryside which are ideal for small children. The Portuguese also have well organized camping and self-catering establishments.

In hotels children under eight are entitled to a 5 per cent discount if they share a room with their parents (or other adults). Many hotels provide cots for babies. Most forms of baby food are available in chemists and supermarkets but imported brands are likely to be more expensive than in the UK.

Public transport is efficient (no problems with children) self-drive cars are readily available. Railway fares are cheap and there are discounts for family tickets (*see* 'Rail Travel', pp. 211–19). It is fun travelling by public transport and people are most obliging and courteous to visitors.

The country is justly famous for its beautiful beaches and there are said to be some 500 miles of sand on the seaboard. The resorts are extremely well equipped and there is any amount of diversion and entertainment for children. The magnetism of the shores is strong but I should certainly take the opportunity of going inland if possible. Children will find interesting rural ways of peasant life seldom seen in Britain – and look out for the silky-coated, long-legged pigs of the Algarve.

Portuguese food is plentiful, well prepared and well cooked, though for some palates it may prove a little too oily at times. As in Spain meals are leisurely and there are many delectable dishes, such as *calde verde* (a broth made of shredded kale and potatoes), *gazpacho* soup (which is served cold), and the national dish *bacalhau* – salted, dried cod prepared and presented in many different ways. Because of the Atlantic seaboard fish and shellfish are first class, especially mullet, halibut, sole, sardines, squid, swordfish, tuna, lobster and prawns. I also recommend *caldeirada*, a fish stew somewhat reminiscent of *bouillabaisse*. Like the Turks, the Portuguese have a very sweet tooth and produce lots of delicious confectionery and sweets. One such delicacy is *barrigas de freira* (which means 'nuns' tummies') and is a mixture of egg, almonds and sugar. There is a good range of soft drinks and the water is safe but I would always be cautious about ordinary tap water.

Like the Spaniards the Portuguese have a large number of spectacular fiestas and festivals which are delightful for children and it would be a great pity not to include one of them in a trip. Some of the more famous are the Tomar Festival of Tabuleiros (a harvest festival which happens every two years); the Golega Fair of St Martin (November); the Lisboa Festival of SS Anthony, John and Peter (June); the Vila Franca de Xira Red Waistcoat Festival (in July, it includes bullrunning and bullfighting); the Viseu Cavalcades of Vil de Moinhos at Montanhas (June); the Ovar Carnival of Costa de Prata (the weekend before Lent); the Porto Festival of St John (June); and the Costa Verde festival of Our Lady of Suffering in August.

J.A.C.

Recommended reading:
Portugal; A Travellers' Guide, Susan Lowndes (Thornton Cox, 1989, £5.95)
The Penguin Guide to Portugal 1990 (Penguin, 1990, £7,99)
Blue Guide: Portugal (A & C Black, 1989, £8.95)

For further information:
Portuguese National Tourist Office, New Bond Street House, 1 New Bond Street, London W1. Tel: (071) 439 3873

Saudi Arabia

Capital Riyadh	**Climate** Desert
Major cities Jiddah, Mecca, Taif, Medina	**Annual weather range** – Riyadh:
	Temperature Max 42°C
Time GMT + 3	(Jun–Aug) Min 8°C (Jan)
Currency Saudi Riyal (SAR) =	*Rainfall* Max 25mm (Apr) Min
100 hallalas	0mm (Jun–Dec)
Language Arabic	

As the Kingdom of Saudi Arabia does not issue tourist visas it is very unlikely that anyone would go to Saudi for a holiday with their children. However, there are many English people working there whose families either live with them for part of the year or who plan to visit. The annual pilgrimage, the Haj, also attracts hundreds of visitors.

For those already living there, the area is more varied and interesting than one would, perhaps, expect of a desert area. Just one example is the cooler mountainous region in the south-west, the Assir.

There are some fairly obvious health precautions that must be taken by everyone who visits the country. Although there are many diseases that are no longer officially present in Saudi Arabia it is wise to be protected against tuberculosis and polio, and should you be planning to leave the major cities, against cholera, typhoid and paratyphoid as well. Malaria is still present in the southern part of Saudi Arabia on both the Gulf and the Red Sea coasts. It is best to check with your doctor exactly which innoculations you need.

Although tap water is safe to drink you may prefer your children to stick to boiled or bottled mineral water. And of course all fruit and vegetables should be washed.

Shoes should be worn at all times: there is bilharzia in many pools and standing water in the mountains; stone fish and other nasties inhabit the shallows at the seaside and there is also a chance of hookworm. The ground also gets hot enough to burn the soles of the feet.

Do not touch any animals, however appealing they may look. There are few pets in the Kingdom and rabies is endemic. Take out comprehensive health insurance before you leave the UK and ensure it covers absolutely every eventuality. Hospital facilities are very good, but expensive.

The climate is severe. Your skin should be protected at all times and children should certainly wear sunhats. It is important that drinking water (bottled) is always available and children especially should be encouraged to drink it. Extra salt is not generally thought to be necessary if you eat a balanced diet.

Remember to wear modest clothes at all times. There are separate facilities for men and women. Small compartments at the rear of buses, for instance, have separate entrances and are reserved for women. Benches and restaurants are similarly segregated although there are 'family' areas in most city hotels and restaurants where men and women can sit together.

There are a few things you should know about etiquette in Saudi Arabia: don't use your left hand to point at people or to hand things to others. Don't allow the soles of your feet to show when sitting, as this can be taken as an insult. Of course, the local inhabitants will be tolerant of mistakes, but you should remember to be respectful of a somewhat more private society than our own. Most visitors quickly understand and adapt to the Saudi laws and customs.

Everything you need for children is readily available in the major towns and things like disposable nappies are in every little corner shop. The local brands are relatively cheap.

P.K-H.

Please Note
Recent political events are such that it is difficult to know the effect they will have on holiday makers. We would advise you to contact the relevant National Tourist Office for further details before travelling.

Recommended reading:
Berlitz Travel Guide: Saudi Arabia (Macmillan, 1985, £3.95)
MEED Guide: Saudi Arabia (MEED, 1983, £9.95)

For further information:
Royal Embassy of Saudi Arabia, Information Centre, 18 Cavendish Square, London WC1. Tel: (071) 629 8803

Scotland *see* **Britain**

Sicily *see* Italy

Singapore *see* Malaysia

South Africa

Capital Pretoria
Major cities Cape Town,
 Johannesburg, Durban
Time GMT + 2
Currency Rand (R) = 100 cents
Languages Afrikaans, English
Climate Wide regional variation
 from temperate to desert to
 tropical
Annual weather range – Eastern
 interior (Pretoria and
 Johannesburg):
Temperature Max 28°C (Dec)
 Min 3°C (Jun–Jul)
Rainfall Max 132mm (Nov–Dec)
 Min 5mm (Aug)
Annual weather range –
 Mediterranean (Cape Town):
Temperature Max 26°C
 (Jan–Feb) Min 7°C (Jul)
Rainfall Max 89mm (Jul) Min
 8mm (Feb)
Annual weather range – Tropical
 (Durban):
Temperature Max 27°C
 (Jan–Mar) Min 22°C (Jul–Aug)
Rainfall Max 122mm (Feb, Nov)
 Min 51mm (May)

The climate is wonderful. In Johannesburg the heat can sometimes get unpleasant, but the Cape has a mainly Mediterranean climate, while Durban is more tropical. Remember, the seasons are reversed, and Christmas means summer. Even South Africa's winter compares favourably with summer in Britain, and along the Natal coast, winter is the height of the holiday season. You will only need light clothes, plus sweaters for winter evenings. Shield your children at first from the sun, which can be very fierce. Inevitably, such a climate means a concentration on outdoor activities. A huge variety of sports and watersports is available, so there's lots for children to do.

The country is spectacular throughout, with a huge variety of scenery. The nicest place to visit is the Cape Coastal Belt, which is incredibly beautiful. Start at Cape Town and go up the Garden Route to Port Elizabeth.

Inland attractions which would appeal to children include the Cango Caves, and the ostrich and crocodile farms of Oudtshoorn, on the edge of the Little Karoo semi-desert plain. Further up the coast, The Transkei and Kwazulu – both so-called black 'homelands' – are well worth visiting.

In Johannesburg you can visit the surface workings of a gold mine and see the mine dancers. Special attractions for children are Santa-rama Miniland in Rosettenville and Gillooly's Farm in Bedfordview. But take care in Johannesburg: muggings are on the increase in the city centre.

You will probably want to visit a game park. The most famous (and largest) is Kruger National Park, along the border with Mozambique, but there are many others worth considering. You can book tours, or go on self-drive visits. You can get bungalow accommodation suitable for families.

Hotels are excellent. Most of them have swimming pools and all the larger ones provide cots and high chairs on request. The game parks will provide cots if these are reserved in advance when booking. Car hire is reasonable, the roads are excellent and you drive on the left.

White South Africa is an African version of California, so life for those travelling with children is relatively easy. Most of the pre-cautions you might need to take in other countries – Zimbabwe or Egypt for example – do not apply if you stay within the white areas. The water is perfectly safe to drink and uncooked foods don't need special treatment. Nappies of all kinds are available everywhere and the standard of health care, should you need it, is extremely high. But you will have to pay for treatment. Anti-malarials are recommended for visiting the Lowveld, Kruger National Park and Zululand. Unless you have come from the Yellow Fever area there are no other special health requirements.

If you want to see the country by train, the Blue Train is the way to go. It's South Africa's deluxe, air-conditioned express train, travelling between Pretoria, Johannesburg and Cape Town, and commonly spoken of as a memorable experience. Overseas tourists staying for less than three months get a 40 per cent reduction on the rail fares – so ask for it.

You won't get to see how black South Africans really live unless you make an effort – like getting a special pass that will allow you to visit a non-white area. There are now organized trips to Soweto. The ex-perience can be an uncomfortable revelation to white visitors who may be expecting fundamental change since the release of Nelson Mandela.

R.E.

Please Note
Recent political events are such that it is difficult to know the effect they will have on holiday makers. We would advise you to contact the relevant National Tourist Office for further details before travelling.

Recommended reading:
Central Africa: A Travel Survival Kit, Alex Newton (Lonely Planet, 1989, £6.95)
The Traveller's Guide to Central and Southern Africa (International Communications, 1990, £7.95)

For further information:
South African Tourism Board, P.O. Box 318, Wimbledon, London SW19 4RZ. Tel: (081) 944 6646

Spain

Capital Madrid	**Annual weather range** – Madrid:
Major cities Barcelona, Malaga, Seville, Valencia, Zaragoza	*Temperature* Max 27°C (Jul) Min 14°C (Dec–Feb)
Time GMT + 1	*Rainfall* Max 53mm (Oct) Min 11mm (Jul)
Currency Peseta (Pa) = 100 céntimos	**Annual weather range** – Balearic Islands (Palma, Majorca):
Language Spanish	*Temperature* Max 29°C (Jul–Aug) Min 20°C (Jan–Feb)
Climate Mediterranean	*Rainfall* Max 55mm (Sep) Min 3 mm (Jul)

As a major tourist country, Spain should hold no fears for holiday-makers with children heading for the main resorts. If in doubt, ask a travel agent about special child facilities at hotels and take the normal precautions over heat, mosquitoes, sun and water.

If you do venture into the interior, things may be a little different. Spain is a child-loving country and many couples, including the young middle-class, still have quite large families. Nevertheless, childrearing is perhaps more relaxed. There is not the same concern about safety, so you will find car seats are not common, and children's playgrounds may not be maintained to a high standard. Also the current concern over sugary foods doesn't seem to have hit Spain yet. Expect your children to be offered sweets, biscuits and crisps as a matter of course. (However, in general, the Spanish diet is much healthier than the British.)

One major difference is the time of meals. Few Spaniards will sit down to lunch before 2 p.m. and 3 is more usual. The evening meal is from 9 p.m. onwards (10 is more common) and you will probably not be served in a restaurant, unless it is a transport or tourist restaurant, before 8 p.m. Spanish children stay up for meals and are more than tolerated in restaurants – very little bad behaviour would be unacceptable. (One solution to Spanish hours is to keep your watch on British time – two hours behind.)

Spain is not noted for its cuisine and children allergic to garlic or olive oil will not be happy, but typical menus usually offer pasta, grilled meat – lamb (*cordero*) and pork (*lomo*) are the most popular – chips, ice cream, fruit and the ubiquitous *flan* (cream caramel), which all but the fussiest eaters should find acceptable. Restaurant meals are nearly always freshly cooked, using the freshest ingredients, and are still very cheap. Child portions are not a special feature but few restaurants would object to providing extra plates and spoons for dividing up meals. Similarly, high chairs are not normally available.

As in most continental European countries, children are allowed in bars in Spain, where soft drinks, ice cream and coffee are served, as well as alcohol. They also usually have televisions and bar-football machines.

Shopping in Spain is a great experience – as long as you have plenty of time. Modernization is overrunning Spain very quickly, and new *supermercados* have brought with them a kind of Sainsbury mentality. But in the market, butchers and fishmongers are a law unto themselves. The best advice is to be bold – and take your own shopping basket. Children, naturally, can tire of the experience quickly, but may be revived by a stop at a *churrería*, a bar or stall serving *churros*, a delicious kind of long doughnut.

Shops are usually open from 9 or 10 a.m. to 1 or 1.30 p.m. and then from 3 or 3.30 p.m. to 7.30 or 8 p.m., but check locally as times can vary according to the season and area.

Disposable nappies and other baby equipment are available in all but the smallest villages and a chemist can usually be relied on to prescribe appropriate drugs for most holiday complaints. Most towns and large villages will have a doctor on duty for accidents and emergencies (ask at your hotel or campsite for details). There are also Red Cross clinics for emergencies.

Spanish children don't seem to be fussed over as much as their Italian counterparts, and the large families mean that older children entertain younger ones. If you are staying in a mainly Spanish area, your children will be the centre of attention and should have no problems making friends even with a language barrier. For older children, football is the universal language, but beware, very young Spanish children, as young as 11 or 12, often own small motorbikes which they use off the main roads in campsites, holiday villages and so on.

When not in swimming costumes, Spanish children are always immaculately dressed. You may find that your younger daughters with short hair will be mistaken for boys since most Spanish girls have their ears pierced at birth and are therefore easily recognized by their earrings.

The Spanish interior has some wonderful sights – Seville, Granada, Segovia, Toledo, Avila – but distances between cities are very great and it's no coincidence that cowboy films are shot in the desert landscape. So, make sure your children are good car travellers before attempting a touring holiday.

C.B.

The Canaries

Like much of mainland Spain the Canaries welcome British visitors and their families. Taking your baby with you should present no particular problems provided you plan sensibly in advance for your baby's (and your own) needs. Forward planning may ultimately help to reduce the cost of your holiday. Remember, even after you have landed on the island you are going to, there may be a journey of one or two hours before you reach your final destination, so go prepared and take your own supplies with you. Even in the airports where baby facilities are advertised it is usually busy and chaotic. It is possible to buy most medication in the pharmacies.

If you have arranged car hire in advance ask for a child seat when booking because they are common and it is not rare to see local children restrained in the rear of cars.

If you are staying in a hotel you will probably be able to arrange for a cot in your room in advance for a small charge. If staying in private accommodation it is difficult to arrange the hire of one. However, most airlines will carry a travel-cot and pushchair, if tied up securely, in addition to the normal adult baggage allowance, at no extra cost. High chairs are also difficult to borrow, though some hotels may have them. A pair of reins tied on to a normal chair may be a satisfactory compromise.

Supermarkets are everywhere and most products found at home can be purchased. Fresh fruit and vegetables are particularly tempting. But tinned foods are expensive, especially prepared baby foods, drinks and disposable nappies. Take as many of these with you as you can to reduce costs. Buy bottled water for children's drinks.

Restaurants are quite tolerant of children. In tourist areas it is easy to find English-style food (if that's what you want), and most restaurants have dishes suitable for children. If you manage to find a restaurant frequented by Spanish families on a Sunday you can enjoy a break while all the children mix and are amused by the Spanish families.

Most children will love the sunshine, beaches and activities available in the Spanish islands, provided they are well protected with a hat and sun cream. Many of the beaches are black and the sand is coarse. Make sure young feet are covered as the black sand absorbs the heat readily, making it very hot. Most beaches have sunbeds and sunshades available for hire. Children are well catered for in the swimming pools and aqua-parks, although at some times of the year unheated pools may be cool for very small children.

As in most holiday destinations other attractions such as zoos, parrot parks and banana plantations welcome families.

All in all you will find the Canaries pleasant, clean and welcoming for an enjoyable family holiday at reasonable cost.

J.H.

Majorca

I spent two weeks in Puerto Pollensa, Majorca in spring, 1987 with my mother and two children, Bryn aged 5 and baby Siân aged 15 months. We went during the Whitsun holidays, as Easter might have been too cold and summer can be too hot for small children and the elderly to enjoy the whole day out in the sun. We had an early morning flight, but it was a Bank Holiday weekend with threats of airport strikes and subsequent long delays, so I took piles of food, juice and nappies. The juice spilt before we even got to the check-in desk and they nearly turned us off the plane when they saw all the junk! Anyway, the journey from Manchester to the resort by plane and bus didn't take long, and we were walking along the beach by the afternoon.

Puerto Pollensa was originally a small fishing village. It still has its harbour and jetty for fishing boats and leisure craft and there are frequent boat trips around the bay every day to the beach at Formentor. We used to save some bread from our meals and throw it into the sea to watch hundreds of small fish rushing in to eat. There is a long promenade of small hotels, shops, bars and restaurants, with a tree-covered walk alongside the beach at one end and huge new white sandy beaches towards Alcudia at the other. Many British people buy or rent villas and apartments here, and the town is full of interesting shops and eating places. It never gets boring. There's little drunkenness or rowdiness about, and we stayed in a small hotel with the locals and their children coming in and out all day, talking Spanish to the children and being very friendly.

The various supermarkets are crammed with good food and we picknicked well on local bread, cold meats and cheeses, fruit and salads. The juices are expensive, but would probably be too heavy to carry from home. We really liked the peach one, however. When I ran out of disposable nappies I found replacing them expensive (about 45p each) and wished I had brought more. Siân didn't wear a nappy on the beach but drank a lot more and used about six per 24 hours. Also you never know if the 'runs' are going to attack.

The mountains are all around and when we were on the beach there was plenty of scenery there too – hills in the distance, trees, flying-boats landing and taking off from a special harbour, and people using the wind-surfing and water-ski facilities. We enjoyed the slower pedaloes which were about £3 per half-hour and chairs or loungers were £3 for the day. Bryn was in the sea so much that he learnt to swim, but I had to put creams on both children to stop them burning. They did get an itchy rash the first few days, but it disappeared without any special treatment. There's a doctor's surgery on the main street, open in the day at various times and all are welcome. Also chemists sell most general medications.

We hired bicycles for about £4 per day and baby seats were £1 extra. This is a very good way of exploring the town and surrounding country. There was a another pretty cove called Cala San Vincente next to Puerto Pollensa which was well worth pedalling to. Also local buses are very cheap, and we just walked down to the bus station at the harbour and got on. There are two old towns nearby to explore, and you could go on a longer trip over the mountains into Puerto Soller. Oranges and lemons are growing everywhere. Just outside Pollensa town five miles away, we found a garden centre full of ornamental clay pots – I wanted them all! We also found plenty of shoe shops and bought a beautiful pair of shoes for Siân for £12 – all leather. The clothes and swimwear shops are full of stylish goods. It is almost worth taking empty suitcases and getting all your holiday teeshirts there.

There isn't a launderette so I washed a few things by hand and was allowed to borrow pegs and use the line on the hotel roof. The sun dried everything in just a few hours. I took a travel iron but didn't need it much. If required, there was a dry cleaners next to the hotel.

Just outside the port there are riding stables and there are small Shetland ponies available for children to use. On Wednesdays the market comes to the town square and the stalls are laid out with fruit, vegetables and piles of olives. There are also leather goods, clothes, pot plants and flowers everywhere.

A tip: everything the children ate stained like mad, e.g. delicious bottled chocolate drinks, local cherries and strawberries, tomato purée in the rice and pasta dishes, so a plastic bib and lots of 'wipes' are necessary.

Many people go back to Puerto Pollensa every year and I can heartily recommend it as a good place to visit with the family.

N.L.

Recommended reading:
Blue Guide: Spain, Ian Robertson (A & C Black, 1989, £13.95)
Spain: The Rough Guide, Mark Ellingham & John Fisher (Harrap–Columbus, 1990, £6.95)
The Penguin Guide to Spain 1990 (Penguin, 1990, £7.99)
Cadogan Guide: Spain, Dana Facaros (Cadogan, 1989, £9.95)
American Express Guide: Spain (Mitchell Beazley, 1989, £5.95)

For further information:
Spanish Tourist Office, 57 St James's Street, London SW1. Tel: (071) 499 0901

Sweden

Capital Stockholm	**Climate** Continental
Major cities Göteborg, Malmö, Uppsala	**Annual weather range** – Stockholm:
Time GMT + 1	*Temperature* Max 22°C (Jul) Min −5°C (Jan–Feb)
Currency Swedish krona (SKr) = 100 ore	*Rainfall* Max 76mm (Aug) Min 25mm (Mar)
Languages Swedish, English	

Sweden is a successful industrial nation with a small population and a very advanced welfare state structure. The standard of living is high and although visitors to the country will probably be impressed by the quality and efficiency of transport and other services, they are likely to be less pleasantly surprised by the cost. It is one of the most expensive European countries to visit but its attractions make the expenditure worthwhile. There are large areas of breathtaking scenery and one can feel completely free and at peace with one's natural surroundings.

Most Swedes own a summerhouse *stuga* so that they escape the city and can relax with the pleasures of water, sun and greenery. The shortness of the summer growing season in comparison with the long dark winter months makes the pleasure of being outside even more intense, and the first warm days of spring brings city Swedes out onto the pavements, stretching their faces to the sun like cats or lizards basking in its warmth. If you plan to visit Sweden in the winter with your family you will need extra warm clothing for outside but all

Swedish houses and flats are through necessity well-heated and insulated against extreme weather. A self-catering holiday or a house swap with Swedes can be a marvellous way to see the country but some visiting families might be surprised how primitive the summer *stugas* can be, with no electricity or sanitation except a chemical toilet. Swedish families feel that the return to basic living is part of the charm of their summer holidays and so it can be, if one is prepared for it! In contrast, visitors are likely to be impressed by the high standard of cleanliness and efficiency in normal Swedish everyday accommodation.

Sweden is one of the easiest places in the world to travel with a child. Most people speak English, there are excellent facilities, plain palatable food and good medical care. The majority of Swedish mothers work outside the home and there is a strong tradition of women's opinions being listened to. This means that in the major cities at least there should be no problems with pram/buggy access, nursing and changing areas, availability of high chairs in restaurants and so on. Some of the larger city stores provide creches and play areas for children and most supermarkets have miniature trolleys allowing your young family to charge alongside you as you shop, which is entertaining for them but can be hazardous for other shoppers and your wallet!

When visiting Sweden we have always travelled by ferry with our car using Scandinavian Seaways (formerly Torline) who provide excellent facilities in the form of playareas, children's competitions, cartoon shows etc. to while away the long journeys.

When planning a family holiday in Sweden be prepared for easy but expensive living in cities and simple, basic living in the country. Distances between destinations can be very great indeed and shops few and far between. There are numerous lakes and rivers providing every form of water sport but care must naturally be taken that children are well supervised as the waters are usually very deep. Mosquitoes can also be a real pest in the summer months.

Recommended reading:
Insight Guides ; Sweden (APA Publications, 1990, £10.95)
Fodor's Sweden (Fodor, 1990, £6.99)

For further information:
Swedish Tourist Office, 3 Cork Street, London W1. Tel: (071) 437 5816

Switzerland

Capital Bern	**Climate** Varies with altitude
Major cities Bern, Zürich, Basel, Geneva, Lausanne	**Annual weather range** – Zürich:
Time GMT + 1	*Temperature* Max 25°C (Jul)
Currency Swiss franc (SFr) = 100 centimes	Min −3°C (Jan)
Languages German, French, Italian, Romansch	*Rainfall* Max 136mm (Jul) Min 64mm (Mar, Dec)

It is not for nothing that the Swiss have a reputation for efficiency: their country is highly organized and it works. Coupled with this is the very high degree of affluence which allows the Swiss to improve, review, rebuild and convert to such an extent that it is possible to say that Swiss services – whether they be transport, telephones, banking, restaurants, postal services, facilities for the disabled or those travelling with young people – are almost without exception of an extremely high order.

Switzerland itself is the country of tourism par excellence: the Swiss have long been accustomed to people from abroad coming to enjoy and marvel at their beautiful country, initially the British, but now also from all over the world. If you speak French, German or Italian to them they will appreciate it but English is spoken to a high standard throughout most of the country and the Swiss, with four languages of their own to learn, enjoy the challenge and opportunity of practising a foreign language with visitors from overseas. But do remember that there are still, I am happy to say, many remote areas, notably in the mountains. Here life is rural, primitive and surprisingly poor: it may be difficult to find someone who understands English or to send a telegram to Bangkok – on the other hand, the mountain people are unfailingly helpful especially where children are concerned. Generally this is true wherever you go in Switzerland, the people will be welcoming, polite and helpful – and children – providing they behave in ways which are not too remote from the high standards of the Swiss themselves – are often the passport to offers of generous assistance and advice.

To come to specifics, in restaurants children are well catered for with high chairs and small portions, especially in the big chain restaurants (Migros, Mövenpick, Coop). The cost of living is high, so go for the chain stores – Migros and Coop are especially reasonable and offer a vast choice of baby goods, including Nestlé milk. The shop on the corner will be more Swiss and enjoyable but much more pricey as well. Parks and open spaces exist in abundance, and in urban areas they usually include a corner with swings and climbing frames. Public transport is fairly spartan (unless you go first class) but is astonishingly punctual (set your watch by it), clean and well organized. Car rental is easy and although I have no experience of baby seats in rented cars I would be most surprised if it created a problem.

Swiss food, unlike that in neighbouring France, tends to be straight-forward, based on milk products, wholesome and excellent. If your baby enjoys cheese and chocolate then you're home and dry! Hotels are generally spotless and will often provide a cot for a child at no extra cost and many of the big supermarkets have facilities for changing and feeding young children.

Above all, don't hesitate to ask. The Swiss are not very good at putting up notices to tell you what they have to offer and if, in the unlikely event that you catch them out and they don't have what you want then they will go to immense trouble to get you something as good if not better.

Our daughter was born there and both our children were brought up there. I hope that these few notes will help you to enjoy this wonderful country as much as we did.

R.T.

Recommended reading:
The Visitor's Guide to Switzerland, John Marshall (M.P.C, 1990, £8.99)
Blue Guide Switzerland, Ian Robertson (A & C Black, 1987, £9.95)
Fodor's Switzerland 1990 (Fodor, 1989, £9.99)
Frommer's Switzerland & Liechenstein, Darwin Porter (Simon & Schuster Inc., 1990, £11.95)

For further information:
Swiss Tourist Office, Swiss Centre, 1 New Coventry Street, London W1. Tel: (071) 734 1921

Thailand

Capital Bangkok	**Climate** Equatorial
Major cities Chiang Mai, Nakhon Ratchasima, Khon Kaen, Udon Thani	**Annual weather range** – Bangkok: *Temperature* Max 35°C (Apr) Min 20°C (Jan, Dec)
Time GMT + 7	*Rainfall* Max 305mm (Sep) Min 5mm (Dec)
Currency Baht (Bt) = 100 satang	
Language Thai	

Thailand means the land of the free and it's important to remember when you consider going there that the country was never colonized. This means that everything about Thailand is entirely its own, even though the US has been a big influence in recent years.

The Thais love children and are unfailingly polite and welcoming to foreigners. Their own children are generally brought up to be quiet and polite. Living is very public because it is a very hot country – everyone is out on the verandah or balcony most of the time – so babies are much in evidence and people are tolerant and sympathetic towards them.

Travelling in modern Thailand is easy. There are excellent hotels providing all the facilities and conveniences you could hope for. They are quite luxurious and everything works. Bangkok's Oriental Hotel is generally thought to be one of the world's best. For the visitor with children there are one or two real bonuses thrown in. The staff in a Thai hotel will be very helpful and go to great lengths to assist you. Medical and nursing care is very good indeed. Doctors are well-trained and thoroughly responsible. You will need to take out medical insurance though, as treatment is not free to visitors. Baby supplies are available in the big hotels and are reasonably priced.

Thai food is one of the great cuisines of the world but it may be a bit of a shock to your children since it is so hot and peppery. In hotels you can get Western food and many of the coffee shops or restaurants have children's menus. Opening hours are long. But do try Thai food. I would recommend the delicious and delicate soups which are excellent for young children. Thais don't eat courses: they sit down to the whole lot at once and there will always be rice and soup available. There is an abundance of wonderful fruit. Our year-old daughter took to papaya at once.

Hotels have pools and terraces where children can play in safety. Bangkok has an excellent zoo with paths and bridges over ornamental lakes. There is a kind of Thai Disneyland outside Bangkok which is also a good outing for the children. Provided you go with recognized tours – and that means air-conditioned buses – getting around the sights should present no problem. Struggling with local taxis and the heat and the impossible traffic would not be any fun, though walking the streets with a pushchair in a town like Chiang Mai in the north would be all right. Unless you are the rugged sort keep clear of local transport with your children. Bus travel in Thailand has its charms, but is also sticky, crowded and not for the faint-hearted. If you want to avoid the cities, go to the beaches of Pataya and Phuket.

After all these reassurances you should be prepared for a number of things. First the climate. It is always very, very hot and humid. Some Westerners sweat all the time, but you do get used to it. The

Thais have several baths a day to keep cool. After dark mosquitoes are a nuisance, but there are creams and sprays available to repel the unwelcome creatures. There are snakes in Thailand but they don't really like people and provided you know where your children are playing, you should have no qualms about this. Don't hesitate to take a trip to Thailand with your children – it is a beautiful country and its people are smiling, charming and incredibly tolerant.

M.H.

Recommended reading
Essential Thailand: All You Need to Know, Christine Osborne (AA, 1990, £3.95)
Thailand, A Travel Survival Kit, Joe Cummings (Lonely Planet, 1990, £7.95)
Insight Guide: Thailand (Harrap–Columbus, 1989, £10.95)

For further information:
Tourism Authority of Thailand, 9 Stafford Street, London W1X 3FE. Tel: (071) 499 7679

Tunisia

Capital Tunis	**Climate** Mediterranean
Major cities Djerba	**Annual weather range** – Tunis:
Time GMT + 1	*Temperature* Max 33°C (Aug)
Currency Tunisian dinar (TD) =	Min 6°C (Jan)
1000 millimes	*Rainfall* Max 64mm (Jan) Min
Languages Arabic, French	3mm (Jul)

It takes about 150 minutes to reach Tunisia from England and thus be transported to one of the most beautiful and exotic countries in the world which has the bonus of 700 miles of beaches whose sands are the texture of caster sugar. A highly civilized country, too, and not only because it was a French Protectorate for seventy-five years.

There are several ideal holiday resorts of outstanding merit: Hammamet, Cap Bon, Nabeul, Sousse, Monastir, Mahdia and the little islands of Zarzis, Kerkenah and Jerba. These (and other places) have been well organized for foreign visitors for many years and there is a wide variety of accommodation available at reasonable prices. Some hotels even have self catering cottages in their grounds. Most holiday sites are near small supermarkets. Many excellent restaurants cater for guests of all means and most palates.

Tunisian cuisine is an interesting blend of Arab and French. Though many children are notoriously conservative about food many, I find (and I include my own), are perfectly capable of being adventurous and experimental and Tunisia is a place to experiment in. You must try proper couscous, for example, with lamb, poultry or fish. And there is *koucha fi kolla* – a dish of young lamb baked with herbs in a jar. Avoid local national dishes that contain the peppery *harissa*. Though it is Mediterranean, the fish is often quite good, especially sea bass, bream, mullet, sardines, prawn and squid. The fruit is superb and, as Arabs like sweet things, there is a splendid range of confectionery (not so splendid for the teeth however). Standard soft drinks are in plentiful supply and the water is good – but, don't drink tap water. Stick to bottled mineral water. Incidentally, be cautious about an excess of chilled or iced drinks. These are a prime cause of stomach upsets.

Some knowledge of French stands one in good stead in hotels, shops and restaurants but many of the staff speak some English as well as Arabic and French. Menus are printed in Arabic and French and sometimes in English.

In summer when it is pretty hot children only need lightweight clothes, but if you are going in September or October, take some warmer things for the evenings. In winter take some warm clothes and waterproofs.

Communications by bus and train are fairly efficient and travel by public transport is entertaining for small children. Car rental is easy and there are good organized excursions. Immunization and vaccination are not necessary. Chemists are quite well supplied but I would play safe and take basic supplies.

There are a number of important and spectacular festivals which children would greatly enjoy. The main ones are the Sahara festival at Douz (January); the hawking festival at El Haouaria (May); the Sirens festival on the Kerkenah Islands (July); the Aoussou Festival at Sousse and the Festival of Kharja at Sid-bou-Said (August).

To the average 4- or 5-year-old a beach or a building seems to look much the same wherever they be and children of this age are not much interested in scenery *per se*. However, an alert and observant 5-year-old could hardly fail to be struck by the differences between Marks and Spencer (or Sainsbury's) and a Tunisian *souk*. In fact, such a child will find the *souks* fascinating and – dare one say it? – 'educational'.

Nor would most children be impervious to the splendour of their surroundings off the beaten track: the pine-clad hills, the orchards, orange and lemon plantations, vineyards, olive groves, date palms; the walled medinas and Berber villages, the black tents of the

Bedouin encampments, the vast plains with their flocks and the long camel trains.

No trip to Tunisia would be complete without a visit to one of the great oases. These are not just large waterholes with a few dozen date palms but cover many acres and support tens of thousands of date palms, bananas, pomegranates and other vegetation. Gabes in the south is an outstanding example, and can be toured in a horse-drawn *caleche*. Moreover, it is a suitable base for excursions (which small children would greatly enjoy) through the *chotts* (vast dried salt lakes gleaming white in the summer sun) to Gafsa, Tozeur, Nefta and Douz. The oasis at Gafsa may also be toured by *caleche*. At Tozeur some 200 different springs form the oasis and there is a zoo, and at Douz there is a marvellous camel market on Thursdays. You may not wish to risk your children on a camel ride but they will certainly enjoy the camel wrestling which is a feature of the Douz festival.

In the far south are extraordinary cave dwellings, weird underground houses (even an underground hotel) and subterranean oil factories where the mills are powered by camels. Should you wish to make a trip into the desert proper (and this is a remarkable experience) you must take full precautions and have plentiful supplies of water and provisions plus, unless you are experienced, a guide.

J.A.C.

Recommended reading:
Essential Tunisia; All You Need to Know (AA, 1990, £3.95)
Discover Tunisia, Terry Palmer (Heritage House, 1988, £4.95)
Where to Go in Tunisia, Reg Butler (Settle Press Hippocrene Books Inc., published in association with Thomson, 1990, £8.99)
Rough Guide: Tunisia, Peter Morris and Charles Farr (RKP, 1985, £5.95)

For further information:
Tunisian National Tourist Office, 7a Stafford Street, London W1. Tel: (071) 499 2234/629 0858

Turkey

Capital Ankara	**Climate** Mediterranean on coast,
Major cities Istanbul, Izmir,	continental inland
Adana, Bursa	**Annual weather range** – Izmir:
Time GMT + 3	*Temperature* Max 33°C
Currency Turkish lira (TL) =	(Jul–Aug) Min 4°C (Jan–Feb)
100 kurus	*Rainfall* Max 122mm (Dec) Min
Language Turkish	5mm (Jul–Aug)

Turkey is a very big country, astonishingly beautiful and varied in almost every topographical feature you can think of, and in much of it comparatively primitive conditions prevail. It is only during the last 50-odd years that it has been westernized. In summer most of the country is hot or very hot; in winter, cold or very cold. The Black Sea coast is the most humid region. Spring and autumn are the ideal seasons for the visitor.

Most visitors go to Istanbul, along the Black Sea coast and down the Aegean or Asia Minor coast to the southern shores. Some go inland, to, for instance, Iznik, Bursa and Ankara; a handful visit the central and eastern regions. I would be chary of these last with very small children.

In the major cities and towns (Istanbul, Bursa, Ankara, Konya, Antalya, Izmir) and along the principal tourist routes you may expect standards of living similar to those in Britain and Western Europe and you will have little difficulty in meeting the basic requirements of babies and small children. Soon after you journey beyond such areas you may easily find essentials difficult or impossible to come by. I would play safe and take with me all the pharmaceutical goods that might be needed.

Almost any kind of accommodation is available for the holiday-maker in traditional tourist areas and proprietors are obliging and helpful in making special arrangements for small children. As ancient codes of hospitality and courtesy in Turkey have few or no equals in the world (total strangers will buy you drinks or have food sent over to you in a restaurant) you may be absolutely sure that children (as well as their parents) will be very welcome. Indeed, little ones will be fussed over, indulged and given mini-VIP treatment. British children, because they are so fair and light-skinned by comparison with the Turks, arouse much curiosity and attention.

In general Turkish hotels are clean and well run, but you may find that the lavatory and washing facilities are not what you are used to. In simpler hotels there are often several beds to a room, so, unless you don't mind sharing the room with other guests, you need to pay for all the beds in a room. Do take note that scorpions have a tendency to turn up in odd places. They particularly like a snug site such as a shoe or slipper.

Small children may not take too readily at first to the food although Turkish cuisine is generally acknowledged to be among the best in the world. Initially, they may find it a little too oily or spicy. In regions frequented by visitors there are very high hotel standards and every effort is made to ensure that guests get what they need or want. The Turks are expert at delicious cold hors d'oeuvres (*soğuk meze*) and also hot hors d'oeuvres (*sicak meze*). These are brought on trays and are a meal in themselves. Meat and fish are also very good and are usually on display in the refrigerators of restaurants. So you choose what you want. It is also standard practise for guests to go into the kitchen and select what they want. Vegetables and salads are good and the fruit is wonderful (especially melons, peaches, figs and nectarines). Always wash and peel fruit. Water, especially spring and well water, is delicious but be wary of tap water. Ask for drinking water. Mineral waters are plentiful and excellent. Soft drinks (particularly pure fruit juices) are very good. Always boil milk. A change in diet may cause tummy troubles so take some suitable medicine.

If you value your children's teeth you will make sure they are not overexposed to Turkish confectionery. The Turks love sweet things and there is a wide range of the most delectable pastries, cakes, tarts and biscuits and many unfamiliar delicacies.

You can buy a fair variety of toys in all the main towns and any amount of standard entertainment is accessible. Children expecially enjoy the *karagöz*: witty and lively puppet shows in the Punch and Judy tradition.

Travelling by public transport is something of an adventure, particularly in out of the way places, but most small children enjoy it very much; and it provides insights into unfamiliar ways of life that surprise children. The markets and bazaars and the old 'oriental' quarters of the cities where modes of life and work have changed little during the last 500 years are fascinating for any observant and inquisitive 4- or 5-year-olds. Traditional rural life in Turkey is equally fascinating.

Seaside resorts are well equipped for small children and I would recommend such places as Bodrum, Marmaris, Fethiye, Finike, Kemer, Alanya and Anamur.

J.A.C.

The first time we took the children to Turkey in 1986 we booked a flight and village room accommodation with SunMed holidays. We left the resort after a week to explore on our own, as we don't particularly like organized tours and felt we weren't getting the feel of real Turkey. The next time we went we just booked a charter flight and a hire car. We went on a night flight to Dalaman airport. (We find flying through the night a good idea with young children, as they are usually asleep soon after take-off and not fidgeting around the plane for five hours. Adults don't feel so good the next day though!) Miraculously, the pre-booked hire car (Avis) was waiting for us at 4 a.m. and the sleeping children transferred to it. Children's car seats or restraint straps don't seem to be available in hire cars in Turkey.

A word about Dalaman airport: it is very poor on facilities, e.g. rock-hard plastic seats and limited refreshment facilities. Young soldiers with machine guns parade around the planes while passengers are disembarking.

Local driving standards aren't too bad outside Istanbul (where they are dreadful), but watch out for the odd car on the wrong side of the road. On country roads wild-looking dogs belonging to gypsies often chase after cars and can be rather frightening.

Although hire cars are convenient for travelling between resorts and for less accessible sites, short excursions are more fun on the extremely efficient and cheap minibus (*dolmus*) network. The locals are often accompanied by the odd hen or goat and lemon-scented cologne is passed around to refresh jaded passengers.

One of our main reasons for visiting Turkey was to see the wonderful archaeological sites, of which there are many. Before and during the holiday we primed the children with elementary versions of Greek myths and legends (e.g. *The Usborne Book of Legends*) so that they are familiar with places like Troy and monsters such as the Chimera whose legendary cave we passed.

Some places we would recommend: Altinkum on the Aegean coast is a relatively new and unspoiled resort with a vast sandy beach. People are very friendly and it is within easy reach of the ancient sites of Ephesus, Didyma, Miletus and Priene. Olu-Deniz near Fethiya has wonderful swimming in either sea or lagoon. The scenery is beautiful but rooms are more expensive here. Kas is an attractive former fishing village; the beach is rocky and a good walk from the centre. A fifteen-kilometre sandy unspoilt beach can be found at Patar, twenty kilometres west of Kas. The resort at Side is more commercialized, but good fun, with lots of sandy beaches and ruins.

Although they are not compulsory, check with your GP about inoculations for such things as typhoid and cholera etc. A hepatitis jab is strongly recommended. Don't let children stroke dogs or cats because of the risk of rabies. On both holidays to Turkey we have had to visit the local doctor when our youngest son developed acute ear infections. The locals were very concerned and eager to help and provided transport to the doctor. The surgeries were basic but the doctors seemed proficient, albeit rather enthusiastic with their prescriptions of antibiotics and pain-killers.

Always carry a loo roll with you. Toilet paper isn't usually provided in accommodation other than hotels and rarely in public lavatories.

The ice-cream vendors are good entertainment for children in the larger resorts. Usually dressed in local costume they play lots of teasing tricks on the children by manipulating ice-cream just out of their reach, to the accompaniment of theatrical shouts and gestures. Adults are also subject to this routine. Children in general are made a great fuss of in Turkey, especially by young men. Complete strangers will buy them ice-creams and give them kisses and cuddles. Although this sort of behaviour is frowned on in the UK, in Turkey it is a genuine expression of hospitality and friendship. Another pastime to provide unexpected fun is a visit to a carpet shop. It is very relaxed, there is no pressure to buy, exotic tea is offered and children are well tolerated. The ritual of unrolling carpet after carpet becomes a game for the children.

S.B.

Recommended reading:
Blue Guide; Turkey (The Aegean & Mediterranean Coasts) (A & C Black, 1989)
Travel Survival Kit: Turkey, Tom Bronahan (Lonely Planet, 1990, £8.95)
The Visitor's Guide to Turkey, Amanda Hinton (M.P.C, 1990, £8.99)
Guide to Aegeaen and Mediterranean Turkey, Diana Darke (Haag, 1989, £9.95)
Guide to Eastern Turkey, Diana Darke (Haag, 1990, £10.95)
Essentially Turkey, C & C Stewart (Croom Helm, 1988, £4.95)

For further information:
Turkish Embassy Information Office, Egyptian House, 170/173 Piccadilly, London W1. Tel: (071) 734 8681

United Kingdom *see* Britain

United States

Capital Washington DC

Major cities New York, Chicago, Los Angeles, Philadephia, Houston, Detroit

Time GMT −5–11

Currency Dollar ($) = 100 cents

Language English

Climate Wide regional variation

Annual weather range – Northeast (Washington DC) – continental:

Temperature Max 31°C (Jul) Min −3°C (Jan)

Rainfall Max 112mm (Jul) Min 66mm (Nov)

Annual weather range – Southeast (Miami) – subtropical:

Temperature Max 31°C (Jul–Sep) Min 16°C (Jan–Feb)

Rainfall Max 234mm (Oct) Min 51mm (Dec)

Annual weather range – Southwest (Los Angeles) – mediterranean:

Temperature Max 28°C (Aug) Min 8°C (Dec–Feb)

Rainfall Max 79mm (Jan) Min 0mm (Jul–Aug)

Annual weather range – Northwest (Seattle) – temperate:

Temperature Max 23°C (Aug) Min 2°C (Jan)

Rainfall Max 142mm (Dec) Min 15mm (Jul)

Americans generally like children and are well prepared for them. Special provisions such as children's menus and a general 'open for business' attitude are found nationwide.

In hotels and motels cots are normally available ('crib' is the word to use – a 'cot' is a camp bed). Apart from hotels in big cities, the flexibility of American lodging means you can expect sleeping room for three or four in almost all categories of rooms. Every hotel room has its own bathroom, WC and television – which can be a godsend for older children.

Renting a car is easy (automatic transmission is the norm) and there is usually a small charge for a child's seat. If you are visiting a small town, try and give the rental company a few days' notice.

Amtrak, which runs the railway system, is roomy and comfortable, but slow and patchy in coverage since most Americans travel by air and road. If you are travelling more than 200 miles, go by air. The many domestic airlines vary in their attention to young passengers, but most will ask parents with children to board first. Do check with your travel agent and remember that there are substantial discounts for American domestic flights if you book before you leave the UK.

Eating out is a family event in the US so you can expect high chairs almost everywhere as well as children's portions and free salad in steak and salad bars (provided the adults buy steaks). It is not just the fast-food restaurants which provide meals quickly; this is a standard feature of most American restaurants so you can eat out with the family and have time to do something else. Americans eat early so it is no problem going for dinner at 6.00 or 6.30 p.m. Supermarkets and shops of all kinds are always open late so you are never stuck if you run out of baby food or nappies. The labelling on most food items is very good. Incidentally, nappies are called 'diapers' in the US and disposables are more expensive than in the UK.

Changing facilities and mother's rooms are not usual, but the WCs are much larger than those in the UK and there is a lot of table-top space so you can change your baby easily.

American museums and zoos are extremely good. There is a wide variety available and those focusing on natural history and the environment are best for little ones. Facilities for the disabled are usually very good and there are ramps everywhere – especially useful for people pushing prams and pushchairs.

National parks, monuments and tourist attractions are very well organized. They are likely to have lots of space with play areas and other features for children. The theme and amusement parks of the Disney organization are found in California and Florida.

Climate varies enormously from north to south and east to west. Make sure you know the temperature ranges of your destinations. Ferocious central heating and air conditioning is common so you may find indoor temperatures uncomfortable. Bring layers of clothing for your children which can be put on or peeled off as necessary. Tee-shirts are essential.

There is no National Health Service in the US so it is vital that you arrange for comprehensive medical and dental insurance before you go. If you have a serious health emergency go to a hospital 'Emergency' room (not 'Casualty'). For problems such as minor cuts or bruises, slight fever, colds or upset stomach go to a 'Primary Care Centre'. These are an alternative to overcrowded emergency rooms and offer immediate attention by trained and fully qualified medical personnel, are usually accessible in shopping areas and often at less cost than hospitals would be. They will ask you how you will pay your bill and expect to see evidence that you can – like a credit card or insurance policy. Outside the big cities the trend is towards all-in-one medical centres with on-site specialists like dentists and paediatricians. Again, you will be asked how you are paying. Credit cards are the norm. One last point – a general practitioner is usually a 'family practice' physician or an 'internist' who specializes in internal medicine.

A-L.N.

For the British family on holiday, America offers infinite opportunities for amusement to parents, teenagers, and toddlers. With no language problem, and with airline deregulation making it cheaper to fly coast-to-coast in the US than to make a much shorter trip in Europe, America is an ideal destination for the British traveller. A sampling of America should include at least one city, one major amusement park and one national park.

Starting a visit to the US in Boston eases the British visitor into America because the older sections of the city, especially those around Beacon Hill, are reminiscent of an English city. Walk the Freedom Trail (marked with a wide red stripe in the pavement), there you'll see the house of Paul Revere, the USS Constitution, and the Old State House, from whose balcony the Declaration of Independence was read. Stroll the streets of Beacon Hill, especially at twilight, when the street lamps are lit.

A sure hit with children will be a visit to Quincy Market, where the scores of food stalls lining the central market building allow each family member to choose their own meal.

Just south of Boston's centre, you'll find Museum Wharf, housing two museums of special interest to young people – the Computer Museum, tracing information processing from the Chinese abacus to today's supercomputers, and the Children's Museum, with its many 'hands on' exhibits, including the very popular Japanese House and the Small Science Factory.

A few miles farther south, you'll reach the John F. Kennedy Museum and Library, with its mementoes of the President's life and career – and its glorious view of Boston Harbor.

A visitor to Florida's Walt Disney World and Epcot Center said, 'Everything there makes you smile. The staff are so wonderful. The place is so clean. And the roller coasters are the most exciting I've ever been on.'

Don't be surprised if the family members most enthusiastic about Disney World are the teenagers and the adults. They appreciate the great humour in the exhibits – the ghosts' dining room in the haunted house, the Peter Pan ride over London. Expect to run into beloved Disney characters anywhere and everywhere. Donald Duck may turn up on water-skis, or you may find yourself breakfasting next to Mickey and Minnie Mouse.

Just a short distance away (no worries about transportation – Disney World provides it) is Epcot Center, where you can take a ride in Spaceship Earth or a Journey into the Imagination. You can also shop and eat around the world in a village with restaurants and shops representing countries around the globe. (The homesick will find a realistic nineteenth-century London street.)

A ten-minute drive from the Disney complex brings you to Sea World, where dolphins, killer whales and sharks cavort in a 150-acre marine park. If Sea World inspires a desire for personal cavorting in the water, you aren't far from some part of Florida's 8,000 miles of coastline, sections of which sport such inviting names as The Gold Coast, The Platinum Coast, The Space Coast, and The Treasure Coast.

The wonder of Yosemite Park was captured by one of its founders, John Muir, who wrote that in the park are '. . . the most songful streams in the world . . . the noblest forests, the loftiest granite domes, the deepest ice sculptured canyons.'

Families can choose any level of accommodation, from the luxurious Ahwahnee Hotel (where Queen Elizabeth II stayed on her California visit) to Curry Village's cabins to a campsite in one of the park's five valleys.

Visitors will find activities for all ages and lifestyles. The more sedentary can tour in one of the park's open-sided buses, each one with a National Park Service guide. The more vigorous can opt for a hike or backpacking jaunt on part of the 773 miles of trails in Yosemite. In winter, there's skiing in the Badger Pass Ski area and skating at Curry Village's outdoor rink. In warmer weather, there's fishing, swimming and boating. All this in the midst of Yosemite, with its famous peaks such as El Capitan and Half Dome, its waterfalls and its magnificent giant sequoias.

From Yosemite, go northward to the area where gold was discovered and fortunes made overnight, or travel northeast to Lake Tahoe, the world's second deepest alpine lake, ringed by mountains that are snowcapped year round. Yearning for urban life? Head for San Francisco – ride a cable car, walk across the Golden Gate Bridge, and sample one of Asia's great cultures in Chinatown.

In planning a family holiday in the US, keep in mind that many American families travel there, and facilities for children tend to be very good – convenient places for changing nappies at the rest stops on interstate highways, menus for children in restaurants and generous discounts for children at hotels and motels.

It is now possible for British citizens to travel to the US without a visa. There are, however, several conditions of entry and travellers are advised to contact the US Embassy in advance on (071) 499 7010 to confirm their eligibility. Although many holiday makers have successfully used this system, if you have time, it is probably safer to obtain a visa in the normal way.

M.E.D.

Recommended reading:
Insight Guides to: North California, South California, the Rockies, N.Y. State, Florida, Texas, New England, Alaska. (APA Publications, 1989, £10.95 each)
Amex Guides to: California/New York/Washington D.C. (Mitchell Beazley, 1989, £4.95 each)

For further information:
US Travel and Tourism, 22 Sackville Street, London W1X 2EA. Tel: (071) 439 7433

USSR

Capital Moscow	**Climate** Continental/arctic
Major cities Leningrad, Kiev, Minsk, Tashkent,	**Annual weather range** – Moscow: *Temperature* Max 23°C (Jul)
Time GMT + 3–12	Min −16°C (Jan)
Currency Rouble (Rub) = 100 kopecks	*Rainfall* Max 88mm (Jul) Min 38mm (Feb)
Language Russian	

People in the USSR are generally very fond of children, but travelling around the country with them can be very difficult. Little provision is made for children, especially infants, at hotels and restaurants because it is not customary for Russians to travel with their offspring. Little attention is paid to children on the airlines, but airports, like big stations, usually have a mother and baby room.

Accommodation at Soviet hotels usually consists of twin-bedded rooms with private bathrooms and televisions. Rooms with more than two beds are unusual and cots are not generally provided.

The easiest way to visit the Soviet Union with children is on a package tour as all transportation, including buses and trains, is then organized for you. Car travel and hiring a car may be complicated because of certain travel restrictions. Public transport, which is very cheap, is usually packed but people willingly give up their seats to children.

Feeding children can also be a problem. There are usually plenty of stalls and coffee bars selling sandwiches, buns and soft drinks, but children are only permitted to eat in restaurants during the day. High chairs are not provided. Travellers with small children are advised to take food with them since milk and other dairy products may be hard to get outside the main cities. There are foreign currency foodstores at the main tourist centres, but the selection is limited. Local super-markets are open from 8 a.m. until 9 p.m. and usually close from 1 until 2 p.m.

Disposable nappies, paper tissues, toilet rolls and waterproof pants are extremely hard to find and bottle teats, baby wipes, plastic tie pants and plastic feeding bottles are simply not available. Baby creams are not always in stock either. No provision is made in WCs for changing babies and public conveniences should be avoided with small children anyway.

There are lots of pleasant children's playgrounds and plenty of circuses and puppet shows for older children. In winter there are opportunities for children to toboggan, ski and skate outside. However, visiting museums and art galleries with small children is frowned upon.

The winters are very cold but the buildings are well heated so light clothing is recommended indoors, however children need to be warmly dressed outside. If you are going to the USSR at a very cold time of year, it is wise to take a pure lanolin cream (with a low water content) to protect your child's cheeks from the frost. In summer it can be very warm, especially in the south. Children certainly need to have sun hats in the Central Asia Republics or on the Black Sea.

The USSR has a national health service, but foreigners are required to pay for medical treatment (payment must usually be made in roubles) unless some kind of reciprocal agreement exists between the respective countries. (Such an agreement exists between the UK and USSR.) Health facilities are provided at large clinics and there is a special clinic for foreigners in Moscow. Mothers with children are advised to arm themselves with antiseptic creams, anti-stomach-upset pills and cotton wool as these may prove hard to find. Bear in mind that if you need something for your child, it is sure to be out of stock!

Please Note
Recent political changes are such that it is difficult to know the effect they will have on holiday makers. We would advise you to contact the relevant National Tourist Office for further details before travelling.

Recommended reading:
Fodor's Soviet Union '90 (Fodor Travel Publications, 1990, £12.95)

For further information:
Intourist Travel Ltd, 219 Marsh Wall, London E14 9FJ. Tel: (071)
538 8600

Wales *see* Britain

West Indies

Antigua	**Barbados**
Capital St John's	**Capital** Bridgetown
Time GMT −4	**Time** GMT −4
Currency East Carribbean dollar (EC$) = 100 cents	**Currency** Barbados dollar (Bds$) = 100 cents
Language English	**Language** English
Climate Tropical	**Climate** Tropical
Annual weather range – St John's:	**Annual weather range** – Bridgetown:
Temperature Max 31°C (May–June, Aug– Sep) Min 21°C (Jan–Mar)	**Temperature** Max 30°C (May–Sep) Min 20°C (Jan–Mar)
Rainfall Max 180mm (Nov) Min 22mm (Feb)	**Rainfall** Max 206mm (Nov) Min 28mm (Feb)

Bright sunshine, cool sea breezes, warm water and sandy, palm tree-fringed beaches give this part of the world a special magic all of its own. Once experienced, the desire to return to the West Indies becomes irresistible and young children need not stand in the way. December to March is high season but April and May are also lovely months to visit, with the bonus that prices drop considerably. from April. The eight-hour flight, with a change of plane at Antigua for Nevis, may seem a long way with a young family, but the promise of guaranteed warmth makes it all worthwhile. For lovers of remote, far-away places island hopping is tempting, but with children, the extra (but not outrageous) expense of a private charter is desirable. In any case it is bliss to be met off the plane and whisked to a small aircraft.

West Indians love children and are welcoming and kind; babysitting and help with housework are easy to arrange. With an apartment or villa, a maid to do the cleaning, washing and ironing is usually, but not always, provided. Cots and high chairs are generally available and hotels will normally organize an early evening meal for children. Fresh food is limited; but plenty is available frozen or canned. Local fruits such as papaya, mangoes and bananas can be found and also locally-grown vegetables, but these are not always in abundance. Hotels are influenced by US cuisine and at lunchtime hamburgers and club sandwiches are always on the menu. Young children may take a few days to adjust their internal clocks and I suggest you arrive with a supply of powdered milk and cereal, so that in a hotel demands for a 6.00 a.m. breakfast can be satisfied.

The temperature ranges from 20°C to 30°C and the sun's piercing rays are made deceptively comfortable by cool breezes. It is very important to protect small children with a strong barrier cream and to make sure that they have hats and long-sleeved coverups. Children need very few clothes, so a holiday in the Caribbean can make an ideal opportunity for potty training; our boys ended their nappy days in Nevis. Disposable nappies, incidentally, are expensive and it is sensible to pack them in the luggage together with pharmaceutical items. Do take insect repellents as you can be bothered by mosquitoes in the evenings.

Car hire is always possible but baby seats are not much in evidence. This is not a real problem since distances are short and most of the roads are not made for speed. Apart from the few towns where congestion can be found, there is virtually no traffic. West Indians are so friendly that it is common practice to stop and offer lifts, especially on a small island like Nevis. This is fun for children and one of the charms of travelling in a part of the world where time has, in some ways, stood still. Although there are few buildings of great historic interest, there is a romantic awareness of the past and reminders of the days when sugar plantations flourished and naval sailing ships were based in Antigua. Horatio Nelson spent his youth in the Caribbean and met and married Frances Nesbit on the island of Nevis.

Armed with buckets and spades, young children will be happy wherever they are taken in these islands. On Nevis there are crabs to creep up on before they disappear down tunnels and pelicans to watch plunging clumsily into the sea. Nevis has no large hotel complexes which makes a marvellous escape from modern urban life. On Antigua remote places can be found, but there is much more sophistication and a full range of water sports, plus the excitement of being taken out to a reef in a glass-bottomed boat to watch the brightly coloured fish. The famous St James beach on Barbados has everything; hotels, apartments, villas and most known water sports, but there is still plenty of room on the pink-tinged coral sand. We have been going to the Caribbean for many years and have been taking our boys ever since they took their first staggering steps. The anticipation is enough to cheer the greyest winter day.

J. deC.

Recommended reading:
Antigua and Barbuda, the heart of the Caribbean Brian Dyde (Macmillan, 1986, £4.75)
Birnbaum's Caribbean 1990 (Houghton Mifflin, 1989, £13.95)
Barbados: The Visitors' Guide F.A. Hoyos (Macmillan, 1988, £13.95)
Fodor: Caribbean 1990 Gail Chason (Fodor Travel Publications, 1990, £11.99)

For further information:
Antigua & Barbuda Tourist Office, 15 Thayer Street, London W1. Tel: (071) 486 7073
Barbados Board of Tourism, 263 Tottenham Court Road, London W1. Tel: (071) 636 9448/9
St Kitts & Nevis, 10 Kensington Court, London W8. Tel: (071) 376 0881

Yugoslavia

Capital Belgrade	**Climate** Mediterranean
Major cities Ljubljana, Zagreb, Sarajevo, Skopje	**Annual weather range –** Dubrovnik:
Time GMT + 1	*Temperature* Max 29°C (Jul) Min 6°C (Jan–Feb)
Currency Yugoslav dinar (YuD) = 100 paras	*Rainfall* Max 198mm (Nov) Min 26mm (Jul)
Language Serbo-Croat	

Yugoslavia is a country well suited to a family holiday with small children. Its 400 miles of Adriatic coastline are very well-equipped with resorts and most of the facilities that you might expect in such a popular region. It has been a favourite holiday area for over 50 years and many hundreds of thousands of tourists from all over Europe go there every year. The coast is especially popular among the British.

The best times to go are May and September. In June, July and August the coast tends to be extremely hot and is very crowded – this despite the fact that the Istrian and Dalmatian shores are not renowned for their beaches. Most of them are made up of rock, pebble and rather gritty sand. At Opatija, the Blackpool of the Adriatic, there are good sandy beaches. In the far southeast, between Ulcinj and the Albanian border, there are 14 kilometres of very broad sandy beaches. This region is also well developed for holidaymakers. Between Budva and Ulcinj there are a number of pleasant small bays with good, though narrow, sandy beaches. Sveti Stefan is one of the most delightful resorts in Europe.

Scattered down the coast there are about a thousand islands, many of which are extremely beautiful, especially Rab, Cres, Lošinj, Pag, Brač, Hvar, Korčula and Mljet. These last two have delightful little secluded sandy beaches, coves, creeks and bays where children can safely potter, paddle and explore.

The islands and little cities that lie on and along the mountainous shores of Dalmatia and Istria are well connected by numerous craft (often hydrofoils). Travel by these is an exciting experience for children (look out for dolphins), and fishing expeditions can be arranged with local fishermen.

Inland travel by public transport still has an element of adventure, especially the train journey from Zagreb to Split across the Karst mountains. There is also a new line from Belgrade to Bar on the coast. This provides one of the most stunning and spectacular trips in Europe and small children love it. Self-drive cars are easily arranged everywhere.

Camping holidays on the coast and inland are popular among children and can be combined with treks, boating on the lakes and journeys by river. The huge national parks are magnificent. They particularly appeal to the town-bred child.

Food presents no problems. In fact, you can eat very well indeed, and all places on the main tourist beat are well equipped to cater for almost any child except, possibly, the chronic food faddist. There is good meat, excellent fish and crustacea on the coast, delicious fruit and salads and a copious range of soft drinks. Water is excellent and Yugoslavs discuss its qualities at various springs and wells as French people discuss wine.

Most inland regions also tend to be very hot in summer so precautions are necessary. Emergency medical aid is very efficient, but do take out insurance.

J.A.C.

Recommended reading:
Blue Guide: Yugoslavia (A & C Black, 1989, £12.95)
Fodor's '90: Yugoslavia (Fodor Travel Publications, 1990, £9.99)
Companion Guide to Yugoslavia, J.A. Cudden (Collins, 1990, £10.95)

For further information:
Yugoslav National Tourist Office, 143 Regent Street, London W1.
Tel: (071) 734 5243 / (071) 439 0399

Zimbabwe

Capital Harare	**Climate** Warm temperate and
Major cities Bulawayo	tropical
Time GMT + 2	**Annual weather range** – Harare:
Currency Zimbabwe dollar (Z$)	*Temperature* Max 28°C (Oct)
= 100 cents	Min 21°C (Jun–Jul)
Languages English, Shona,	*Rainfall* Max 196mm (Jan) Min
Ndebele	0mm (Jul)

It's a shame that the vast majority of travellers to Zimbabwe – Southern Rhodesia in the old days – go there because of some sort of connection with the place; very few go there as independent tourists with no ties. This is very likely because Zimbabwe is still popularly thought of as a dangerous country, because of its black socialist government and the war being fought in Mozambique next door. None of these factors should put you off: Zimbabwe is an amazingly beautiful, friendly country.

Musts for visitors: obviously Victoria Falls, Lake Kariba and Hwange Safari Park. Kariba has a string of lake shore hotels, all with pools and stunningly beautiful. Hwange is without doubt one of the finest game reserves in Africa. Some of the safari tour companies in the park will accept children in their game drives – though mine simply spent the journey asleep. Locals will recommend a trip to Nyanga, which sparks off memories of the Scottish Highlands: very beautiful and slap on the border with Mozambique (but safely away from the fighting). There are some breathtaking views and a huge variety of mountain landscapes. The ruins of Great Zimbabwe are a mysterious reminder of an ancient African civilization, and of course there are the main towns, Harare and Bulawayo, both pleasant and interesting.

The climate is close to perfect, with the days mostly dry and sunny. In summer the heat rises and October is the hottest month. Small children will need some protection from the sun – sun block, and sun hat. They may be affected by heat rash when they first arrive. Keep them cool with lots of drinks, and for tiny babies, a sun canopy over the buggy. My 7-month-old adapted to the hot weather and the relaxed, luxurious lifestyle with great ease and pleasure.

Because of the historical connection with Britain, food everywhere can best be described as old-fashioned English, with some Italian, French, Greek and Indian restaurants in Harare and Bulawayo. Major hotels have standard international cuisine, welcome children and have high chairs.

The Zimbabwe Sun group of hotels, a large chain of good hotels, accommodate children free when sharing with parents. The tourist industry is in the doldrums right now, and hotels are extremely attractively priced. It's possible to travel right round Zimbabwe on a package tour for ridiculously low amounts.

Because of the distances involved, air travel is preferable, though both trains and coaches are of a reasonable standard. Car hire is expensive but the roads are completely empty and very good. Take a small battery fan to cool your child during a long hot journey.

Malaria tablets are essential for travellers even though locals will boast they never take them. They should be taken at least one month before departure, for the whole trip and for six weeks afterwards. This aftercare is particularly important to maintain protection. Take both daily and weekly tablets, but check with your doctor about the correct children's dose.

Never let children swim in rivers or dams because of the dangers of bilharzia. The water in towns, hotels and swimming pools is from purified central water supplies or boreholes and is therefore perfectly safe. Use insect repellent after sundown, and a mosquito net (easily available everywhere). Cover arms and legs. AIDS is prevalent in Africa, so if possible take an emergency supply of syringes, needles and stitches and try not to need a blood transfusion.

There are no disposable nappies or baby wipes available in Zimbabwe. Bring your own, or get them from South Africa or Botswana. All washing, including terry nappies, must be ironed before being worn. This is because the imfulu fly lays its eggs on anything damp. Once developed the larvae bore their way under the skin and can be quite painful. Ironing kills them off.

Bring your own kettle if you need boiled water – at least that way you can be sure what you're getting. Electric plugs are three point square and the same voltage as in Britain.

R.E.

Recommended reading:
African Safari, M. Notting (Global Travel, 1987, £9.95)
Africa on a Shoestring (Lonely Planet, 1989, £14.95)

For further information:
Zimbabwe Tourist Office, Colette House, 52-55 Piccadilly, London W1. Tel: (071) 629 3955

Contributors

Susan Brearley is an infant school teacher and mother of two boys. She has forsworn package holidays forever and discovered the pleasure of do-it-yourself travel.

Cath Bruzzone is a working mother with two daughters. She is married to an Italian and spends every summer in Spain with her family.

Anna Carragher was born and brought up in Belfast. She now lives and works in London and has three well-travelled children.

Judy Carreck is a sociology graduate of Bristol University. She has travelled widely and worked for Action Aid in Nepal. She is now pursuing a career in publishing.

Mary Cornell is a teacher of history and has two children. She and her husband lived in Italy for nearly three years and make regular return trips on holiday.

J.A. Cuddon, educated at Douai and Brasenose College, Oxford, is a novelist, playwright and lexicographer. He has also published several travel books and numerous articles on travel worldwide. He is married with three young children.

Christine Davies is married with two children and lives in Buckinghamshire. She teaches at a centre for mentally handicapped adults.

Jan de Carle spent her career in publishing and is the author of several cookery books. She is now married with two sons.

Mary Elizabeth Devine is a university teacher and travel writer who commutes between Chicago and Boston. She lives in Massachusetts.

Rosalind Erskine is a single parent working in television. When her daughter Sophie was 7 months old they both went on a three-month research trip to the front-line states in Africa and emerged none the worse for wear.

Janet Hadley is a former teacher who enjoyed holidays in a number of countries, including Egypt, Czechoslovakia and Turkey. Now a full-time mother, she is learning through experience the best way to travel with young children.

Maggie Hartford is a journalist on the *Oxford Times* and has two young children. She has a French sister-in-law, and Dutch friends and has had truly awful – as well as good – experiences travelling with children.

Angela Hogg has mopped up children and orange juice around Europe, the Far East, India and Jordan. Currently living in Jidda, Saudi Arabia, she is particularly keen to find out how Saudi women tick.

Malcolm Hossick makes educational films. He once taught English to the children of the King of Thailand and makes frequent visits there with his family.

Wayne Jackman has been a children's TV presenter for ten years, has written many children's books and has three children himself.

Ernest R. Jones is the chairman and chief executive of Mercury Insurance Services Ltd., a specialist emergency assistance company.

Fe Corcilles Kaplan was born in the Philippines. She has travelled extensively in the Philippines and throughout East Asia with her daughter Monica.

Fredric M. Kaplan is author of *The China Guidebook* and owner of a travel agency in New Jersey, US. He has made frequent short trips to Asia accompanying his young daughter.

David Kewley has travelled the world extensively. Some of the more unusual places have been Malaysia, Japan, Afghanistan, Uganda, Lesotho, Mexico and Iran. He works in publishing and has recently begun to gain a different perspective on travel through the arrival of his daughter Kate.

Ettie Knatchbull-Hugessen has four children. She spent five years living in Saudi Arabia, making regular trips to Britain. On the way back from Saudi one year, Ettie spent a long holiday in Cyprus.

Peter Knatchbull-Hugessen lived in Arabia for nearly five years.

Jan Marsh is a freelance writer and editor and mother of now grown children who remembers what it's like to travel with young ones.

Jan Maulden is a well-travelled publisher with one daughter. She has lived for a year in South America, working in Brazil and Peru, and travelled to out-of-the-way places, including two months on the Amazon. She also lived and worked for a year in a small bush town in Nigeria.

Su Ong was born and brought up in Malaysia. She has worked as a teacher and publisher, specializing in English as a Foreign Language, and travelled widely. Su lived in Britain for fourteen years before returning to the Far East to live in Japan where she had her daughter.

Amia Raphael has been a frequent visitor to Israel over many years. She often took her children to the country when they were little.

Jane and **Robert Rogers** live in Herefordshire with their two small daughters Catherine and Eleanor. Eleanor was born in New Zealand and the Rogers family travelled around the North Island during a four-month stay with Jane's parents, who farm on the Kaipara.

Kathy Rooney lives in London and is the mother of two long-suffering children.

Sheila Sang is Consumer Editor for *Essentials* magazine, has worked for the Consumer Association, and also freelances as a researcher and writer.

Luba Selzer was born in Germany and is an economics graduate and chartered accountant. After having worked for a large firm of accountants and a well-known merchant bank she and her husband started their own business services company. They have two children, Simone and Elizabeth.

Richard Taylor is married with one son and one daughter. He recently spent nearly eight years living in Geneva and works in the field of international development and education.

David Waines is a lecturer in the Department of Religious Studies at the University of Lancaster. He was born in Canada and has spent a great deal of time in Egypt.

Marie Wells was born and brought up in Corfu. She is married to an Englishman, has three children and operates her own villa holiday business.

Ruth Widen is married to a Swede and has travelled around the country with her husband and son several times.

Section 2

Choosing and planning your holiday

Where should we go and what should we do?

Most people take one major holiday a year. After poring over brochures and parting with hard-earned cash, the next six months are spent in anticipation of a few weeks in the sun. The summer holiday is probably the single biggest and most important yearly purchase for the average family. When you think how much your well-being can hinge on that break, it's no wonder that the decision-making can be fraught rather than fun, and through insufficient planning you can easily make expensive mistakes.

This section of the *Family Travel Handbook* avoids the time-consuming and sometimes confusing wade through piles of brochures. It describes what is on offer from different tour operators and travel companies. At a glance you can see the destinations available, assess what kind of holiday is on offer and judge whether their price range fits yours. Each entry focuses on the facilities available for families, and you can quickly discover if cots and high chairs are easily available, or whether there are children's clubs and entertainment.

The companies listed cover almost every country in the world, so if you fancy a change of destination, you have the facts at your fingertips. If the kind of change you are considering is in the *type* of holiday rather than the destination, this section is invaluable. We cover sixteen types of holiday, from cycling to safaris, from home-swapping to traditional hotels. There is useful information to help you choose car rental companies, or to find out about the major air, sea and rail carriers.

All the companies are listed alphabetically within each section. You can take time to consider what you want from your holiday and who is best equipped to supply it. Whether you like to have every tiny detail planned in advance, or to travel independently, this section has information relevant to you and your needs.

In general, the prices quoted are for the 1990 season. They are intended as a guide to the character of the company's programme and special offers and specific prices should always be checked before booking.

To help us get better information and more cooperation from operators and their agents please always mention the *Family Travel Handbook* when you make a booking or ask for a brochure.

We'd also be interested to hear of your experiences, both good and bad. Write to us at: Reference Book Department, Bloomsbury Publishing, 2 Soho Square, London W1V 5DE, marking your envelope '*Family Travel Handbook*'.

Camping, Caravan Sites & Mobile Homes

One of the advantages of a self-catering holiday in a tent, caravan or mobile home is that for a relatively low cost you can enjoy a holiday that allows you to really 'please yourselves'. The independence of self-catering holidays is a great advantage to those with children – there are no stuffy and formal hotels or unsympathetic landladies to cope with and your family can eat when and whatever you please.

To put minds at rest, we need to define what you can actually expect from a camping site. However idyllic the setting, it is important to remember that if you chose to pitch your own tent or caravan in a farmer's field, you cannot expect even the most basic of facilities. You are on your own. There may not be anyone around to help you put your tent up in the pouring rain, help you to dig your car out of the mud and, ninety nine times out of a hundred, no washing or toilet facilities. All of these problems seem trivial in the blazing sunshine, but it is best to imagine the worst before plunging into a 'back to nature' mood. Farmers can often be extremely helpful, but they will never tolerate fools. If you *are* planning to take this option, it is important that you make sure you follow the rules of the Country Code. All its rules are common sense, but it really is essential reading. This section of the book includes many organised campsites with toilet and shower blocks and many have shops and entertainment, making them ideal for families. Another advantage of such sites is that there will be other children for your family to play with! Details of campsites in any particular area in Britain can be obtained by contacting the relevant tourist board, the Camping and Caravanning Club or the National Caravan Council (see Useful Addresses pp. 355–63).

One of the most civilised form of camping is a holiday at a site where luxury tents are ready-pitched and fully equipped for your use. If you are expecting khaki-coloured army-surplus tents, think again. Most family tents are large, 'bungalow-style' tents divided into separate rooms by zipped partitions. They all have transparent window panels and the tent sides can be raised to extend your living space when the weather is good. Inside they may have all mod cons, and some even have their own separate toilet tents. All these facilities should be checked before booking.

If you are wondering what the difference is between a caravan and a mobile home, the answer is, not a lot. Some companies make a distinction, apparently based on the caravan's lack of a plumbed in toilet and shower, but they often do not differ in size and they are both completely stationary! It is probably worth the extra expense in having your own toilet and bathroom facilities; traipsing through wet grass with children in the early hours is not much fun. Many caravans have a television which will prove its worth ten times over should the weather be bad. You can often hire linen and pillows and sometimes the site owner may supply basic groceries on request – check with the site for details of facilities available well in advance. With many sites giving much thought to families, this type of holiday can be ideal for those travelling with children.

When comparing what companies have to offer, the cheapest deal does not necessarily represent the best bargain. It is essential to compare the site facilities before deciding on your destination. These vary from the basic to the fantastic and should be a major factor in any decision you make. A self-catering holiday obviously appeals because of the money that can be saved, but do you really want to cook every day? The take-away food outlets and cafes on some sites could be a terrific advantage. How far is the site from the nearest town or beach? Is there a regular bus service? Is there a swimming pool? What can you do if it is wet? Finally, most parents appreciate some time alone together on holiday, so look out for those sites that offer organised children's games and babysitting facilities.

Prices

Unless otherwise stated 1990 prices have been quoted. These are intended only as a guide to the type of holiday offered and travellers should check with the company concerned for 1991 pricing details.

ATLANTIC COAST CARAVAN PARK
53 Upton Towans, Hayle, Cornwall
TR27 5BL
Tel: 0736 752071

UK (Cornwall)

Holidays in 4–6 berth luxury caravans. All have electricity and gas supplies, shower, WC, fully-equipped kitchen, colour TV and heating. The site is located at the eastern end of St Ives Bay, with room for tents and touring caravans. Facilities include some electric hook-ups, showers and WCs, washing and drying machines, ironing facilities, and shop.
Prices   (per caravan per week)
£205–£285 (mid-July)
Where space permits, extra people pay £10 each per week.

BEACH CAMPER
2 St Ann's Square, Manchester M2 7HJ
Tel: 061 834 0700 *or* 071 488 9495 *(London)*, 021 632 6621 *(Birmingham)*, 0223 350777 *(Cambridge)*

Fr   Sp   UK

Tent and mobile home holidays on sites in southern England, northern Spain and throughout France. The bungalow-style tents sleep 6 people in 3 bedrooms and have electricity and gas supplies, fully-equipped kitchen, living room and patio furniture. Bedding and pillows are not supplied. The mobile homes sleep 6, are similarly equipped to tents, but also have shower and WC. Pillows and blankets are supplied. Cots are provided free on request when booking. The sites usually have shopping, laundry, shower, WC and games facilities, including swimming pool. None are far from the sea.
Prices   A fortnight in a mobile home in mid-July costs £610 (Bretignolles sur Mer).
Discounts   On self-drive holidays children under 10 travel free on all dates.

This applies only to short Channel crossings, e.g. Dover–Calais. If you take a longer sea crossing, children are charged for seat/cabin plus insurance. 10–14s pay half additional adult rate.

BECKS HOLIDAYS
Southfields, Shirleys, Ditchling, Hassocks, W. Sussex BN6 8UD
Tel: 07918 2843

Fr

Caravan holidays on 4 sites in Brittany and the Vendée. The caravans sleep 6 or 7 and have electricity and gas supplies, mains water, shower, WCs, fully-equipped kitchen and patio furniture. Cots are available free on request. Blankets and pillows are provided. All sites have resident couriers, swimming pools (including children's pools), shops, bar, restaurant, take-away meals, laundry facilities and children's play area. Additional facilities include showers, WCs, guest rooms, TV room, tennis courts and bicycle hire (not all available at all sites).
Prices   (per adult per week)
Low   £78–£116
Mid   £97–£228
High   £149–£378
Discounts   Children under 4 go free and 4–13s pay £15–£30 each. Each child must pay £9.50 insurance.

BRITTANY CARAVAN HIRE
15 Winchcombe Road, Frampton Cotterell, Bristol BS17 2AG
Tel: 0454 772410

Fr

Mobile home holidays in Brittany and on the west coast, inclusive of self-drive travel arrangements. Mobile homes have gas and electricity supplies, running water, portable flush WC and fully-equipped kitchen and include showers.

Patio furniture and pillows supplied. Cots are available free in any accommodation on request. Most sites are close to the beach and have shops, bar, restaurant, take-away meals, showers, WCs, laundry facilities, children's play area and sports facilities. Some sites have swimming pools and evening entertainments.

Prices   The company has 5 seasons and the prices quoted cover mobile home hire and a short ferry crossing for 2 adults plus a car.

Low season (May): £288
High season: £878

Discounts   Children under 4 go free all season. From April to mid-June the first child under 13 also goes free. Additional children pay £15 each.

CABERVANS
Luxury Motor Homes, Caberfeidh,
Cloch Road, Gourock, Scotland
PA19 1BA
Tel: 0475 38775

Eur   UK

Motorhomes and caravans (2–7 berth) all with shower and fully-equipped kitchen. Extra charge for sleeping bags and sheets, if required. Drivers must be over 25.

Prices   (excluding VAT)
2-berth home: £200–£400
4-berth home: £240–£400
6/7 berth home: £320–£500

CANVAS HOLIDAYS LTD
Bull Plain, Hertford, Herts SG14 1DY
Tel: 0992 553535

Aus   Fr   Ger   It   Sp   Swi   Yug

Experienced and award-winning company specializing in tent and mobile home holidays. Accommodation is also available in log cabins. Bungalow-style tents have three bedrooms to sleep 6

people, electricity and gas supplies, fully-equipped kitchen, living room and patio furniture. Bedding and pillows are not supplied. Optional extras include your own toilet tent, a children's pack of cot and high chair (£1.50 per night) and a beginner's tent for children who want to try camping on their own (£2.50 per night). Mobile homes have two bedrooms and sleep 6–8 people. All are similarly equipped to tents, but have hot and cold running water, shower and WC. Blankets and pillows are supplied, but not linen. Children's couriers operate in selected camps, organizing games and activities. Special children's clubs everywhere, with treasure hunts, plus children's pack including scrapbook, nature trail book and 'passport'. Babysitting and baby patrols can be arranged for a small fee. Most sites have swimming pools and the company provides free watersports equipment at many sites with free instruction at selected camps. All have shopping, laundry, shower, WC and games facilities.

Prices   (two weeks)
Low season, 2 adults: £145
High season, 2 adults: £649

Discounts   Infants 0–3 free; 4–13 free, excluding high season (high season £14 per holiday); teenagers £19–£34 per holiday. All pay insurance of £13.

CAREFREE CAMPING LTD
126 Hempstead Road, Kings Langley,
Herts WD4 8AL
Tel: 0923 261311

Fr   H   Sp

Camping and mobile home holidays on 41 campsites. Spacious tents sleep 8 and have electricity and gas supplies, fully-equipped kitchen, living room and patio furniture. Bedding and pillows are not supplied. Luxury mobile homes sleep 8 and are similarly equipped to tents, but have proper bedrooms, a wardrobe with hanging space, hot and cold running water, shower, WC, fridge, oven, gas fire and patio furniture. Blankets and pillows are supplied.

All sites have showers, WCs, ironing and play facilities. On 27 sites a courier is available 6 days a week to arrange fun and games for children under 14. An evening baby-visiting service is also available by arrangement. Cots and high chairs may be booked costing 50p per night. Baby baths may be borrowed from the couriers on-site.

Prices   (for 2 adults and up to 4 children with car, including short Channel crossing and 14 nights' accommodation in a tent)

Low   £229
High   £625

There is a supplement of £10–£21 per party per night for a mobile home.

One-parent families   may deduct the cost of one extra adult from the basic price.

CARISMA HOLIDAYS LTD
Bethel House, Heronsgate Road, Chorleywood, Herts WD3 5BB
Tel: 09278 4235

Fr

Mobile home and tent holidays on 6 sites, all with their own private beaches, in south-west France, Vendee and Brittany. The mobile homes have 6–8 berths, gas and electricity supplies, hot and cold running water, shower, WC, fully-equipped kitchen and patio furniture. No bedding or linen supplied. Bungalow-style tents sleep 6 in 3 bedrooms. They have a fully-equipped kitchen, living room and patio furniture. No bedding or linen. Couriers on-site organize children's games and family entertainment, and will babysit for a small charge. Facilities on-site include shop, bar, restaurant, take-away meals, hot showers, WCs, sports and laundry facilities, children's play area, swimming pool. A doctor is available daily on each site.

Prices   (per mobile home, per fortnight)

£536 (July, all destinations for family of four, including car-ferry)

Discounts   Children under 4 travel free.

EUROCAMP TRAVEL LTD
Edmundson House, Tatton Street, Knutsford, Cheshire WA16 6BG
Tel: 0565 3844

Aus   Bel   Fr   Ger   Ire   It   Lux
Sp   Swi   UK   Yug

Tent and mobile home holidays on 200 sites. Bungalow-style tents sleep 6 in 3 bedrooms, have electricity and gas supplies, fully-equipped kitchen, living room and patio furniture. Bedding and pillows are not supplied. Mobile homes sleep 6–8, are similarly equipped to tents, but also have hot and cold running water, shower and WC. Blankets and pillows are provided. Cots available in all accommodation on request. All sites have shops, bar, restaurant, take-away food, hot showers, WCs, washing and drying machines, ironing facilities, play areas, sporting facilities and swimming pool. A children's courier service operates on 73 sites, organizing games and activities for children of all ages. A baby-sitting service is available at an hourly rate and children under 15 receive their own travel pack of information, games to play, etc. Baby packs of high chair, playpen and baby bath are available on selected sites for £1 a night per pack. Travel arrangements, including ferries, motorail and flights can be arranged on request.

Prices   (per car with 2 adults for 2 weeks, including insurance and short sea ferrty crossing). For holidays in tents:

Low   £274.40
Mid   £540.40
High   £680.40

Mobile home holidays extra.

Discounts   On travel-inclusive holidays, children up to nine are free, but insurance cover of £12.70 must be paid. Children aged ten to thirteen are free from 25 August–5 July, but must pay a supplement of £43 at other times.

GOODFELLOW HOLIDAYS LTD
10 Martin Close, Hatfield, Herts
AL10 8QS
Tel: 07072 62727

Fr

Mobile homes in Benodet, Brittany. The mobile homes sleep 6 and have electricity and gas supplies, hot and cold running water, shower, WC, fully-equipped kitchen and patio furniture. Pillows are provided, but no other bed linen is available. The site includes showers, WCs, hot-water supplies, bar, restaurant, crêperie, laundry, swimming and paddling pools, tennis courts and table-tennis facilities.
Prices   (per fortnight)
For 6 people in mid-July: £515
Discounts   All children under 14 stay free all season.

HAVEN HOLIDAYS
Swan Court, Waterhouse Street, Hemel Hempstead, Herts HP1 1DS
Tel: 0442 233111

UK

Self-catering holiday parks and villages at coastal resorts in England and Wales. Parks are small, medium and large, with corresponding levels of entertainment. Most have pools, indoor and outdoor games, bars, shops, restaurants, launderettes and evening entertainment for both adults and children. Cots can be booked. Accommodation is in 4–8 berth caravans or 2–3 bedroomed chalets and villas.
Prices   (6-berth caravan in Dorset per week, inclusive of gas, electricity, colour TV, linen, crockery and utensils)

£105 (September), £244 (June), £205 (July) or £320 (August).
Discounts   Book 14 nights get £25 off. Book second holiday in same year get £25 off. Short breaks at 50% discount.

HAVEN FRANCE AND SPAIN
Northney Marina, Northney Road, Hayling Island, Hants PO11 0NL
Tel: 0705 466111

Fr   Sp

Mobile homes and tents on established sites, on the French coast, the Auvergne, the Dordogne and the Loire, but including 2 on the Costa Brava. Mobile homes have 7–8 berths (some intended for children rather than adults), shower, WC and kitchen. Tents sleep 6. Crockery and utensils are provided, but bring your own linen. Cots provided free. The sites have restaurants and swimming pools, and most provide children's play areas and games. French Motorail connections on request.
Prices   (including ferry, gas and electricity)
Two adults sharing a mobile home for 2 weeks in south western France: from £411–£950; sharing a tent £258–£689.
Discounts   Children under 14 go free.

HOLIMARINE
171 Ivy House Lane, Bilston,
W. Midlands WV14 9LD
Tel: 0902 880800

UK

Family holiday parks in south-west England and Suffolk. Sites have swimming pools, paddling pools, playparks and indoor sports, tennis, snooker and amusements. There are also free discos, daytime entertainment, and cabaret shows in the evenings for both children and adults. Accommodation is in luxury lodges, maisonettes, villas or caravans half-board or self-catering, according to site. All are equipped with fridge, TV, bath or shower, crockery and utensils. Bring your own linen and towels. Cots available (free) at most sites but there is no organized baby-sitting. There is a children's club and a supervised crèche on every site.

Prices   (per property per week, including gas and electricity)
5-berth caravan: £80–£290
4-person flat: £80–£320

MATTHEWS HOLIDAYS
8 Bishopmead Parade, East Horsley,
Leatherhead, Surrey KT24 6RP
Tel: 04865 4044/5213

Fr

Mobile home holidays in south-west France. Accommodation is available in 3 sizes, sleeps 6, has gas and electricity supplies, fully-equipped kitchen and patio furniture. Blankets and pillows are supplied. The largest accommodation has a WC and shower, while the medium has WC only. Shower and WC blocks are on all sites for mobiles without these facilities. In addition, some sites have their own shops, bar, takeaway meals, laundry, irons and sports facilities, including swimming pool; others use nearby facilities in local towns.
Prices   average price per unit in Benodet, July/August)
£728 per fortnight, excluding travel.
£852 per fortnight, including travel for 2 adults with 3 children under 14 via Dover. Other routes possible.
Discounts   On travel-inclusive holidays, three children under 14 travel free on all dates.

THE MOUNT HOLIDAY PARK
Par, Cornwall PL24 2BZ
Tel: 072 681 2616

UK (Cornwall)

Caravan and chalet holidays on a site close to the sea, between Fowey and St Austell. All caravans are fully serviced, with mains drainage, fully-equipped kitchen, gas and electricity, colour TV, WC, hot and cold water and a shower. Chalets have 2 bedrooms and sleep 6 people. They are fully serviced and have colour TV. Blankets and pillows are supplied in all accommodation, but own linen must be provided. Cots can be hired for £3 per week. Facilities on site include an adventure playground, shop, launderette and ironing room. There is a restaurant in a central club-house which stages evening entertainment throughout the summer season. Sports facilities, including golf and riding are available nearby. It is the park's policy to accept only family bookings.
Prices   (per fully-serviced caravan or chalet per week)
6-berth caravan: £165
8-berth caravan: £270

ROMANY CARAVAN HOLIDAYS
c/o NORTHUMBRIA HORSE HOLIDAYS
(*see* **Special Interest Holidays**)

UK (Norfolk)

Romany caravan holidays in the Waveney Valley in Norfolk. The horse-drawn caravans sleep 4–5 people, have modern interiors and are fully equipped. Gas is provided free for lighting and cooking. You can meander along quiet country lanes, staying overnight at the Waveney Valley home base, or at one of the selected parking sites. Before starting out tuition is given in hitching up and handling your horse, which has been specially chosen for its friendly temperament.
Prices   (per week's rental)
Low   £199
High   £274

SEASUN HOLIDAYS LTD
71/72 East Hill, Colchester, Essex
CO1 2QW
Tel: 0206 869888

Fr It Por Sp

Self-catering holidays by coach, car and air to seaside resorts on the Mediterranean and the Algarve. Accommodation is in apartments, mobile homes, chalets, caravans, cabins and tents. All are fully-equipped, although a returnable deposit is payable on some sites from which gas, electricity and laundry costs are deducted. Most of the sites provide day and night entertainment with swimming pools, mini-golf, mini-olympics, inflatable castles, water slides, competitions, laundry rooms, shops and restaurant.
Prices   (per adult per fortnight, including coach travel and ferry crossing)
Tents: £69–£250
Cabins and caravans: £79–£300
Mobile homes: £99–£400
Apartments: £99–£450
Discounts   Under-3s go free provided they do not occupy a seat. Children aged 3–16 receive discounts of £15–£40, (high season), with many free places in low season.

SOLAIRE INTERNATIONAL HOLIDAYS
1158 Stratford Road, Hall Green,
Birmingham B28 8AF
Tel: 021 778 5061

Fr Sp

Mobile homes, caravans and tents sleeping 4–8 people at many sites in France and 2 in Spain. Crockery, utensils and pillows are supplied (bring your own bedding), and the homes and caravans have their own shower and WC. Sites include all modern facilities and many provide play areas for children (contact company in advance for details). All have swimming pools. Cots can be booked in advance free of charge. Travel by ferry and coach/own car service available to some sites.
Prices   (per 2 adults, per fortnight, including ferry crossing)
Brittany: £199–£498
(An extra adult would pay £30–£50. Add £8–£16 if hiring a mobile home)
Discounts   Children under 14 travel free
Children aged 14–16 pay £22–£36 per fortnight
Some sites offer special discounts for long bookings.

TREBLE B HOLIDAY CENTRE
Looe, Cornwall PL13 2JS
Tel: 05036 2425

UK (Cornwall)

Family-run site two miles from sea for people wishing to bring their own tents, tourers, caravans and equipment. Chalet and caravan rental also available. All rented accommodation is fully equipped but bed linen and towels are not provided. Caravans are 6–8 berth with electricity, shower, WC, TV and fridge. Site has shower and WC facilities, water and drainage points, electricity, battery charging and ice-pack hire services. There are shops, a launderette, swimming pool, children's play area, TV lounges and games facilities. Family entertainment is staged nightly during the months May to September. Cots and high chairs may be hired for around £5 per week in rented accommodation only (no more than one of each per family).
Prices   (per week in 6-berth caravan, including gas and electricity)
Peak   £290
(to pitch a tent or caravan, price for first 2 people)
Peak   £8.00 per night
Low   £4.90

ULEY CARRIAGE HIRE
Weavers Workshops, The Street, Uley,
Glos GL11 5TB
Tel: 0453 860288

UK (Cotswolds)

Seven-night tours of the Cotswolds in horse-drawn Romany caravans, which sleep 4. Calor gas cooker, crockery, cutlery and chemical WC provided (no linen). An instructor will accompany you on the first day, and is on 24-hour call after that. Most stops are at pubs or farms with washing facilities. Cots might be available (enquire when booking).
Prices (per caravan and horse per week)
Low   £250
High   £350

WELCOME CARAVAN COMPANY
18 King's Drive, Thames Ditton, Surrey
KT7 0TH
Tel: 081 398 0355

Fr

Holidays in mobile homes, 12 at coastal sites and one in Paris. All homes sleep 6 and have hot and cold water, shower, flush WC, fridge, gas cooker and oven, bedding (no linen), crockery and utensils. All sites have shops, restaurants and swimming pools. Camping cots can be hired for £5 per week.

Prices (per 2 adults sharing a mobile home for 2 weeks, including ferry via Dover and Calais)
Brittany: £325–£625
(Each extra adult pays £35–£45, and each child aged 4–13 pays £25–£30.)
French Riviera: £418–£775
Discounts   All children under 14 go free in low and mid season but *all* children pay £9 travel insurance.

WESTENTS LTD
11 Vernon Avenue, Edgerton,
Huddersfield, W. Yorks HD1 5QD
Tel: 0484 510544

Fr

Camping holidays on 3 sites in France. The bungalow-style tents sleep 6 in 3 bedrooms and have gas supply, electricity, fully-equipped kitchen with fridge, living room and patio furniture. Bedding and pillows are not provided. Cots are available free on request. All sites have shop, take-away food, play area, sports facilities, swimming pools, showers, WCs, washing and ironing facilities. A bar is also available on 3 sites. Beaches are 1–3km away. Couriers organize children's games and evening entertainments for all.
Prices   A fortnight in a mobile home, including short sea crossing, costs £580–£750 in peak season.
Discounts   All children under 14 go free throughout season, but insurance of £11 each must be paid.

Canal holidays

Self-catering waterway holidays have always been popular, both in the UK and abroad, but how practical are they for families with young children? One of the difficulties on boats is the confined space which can be a problem with toddlers and energetic youngsters. The craft used by the companies listed in this section have 2–12 berths (beds or bunks), and without exception, all recommend that you hire a larger boat than you actually need. This gives you room to move around comfortably and store all the paraphernalia that babies require. Having pored over the brochures for some time, we conclude that this is sound advice and not just a tactic to get more money out of you.

Most companies feel that carrycots would be fine on a boat, but children of toddling age could be quite a problem unless carefully confined. All companies can provide cotsides which are supposed to stop small children falling or clambering out of bed. However, Mrs S. Austin of Chingford wrote to us with some useful information on this subject after a 'disastrous' holiday on the Norfolk Broads:

'Cotsides do not extend to the full length of the berth. Therefore, if your toddler should wake in the night, she can crawl to the end of the bed and fall to the floor – a drop of some three feet. We were lucky to have hired a bigger boat as we folded the extra blankets to form a makeshift barrier at the foot of the bed, thus preventing a possible visit to the local hospital.'

Having hired an older style craft arranged on two levels, Mrs Austin also discovered the advisability of having all the cabins on one level so there would be no steps for children to trip over or fall down.

On the question of safety, all the companies supply buoyancy aids (except for babies) and children are advised to wear them at all times. Ideally, at least two members of the family group should be able to swim. It is essential to have a minimum of two adults on the boat as steering and mooring is a four-handed job. For this reason, a single parent with young children would not be advised to take a boating holiday.

Boats are priced according to the number of berths, and the fee is a fixed one. There are no discounts for children, except sometimes where the boat has a variable number of berths, say 4–6. This means that the basic hire fee is calculated on four berths, and the extra two can be used by children (normally under 12 years) at no extra charge. To take advantage of this you must take your own linen or sleeping-bags; an extra person charge will be levied if the hire company supplies linen.

Always enquire before booking what the price includes. You may have to pay extra for fuel, moorings, linen or bicycle hire. It is important to remember when loading your car or struggling on to the train that television reception from canal or river level is notoriously poor!

Prices

Unless otherwise stated 1990 prices have been quoted. These are intended only as a guide to the type of holiday offered and travellers should check with the company concerned for 1991 pricing details.

ADVENTURE CRUISERS

Catforth, nr Preston, Lancs PR4 0HE
Tel: 0772 690232

UK (Lake District)

A small hire cruise company specializing in holidays on the Lancaster Canal, which runs between Preston and Twitfield in the Lake District – a distance of 43 lock-free miles. The 6–8 berth narrowboat is modern with electricity, hot and cold water, shower, WC, fully-equipped kitchen and central heating. Day-hire is also available. Fuel is not included in the hire cost. Cotsides can be provided, but not cots. The company will make up beds for small children. Buoyancy aids are provided free. Small dogs may also travel for an extra charge, but the company must be notified when booking (UK residents only).
Prices (per week)
for 2 people: £420
for 8 people: £480
Other prices on request
Discounts Children under 2 travel free.

BLAKES HOLIDAYS

Wroxham, Norwich, Norfolk NR12 8DH
Tel: 0603 782911 (all British waterways, Norfolk Broads, Thames, Cambs, canals and rivers, Scotland).
0603 784131 (Ireland, Holland, Denmark, France)

Den   Fr   Hol   Ire   UK

Established over 80 years, this company arranges the hire of cruisers, narrowboats and yachts of 2–12 berths. All craft have electricity, hot and cold running water, shower, WC, fully-equipped kitchen and some form of heating. Bed-linen is supplied, but there are usually extra charges for fuel, pets and TV. Brief instruction is provided free on steering cruisers. Sailing tuition is available at £6 per hour. Cotsides are often free on request.

On European holidays, ferries, rail and/or air connections can be arranged. Sailing boats tend to be smaller — usually 2–6 berths. The holidays cover canals, rivers, lakes and fjords. On many trips bicycle and canoe hire is available from certain locations for a nominal weekly charge.

Prices   (per cruiser per week on UK canals/rivers)

The company has 8 price bands, A–H according to season. Prices shown cover smallest to largest boats.

Low (A)   £165–£627
Mid (D)   £220–£836
High (H)   £275–£1045

For holidays in Ireland and abroad craft are individually priced. A 4-berth Burgundy cruiser, for example, ranges from £300–£600.

Discounts   Children in carrycots travel free. On UK holidays any extra people aged 12 and under may occupy any extra berths on the boat free of charge.

BLISWORTH TUNNEL BOATS LTD

The Wharf, Gafton Road, Blisworth, Northants NN7 3BN
Tel: 0604 858868

UK (Midlands)

Narrowboat holidays and dayboat hire on a variety of canals in the midland system. Narrowboats have 2–12 berths and include shower, WC, cooker, hot and cold water, heating, crockery and utensils. Linen is not provided. Some boats have cotsides that can be bolted on to a bunk (enquire when booking).

Prices   (per narrowboat, per week, including fuel, gas and car parking)
4-berth boat: £343–£572
6-berth boat: £416–£693
(day boat, peak season)
Full day (9.30–19.00): £60
Half day (9.30–14.00/14.00–19.00): £35

BRIDGEWATER BOATS

Castle Wharf, Berkhamsted, Herts
Tel: 0442 86 3615

UK (England)

A helpful family company offering 2–8 berth narrowboats. All holidays start from the medieval market town of Berkhamstead but you can go as far as London, Stratford and Oxford, depending on duration of holiday. All boats have electricity, hot and cold running water, shower, fresh-water flush toilets, fully-equipped kitchen and heating. Bedding is supplied, but there is an extra charge for bedlinen. Cotsides are available if requested when booking. Lower bunks have been specially designed to fold down to make a play-pen during the day. Some boats are also equipped with a 'running line' – a rope attached to 'eyes' on the deck – to which toddlers can be harnessed so they can move around without fear of falling in. It is recommended that you take an extra berth for a baby to allow room for all their paraphernalia. Dogs, but not cats, may travel for a small extra charge (UK residents only).

Prices   (per 4-berth boat)
Low   from £300
High   from £580

Discounts   Children in carrycots travel free.

CLAYMOORE NAVIGATION LTD

The Wharf, Preston Brook, Warrington, Cheshire
Tel: 0928 717273

UK (Cheshire, Lancs, Yorks, N. Wales)

Narrowboats (3–10 berths) for hire on many canals and rivers. All boats have electricity, hot and cold running water, shower, WC, fully-equipped kitchen, stereo cassette player and central heating. Bed-linen supplied. Cotsides and buoyancy aids provided free if requested in advance. Basic hire fee also includes all fuel and cancellation insurance. Pets may travel free (UK residents only). TV and hairdryer may be hired for a small extra charge.

Prices   (per 4-berth boat, per week)
Low   £245
High   £510 (July–August)

Discounts   Children under 2 are free, provided you supply their bedding.

CORSAIR CRUISERS LTD
Upton Marina, Upton-upon-Severn,
Worcs WR8 0PB
Tel: 081 763 1647

UK (Worcs, Glos)

Cabin cruising on the Severn and Avon
rivers, around Worcester, Gloucester
and the Vale of Evesham. Cruisers are
4–7 berth and equipped to a high standard with cooker, fridge, shower, WC,
hot and cold water, central heating,
crockery, utensils, bedding, TV, hairdryer and shaver-socket. Linen and gas
are included in basic hire fee.
Prices (per 4-berth boat per week with
2 people sharing)
£258–£430
Extra people are charged £25 at certain
peak times, and £15 at other times. Pets
are charged £18, and there is a car parking fee of £7.
Discounts Children under 5 go free at
all times; 6–12s pay £25 at peak times,
and go free at all other times.

FRENCH COUNTRY CRUISES
Andrew Brock Travel Ltd, Barley Mow
Workspace, 10 Barley Mow Passage,
London W4 4PH
Tel: 081 995 3642

Fr

Pénichettes (5–12 berth French design
cruisers) for hire in most regions of
France. All boats have electricity, hot
and cold running water, shower, WC,
fully-equipped kitchen and some form
of heating. Bed-linen supplied. Buoyancy aids and cotsides available free on
request. Fuel is not included in the basic
hire fee.
Prices (per person per week)
Low £133–£275
Mid £168–£364
High £226–£503
Discounts None for children, except
on holidays inclusive of Channel crossing: approximately £12–£15 off.

HORNING PLEASURECRAFT LTD
Ferry View Estate, Horning, Norwich,
Norfolk NR12 8PT
Tel: 0692 630128

UK (Norfolk)

Self-drive cruisers for hire on the
Norfolk Broads. All boats, from 2–10
berths, have electricity, hot and cold
running water, shower, WC, fully-
equipped kitchen and heating.
Bed-linen supplied. Colour TV included.
Fuel is not included in the hire fee.
Prices (4-berth cruiser per week)
Standard: £260 (low); £430 (high)
Luxury: £390 (low); £650 (high)

HOSEASONS HOLIDAYS LTD
J34 Sunway House, Lowestoft, Suffolk
NR32 3LT
Tel: 0502 501010 *(UK)*
0502 500555 *(France and Holland)*

Fr Hol UK

Narrowboats, cruisers, sailing boats
and stationary houseboats (2–12
berths). All boats have electricity, hot
and cold running water, shower, WC,
fully-equipped kitchen and some form
of heating. Bedding and linen supplied.
Buoyancy aids and cotsides available
free on request. Fuel is not included in
basic hire fee. Pets may travel for an
extra cost (£17) (UK residents only).
Bicycle and/or dinghy hire may be
arranged if requested when booking. All
travel arrangements to your destination
can also be arranged on request.
Prices (per boat per week in UK; per
person per week abroad, including return ferry crossing)
4–6 berth boat in UK: £275 (low),
£450–£600 (high)
Luxury cruiser in UK: £600–£650
4–6 berth boat abroad: £150–£250
Discounts Under-4s travel free on
Continental holidays, but are charged
for accommodation if they occupy a
bed. Babies in their own cots are free.

HOTEL BOAT HOLIDAYS LTD
Braunston Marina, Braunston,
Nr. Daventry, Northampton NN11 7JH
Tel: 0788 891107

UK (England)

Hotel boats operating on most canal systems around the country, offering luxury cruises with a crew to do all the strenuous work. Accommodation is in double and single berths, some with en-suite bathrooms. Guests normally number 6–10. All meals are inclusive. Suitability of trip for children can be discussed on enquiry.
Prices (per 6 berth boat per week)
From £200
Children's prices are negotiable.

NIVERNAIS CRUISERS LTD
Bosworth House, The Thoroughfare,
Woodbridge, Suffolk IP12 2QE
Tel: 03943 2077

Fr

Cruisers for hire on the Nivernais Canal in Burgundy (2–11 berths). All have electricity, hot and cold running water, shower, WC, fully-equipped kitchen and some form of heating. Bedlinen supplied. Apparently, there is no room on board for cots. Fuel costs are not included in the basic hire fee. Bicycle hire is available from base.
Prices Details available on request
Discounts Children under 3 go free. On 2–4 berth boats there is no supplement for extra people.

SIMOLDA LTD
Basin End, Nantwich, Cheshire
CW5 8LA
Tel: 0270 624075

UK (North, Central)

Narrowboat holidays on the Midlands canal system. Choice of 4-6 and 6-8

berth boats, all with shower, hot and cold water, WC, cooker, central heating, bedding, linen, crockery and utensils. Bolt-on cot sides available (no charge). Gas, fuel and car parking are included in the basic hire fee.
Prices (per 4-6 berth boat per week, with 4 people sharing)
Low £290
High £570
Extra people are charged £18.50 per week. TV £5.75 per week extra.
Discounts Children under 4 go free; 4–14s pay £9.50 per week. There is no charge for pets. 5% discount is offered for 2 consecutive weeks.

VIKING AFLOAT
Lowesmoor Wharf, Worcester
WR1 2RX
Tel: 0905 28667

UK (Shropshire, Worcester)

Narrowboats (2–10 berths) for hire from bases in Worcester and Whitchurch. All have electricity, hot and cold running water, shower, WC, fully-equipped kitchen, central heating and radio/cassette player. TV may be hired for a small extra charge. Linen supplied. Fuel is included in the basic hire fee. No extra charge for cotsides, buoyancy aids and pets (UK residents only).
Prices (per boat per week)
4-berth: £288 (low); £480 (high)
6-berth: £414 (low); £690 (high)
Discounts On some boats very small children may travel free, depending on the size of the boat. Advice given on request.

Car Rental

There is really no question about it – car hire is an expensive business, but it allows such freedom on holiday that the benefits may outweigh any doubts about 'splashing out'.

On top of the basic hire charge, which can be calculated on a daily, weekly or monthly rate, you have to pay local taxes and insurance. Do not be tempted to take out minimum insurance. In Greece and Spain, for example, the minimum does not cover you against claims made by passengers. Most companies recommend taking out additional insurance against personal injury (PAI), and Collision Damage Waiver (CDW) which rules out your having to pay for any damage to the car. Be sure to read the small print carefully. Several companies have rules of hire that may seem peculiar on first reading.

Rates vary a great deal from company to company and country to country. Note too that it is usually cheaper to book your hire car from the UK before departure than on arrival at your destination.

Should you require them, baby seats and roof racks can be fitted in most hire cars if you request them when booking. There is usually a charge for this.

It is unwise to drive a car in a foreign country unless you are conversant with the local rules of the road. The AA and RAC have useful leaflets outlining the rules applicable in various countries. As in the UK, ignorance of the law is no defence, so do find out the basics before you go. Many countries require by law that you carry certain emergency equipment. Check that this is provided by the hire company before departure. (See also Fly/Drive Holidays.)

Prices
Unless otherwise stated 1990 prices have been quoted. These are intended only as a guide to the type of holiday offered and travellers should check with the company concerned for 1991 pricing details.

AVIS

Trident House, Station Road, Hayes, Middx UB3 4DJ
Tel: 081 848 8733

Worldwide

Avis has 3900 offices in 135 countries.
Worldwide Super Value   is the best current Avis deal. European car rental is fully inclusive of local tax, third-party insurance, PAI, CDW and mileage. For US car rental, all insurance elements are optional extras. The cost varies depending on the country and what size and type of car are involved.
One-way rental   The car may be picked up in one city or country and dropped off in another, but there may be a fee, depending on the locations involved.
Personally Yours service   Once you have booked your car you may request a free personalized itinerary based on your particular interests — anything from castles and palaces to shopping and crafts; available for Austria, France, Germany, Eire, Italy, Spain and Switzerland, and Florida, California, Arizona, New Mexico and Nevada in the US. These itineraries give detailed directions to get to your destination, the major sites of interest, times and prices of admission, and a list of family-run hotels.
Baby seats   Must be requested when booking. Availability and cost vary from country to country.
Booking   For super value at least 7 days in advance for a minimum of 3 days.
Payment   Cash, major credit cards, Avis charge card or Avis travel vouchers.
Example   Alicante = £34 per day (fully inclusive except petrol). If booked 7 days in advance, a week's rental is available for the price of 6 days.

EUROPCAR UK LTD

Bushey House, The High Street, Bushey, Watford, Herts WD2 1RE
Tel: 0532 422233
081 950 5050

Worldwide

Over 4600 offices in 122 countries. Affiliated to National car rental in the Caribbean, US and Australia, Tilden Rental in Canada and to Nippon Rent-a-car in Japan.
Super Drive   is the best current Europcar deal in Europe, Africa, the Middle East, Caribbean, US, Canada, Latin America and Australia. Rates include unlimited mileage and third-party insurance, except in Canada where 1050 km are free, and you're then charged by the kilometre. Rates are guaranteed in either sterling or dollars. Excess hours may be charged.
One-way rentals   (picking the car up in one city or country and dropping it off in another) is possible in some locations, but may be charged. Ask when booking. (There is no one-way rental charge in UK.)
Baby seats   Must be requested at time of booking. Availability and cost vary from country to country.
Booking   48 hours in advance for US, Caribbean and Australia. 24 hours in advance for all other regions.
Payment   Full or part payment by cash, major credit card, or Europcar/National/Tilden credit card. Local taxes, insurance and petrol deposit may be paid when you collect the car.
Deposit   100% of cost required if paying by cash. If rental is arranged through a travel agent, a deposit will be required at start of rental to cover optional insurance, petrol, damage liability and extra days. If you do not purchase CDW, you may have to pay an additional deposit to cover damage liability — this is refundable on return of the car undamaged.
Example   Super Drive deal for a category A car in Spain (1 week) = £168 (inclusive of CDW, PAI and local taxes).

HERTZ (UK) LTD
Radnor House, 1272 London Road,
London SW16 4XW
Tel: 081 679 1799

Worldwide

Hertz has 4800 offices in 130 countries, including 2000 airport locations.
Europe on Wheels is the best current Hertz deal. It covers 26 European countries, including Morocco, Tunisia and Israel, and provides CDW, local taxes and unlimited mileage.
One-way rental In most countries cars can be rented in one town and left in another free of charge. It is usually possible to start rental in one country and end it in another; details should be checked when you book.
Baby seats must be requested at time of booking. Availability and cost vary from country to country, but sometimes they are free.
Booking Usually 7 days in advance with the exception of rentals in selected resorts where the advance booking requirement is 24 hours. Europe on Wheels programme should be asked for at the time of booking.
Payment Details given on request.
Deposit Required prior to rental if payment is prepaid in the country of residence, or if made other than by accepted credit card at place of rental. These conditions vary from deal to deal.
Example Spain (1 week, Europe on Wheels) = £161, exclusive of PAI.

EURODOLLAR RENT A CAR LTD
3 Warwick Place, Uxbridge, UB8 1DE
Tel: 0895 33300

Worldwide

Partnership between Swan National in the UK and Dollar Rent-a-Car in the USA.
Eurodrive Leisure rates are available in 14 European countries, but apply only if pre-booked at least 3 days prior to commencement of rental.
One-way rental (picking the car up in one city or country and dropping it off in another) is available free of charge between EuroDollar locations in some countries. Ask when booking.
Baby seats Must be requested at time of booking. Availability and cost vary from country to country.
Booking 3 days prior to rental. Minimum rental is 3 days.
Payment With most major credit cards or cash.
Deposit Petrol deposit refundable on return of car.

WORLDWIDE CARS LTD
34 Ship Street, Brighton, Sussex
BN1 1AD
Tel: 0273 205025

Eur UK US

A company specializing in car hire in the Balearics, Canaries, Portugal and Spain. Prices are inclusive of local tax, comprehensive insurance, unlimited mileage, CDW and delivery to the airport. As PAI is not included, holidaymakers are recommended to check their own holiday insurance to ensure they have cover.
Baby seats Available at most destinations and always free. Ask when booking.
Booking Preferably at least 7 days in advance.
Payment Payable in full before departure.
Deposit Small amount required to confirm booking. Fuel may be paid on arrival.
Example Alicante (1 week) = £109 (collected from airport any time of day or night).

Coach Transport and Coach Tours

Coaches are probably unbeatable as a fast, cheap method of getting from A to B. They cost considerably less than planes and trains and allow the whole family, including the usual driver, to enjoy the scenery and arrive at the destination relatively refreshed. Camping and skiing companies most frequently offer coach travel as a cheap alternative on their holidays, but think hard before embarking with young children on what may be an eighteen-hour journey in cramped conditions.

In researching this section, we found no coach operator offering any special on-coach facilities for children. The most you can hope for are WCs and video films, with some long-distance companies having a drinks and snacks service. Most large operators will have cushions and covers for hire, but it can be a good saving to take your own; a sleeping bag rolls up very small and can easily take two children. Read the section on avoiding boredom (pp. 318–9) and think about investing in a personal stereo with connections for two pairs of headphones and some story tapes.

However, many of the companies we list advise against taking very young children on coach trips, and several don't allow them anyway. Coach tours, by their very nature, involve a lot of travel and are not ideal for youngsters with high energy levels and short concentration spans.

If you plan to do a lot of independent travelling by coach, it is worth investigating the special passes and discount tickets that are available. Generally speaking, the longer your stay, the greater the discount. Long-haul operators, such as Greyhound, change their offers from year to year.

Prices
Unless otherwise stated 1990 prices have been quoted. These are intended only as a guide to the type of holiday offered and travellers should check with the company concerned for 1991 pricing details.

CLANSMAN MONARCH HOLIDAYS
St Andrew Square Bus Station,
Edinburgh EH1 3DU
Tel: 031 556 2126/7 or 0800 833991

UK (Scotland)

Coach tours lasting 2–7 days, including special interest tours from April to September. The coaches have reclining seats, arm rests, air suspension and forced ventilation. Accommodation is in hotels and the availability of such things as cots and high chairs varies.
Prices (per person, including full board and entrance fees)
Cheapest 2-day tour: £63
Dearest 7-day tour: £320
Discounts Discounts are given at the discretion of individual hotels, and will be quoted on request.

COSMOSAIR
Cosmos House, 1 Bromley Common,
Bromley, Kent BR2 9LX
Tel: 081 464 3444 or 0272 277404 (Bristol), 021 236 9621 (Birmingham), 061 493 9393 (Manchester), 031 226 3521 (Edinburgh)

Eur

Sea/coach and air/coach holidays to most European destinations. All departures are from London or a Channel port. Free coach connection to and from Dover from 90 locations in the UK. The coaches have WCs but no other facilities.
Prices (per adult, half board)
Tyrol (6 days): £158–£187
Black Forest (9 days): £198–£230
Italy (15 days): £339–£386
Discounts Children under 7 are not allowed on any of these tours. A 10% discount for children aged 7–12 is available if they share a room with 2 full fare-paying passengers, provided the tour chosen includes at least one week in a resort.

COTTER COACH LINE
12 Crimea Street, Anderston, Glasgow
G2 8PW
Tel: 041 221 8921 or 071 730 0202 (London)

UK

Twice-daily coach journeys between London and Scotland. The coaches have WC and wash facilities, stewardess service for food and refreshments, video TV and private headphones.
Prices London—Scotland £16 single, £28.50 return.
Discounts Children under 12 pay half fare when accompanied by an adult.

EVAN EVANS TOURS
26–28 Paradise Road, Richmond,
Surrey TW9 1SE
Tel: 071 930 2377

UK

Coach tours to most parts of the UK lasting from 1½ hours to 4 days, led by experienced guides. The coaches are air-conditioned and some tours include accommodation and lunch and/or dinner. The availability of cots, high chairs and child-minding varies from hotel to hotel, but we are informed that this is 'generally pretty good'.
Prices (per adult) These range from £7 for the cheapest 1½ hour tour, to £300 for a 4-day tour.
Discounts Special prices are offered to children under 17 and on extended tours (ie. tours with accommodation) children get a 10% reduction on the tour price.

FRAMES RICKARDS
11 Herbrand Street, London WC1N 1EX
Tel: 071 837 3111 (sightseeing)
071 637 4171 (tours)

UK

Tours to most parts of the UK lasting from half a day to 11 days. Coach tours of more than one day are not recommended for children under 12. The company will advise on suitable tours for children, which are usually day trips in and around London to such places as Oxford, Warwick Castle and Stratford-upon-Avon.

Prices (per adult)
Half-day tour (all year round): £9.50
4-day 'Quick Look at Britain' tour: £195 (low)–£225 (high)
11-day tour (high season only): £525 (approx)

Discounts 20% discount on some longer tours for children aged 5–14. Special discounts may be available on day trips (details on request).

GREYHOUND WORLD TRAVEL
Sussex House, London Road, East Grinstead, W. Sussex RH19 1LD
Tel: 0342 317317

Can   US

The principal coach operator in North America. Some excellent deals are available, but must be purchased in the UK rather than at destination. Organized tours are available in conjunction with Jetsave Holidays (*see* **Fly/Drive**). The coaches all have air-conditioning, WCs and reclining seats. No special facilities for babies.

Prices The 1990/1 rates for Ameripass are:
4 days: £49 (valid Monday–Thursday). No extensions.
Longer passes are refundable if unused; extensions cost £10 per day.
7-day pass: £85
15-day pass: £135
30-day pass: £170

Discounts On bus travel only, under-5s are free. Children aged 5–11 pay half adult fare. On organized tours children under 12 pay half the adult fare provided they share parents' accommodation.

NATIONAL EXPRESS LTD
Ensign Court, 4 Vicarage Road, Edgbaston, Birmingham B15 3ES
Tel: 021 622 4373 *or* 071 730 0202 *(London)*, 061 228 3881 *(Manchester)*, 0329 230023 *(Fareham)*

UK

The largest coach operator in the UK serving hundreds of places daily. For travel information telephone your local enquiry centre; the number will be in the phone book.

Prices There is a huge range, impossible to cover here. Your local enquiry centre will supply details.

Discounts On travel within the UK children under 5 are free provided they do not occupy a separate seat. Children aged 5–15 get about one third off standard adult fares. People aged 16–23 can buy a discount coach card for £5, which is valid for 12 months and gives the same discounts.

SONATA LEISURE LTD
227 Umberside Road, Selly Oak, Birmingham B29 7SG
Tel: 021 472 8636

Bel   Fr   Ger   Hol   It   Sp   UK

Continental coach tours arranged, as well as weekend city breaks to Paris, Bruges, Amsterdam and many UK cities. Cots and high chairs may be available in some accommodation on request.

Prices (per adult) 8-day tour to Nice with bed and breakfast: £130

Discounts Small children not occupying a seat or separate accommodation go free. Children up to 12 receive 10% discount on the adult fare.

WALLACE ARNOLD
Gelderd Road, Leeds LS12 6DH
Tel: 0532 636456 *(Leeds) or* 081 686
2378 *(London)*, 0382 27321 *(Scotland)*

Eur   UK

Long-established coach company offering tours throughout the UK and to
most European destinations. Special
requirements, such as cots, must be
requested when booking. Wallace
Arnold also offer air holidays to
European destinations and some long-
haul packages (Canada, USA and South
Africa).

Prices   Prices vary greatly and details
should be confirmed direct.

Discounts   Details of child discounts
are available on request and vary from
holiday to holiday.

Cottages, Gîtes & Farmhouses

The cottage industry, as the length of this section suggests, is a large one. We list companies, large and small, who offer various grades of accommodation mainly in the UK, Ireland, France and Italy. Properties vary enormously – from period cottages to modern bungalows. Our descriptions are necessarily brief, but we hope they will help you to make an initial selection and to find a company that caters for your needs. To save space and needless repetition we state here that all properties have gas and/or electricity supplies, running water, fully-equipped kitchen and bathroom and at least an adequate standard of furnishing.

When choosing your holiday home, do read the small print carefully and compare what is included in the price. In some properties gas and electricity are metered, or a charge may be levied at the end of your stay for the amount consumed. Note too that linen is not usually supplied, although it may be available for hire. Where cots, high chairs and any other children's facilities are provided we say so and quote the fee where appropriate.

If you choose to holiday in France, chances are that your cottage will be called a gîte. This is usually a building that has been renovated with the help of a government grant. Gîtes are usually found in the more rural parts of France and have to meet standards specified by the government. Do not expect luxury, however. They offer simple, clean accommodation but do not necessarily have such things as armchairs. Several companies, Brittany Ferries being one of them, offer gîtes which are not part of this government scheme. The name has simply come to mean a cottage with a basic level of comfort.

If you wish to rent a gîte in a particular part of France, you can obtain lists from the *département* in question. Addresses are available from the French Tourist Office. Note that the best properties are snapped up by Christmas, so book early to avoid disappointment.

Farmhouse holidays tend to fall into two categories: either you rent the property as you would a gîte or cottage, or you can take a chambre d'hôte holiday, which means that you have bed and breakfast in the farmhouse and get to know the family. In some places an evening meal may also be provided. We have had enthusiastic reports from families who have taken chambre d'hôte holidays; they consider them the ideal family holiday as real friendships can form and the French tend to make a great fuss of the children, perhaps leaving you free to do some exploring on your own.

Before you book a property you should read Kathy Rooney's article on pp. 301–5 that gives advice on the kinds of questions to ask a holiday operator about their properties.

Prices
Unless otherwise stated 1990 prices have been quoted. These are intended only as a guide to the type of holiday offered and travellers should check with the company concerned for 1991 pricing details.

ALLEZ FRANCE
27 West Street, Storrington, W. Sussex
RH20 4DZ
Tel: 0903 745793

Fr

This company says it is experienced in dealing with family groups. It offers a selection of properties ranging from tiny country cottages to large seaside villas in most areas of France. A service charge of £3 per person per week is payable for water, gas, electricity, agent's fees and taxes. Cots are available in many places, either free or for a small charge. High chairs are not usual in France. Childminding can sometimes be arranged locally, depending where you stay. Also a selection of family-run hotels of character, many ideal for family groups.
Prices   (per week for 4–9 people)
Low: from £300
High: up to £3000
Discounts   Children receive standard ferry discounts. Infants free (or nominal charge).

AMARO COTTAGE HOLIDAYS
22 High Street, Alton, Hants GU34 1BN
Tel: 0420 88867

UK

Large selection of properties from converted stables to country mansions in many picturesque areas of England, Scotland and Wales. Up to three-quarters of the properties have cots and high chairs, but baby-sitting is not widely available.
Prices   (per family of 4 per week in a mid-range property)
Low: £100–£125
High: £220–£270
Discounts   Children under $2\frac{1}{2}$ are free.

AULTBEA HIGHLAND LODGES
Torliath, Drumchork, Aultbea,
Achnasheen, Ross-shire IV22 2HU
Tel: 0445 731233/731268

UK (Scotland)

Purpose-built holiday homes on a 23 acre site overlooking the fishing hamlet of Aultbea on the north-west coast of

Scotland. Cots and high chairs may be hired for £7 per week and childminding can be arranged locally. STB class and grading — 4 crown facility — highly commended.

Prices range from £188 for a couple in low season to £467 for 6 people in high season. A family of 3–4 would pay around £209–£389 per week. From January–April 3-day mini-breaks for 4 people cost from £90.

Discounts Children under 2 are free.

B+I LINE UK LTD
East Princes Dock, Liverpool L3 0AA
Tel: 051 236 8325

S. Ire

Self-catering holidays with a choice of accommodation in cottages, caravans, river cruisers or holiday villages. 'Village' amenities include shops, launderette, children's playroom, enclosed playground, TV room, showers and sports. Hire of touring caravans can be arranged on request. Cots and high chairs are usually available in all locations.

Prices (per family of 4 per week in a cottage)
£235 (May–June)
£420 (July–August)

Discounts Children travel free with all self-catering holidays.

BATH HOLIDAY HOMES
3 Frankley Buildings, Bath BA1 6EG
Tel: 0225 332221

UK (Bath)

Historic houses, cottages and flats for rent in and around the city. Some properties specify minimum ages for children, and some do not allow children at all. Some offer free use of cots and high chairs, but at other properties such equipment can be hired by arrangement.

Prices (per property per week)
Low: from £170
High: from £220

BELL-INGRAM SELF-CATERING HOLIDAYS
Durn, Isla Road, Perth PH2 7HF
Tel: 0738 21121

UK (Scotland)

Selection of cottages and country houses ranging from rural simplicity (sleeping 2) to various lodges on their own estates (sleeping up to 15). Some accommodation is classified by 'crowns'; all are illustrated. Cots and high chairs are free, where available.

Prices (per property per week)
Low   £75–£375
Mid   £85–£425
High   £100–£500

BLAKES COUNTRY COTTAGES
(see also **Canal holidays**)

Ire   UK

Wide selection of cottages, farmhouses, bungalows and apartments. Some are individual properties of great character or historical interest, while others may be purpose-built holiday villages. Around 90% of the cottages have cots, and some can provide high chairs and baby-sitting. Many cottages have farm animals nearby, which might interest families with young children. Some groups of cottages have facilities, such as swimming pools and jacuzzis. Most properties in the brochure are illustrated with floor plans.

Prices (average 1990 prices for 4 people)
Low   £160
High £304

However, the cheapest 3-person cottage in January–April is £75, and the dearest is £575.

Discounts For holidays in Ireland, children up to 14 can travel free at certain times.

BOWHILL'S
Mayhill Farm, Swanmore,
Southampton SO3 2RD
Tel: 0489 877627/878612 or 0329
833093

Fr It Por

More than 300 'hand-picked' villas and farmhouses in France. The emphasis is a distinctive blend of character and amenities. Most properties are carefully converted historic places with lots of character, some are modern and have a selection of swimming pools. Cots are available in some locations, usually free. Baby-sitting and cleaning can also be arranged locally, depending on the location. Ferries, overnight hotel stops and motorail transfers can be arranged for self-drive holidays. Fly-drive arrangements can also be made. Two-centre holidays available.
Prices (per adult per fortnight, including Channel crossing with car and insurance)
Average cottage: £93 (low), £105 (mid), £130 (high).
Villa on Côte d'Azur with pool: £352 (low), £476 (mid), £721 (high).
Discounts Under-4s are free. Children aged 4–13 each receive £10.10 discount.

BRITTANY DIRECT HOLIDAYS
362 Sutton Common Road, Sutton,
Surrey SM3 9PL
Tel: 081 641 6060

Fr (Brittany)

Illustrated brochure of forty gîtes, cottages and houses. The company also offer holidays in hotels and chambre d'hôte. Colour interior/exterior photos supplied when booking. Cots, where available, cost £5 per week to hire. Most places offer baby-sitting which is arranged locally. Many also offer a starter pack of groceries. In addition to the packages described above, Brittany Direct also organize fly-drive and golfing holidays. On the latter, junior participants are eligible for discounted green fees (details available on request).
Prices (per property per week for 2 adults, including ferry crossing)
Low: from £300
High: up to £500
Discounts Children receive standard ferry discounts.

BRITTANY FERRIES GITES HOLIDAYS
(see **Ferries**)

Fr

Over 1500 holiday homes comprising gîtes, villas and apartments in west, south-west and the south of France, Normandy and Loire Valley, Burgundy, Franche Comte, Limousin, the Auvergne, Rhône Valley and the Alps. The properties represent the finest selection of France's rural and seaside accommodation and are graded 1–9 (very comfortable to basic) by Brittany Ferries. Cots and/or children's beds are available in many places.
Prices (per adult per week, including return ferry crossing with car)
Grade 9 gîte: £60–£149
Grade 1 gîte: £85–£237
Discounts Under-4s are free all year. Children 4–13 pay £13 a week in low season and £21 in high season.

CASAS CANTABRICAS
31 Arbury Road, Cambridge CB4 2JB
Tel: 0223 328721

Sp

Family-run company offering a small selection of privately-owned cottages in Cantabria, northern Spain. Most properties are in villages or rural situations, and all are within easy reach of the sea. The availability of cots and high chairs varies. Details on request. Baby-sitting may be arranged locally.
Prices (per property per week)
Low: £95–£310
Mid: £125–£410
High: £175–£565

CERBID'S QUALITY COTTAGES

Cerbid, Solva, Haverfordwest, Pembs
SA62 6YE
Tel: 0348 837874

Fr   UK (Wales)

Family company offering a wide variety
of privately-owned cottages throughout
France and Wales. Cots available on request. Baby-sitting can be arranged in
some locations. Linen and heating is
usually inclusive. Pets welcome.
Prices   (per property per week)
Wales: £99–£660
France: £390–£5300 (including short
ferry crossing for two adults with a car).
Discounts   In summer small families
receive a £10–£40 discount, depending
on property chosen.

CHARACTER COTTAGES LTD

34 Fore Street, Sidmouth, Devon
EX10 8AG
Tel: 03955 77001

UK

Large selection of cottages throughout
England, and a smaller selection in
Wales, Scotland and Ireland. Cots and
high chairs are supplied in some locations. Baby-sitting can sometimes be
arranged locally for about £1.50 per
hour.
Prices   (middle-range property for
family of 4 per week)
Low: £120
High: £210

COAST AND COUNTRY HOLIDAYS

15 Town Green, Wymondham, Norfolk
NR18 0PN
Tel: 0953 604480

UK (Norfolk, Suffolk)

Cottages and houses of all periods for
rent. Around 90% of properties have
cots and the vast majority supply them
free of charge. Some also have high
chairs and will arrange babysitting.
Prices   (per family of 4 per week)

Low: from £80
High: from £200
(per group of 9 per week)
Low: £179
High: £312

COASTAL COTTAGES OF PEMBROKESHIRE

Abercastle, nr Haverfordwest, Pembs
SA62 5HJ
Tel: 0348 837742

UK (Wales)

Large selection of cottages in
Pembrokeshire ranging from modern
bungalows to old farmhouses, all in
coastal locations. All cottages have free
cots and high chairs. Babysitting can be
arranged in less remote places.
Prices   (per 4-person property per
week)
Low: £80–£130
High: £180–£425

CORNISH TRADITIONAL COTTAGES LTD

Lostwithiel, Cornwall PL22 0HT
Tel: 0208 872559

UK (Cornwall)

Extensive selection of properties
ranging from traditional cottages to
converted boat-sheds and chapels. Cots
and high chairs are available free of
charge in some properties; check details before booking. Baby-sitting can
usually be arranged locally through the
property owner or housekeeper.
Prices   (per family of 4 per week)
Low: £84–£120
High: £220–£350

COTTAGE HOLIDAYS

Lansdowne Place, 17 Holdenhurst
Road, Bournemouth BH8
Tel: 0202 25545 *or* 0202 295006
(24-hour)

UK

Wide selection of coast and country
properties in most popular holiday

areas in England and Wales. All are categorized according to the degree of comfort. Cots are supplied free in many locations, with high chairs and baby-sitting available at some cottages.
Prices   (per property per week)
£88–£625
The average summer price for a 4-person property is about £220–£270
Discounts   For summer bookings confirmed before 31 January, there is a low deposit of 20% only required. A 10% discount is available on the second week of a 2-week holiday. (These discounts apply to many properties.)

A COTTAGE IN THE COUNTRY
Thames and Chilterns Tourist Board, 8 Market Place, Abingdon, Oxon
OX14 3UD
Tel: 0993 779207

UK (Oxfordshire, Cotswolds, Thames Valley and Chilterns)

A varied selection of properties in town and country locations. Tourist Board inspected. Many with an inclusive price, i.e. linen, heating and electricity. Some offering tennis court or swimming pool.
Prices   (per property per week)
Low   £60–£250
Mid   £65–£450
High   £70–£650

COUNTRY HOLIDAYS
Spring Mill, Earby, Colne, Lancs
BB8 6RN
Tel: 0282 445533

UK

Extensive selection of inspected and graded period and modern properties throughout England, Scotland and Wales. All properties suitable for children have cots, and many have high chairs and automatic washing machines. Baby-sitting may be organized with some owners.
Prices   (per property per week)
Low   from £72
High   from £147

COUNTRY SERVICES
Union Road, Kingsbridge, Devon
TQ7 1EF
Tel: 0752 881570

UK (Devon)

Cottages in waterside or rural settings. Cots and high chairs can both be hired for £5 each per week; linen hire £5 per week. Baby-sitting can be arranged at some cottages. Many cottages accept pets.
Prices   (per property per week)
Low   £70–£230
Mid   £85–£315
High   £150–£580

COUNTRYSIDE COTTAGES
Vale House, Gillingham, Dorset
SP8 4LD
Tel: 0747 824778

Mal   UK

A selection of traditional and modern cottages in the Cotswolds and throughout southern England except Cornwall, plus a few apartments in Malta. All properties are illustrated with floor plans. Cots and high chairs are provided free where available, and baby-sitting can be arranged at most cottages.
Prices   (per property per week)
Low   £84–£214
Mid   £96–£202
High   £140–£326

DALES HOLIDAY COTTAGES
Otley Street, Skipton, N. Yorks
BD23 1DY
Tel: 0756 799821/790919

UK (Yorkshire and Northumberland)

Mostly traditional, locally-owned cottages, sleeping from 2–11 people. Cots and high chairs are free where available, but linen hire may be extra.
Prices   (per property per week)
Low   £90–£140
Mid   £120–£160
High   £170–£280

DIEPPE FERRIES HOLIDAYS

17 Market Street, Weymouth Quay,
Weymouth, Dorset DT4 8DY
Tel: 0305 777444

Fr   Sp

Holidays available in gîtes (government
approved), hotels, villas, caravans and
on camp sites in several parts of France.
The brochure gives detailed descriptions of sleeping arrangements; many
properties have children's beds but not
cots.
Prices   (per adult per week, including
ferry crossing)
Low   £82–£109
Mid   £100–£130
High   £135–£190
Discounts   Under-4s go free; 4–14s
pay £12 each.

DISCOVER BRITAIN HOLIDAYS

Shaw Mews, Shaw Street, Worcester
WR1 3QQ
Tel: 0905 613746

UK

Personally inspected farms and cottages in all parts of England, Scotland
and Wales. Cots, high chairs and folding
beds are free where available. Special
facilities like helping on the farm, swimming and riding are by arrangement
with the owner, as is baby-sitting.
Properties are graded from 'homely' to
'best' family accommodation. Both bed
and breakfast and self-catering accommodation is available.
Prices   (per self-catering property per
week)
Low   £91–£325
Mid   £85–£304
High   £103–£385
Bed and breakfast (per night)
Adults   £15.00
Children   £9.00

DUNAIRD CABINS

St Mary's Road, Birnam, Dunkeld,
Perthshire
Tel: 03502 262

UK (Scotland)

Ten octagonal pine cabins in a two-acre
woodland setting. Each cabin sleeps
4–6 people. Cots, high chairs and safety
rails for bunk beds are supplied free.
Baby-sitting   can   sometimes   be
arranged with the owners. A playpark is
available nearby.
Prices   (per week per 4 people)
Low   £100
Mid   £170
High   £250

ENGLISH COUNTRY COTTAGES LTD

Grove Farmbarns, Fakenham, Norfolk
NR21 9NB
Tel: 0328 864041 *(English cottages)*
0328 851341 *(Welsh cottages)*
0328 864011 *(Scottish cottages)*

UK

Extensive selection of over 2400 carefully inspected properties, ranging from
cottages and farmhouses to country
houses and mansions, sleeping 2–20
people. The company offers countryside, waterside and seaside locations.
Some properties in the grounds of
country hotels offer hotel-style facilities
and a selection of sports. Properties are
categorized A-Z, from small to large and
simple to deluxe, with all grades being
well represented. Cots are available
(free) in most cottages. Many offer
baby-sitting by arrangement, high
chairs, children's games rooms and
equipped play areas. A few properties
do not allow children. Short breaks (3
nights) available September to May.
Prices   (per property per week)
Off-season   £99–£501
Peak season   £186–£714

FARM AND COTTAGE HOLIDAYS
5 Fore Street, Bideford, Devon
EX39 3PW
Tel: 0237 479146

UK (Devon, Somerset, Cornwall)

Self-catering or half board family holidays. Properties are graded from basically to plushly furnished. Nearly all properties have cots, some offer microwaves, washing machines, videos, etc. Some have linen for hire and many offer baby-sitting by arrangement.
Prices (self-catering property per week)
Low   £80–£199
Mid   £100–£345
High   £110–£505
(half-board accommodation per adult per week)
Low   £89–£165
Mid   £99–£195
High   £109–£195
Under-2s sharing parents' room pay £7 each per week.
Discounts (available on half board only)
Under-5s pay 50% of adult rate, under 12's pay 70% of adult rate. 12's and over pay adult rate. Children under 2 pay £10 for cot.

FELINDRE
51 Church Street, Stoke-on-Trent, Staffs ST4 1DQ
Tel: 0782 744865

UK (Wales)

Nine very comfortable cedarwood bungalows and three cottages set in nine acres of Pembrokeshire National Park near St Davids. The following children's facilities are all supplied free: cots, high chairs, pushchairs, baby baths, potties, nappy buckets and toilet trainer seats.
Prices (per property per week, excluding VAT)
Low   £69
High   £249

FERMANAGH LAKELAND
Lakeland Visitor Centre, Eniskillen, Co. Fermanagh
Tel: 0635 323110/325050

UK (N. Ireland)

The company specializes in fishing, boating and cruising holidays. Wide choice of lakeside hotels, guest houses and self catering chalets, many of which offer special facilities for children. Activity Centres for groups and individuals offering instruction in canoeing, caving, windsurfing, pony trekking, etc.
Packages special package holidays can be arranged for those travelling by ferry.
Prices (self-catering property per week)
£80–£300
(double room with B+B per night)
£16–£60
Discounts Some available for OAPs and children and vary according to establishment.

FINNCHALET HOLIDAYS LTD
Dunira, Comrie, Perthshire PH6 2JZ
Tel: 0764 70020

Den   Fin   Swe

Chalet, farm and hotel holidays. Farm holidays include full board and the brochure lists animals kept on the farm. Most properties have family bedrooms but no cots. The owners mostly speak English. Baby-sitting is generally available. Free cots on ferry crossing.
Prices (including full board, ferry crossing plus berth and twice-weekly sauna)
Finland: £408
Denmark: £265, £364–£415 (July, August)
Discounts Babies go free. Under-11s receive a discount of £11 per day. Under-16s receive a discount of £58 for Finland and £49 for Denmark.

FOREST HOLIDAYS

Forestry Commission, 231 Corstorphine Road, Edinburgh EH12 7AT
Tel: 031 334 2576/0303

UK (Cornwall, Yorkshire, Scotland)

Selection of cabins and cottages located in open countryside, in woods or near water. Bed-linen included. Pets welcome. Short breaks also available. Send for free colour brochure.
Prices   from £60 (3 nights)–£105 (7 nights)

FRANCOPHILE HOLIDAYS

Matheran House, Newlands, Daventry, Northants NN11 4DU
Tel: 0327 300565

Fr

Selection of private and independently-run houses, villas and apartments. The brochure has interior photos, plans and lots of useful advice about the suitability of each property for young children. Children's beds are generally available, but there are few cots. Babysitting is widely available on request.
Prices   (per property sleeping 4 people for 14 nights)
Low: £548
High: £886
(per property sleeping 16 people for 14 nights)
Low: £837
High: £1388

FREEDOM HOLIDAYS LTD

40 New Street, St Helier, Jersey, Channel Islands
Tel: 0534 25259

UK (Jersey)   Fr

Selection of cottages and flats in country and suburban locations. Where available, cots are provided free. Elsewhere the hire of cots, high chairs and all other baby equipment can be arranged. Baby-sitting may be offered in some properties.
Prices   Studio apt. (couple and child per week)
Starts at £105

FRENCH AFFAIR

34 Lillie Road, Fulham, London SW6 1TN
Tel: 071 799 1077

Fr

Hand-picked cottages and houses with detailed descriptions of accommodation. Some properties offer free cots, and baby-sitting is available by arrangement.
Prices   (per property per person for 1 week, including ferry crossing)
From £75
Discounts   Children receive standard travel discounts (see **Ferries**).

FRENCH COUNTY COTTAGES

Anglia House, Marina, Lowestoft, Suffolk NR32 1PZ
Tel: 0502 517271

Fr

Self-catering holidays in cottages, gîtes and villas. A selection of family-run hotels and motels are available for stops en route. Cots are provided in some locations.
Prices   These are calculated on the number of adults in the party. A 4-person gîte in Brittany for 1 week, inclusive of travel arrangements and insurance/car insurance would cost:
Low: £95 approx.
Mid: £112 approx.
High: £135 approx.
Discounts   On self-catering and farmhouse holidays under-4s are free. Children aged 4–13 each receive a £12 discount and travel free outside July and August depending on ferry company and date.

FRENCH LIFE
26 Church Road, Horsforth, Leeds
LS18 5L
Tel: 0532 450443

Fr

Choice of holidays in gîtes or farm-houses, but the brochure also covers mobile homes, chalets, tents, villas and apartments. When booking a gîte or farmhouse you only pay for the number of adults in your party rather than the sleeping capacity of the accommo-dation. Cots free, where available.
Prices (per property per week for 2 adults, including ferry crossing)
From: £189
Discounts Under-14s travel free.

GAER COTTAGES
Cribyn, Lampeter, Dyfed SA48 7LZ
Tel: 0570 470275

UK (W. Wales)

Nine cottages converted from an old farm building. Some sleep up to 9 people. Bedding, including cot bedding, is supplied, as are towels, soap and detergent. Each cottage has a washing-machine. There is an enclosed chil-dren's play area, and nearby is a picnic area, woodland trail and small river. Cots and high chairs are supplied free on request. A list of reliable local baby-sitters is available.
Prices
3 people sharing: £194 (low); £314 (high)
9 people sharing: £249 (low); £395 (high)

GITES DE FRANCE LTD
178 Piccadilly, London W1V 9DB
Tel: 071 493 3480

Fr

A handbook listing over 2500 rural properties throughout France. Accom-modation tends to be simple and the availability of cots, high chairs and baby-sitting varies from place to place. To obtain the handbook you must be-come a member, which costs £3. This also entitles you to a list of *Chambres d'hôte* and *Logis de France* (family-run hotels). A new handbook for 1991 de-tails properties in Belgium.
Prices (per 4-person gîte per week)
From: £90
Discounts Children under 14 travel free with Sally Line.

GORDON HOLIDAY COTTAGES
118 Kidmore End Road, Emmer Green, Reading, Berks RG4 8SL
Tel: 0734 472524

Fr UK

Small selection of self-catering proper-ties in Scotland, Brittany and some parts of England, ranging from cottages to large farmhouses sleeping 8. Cots may be hired. Some properties have facilities, such as mini-golf, for children, and some have been adapted for the disabled.
Prices (per property per week)
Low: £150–£200
Medium: £180–£300
High: £230–£350

HAYWOOD COTTAGE HOLIDAYS
Lansdowne Place, 17 Holdenhurst Road, Bournemouth, BH8 8EH
Tel: 0202 555545 *or* 0202 295006
(24-hour brochures)

UK

Wide selection of coastal and country properties in most popular holiday areas in England and Wales. All are categorized according to the degree of comfort. Cots are supplied free in many locations, with high chairs and baby-sitting available at some cottages.
Prices (per property per week)
£88–£625
The average summer price for a 4-person property is about £220–£270.
Discounts For summer bookings con-firmed before 31 January, there is a low

deposit of 20% only required. A 10% discount is available on the second week of a 2-week holiday. (These discounts apply to many properties).

HEATHERWOOD PARK
Dornoch, Sutherland, Scotland
Tel: 0862 810596

UK (Scotland)

Luxurious Norwegian bungalows set in private Scottish parkland close to local village shops and amenities. Cots are provided on request. Golf and tennis are available nearby.
Prices (per week per 5 people)
Low £150
High £250

HOLIDAY COTTAGES
Water Street, Skipton, N. Yorks
BD23 1PB
Tel: 0756 700510

UK (Cumbria, Derbyshire, Yorkshire)

Cottages and houses ranging from converted barns to country farmhouses in the Yorkshire Dales, Moors, Peak and Lake District. Cots and high chairs are available at most properties free of charge.
Prices (per property per week)
Cottages: £65–£150 (low); £140–£400 (high).

HOLIDAY HOUSES DUMFRIES AND GALLOWAY
G.M. Thomson & Co, 27 King Street, Castle Douglas DG7 1AB
Tel: 0556 2701/2973

UK (Scotland)

Collection of personally inspected houses, sleeping 2–16 people. Many properties are classified with 1–5 crowns (basic – outstanding) by the Scottish Tourist Board. In addition some are graded approved – highly

commended. Cots are free where available and there may be some baby-sitting by arrangement.
Prices (per property per week)
Low £85–£540
Mid £105–£640
High £540–£850

HOLIDAY SCANDINAVIA LTD
28 Hillcrest Road, Orpington, Kent
BR6 9AW
Tel: 0689 24958   Fax: 0689 35807

Den Fin Nor Swe

This company offers a selection of purpose-built chalets in holiday villages plus hotel package holidays in all areas of Sweden, Denmark, Finland and Norway. Hotel cheques can be purchased in advance for moderate to first-class accommodation. The chalets are comfortably furnished and all have a fully-equipped kitchen. All 'villages' offer a variety of sports facilities and children's play areas or swimming pool. This company also offers activity holidays (see **Special Interest Holidays**).
Prices (per chalet per week for 2 people, including ferry and transportation of car)
Winter from £195 per person
Summer from £269 per person
Discounts Under-4s travel free. Children aged 4–15 receive a reduction of £55 in summer, £19 in winter.

HOLIDAYS IN LAKELAND
Stock Park Mansion, Newby Bridge, Ulverston, Cumbria LA12 8AY
Tel: 05395 31549

UK (Cumbria)

A selection of 250 houses, flats, cottages and caravans located throughout Cumbria. Some properties are AA-listed and registered with the English Tourist Board. The brochure gives detailed instructions on how to reach each property. Some places do not allow children.

In those that do, cots and high chairs may be available free, or may be hired at some properties for £6–£9 per week.
Prices   (per property per week)
Low   £75–£370
High   £125–£630

HOME FROM HOME
2a Queens Road, Mumbles, Swansea
SA3 4AW
Tel: 0792 360624/368078

UK (S. Wales)

Large selection of cottages, houses and flats in Swansea Bay, Mumbles and Gower. Cots included in properties or can be with all other baby equipment. Baby-sitting can be arranged.
Prices   (per property per week)
Low: £75–£200
High: £150–£400

HOSEASONS HOLIDAYS LTD
(see **Canals***)*
Tel: 0502 500500
0502 500555 *(Continent)*

Bel   Den   Fr   Ger   Hol   UK

Bungalows, chalets, cottages and mobile homes throughout the UK, with gîtes, cottages and bungalows available in mainland Europe. Many properties are sited in purpose-built holiday villages which have ample shopping, leisure and sports facilities. There are often special entertainment programmes for adults and children. At some holiday parks you have the option of being self-catering or taking half board. Cots and high chairs are generally available for around £7 each per week. Baby patrols or baby-sitting can also be arranged on request in many locations.
Prices   (per property per week in UK; per person per week abroad, including ferry crossing)
UK cottages: from £75 (low); £300–£600 (high).

Continental cottages: from £75 (low); £100–£150 (high).
Discounts   UK: special two-week offers, senior citizens' and children's discounts, plus Easter and Spring bank holiday offers. Under-4s travel free on Continental holidays, but are charged for accommodation if they occupy a bed. Babies in their own cots are free.

JUST FRANCE
1 Belmont, Lansdown Road, Bath
BA1 5DZ
Tel: 0225 446328

Fr

Large brochure offering self-catering holidays throughout France in gîtes or cottages. Some have cots available free, some hire them for £5–£10 per week, paid locally.
Prices   (per property per week, including ferry crossing for 2 people)
Low   from £215
Mid   from £229
High   from £249
Discounts   Children receive standard travel discounts (see **Ferries**). If you book a ferry crossing as well as one week's accommodation through this company (before July 13 or after Sept 2), parties of 8 or more adults or children over 4 receive free ferry travel.

KILMINORTH FARM
c/o TREBLE B HOLIDAY CENTRE
(see **Camping***)*

UK (Cornwall)

Seventeen 'superior country cottages' which appear to be both interesting and comfortable. Cots are supplied free and high chairs are available on request. From May–September tenants have free access to facilities at the Treble B Holiday centre two minutes away.
Prices   (2 people per week)
Low   £95
High   £300

LA FRANCE DES VILLAGES
Model Farm, Hattlesden, Nr Bury St
Edmunds, Suffolk IP30 0SY
Tel: 0449 737664 *(reservations)*
0449 737678 *(brochures)*

Fr

A small family-run business offering
accommodation of a high standard in
France. Includes hand-picked chateaux,
farmhouses, mills and village houses,
many with pools. Linen provided.
Prices (per person, based on family of
4 with car for fortnight, including ferry
crossing)
£95–£475
Discounts Available on self-drive
holidays

MACKAY'S AGENCY
30 Frederick Street, Edinburgh EH2 2JR
Tel: 031 225 3539

UK

Wide selection of cottages, mainly in
Scotland, but some available in north-
ern parts of England. Cots and high
chairs are usually available, often free.
Baby-sitting can usually be arranged
locally, except in very remote areas.
Prices (average per week, per family
of 4)
Low £65
High £225

MANN'S HOLIDAYS
20a Gaol Street, Pwllheli, Gwynedd
LL53 5DB
Tel: 0758 613666

UK (N. Wales)

Detailed brochure of cottages, farmhouses and caravans. All properties, except caravans, are approved by the
Wales Tourist Board. Where available,
cots are free. Children especially welcome at all properties.
Prices (per property per week)
A caravan or small cottage several
miles from the sea ranges from

£40–£120. A beautifully-furnished
house overlooking the sea ranges from
£120–£390.

MILKBERE HOLIDAYS
15 Harbour Road, Seaton, Devon
EX12 2LZ
Tel: 0297 22925

UK (Devon, Dorset)

A selection of eighty cottages, flats and
caravans ranging from the simple to the
luxurious. All are equipped to English
Tourist Board standards. Cots and high
chairs are free in some properties, but
may be hired in others. Baby-sitting can
be arranged in some locations.
Prices (per property per week)
Low from £85 for a small property
High £350 for a large property

NATIONAL TRUST FOR SCOTLAND
5 Charlotte Square, Edinburgh
EH2 4DU
Tel: 031 226 5922

UK (Scotland)

Selection of thirty-two holiday flats and
cottages. Each property contains a
sheet giving useful information on the
locality plus leaflets advising what to
see. Cots free where available, but if
you are taking small children you are
asked to provide rubber undersheets for
the beds. Properties sleep up to 10
people. 'Guide To Properties' brochure
available on request from the
Publications dept. (price £1 inc. P&P).
Membership details also available.
Prices (per 4-person property per
week)
Low approx. £90
High approx. £370

DAVID NEWMAN'S EUROPEAN COLLECTION
Box 733, 40 Upperton Road,
Eastbourne BN21 4AW
Tel: 0323 410347

Fr

Gîte and apartment holidays in many

parts of France. Cots may be available in some locations on request.

Prices (per property per fortnight, including ferry for car with 2 adults and 2 children)

Low   £450–£580
High   £580–£750

One-week holidays are available in low season and range from £350–£450 per property. A third child is charged £15 for the ferry.

NORTH NORFOLK HOLIDAY HOMES

Lee Warner Avenue, Fakenham,
Norfolk NR21 8ER
Tel: 0328 855322

UK (Norfolk)

Personally inspected properties ranging from fishermen's cottages to converted stables, barns and even a hall. The brochure gives helpful descriptions of properties, including information about games provided, lawns to play on and other leisure facilities. Children are obviously welcome at a great number of the properties. Cots and high chairs are free where available, but cot linen is not provided. Many houses offer baby-sitting by arrangement.

Prices (per property per week)

Low   £77–£250
Mid   £94–£300
High   £115–£400

NORTH WALES HOLIDAY COTTAGES AND FARMHOUSES

Station Road, Deganwy, Conwy,
Gwynedd LL31 9DF
Tel: 0492 582492

UK (N. Wales)

Large selection of cottages and farmhouses, ranging from converted chapels to a gamekeeper's lodge. Most are privately owned and offer free use of cots. Some are owned by the National Trust and a travelling cot is supplied in most properties. High chairs and baby-sitting can be arranged in some locations.

Prices (average per week, per family of 4)

Low   £89
High   £350

OWNERS HOLIDAY LETTING CONSORTIUM

Moore House, Moore Road,
Bourton-on-the-Water, Cheltenham,
Glos GL54 2AZ
Tel: 0451 20927

UK (Cotswolds)

Small selection of characterful cottages and houses. Most properties have washing machines and can organize cots, and baby-sitting. All have colour TV, and some allow dogs.

Prices (per family per week)

Low   £100–£278
Mid   £144–£226
High   £199–£278

PEAK AND MOORLAND FARM HOLIDAYS

Self-catering: Miss J. Salt, Stonesteads Farm, Waterhouses, Stoke-on-Trent, Staffs ST10 3HN
Tel: 0538 308331

Bed & breakfast: Mrs J. Lomas, Lydgate Farm, Aldwark, Grange Mill, Wirksworth, Derbyshire DE4 4HW
Tel: 062 985250

UK (Peak District, Staffs)

A group of farmers and their wives offering bed and breakfast or self catering accommodation in their farmhouses. All those involved are registered with the English Tourist Board. Guests are welcome to get involved with the farm work where practicable. Where available, cots are free.

Prices B+B per person per night: £10–£25

Self-catering property per week: £90–£280

Discounts   On B+B only several farms offer varying discounts for children. For example, one offers free accommodation for under-3s and half price for 3–16s sharing parents' room.

POWELL'S COTTAGE HOLIDAYS

Dolphin House, High Street,
Saundersfoot, Pembs
Tel: 0834 812791

UK (Wales, S.W. England)

Wide range of personally inspected cottages, farms, bungalows, flats and houses. Cots are free and available in nearly all the properties, but you must supply your own cot linen.
Prices   (per property per week)
Low   from £75
High   £78–£800

LES PROPRIETAIRES DE L'OUEST

34 Middle Street, Portsmouth, Hants
PO5 4BP
Tel: 0705 755715

Fr

Small, helpful company offering a selection of personally inspected gîtes and apartments in Brittany, the Dordogne, the Pyrenees, Vendée, Languedoc–Rousillon and Provence. Descriptions are usefully detailed. Cots are available in many places.
Prices   (per person per week, including short Channel crossing; e.g. in party of 4)
Low   from £70–£75
Discounts   Children under 4 are free; 4–13s pay £14–£20 each, depending on season and length of stay.

QUALITY COTTAGES

Cerbid, Solva, Haverfordwest, Pembs
SA62 6YE
Tel: 0348 837871

Fr   UK (Wales)

Family company offering a wide variety of privately-owned cottages throughout France and Wales. Cots available on request. Baby-sitting can be arranged in some locations. Linen and heating is usually inclusive.
Prices   (per property per week)
Wales: £99–£700
France: £600–£6000 (including short ferry crossing for 2 adults with a car).
Discounts   In summer small families receive a £10–£40 discount, depending on property chosen.

RECOMMENDED COTTAGE HOLIDAYS

Birdgate, Pickering, N. Yorkshire
YO18 7AL
Tel: 0751 75555

UK

Personally inspected cottages all over England. Cots and high chairs are available in most properties, but may be supplied by arrangement for an extra charge, if not.
Prices   (per property per week)
From: £75

RENDEZVOUS FRANCE

Holiday House, 19 Aylesbury Road,
Wendover HP22 6JG
Tel: 0296 696040

Fr

Choice of gîtes, cottages and villas throughout France. Very few provide specific children's accommodation, but where available, cots, bunks or children's beds are free.
Prices   (per property per week for 2 people, including ferry crossing)
Low   £290–£335
Mid   £340–£430
High   £375–£455
Discounts   Children receive standard travel discounts for sea travel.

SEALINK HOLIDAYS
(see **Hotels** and **Holiday Centres***)*

Bel   Fr   Ger   Hol   Ire   Sp   Swi

A wide selection of self-catering accommodation: gîtes in Normandy; bungalow parks in Belgium, Germany and
Holland (many with swimming pools,
tennis courts and children's playgrounds); apartments and chalets in
Spain, Switzerland and France, where
there is an extensive range of gîtes;
holiday homes and farmhouses in Cork,
County Clare, Mayo, the Waterford
Coast, Kerry and Limerick. All properties are fully equipped. Mobile homes
and caravans are also available.
Prices   (per person per week, including ferry crossing with car)
Gîtes: £79–£132 (low);   £118–£162
(high).
Apartment in France: £78–£169
Discounts   Children under 14 are free
if the holiday is booked before the end
of March. After this date, each child
booked pays £15.

SECRET SPAIN
Model Farm, Rattlesden, Nr Bury St
Edmunds, Suffolk IP30 0SY
Tel: 0449 737850 *(brochures)*; 0449
737664 *(reservations)*

Sp

A small family-run firm offering self-
catering holidays in traditional houses
on the coast and in the mountains of
northern Spain. Catered holidays in
small hotels also available. Self-drive,
using the ferry from Plymouth.
Prices   (per person per fortnight,
based on a family of 4 with car)
£109–£249

S.F.V. HOLIDAYS
Summer House, Heines Road,
Summertown, Oxford OX2 7PU
Tel: 0865 57738

Fr   It   Sp

Personally chosen selection of over 500
gîtes and villas with two to ten bedrooms throughout France. The brochure has exterior photos of each
property and a comprehensive description of facilities, including gardens suitable for children. Most properties
overlook, or are within easy walking distance of, the sea. One property offers
free use of bikes. Cots are free and available in all properties if requested when
booking. The company holds a list of
baby-sitters and nannies and can make
arrangements for you in those areas
where it is available. There is also a
children's club.
Prices   (per property per week, including ferry crossing)
Low   £250–£500
Mid   £350–£600
High   £400–£700
Discounts   Children receive standard
sea-travel discounts.

SHAMROCK COTTAGES
50 High Street, Wellington, Somerset
TA21 8RD
Tel: 0823 660126 *or* 062 76104
(Tipperary)

Ire

Selection of country cottages throughout Ireland, many registered with the
Irish Tourist Board. Cots and baby-
sitting are available in some locations
by arrangement with the owner.
Prices   (per property per week, including return ferry crossing for a car and
two adults)
Simple cottage: £175 (low), £230 (mid),
£350 (high).
Luxurious house: £256 (low),   £380
(mid), £609 (high).
Extra adults pay £12–£18 each, depending on the crossing.
Discounts   All children are free.

SHAW'S HOLIDAYS

Y Maes, Pwllheli, Gwynedd LL53 5HA
Tel: 0758 612854/614422

UK (N. Wales)

Mainly unillustrated brochure of approximately 750 inspected cottages, flats, houses and caravans. Cots, high chairs and baby-sitting are available in some locations by arrangement. Where permitted, a child in a cot does not count towards the maximum occupancy of the property. Some properties have children's playgrounds.

Prices   (per week per family of 4)
Low   £80
High   £300

SUMMER COTTAGES LTD

1 West Walks, Dorchester DT1 1RE
Tel: 0305 266877

UK

Bulky brochure with 770 personally inspected properties catering to all tastes. The brochure shows photos of each property and gives useful information, such as the location of the nearest swimming pool or stables. Cots and high chairs are free where available. Two houses also offer pushchairs. Some places offer baby-sitting by arrangement.

Prices   (per property per week)
Low   £56–£425
High   £129–£580

SUNVISTA HOLIDAYS LTD

5a St George Street, Warminster, Wilts
BA12 8QA
Tel: 0985 217373

Fr

Selected, personally inspected cottages and villas in many areas of France; also hotel touring holidays.

Prices   (based on a house for four, including short ferry crossings and insurance)
Low   £375–£1400
High   £600–£2350

STATTON CREBER

32 Causewayhead, Penzance, Cornwall
TR18 2SP
Tel: 0736 60070

UK (Cornwall)

Choice of 60 flats, cottages and houses, traditional and modern. Baby equipment is available for hire on a daily or weekly basis and includes baths, bouncers, buggies, cots, high chairs, papooses, slings, prams and pushchairs, ranging from £2–£10 per week.

Prices   (per property per week)
Low: £74–£169
Mid: £84–£209
High: £104–£375

VACANCES

28 Gold Street, Saffron Walden, Essex
CB10 1EJ
Tel: 0799 581479

Fr

Family-run company offering a choice of farmhouses and about 300 cottages, some of which are converted watermills and one which is a converted pigeon loft. Cots are free where available; many properties offer children's beds or bunks.

Prices   (per property per week, including ferry crossing)
Low: £173–£448
Mid: £252–£527
High: £282–£557
Discounts   Children receive standard sea-travel discounts.

VACANCES EN CAMPAGNE/VACANZE IN ITALIA

Bignor, Pulborough, W. Sussex
RH20 1QD
Tel: 07987 433 *(France)*
07987 426 *(Italy)*

Cors   Fr   It

Large selection of 'up-market' country cottages, houses and farmhouses in many regions of France and Italy, including Corsica. The company stresses that in mainland France none is close to the coast, so these properties are strictly for country-lovers. All are fully equipped and well furnished. Linen is included in Italy but is usually extra in France; heating is always extra. Where available, cots are provided free. Baby-sitting is sometimes available locally for a small charge, and a maid service is offered in some locations. Travel arrangements at advantageous prices can be made on request.

Prices   (per property per week, including short Channel crossing for 2 adults and 2 children with a car)
Basic farmhouse in Normandy: £290–£470
Mid-range farmhouse in Normandy: £384–£642
A large château in the Auvergne for 4 adults and 4 children ranges from £542–£851.
Farmhouse in Tuscany sleeping 4 from £226–£478
Discounts   Children under 4 travel free on ferry; reduced prices for children under 14.

VFB HOLIDAYS LTD
Normandy House, High Street, Cheltenham, Glos GL50 3HW
Tel: 0242 526338

Fr

A wide selection of regularly inspected gîtes, country cottages and houses throughout France. Although the brochure is unillustrated, the company has a two-stage booking process which means that bookings are made on the basis of having seen 4–6 colour photographs of the property, so that you know exactly what you are getting. Cots are available in a few places – children's beds are more common. At some properties baby-sitting can be arranged.

Prices   (per person per fortnight, including ferry crossing with car)
4-person gîte: £90–£100 (low); £120–£145 (high).
4-person villa on Côte d'Azur: £155 (low); £235 (high).
Discounts   Children under 4 pay £5 each, but do not pay for accommodation; 4–13s receive a reduction of £7 each.

WELSH HOLIDAYS
Snowdonia Tourist Services, High Street, Porthmadog, Gwynedd LL49 9PG
Tel: 0766 513837/513829

UK (Snowdonia)

Selection of cottages in sea and mountain locations around Snowdonia National Park. Cots and baby-sitting are frequently available.
Prices   (mid-range cottage, per family of 4 per week)
Low   £99
High   £185

WINDERMERE LAKE DISTRICT HOLIDAYS
Loray House, Queens Drive, Windermere, Cumbria LA23 2EL
Tel: 09662 3627

UK (Lake District)

Illustrated brochure of cottages and apartments around Lake Windermere. Cots may be hired for £8 per week, and high chairs for £7 per week.
Prices   The average price for a cottage for 4 during high season is £175 per week. From March–July cottages start from £100.

Cruises

Cruises have the image of being leisurely holidays for the privileged and elderly, but this is by no means universally so. Needless to say, voyages of long distance and duration can be very expensive. However, many companies offer short breaks and special offers.

Cruise ships are frequently lively and action-packed, attracting adults and children of all ages. There are many theme-based cruises, with daily lectures and film shows preparing you for shore trips to sites of special interest. These may seem highly attractive to an adult enthusiast, but check the provision made for children's entertainment before booking tickets for the whole family. Many ships have special children's facilities – clubs, playrooms, qualified attendants and baby-sitters. You will usually find medical staff aboard too. The sports and leisure amenities are frequently impressive, and the price, of course, includes free access to everything, including evening entertainments. Compare this to a similar land-based holiday, and it all adds up to very good value.

However, there are some possible drawbacks to taking a cruise with children. Do consider very closely the length of time you'll be on board and the facilities available. If babysitting is not part of the service, you may find it impossible to have any time to yourself and mealtimes could be something of a problem. If possible, try to find out if children are a regular feature of the cruise you plan to take. If they're not, you might find your child companionless and that you have to provide entertainment and supervision every waking moment.

If large cruise ships do not appeal, there are many small companies offering cruises, usually on luxury yachts sleeping up to twelve people. Obviously they do not have such a comprehensive range of entertainments and activities, but they do offer a more intimate atmosphere and greater flexibility.

Prices
Unless otherwise stated 1990 prices have been quoted. These are intended only as a guide to the type of holiday offered and travellers should check with the company concerned for 1991 pricing details.

CHANDRIS LTD
5 St Helen's Place, London EC3A 6BJ
Tel: 071 588 2598

Baltic Bl. Sea Crb Egy Gr Isr
It North Cape Tur Yug

Fly/cruises from London lasting 7, 8, 13 and 15 days. Full programme of entertainments available with a wide variety of free sports and activities. Excellent restaurant facilities. Fuel surcharges may be levied at the company's discretion. Port taxes of £35–£70 may also be payable.
Prices (per adult) A 4-berth cabin with shower and WC costs from £635–£1005 (7–8 days); £760–£1455 (11 days).
Discounts These apply to children sharing parents' accommodation. On 7- or 8-day cruises children under 2 travel free on the ship; but pay for the flight; 2–12s pay a child rate from £455 (including flight); 13–17 pay a teenager rate from £495 (including flight). Senior citizens get 10% discount (excluding flight).

COSTA LINE CRUISES
Albany House, 324 Regent Street,
London W1K 5AA
Tel: 071 436 9431

Ala Aus Crb Far East It Med
S.Am US

Italian company offering cruises to the Caribbean and throughout the Mediterranean. Cruises start at Fort Lauderdale, Florida and Genoa or Venice. All ships have good sports, leisure and restaurant facilities; some have a children's playroom. High chairs and cots are available on board the ships at no extra cost, and childminding can be arranged. Caribbean cruises can be combined with a 7-day stay in Florida, visiting sights such as Disneyland. *Note*: 2-bed cabins have pull-down berths for children.
Prices Caribbean cruise (per adult per fortnight in a 2-bed cabin with full

board, including 7 nights' accommodation in Florida and return flight)
Low £795
High £1120
Mediterranean cruise (per adult per week in a 2-bed cabin with full board, including return flight)
Low £650
High £695
Discounts On Caribbean cruises children under 12 receive a 20–50% discount, depending on accommodation. On Mediterranean cruises under-12s who share parents' accommodation pay half fare. A family reduction of 10% is available on May, June or October departures, and 5% on July or September departures.

CTC LINES
1 Regent Street, London SW1Y 4NN
Tel: 071 930 5833

Aus Baltic Bl.Sea Can.Is Crb
Far East N.Cape S.Am Sca
USSR W.Med

Anglo-Russian company offering worldwide cruises, starting from London or Southampton. The company will apply for Russian visas on your behalf, if you wish. Cabins have 2, 3 or 4 berths. Cots can be supplied for children under 3, but must be requested when booking. Cinema, leisure and restaurant facilities on board. Special activities are organized for children on cruises during school holidays.
Prices (per adult per fortnight to Canaries in 4-berth cabin)
From £637
Discounts These are available for children in all sizes of cabin, provided there are as many adults as children in the cabin. Children under 3 receive 90% discount, 3–5s receive 75%, 5–12s receive

50%, and 13–19s receive 25%. Special children's prices are available on shore excursions.

CUNARD
South Western House, Canute Road, Southampton SO9 1ZA
Tel: 0703 34166 *or* 071 491 3930

Bl.Sea Crb Ice Med Mex Sca
S.Am UK US

Cruises lasting 2-40 days on luxury ships, including the QE2. On-board facilities range from shops to saunas, swimming pools, gymnasium, theatre and library, plus gourmet restaurants and an extensive (free) programme of entertainments. All cabins have private shower and WC; some also have baths. Some ships have playgroups with nursery nurses.
Prices   (per double room)
QE2: £220 for 2-day cruise in lowest grade cabin; £10,015 for 24-day cruise in highest grade cabin
Vistafjord: £8,460 for 27 days (highest grade cabin); £695 for 6 days (lower grade cabin)
Princess: £2,110 for 15 day holiday; £800 for 8 day holiday
Discounts   Some discounts available for children under 2.

EQUITY CRUISES
77–79 Great Eastern Street, London EC2A 3HU
Tel: 071 729 1929

Ala Can Crb Egy Med Mex
N.Af Sca S.Am S.Pac US

Large company offering cruises from a number of cruise lines: Carnival, Cycladic, Holland America Line, La Palma (Intercruise), Majestic, Regency, Sea Cloud, Siosa and Star Lauro. Fly/cruise and cruise/stay holidays are available. The ships offer various degrees of comfort with some sports and recreation facilities. Some are fully air-conditioned.
Prices   Each company represented has several different ships and each calculates costs differently. Some quote separate rates for low and high season, others add a supplement to the basic rate for different seasons. The best family deal is a 4-berth cabin, but not all the ships appear to have them. The pricing system is rather complex and the destinations and durations extremely varied. Some 7-day cruises start at £500 per adult, but thereafter the possibilities are endless. Our impression is that there are some reasonably priced cruises available, but it's worth phoning the company for advice.
Discounts   Like prices, each company calculates differently. Discounts on children's fares can be up to 60%.

P & O CRUISES
(*part of* P&O *q.v.*)
Tel: 071 831 1331

N.&W.Af Au Can Egy Fr Gib
Gr HK It Por Sca Sp Tur
US USSR

12- to 33-night cruises aboard either the *Canberra* or the *Sea Princess*. Free entertainments programme and use of extensive sports facilities. The Junior Club for children aged 2–12 is generally open from 9.00 a.m.–8.00 p.m. (except lunchtimes). A special children's tea at 5.15 leaves parents free to enjoy dinner alone. Baby foods and a night nursery (*Canberra* only) are provided for children under 2, but no childminding facilities are available for this age group during the day. Babies under 6 months are not allowed on these cruises. 'Family cabins' sleep 4 in bunk beds and are only available on the *Canberra*.
Prices   (per adult)
£799 (12 nights); £895 (14 nights); £1090 (17 nights); £1599 (25 nights).
These prices apply to 4-berth family cabins which have handbasins only.

Larger cabins with private facilities are more expensive.

Discounts   Depending on the length of cruise and choice of accommodation, children receive the following discounts. 6 months–under 2 receive 70% discount. 2–11s 60% discount. 12–16s 40% discount.

Cycling

Perhaps this isn't the most obvious choice of holiday if you have young children, but it can be one of the most rewarding for all concerned. The benefits of fresh air and exercise are self-evident, but you also have the advantage of seeing unspoilt countryside at a leisurely pace and going back to your hotel's creature comforts at night. All the tours are graded for difficulty, so if in doubt of your ability, choose something easy to start.

None of the tour operators offering organised hotel-based cycling holidays recommend taking children still in nappies, particularly if they're not dry at night. However, children aged 3, 4 and 5 can have a lovely time sitting in a child seat on the back of your bike. Some companies warn of an in-between time around the ages of 5–7 when children are too big for a child seat, but too young to handle a small bike with gears. After this time they often can handle such a bike, and on the quiet lanes and roads chosen for these tours, have no problem cycling up to forty miles a day – sometimes leaving parents panting in their wake! Obviously you need to have some idea of your child's stamina and road sense, so it's wise to check out both at home before embarking on a cycling holiday abroad.

You'll generally find hoteliers and restaurant owners very helpful about providing children's meals – even if your offspring demand egg and chips rather than boeuf bourgignon. Lunches are left up to you and picnics tend to be the norm.

A word of warning about luggage. Unless the company offers to transport your suitcases from stop to stop or offers panniers to transfer your belongings to, avoid bringing suitcases in the first place; your own panniers or a rucksack are much easier to handle on a bike.

Prices
Unless otherwise stated 1990 prices have been quoted. These are intended only as a guide to the type of holiday offered and travellers should check with the company concerned for 1991 pricing details.

BELLE FRANCE

Bayham Abbey, Lamberhurst, Kent
TN3 8BG
Tel: 0892 890885

Fr (Auvergne)

Two-week cycling holidays in July and
August only, with emphasis on a gentle
pace. The price includes return travel
from London, half board accommodation, hire of touring bicycles, maps,
information packs, baggage transport
between stops and holiday insurance.
Children are welcome provided they
can fit on to the firm's smallest bikes
(the minimum age is about 7 years).
Walking holidays are also available
(minimum age 14 years).
Prices   These vary according to
method of travel.
Air & train: £520
Hovercraft & train: £500
Self drive: £450
Discounts   Hotel: £2 reduction for children per night in an extra bed in a
double-bedded room. Travel: £20 reduction by air/coach & train for under-
12s; £10 reduction by car with two
adults for under-14s.

CYCLING FOR SOFTIES

Lloyds House, Lloyds Street,
Manchester M2 5WA
Tel: 061 834 6800

Fr

Award-winning company offering 7, 9
and 14-night cycling holidays. The cost
includes all travel arrangements,
accommodation and half board in small
hotels, lightweight bicycles and all
other necessary equipment. Suitcases
are left at the home-base hotel on each
tour and belongings are carried in panniers on your bicycle. Various types and
sizes of bicycle are available, including
small ones for children aged 7 up.
Children to around the age of 4 may be

carried in child seats, provided free on
request. All hotels used are happy to
supply children's meals if given a little
warning. Babysitting is not available.
Prices   (per adult per week)
Low   £327
High   £370
Discounts   Children receive a £45 reduction each on the adult price.

CYCLORAMA HOLIDAYS

The Grange Hotel, Grange-over-Sands,
Cumbria LA11 6EJ
Tel: 04484 3666

UK (Cumbria)

Leisurely touring cycle holidays in the
Lake District, lasting from 4–7 days,
with a choice of easy, moderate or
strenuous routes. Cycles can be hired, if
you prefer not to take your own. Price
includes bed and breakfast in hotels or
guest houses (dinners can be included
for 4 evenings), maps, information
packs and baggage transport service.
Three- or four-day mini breaks are also
available at the Grange Hotel only.
Minimum age for children is usually 9
years. Walking holidays are also on
offer, and children of any age can be
taken on some, but not all, of the routes.
Prices   (per adult)
£150–£252 depending on choice of
route for six nights. Add on about £17 if
hiring a cycle.
Children up to 15 years, sharing accommodation with 2 adults, pay £6 for 2–3
nights and £10 for 5–7 nights (meals
extra). Add on £5–£7 if hiring a cycle.
Discounts   Available for small groups.

JUST PEDALLING
9 Church Street, Coltishall, Norfolk
NR12 7DW
Tel: 0603 737201

UK (East Anglia)

Seven-day cycling holidays and short breaks. The cost includes bed and breakfast in guest houses, bicycle hire and all necessary equipment. Take your own bike if you prefer. Child seats are provided on request. A Deluxe tour offers accommodation in period houses of special interest.

Prices   (per adult per week)
£135 plus £20 bicycle hire

Fly/drive

Most major airlines and many travel agents can arrange fly-drive packages for you on request, but those we list here are established operators, mainly offering deals to the USA and Canada.

If you plan to stay in a resort or a city with good facilities on the doorstep, or a reliable system of public transport, it would be an unnecessary expense to hire a car and have the additional problems of parking. However, for independent holidaymakers who do not want to be tied down and want to see the most of a huge place like America, a car is more an essential than a luxury.

Cars come in all sizes, from Economy (Fiesta etc.), to Luxury (Granada and estate cars). In the US, most are automatic and have air-conditioning. Child seats are compulsory in many states for children under 5. These are usually available for a small charge.

The way fly-drive holidays are put together varies from company to company. Watch out for deals that offer lots of free gifts, such as flight bags, duty free vouchers and cameras. They do not necessarily offer better value and may have complicated exclusion clauses. Car rental offers no discounts for children or families, but some states, particularly California and Florida frequently offer one or two weeks' very low or free rental. This does not include any insurance, tax or collision damage waiver (see **Car Rental** introduction for further information). Specific children's discounts are often available and you should contact the companies concerned for further details.

Accommodation vouchers may be purchased in advance in the UK and do offer a genuine saving on what you might pay on the spot. However, you can make a saving yourself if you're prepared to stay in independent motels and trust to luck that rooms will be available. Remember – America is a mobile nation and places to stay are thick on the ground. In European destinations it is advisable to reserve accommodation in advance, particularly if you holiday in peak season.

Prices
Unless otherwise stated 1990 prices have been quoted. These are intended only as a guide to the type of holiday offered and travellers should check with the company concerned for 1991 pricing details.

EUROJET
Quo Vadis Ltd, 243 Euston Road,
London NW1 2BT
Tel: 071 387 6122

Fr   It

A go-as-you-please programme, with or
without planned itinerary, plus City
Break packages with charter or scheduled flights. Car rental is arranged with
EuroDollar in France and Maggiore
Rent-a-Car in Italy, who have offices in
all airports and major cities. Rental includes CDW, PAI, local tax and unlimited mileage. Accommodation can
be arranged in hotels (France) or villas
(Italy), and cots and baby-sitting can
usually be arranged on request.
Prices   (per adult per week, based on 2
people sharing, including scheduled
flight and rental of Group A car)

Rome		Nice	
Low	£257	Low	£235
High	£293	High	£271

Discounts   Under-2s fly free and are
charged £15 for the car. Children aged
2–11 receive 25% off chartered flights;
scheduled flight discount varies. Other
discount details on request.

INTASUN FLY/DRIVE
Intasun House, Cromwell Avenue,
Bromley, Kent BR2 1AQ
Tel: 0274 760022

US

Fly/drive holidays and motorhomes
available in Florida and California.
Discover America hotel pass available
for use with some hotel chains.
Prices   Florida fly/drive prices from
£279 per adult for one week.
Discounts   Child reductions available
up to age 16.

JETSAVE
Sussex House, London Road, East
Grinstead, West Sussex RH19 1LD
Tel: 0345 327711 *(London depts.)*
0345 045599 *(Manchester depts.)*

Can   US

Fly/drive holidays, with the option of
purchasing accommodation vouchers.
The vouchers are valid in over 3000
hotels and may be purchased in
advance for £29–£38 per night with
supplements ranging from $1–$95 per
night. Cots and high chairs are not
supplied, but can be requested locally.
Car hire is provided through Alamo
Rent-a-Car.
Prices   Flights from around £262 per
adult – with car hire starting from £79
per week including Collison Damage
Waiver.
Discounts   On many flights under-2s
travel free (no seat). On others they pay
10%. Children aged 2–12 receive up to
33% discount.

MAGIC OF ITALY
227 Shepherds Bush Green, London
W6 7AS
Tel: 081 748 7575

It

Motoring and fly/drive holidays. If you
take your own car, the company organizes ferries. Fly/drive holidays offer
flights to 9 Italian cities and car hire,
which includes local taxes, third-party
insurance, CDW and unlimited mileage.
A variety of companies are used for car
hire.
Prices   (per adult per week, based on a
family of 4)

Low	£199–£235
High	£209–£245

Discounts   These are based on children sharing accommodation with
parents. Under-2s pay £20 on any holiday; 20% off 'motoring' holidays for
under 12 years sharing a room with two
adults in hotels. £20 reduction for children under 12.

MUNDI COLOR HOLIDAYS
276 Vauxhall Bridge Road, London
SW1V 1BE
Tel: 071 834 3492

Por Sp

Fly/drive specialists offering extensive tailormade hotel, *parador* and a few self-catering apartment holidays in Spain, plus *pousada* holidays in Portugal. Two-centre holidays can be arranged on request. Many hotels offer swimming pools, children's play areas and sports facilities. Baby-sitting can be arranged on request in some hotels.
Prices   (per adult per week, B+B including flight)
City hotel: from £230
Fly/drive (12 days): £606, eg. H/B + Avis car
Discounts   Under-2s pay £25 for travel (no seat); cots and meals payable locally. Children aged 2–7 receive a 25% discount and 7–11s receive 20%, provided they share parents' room. (Minimum of 2 persons £45 discount p.p.)

NORTHWEST FLY/DRIVE USA
PO Box 45, Bexhill-on-Sea, E. Sussex
TN40 1PY
Tel: 0345 747800 (toll free), 0424 224400 *(Bexhill)*, 061 499 2471 *(Manchester)*, 041 226 4175 *(Glasgow)*

US

Scheduled flights from Gatwick and Glasgow to Minneapolis/St Paul, Boston and New York. Accommodation vouchers may be purchased from £24 per night for 1–4 people, giving access to a wide range of motel/hotel chains. Car hire can be arranged through Alamo, Avis, Hertz or National.
Prices   (per adult for a mid-week return flight)
To Boston: £298 plus £10 departure tax and free car hire for 1 week, provided 2 adults travel (low); £388 plus £10 departure tax, plus free car hire for 1 week (high).
To Minneapolis: £319 plus £10 departure tax, plus free car hire for 1 week

(low); £409 plus £10 departure tax, plus free car hire for 1 week (high).
Additional weeks of car hire are £40 per week.
Discounts   Under-2s pay 10% of adult fare. Children aged 2–12 pay 67%.

PAN AM HOLIDAYS
Clipper House, Building 451, Southern Perimeter Road, Heathrow Airport, Hounslow, Middx TW6 3LP
Tel: 081 750 9474

US

Scheduled flights from Heathrow to 16 US cities. Accommodation vouchers, costing £25 each, may be purchased in advance, and are valid in 3000 locations. Car hire is provided by Avis and Alamo.
Prices   (2-week holiday to Miami with a medium-sized car for 2 adults and 2 children)
Low (mid-week): £1508
High (mid-week): £1742
Add on £33 each for holiday insurance; under-2s are included free in parents'.
Discounts   The above prices for a family of 4 are based on children under 2 paying 10% for flight, and 2–11s paying 67%. Bonus discounts on hotel vouchers, car hire and travel insurance are available for adults and children on fly/drive packages, with or without accommodation: adults may deduct up to £30 each, and 2–11s may deduct up to £15 each, provided departures from London are *not* on a Saturday.

PEREGOR TRAVEL
146 High Street, Ruislip, Middx
HA4 8LJ
Tel: 08956 39900

Can Crb Mex US

Fly/drive and tailor-made holidays to a wide variety of destinations. There is also a choice of airline, car hire and hotels.

Prices (per adult per week, fly/drive with simple accommodation)
Orlando: from £369
Discounts These depend on which airline you travel with and the holiday package you choose. Quotations are given on request.

US AIR FLY/DRIVE
Valley USA, 546 Burnley Road, Crawshawbooth, Rossendale, Lancashire BV4 8NE
Tel: 0706 212333

US

Daily flights from Gatwick to Charlotte, with internal connections to 49 cities in the states of Florida, N. Carolina, S. Carolina and Virginia. Accommodation vouchers worth £25 each may be purchased in advance and are valid in over 2000 hotels. All rooms sleep up to 4 people. There may be an additional charge for cots. Car hire is arranged through Alamo and offers unlimited mileage. Collision damage waiver is included.
Prices available on request from Valley USA
Discounts Discounts for infants (under 2s) and children (2–11s) available on request.

POUNDSTRETCHER FLY/DRIVE
Atlantic House, Hatelwick Avenue, Three Bridges, Crawley, West Sussex RH10 1NP
Tel: 0293 518060 *or* 061 493 3344

Can US

Scheduled flights with British Airways to 22 destinations in the USA and Canada. Fully inclusive pre-planned fly/drive tours and independent travel arrangements including Hertz car hire, hotel accommodation, air passes around America, motorhomes and go-as-you-please hotel vouchers. Pre-paid accommodation vouchers worth from £13–£33 each, are offered by 4 major hotel chains.

Prices Start from £399 for a fly/drive package to Florida.
Discounts To the USA under-2s pay 10% of full fare. Children aged 2–11 pay 67%. To Canada under-2s pay 10% of the full fare. Children aged 2–11 pay 75%.

TWA FLY/DRIVE
TWA Getaway, 34 The Mall, Bromley, Kent BR1 1TS
Tel: 081 313 0550

US

Scheduled flights to more than 100 cities across America with Alamo and Avis car deals available for up to 7 days free. Accommodation vouchers may be purchased in advance for use in 3 hotel chains. In addition there are tours which include national parks. Escorted coach tours are also available.
Prices (per adult per mid-week flight)
New York: £339 (low); £429 (high)
Los Angeles: £449 (low); £569 (high)
Car hire is free in Florida, California and Hawaii for one week, and for further weeks £40 per week in Florida, £65 in California. Special rates apply to the rest of the USA.
Discounts Children sharing hotel accommodation with parents usually stay free. For children up to age 12 special fares apply.

UNIJET
'Sandrocks', Rocky Lane, Haywards Heath, West Sussex RH16 4RH
Tel: 0444 458611, 081 668 0313 *or* 061 834 8483 *(International flights)*
0444 458181, 081 660 8079 *or* 061 3833 0055 *(European flights)*
0444 459191 *(American holidays)*

Worldwide

Flights to 17 destinations in the US, plus Canada, Australia, Mexico, New Zealand, Far East, S. Africa and S. America. Accommodation vouchers may be purchased in advance for 4 major hotel chains. Car rental is provided through Avis and Alamo, and sometimes up to 2 weeks free rental may be on special offer. Connecting flights within the UK can be arranged on request.

Unijet America offers a comprehensive programme of holidays, featuring self catering, one, two and three centre holidays, coach tours and fly cruises.

The company also operates fly/drive deals to Gibraltar, Greece, Malta, Portugal, Spain and Turkey (some destinations available in summer only).

Accommodation vouchers are not available.

Prices (per adult per week, fly/drive to Florida)
From £355; hotels range from £27–£35 per night.

Discounts Under-2s are charged £15 to cover airport taxes in Europe, but pay 10% on intercontinental flights. Children aged 2–11 receive £10–£50 discount on European charter flights, and 25–33% discount on scheduled intercontinental flights.

Holiday Centres

The growth of holiday centres has been a rapid one. Where once the name brought to mind only large organizations, such as Butlins and Warners, there are now literally hundreds of establishments, from caravan sites to luxury hotels, which describe themselves as holiday centres.

What do they offer? They vary a great deal but the list is usually impressive. Most gear themselves to the family market and try to cater for all interests and preferences. Firstly, accommodation is available in anything from rooms to suites, from traditional chalets to high-tech 'lodges'. Most offer self-catering facilities, but many also offer full and half board so you can have a rest from cleaning and cooking.

The great advantage of holiday centres is that you are free to do what you like when you like and you don't have to go far or pay for it. Everything from archery to trampolining is free – often with free qualified instruction. The exceptions to this are sports such as riding and windsurfing, where special equipment is necessary and must be hired at an hourly rate. A great boon for parents are the funfair rides and massive swimming pools with impressive water slides which children can spend the entire holiday on, if they choose, at no extra cost. In the evening there are often professional shows with 'big name' entertainers.

Teams of hosts and hostesses (Redcoats, Bluecoats, or whatever) are constantly around in the larger centres to organize activities, keep an eye on children and generally help things go with a swing. And although most centres offer entertainments for virtually every hour of the day, there is no obligation to join in, and there are plenty of places to sit quietly and relax.

If you dread hearing your children claim, 'I'm bored', take them to a holiday centre and those words won't have a chance to pass their lips!

Prices

Unless otherwise stated 1990 prices have been quoted. These are intended only as a guide to the type of holiday offered and travellers should check with the company concerned for 1991 pricing details.

BARROWFIELD HOTEL

Hilgrove Road, Newquay, Cornwall
TR7 2QY
Tel: 0637 878878

UK (Cornwall)

An Ashley Courtenay Recommended
Hotel, with 5 crowns and a 'commended' quality grading from the
English Tourist Board. Accommodation
is in luxury en-suite rooms, penthouse
suites and family suites. Facilities include indoor and outdoor swimming
pools, spa baths, saunas, gymnasium,
solarium, games room, coffee shop,
snooker room, launderette and hair-
dressing salon. Nightly entertainment
in peak season. Short breaks also
available.

Prices (per person half board)
3 days from £76
7 days from £123

BEVERLEY PARK HOLIDAYS

Goodrington Road, Paignton,
South Devon TQ4 7JE
Tel: 0803 843887

UK (Devon)

A large number of 4-, 5- and 6-berth
caravans set in 20 acres overlooking the
sea at Goodrington Sands near Paignton. All caravans have a WC, hot and
cold water, bath or shower, fridge and
colour TV. Blankets, china and cutlery
are provided, but bring your own linen
and towels (and rubber sheets for children). Linen may be hired on arrival, if
you wish. Cots are available for £5 per
week. Amenities include a launderette
with drying and ironing facilities,
heated indoor and outdoor pools, children's pool, spa bath, crazy golf, children's playground, games room with
table tennis and pool and tennis court.
There are two shops, a take-away food
bar and restaurant. Free evening entertainment is provided, but no baby-
sitting services are available. There is
also a touring site where campers have
full use of all the facilities.

Prices (per caravan, inclusive of gas
and electricity)
4-berth: £75–£200
5-berth: £90–£255
6-berth: £105–£380

BRIGGS HOLIDAY HOMES

Head Office: Welford-on-Avon, Warks
CV37 8HA
Tel: 0789 750532

UK (Devon)

Brick-built 4- and 6-berth holiday terraces set in Norton Park, South Devon
within a few miles of the safe sandy
beaches of Blackpool Sands, Sugary
Cove and Slapton. The terraces have
bathrooms, fitted carpets, an electric
fire and ironing facilities. Blankets,
pillows, crockery, cutlery and cooking
utensils are provided, but bring your
own linen and towels. Amenities in the
centre include a heated outdoor pool
and paddling pool, a children's playground, darts, table tennis, billiards and
snooker, a supermarket, take-away
meals, a bar and nightly entertainment.
Cots can be hired for £7.50 per week.
Electricity is metered.

Prices (per property per week)
4-berth: £60–£180
6-berth: £70–£230
Detached: £70–£240

BUTLINS HOLIDAY WORLDS AND HOTELS

Bognor Regis, W. Sussex PO21 1JJ
Tel: 081 809 4649 *(Brochures)*

UK

Catered and self-catering holidays in
five Holiday Worlds and five hotels. A
variety of accommodation is available.
'County suites' (at 3 centres only) have 1
or 2 bedrooms sleeping up to 6 people.
Standard accommodation is in comfortable bedrooms sleeping up to 3 or 5.
All catered accommodation has private
bath or shower and a maid service. Full
board is available at off-peak times.

Self-catering accommodation is in chalets and caravans sleeping up to 7 people. They have a bathroom and fully-equipped kitchen. All centres have good shopping facilities plus snack bars, restaurants, bars and free entertainments. There is also free qualified instruction in a wide variety of sports. Redcoats organize special clubs for 6–9s and 9–13s, with one centre offering special activities for 13–16s. Nurseries are available for children under 6 where they can be left for short stays in the care of qualified staff. A child-listening service is also offered at night. Infants up to 9 months may be left in a free nursery at night with qualified nurses. Special facilities include nappy-changing and mothers' room, launderette and ironing room. Pushchairs and cots may be hired. Butlins hotels offer many of the same facilities.
Prices   Phone 0800 222555 for price details.
Discounts   Children under 2 go free on all catered holidays; 2–14s pay 50% at all centres. On hotel holidays children under 4 are not accepted. The Metropole at Blackpool is an adults only hotel.

CENTER PARC

Center Parcs Ltd, Head Office, Rufford, Newark, Nottinghamshire NG22 9DP
Tel: 0623 411411 (*reservations*); 0272 244744 (*brochures*)

UK (Suffolk, Nottingham)

Two all-season holiday centres in Sherwood and Elvedon Forests. Accommodation is in 1-, 2-, 3- and 4-bedroom villas, or apartments. Each villa has a private terrace, fully-fitted kitchen, bathroom, separate WC, radio and television with two video channels. Linen is provided and there is no charge for gas and electricity. A cot, playpen and high chair can be provided free of charge. Amenities include a sub-tropical swimming dome with waves, water-chutes, saunas, whirlpools, wild water rapids and baby and toddler pool. A playschool and kindergarten are available and

baby-sitting can be arranged (all at extra cost). At Sherwood outside the dome facilities include a children's playground, nature trails, a BMX bike track, tennis courts, windsurfing, canoeing and fishing. On some outside activities you have to pay for the hire of equipment such as windsurfers, BMX bikes and tennis courts. There is an international selection of restaurants, all of which serve children's portions. Weekend and midweek breaks are available.
Prices   (per villa per week in Sherwood Forest)
2-bedroom: £217–£374
3-bedroom: £215–£502
4-bedroom: £272–£676

CLUB MEDITERRANEE
(*see* **Hotels**)

LA COLLINETTE HOTEL
St Jacques, St Peter Port, Guernsey, C.I.
Tel: 0481 22585

Ch.Is. (Guernsey)

Situated at the top of a hill overlooking St Peter Port, this hotel has 30 bedrooms, all with private bathrooms. Facilities include a large outdoor swimming pool, a children's pool, a spa, sauna and solarium and a launderette. There is a children's high tea at 6 p.m. and all bedrooms have an automatic baby-listening service. Membership of a local sports and leisure complex, with use of their heated indoor pool, flumes, tennis and squash courts, snooker and other facilities, is included if you book a travel-inclusive holiday with Channel Islands Travel Centre. Details of these prices can be obtained on request. Cots are available free of charge. AA 3-star and Good Hotel Guide recommended.
Prices   (per adult per week, half board)
£147 (Nov–March)
£150 (April)
£154 (early May and all Oct)

£196 (mid May–end June and 20–30 Sept)

£206 (1 July–19 Sept)

Discounts Children sharing parents' room receive 50% discount. Children under 4 are free, apart from meals.

CORTON BEACH HOLIDAY VILLAGE

The Street, Corton, Suffolk NR32 5HS
Tel: 0502 730200

UK (Suffolk)

A family-run holiday village overlooking the beach at Corton. Accommodation is in villas which sleep 4–6 or 6–8; most have a sun patio. All are fully equipped with a modern kitchen and bathroom and a colour TV with a free video channel. There are some luxury villas with three-piece suites. The village has heated swimming pools, a toddlers' pool, a full-sized Krypton Factor assault course, an adventure playground, organized children's activities and a resident children's entertainer. There is a cafe and take-away food. Scuba-diving and horse-riding can be arranged, and jetskiing and clay pigeon shoots are run by the owners. Linen is provided, but not towels. A cot and high chair may be hired for £7 per week. A baby-sitting service is available at £1.75 per hour. Electricity is metered.

Prices (per villa per week)

£85–£300, depending on time of year and size and standard of villa.

EURO HOTEL

Esplanade Road, Pentire, Newquay, Cornwall TR7 1PS
Tel: 0637 873333

UK (Cornwall)

Overlooking Fistral Bay with its surf and mile-long stretch of sand, this hotel offers accommodation in double and family rooms, the largest of which can sleep 2 adults and 3 children. All rooms are en suite with satellite colour TV, direct dial telephone, tea- and coffee-making facilities, and baby-listening intercom. There are laundry and ironing facilities, as well as a heated drying-room. Cots and high chairs are included in the price. Children's facilities include tea for under-7s served at 5.30 p.m., a crèche supervised by a qualified nanny in high season and a playground. The hotel has a heated indoor pool and children's paddling pool, a games room, sauna, solarium and spa bath. There is ample parking.

Prices (per adult per week, half board)

£148–£289

Discounts One child under 10 sharing with 2 adults goes free.

FLAMINGO LAND HOLIDAY VILLAGE

Kirby Misperton, Malton, N. Yorks
YO17 0UX
Tel: 065 386300

UK (Yorkshire)

Fully-equipped 6-berth caravans a short walk from Flamingo Land Zoo and Family Fun Park, whose rides and shows are free to guests. All caravans have a shower room and WC, kitchen with fridge and a TV. On-site facilities include a heated indoor swimming pool, fitness centre, sauna and jacuzzi, children's play area, splash pool, shop, games room, launderette and take-away food. Cutlery, crockery, blankets and pillows are provided, but not linen. Gas and electricity are free. In the Fun Park there are children's roundabouts, a circus, a Formula One car track, high-flying chairs, a looping roller coaster, a log flume and many other attractions. The zoo is the largest privately-owned zoo in Europe and has regular dolphin, seal and parrot shows. In the village there are video shows and a disco every evening to which children are welcome. A cotside can be attached to the bottom bunk free of charge.

Prices (per caravan per week)

£140–£195, depending on season and size of caravan.

JOHN FOWLER HOLIDAYS

Marlborough Road, Ilfracombe, Devon
EX34 8PF
Tel: 0271 866666

UK (Cornwall, Devon)

Holiday villages offering accommodation in bungalows, apartments, chalets, caravans and one motel. All self-catering accommodation is fully equipped with hot and cold running water, private bathroom, WC, pillows, blankets and colour TV. Village amenities include swimming pools, children's play areas, sports facilities, sauna, solarium, club house with bar, games room, disco and restaurant. The motel accommodation has free access to all village facilities. Accommodation is in double rooms or family rooms which sleep up to 4. Chalets and caravans sleep up to 8 and have free access to a similar range of village amenities. Cots may be hired for £5 per week.

Prices   (per property per week)
Bungalow: £49–£99
Cottage: £89–£249

HOBURNE HOLIDAYS

261 Lymington Road,
Highcliffe-on-Sea, Christchurch, Dorset
BH23 5EE
Tel: 0425 277661

UK (Devon, Dorset, Gloucestershire, Hampshire)

This company, with seven awards from the English Tourist Board for 1991, has caravan parks and holiday villages in Bashley Park, New Milton, Barton-on-Sea, Christchurch, Dunster near Minehead, Cirencester, Goodrington and Woolacombe. Accommodation is in furnished chalets, caravans and holiday flats. There are also facilities for touring caravans and tents. The holiday homes are equipped with electricity, colour TV, running water, WC, shower and kitchen. Cutlery and crockery is provided, but not linen and towels. Site facilities vary, but can include a heated swimming pool and paddling pool, tennis courts, crazy golf, an amusement arcade, pool room, skittle alley and 9-hole golf course. All sites have a shop, launderette, children's playground, cafe, bar and take-away food. A small charge is made for tennis, golf, putting, snooker and table tennis. There is a special Hoburne Holiday Club with entertainment and activities for children. Cots must be booked in advance.

Prices   (per property per week)
Caravan: £100–£300
Flat: £125–£300
Chalet: £125–£300

HOLIDAY CLUB PONTINS

Pontins Ltd., P.O. Box 100, Sagar House, The Green, Eccleston, Chorley, Lancs. PR7 5QQ
Tel: 0257 452452

UK

Holiday Centres, Villages and Chalet Hotels in 21 locations throughout England, Wales and the Channel Islands, providing accommodation for up to 7 persons in either 1 or 2 bedroom chalets. Each chalet has washing facilities, toilet and lounge with self catering chalets having a fully-equipped kitchen. Colour TVs are provided in most chalets. Full board, half board and self catering options are available, full board providing three full meals each day with either self service or table service. Facilities include shops, restaurants, take-away food, swimming pools and many exciting sports activities. There is also a special Childrens Club which has supervized activities, and a special Captain Croc character who helps provide fun and games. Each location provides nightly entertainment programmes.

Prices   (per week)
Self-catering chalet for 4: from £165 in low season, and from £233 in high season.
Full board, per person: from £135 in low season, and from £175 in high season.

Discounts   Children under 2 go free. At 11 centres in early and late season 1 child between 2 and 9 goes free with every parent booked. At certain centres in high season 1 child of this age goes free when accompanied by 2 parents. 'Free' children must share parents' room. Children aged 10–15 pay about 50% of the full adult rate.

LADBROKE HOLIDAYS

Caister Holiday Super-centre,
Caister-on-Sea, Great Yarmouth,
Norfolk NR30 5NQ
Tel: 0493 720243

UK

Holiday centres and villages throughout the UK. Accommodation is available in rooms, apartments, chalets, villas, flats, 'hydeaways', caravans and tents, and may be self-catering, full or half board. All fully serviced (apart from tents); electricity metered in some locations. All kitchens are fully equipped. Linen may be hired when not included in cost. Cots are available for hire, but should be requested in advance. Baby-listening patrols available in some locations. 'Hydeaways' are high-tech timbered cabins with 3 bedrooms, bathroom, kitchen and private garden. Caravans sleep 6–8. Bungalow-style tents sleep 6. All entertainments and most activities are free at all centres. Good shopping and sports facilities are available, but vary from site to site. Amenities for children and young babies include playgroups, nurseries, playrooms, toys, nappy service and paddling pools. Special club for children aged 4–10 offering full entertainment programme run by experienced leaders.
Prices   (per caravan per week, self-catering)
£85–£400
Discounts   Under-2s go free on half-board holidays (Caister and Devon coast). Free holidays are occasionally available as special late offers and apply to one child under 10 accompanied by one full-paying adult.

LANTEGLOS HOTEL AND VILLAS

Camelford, Cornwall PL32 9RF
Tel: 0840 213551

UK (Cornwall)

Lanteglos is set in twenty acres of wooded gardens and fields near the north Cornish coast. Accommodation is in double rooms, family rooms and family suites, all with radio and baby-listening intercom. All rooms have TV, tea and coffee-making facilities and direct-dial telephones. Cots, high chairs and nappy buckets are available at no extra charge. There is a special children's supper for under-8s. Children's facilities include early evening entertainment, such as Punch and Judy, magicians, discos, an indoor play area and a wooded adventure playground with swings, climbing structures, swing bridge and fort. There is a television lounge with a video channel and cartoons, and a games room with table tennis, pool table and machine games. Lanteglos has an outdoor swimming pool, paddling pool, tennis, squash and badminton and golf at a club adjoining the hotel grounds. A new indoor swimming pool and leisure complex are planned for 1991. It also has a shop and a launderette.

The self-catering villas (which are suitable for disabled people) have 2 bedrooms, a fully-equipped kitchen and bathroom, colour TV and baby-listening intercom. There are also 22 three-bedroomed luxury Scandinavian lodges which accommodate up to 6 people. A cot or extra bed may be hired for £10 per week. Parents must bring their own waterproof sheets and bedding for the cot. Electricity is metered. Families staying in the villas and lodges have full use of all the hotel's amenities and grounds.
Prices   (per adult per week, half board in hotel)
Low: £190
Mid: £215
High: £250
Lodges: £165–£425 per week.
Discounts   One child under 5 is free in high and mid season, 2 children in low

season. Additional children pay as follows: babies up to one year £30, 1–4s 30%, 5–7s 50%, 8–10s 66%, 11–14s 75%. Discounts are available from the hotel for various local attractions.

PEEBLES HOTEL HYDRO
Peebles EH45 SLX, Scotland
Tel: 0721 20602

UK (Scotland)

A privately-owned hotel about 20 miles from Edinburgh. It has an abundance of leisure and sports facilities for some of which a charge may be made, e.g. riding and fishing. For children the facilities include a playground, playroom, games room, organized activities (in high season), children's high tea, baby foods, cots, high chairs, baby-listening and baby-sitting. In addition there are laundry and ironing facilities and a hotel shop. Accommodation is in double rooms or family suites consisting of a parents' room and a small, separate children's room.

Prices   (per adult per night for a family suite with half-board, calculated on 7 nights' stay)
Low   £45.25–£47.15
High   £53.25–£55.50

Discounts   Children aged up to 16 pay a reduced daily rate based on the nature of accommodation, length of stay and age. This works out around £5.23–£15.75 per night and includes the cost of high tea. There is an extra charge of £7.50 per child if dinner is required. Children not sharing parents' room pay 50% of the adult rate.

One-parent families Special offers are occasionally available.

PONTINS
(*see* HOLIDAY CLUB PONTINS)

RADFORDS COUNTRY HOTEL
Lower Dawlish Water, Dawlish,
S. Devon EX7 0QN
Tel: 0626 863322

UK (Devon)

Set in 6 acres of gardens and fields, Radfords can accommodate up to 37 families in large family bedrooms and 2-bedroom family suites. The bedrooms have baby-listening intercoms and a bathroom complete with airing cupboard and drip-drying area. There is an early tea for children, although they are also welcome to eat in the dining room in the evening; and parents can prepare baby foods at any time. Facilities include an indoor heated pool and a children's pool, supervised by a qualified lifeguard, a jacuzzi and spa bath. There is a colour TV lounge, a playroom and a games room with skittle alley, pool, darts, table tennis and bar billiards. Several mornings a week there is a free playgroup. Reliable babysitters are also available at no extra charge. Children's activities include swimming galas, parties, discos, entertainers and horse-riding. The Radford Club for 5–12 year-olds meets three days a week for indoor and outdoor activities.

Prices   (per adult per week, half board)
Low   £180
Mid   £240
High   £250

Discounts   Children are entitled to a discount which ranges from free to half the adult rate in a family room, and one-third to three-quarters of the adult rate in a 2-room suite.

THE SAUNTON SANDS HOTEL
nr Braunton, North Devon EX33 1LQ
Tel: 0271 890212

UK (Devon)

A 4-star hotel with sweeping views over Barnstaple Bay and the 5 miles of Saunton Sands. Accommodation is in twin or double rooms, most of which have room for a third bed or cot. There are also some rooms with a single or twin-bedded room en-suite sharing a private bathroom. All bedrooms have a bathroom, colour TV and baby-listening intercom. Children's teas are served between 5 and 6 p.m. Facilities include a large indoor heated pool with a paddling pool, sauna, spa bath and solarium, a fitness area, squash, tennis, putting green, table tennis, billiard room, mini cinema, a children's games room and a nursery staffed by an experienced nanny from 9 a.m.–5 p.m. where children can be left for an hour or two free of charge. There is a wide programme of entertainment especially for children. The hotel also has fully furnished self-catering apartments and suites on a separate tariff.

Prices (per adult per day, half board)
Low   £60–£72
High   £64–£77
Special seasonal break rates also apply.

Discounts In low season when children either share parents' room, or 2 children share a single room, under-2s are free, 2–5s pay 40%, and 6–11s pay 60%. Where there are more than 2 children and another room is needed, the first additional child is charged the adult rate and the second one, if 2–5 pays 60%, if 6–11, pays 75%.

In high season when children either share parents' room, or where 2 children share a single room, under-2s pay £3.50, 2–5s pay 50%, 6–11s pay 70%, 12–13s pay 90%. The first additional child in a separate room is charged the adult rate, the second additional child, if 2–5 pays 66%, if 6–11 pays 75%, if 12–13 pays 90%.

SAVOY COUNTRY CLUB
Yarmouth, Isle of Wight PO41 0RJ
Tel: 0983 760355 or 081 870 2723

UK (Isle of Wight)

Awarded 3 'sea-horses' rating by the Isle of Wight Tourist Board, this club offers catered and self-catering holidays in brick-built chalets. All have bathroom, central heating, carpets, radio, colour TV and baby-listening intercom. Self-catering chalets have fully-equipped kitchen and bed-linen is supplied. Electricity is free in all but the standard chalets. Cots and high chairs are available at no extra charge. Amenities include a toddlers' nursery supervised by a resident nanny, the Skylark Club, which organizes a wide range of children's activities and trips to places of interest. The centre has 2 heated indoor pools (swimming lessons available), a spa bath, sauna, steamroom, sunbeds, gym, nature trail, fitness trail, fully-equipped playground and video games room. An indoor sports hall offers many activities, including squash, table tennis, snooker and indoor soccer. Children's meals are available and there is a special dance time for them in the ballroom in the evening. The children's entertainment programme, baby-listening service and resident nanny operate from 25 May to 7 September.

Prices (per adult per week, full board)
£140–£234. A supplement of up to £30 is payable on some chalets.
(per self-catering property per week)
4–6-berth: £150–£260 (low); £435–£545 (high).

Discounts Babies under 6 months in carrycots are free. One child under 6 in catered accommodation is free before 27 July and after 31 August. Children under 3 in catered accommodation pay £24, 2–5s pay £58–£75, 6–11s pay £77–£125, and 12–15s pay £96–£161. If you pay in full by 31 January, there is a £10 discount per adult, £5 per child over 2, per week on a fully-inclusive holiday, and a £12 discount for self-catering bungalow.

SEALINK HOLIDAYS
(see **Hotels** and **Villas***)*

Hol

Self-catering accommodation around the Center Parc in Holland, a sub-tropical swimming dome with facilities including waterslides, wave-pool, shallow children's pool and play area. (For further details of these facilities see CENTER PARC entry in this section.) The bungalows are available for 3-, 4- and 7-night stays. Similar facilities are available at the Normandy Center Parcs and the Trabolgan Holiday Centre in Ireland. Prices include heating, lighting and cooking facilities, entrance to dome, linen, cleaning and tourist tax.
Prices (per adult per week, including return travel for car and passengers) £102–£147
Discounts Children under 14 free if holiday is booked before end of March, otherwise they pay £15 each per holiday.

SUSSEX BEACH HOLIDAY VILLAGE
Bracklesham Bay, West Sussex
PO20 7JP
Tel: 0243 671213

UK (Sussex)

Self-catering and catered holidays by Bracklesham Bay, a secluded and safe beach near Chichester. Accommodation is in 2-, 4- and 6-berth bungalows with fully-equipped kitchen, bathroom and WC, carpets, electric fire, radiator and colour satellite TV. Self-catering bungalows are not provided with linen and cots may be hired per week. Electricity is metered. The village has a shop, a restaurant, cabaret club, village pub and a launderette. Younger children can join the Effelump Club, which has a busy programme of films, cartoon shows, fancy dress parties, talent contests and games. There is also an adventure club for 10–15 year-olds. Membership of these clubs and all the facilities in the village is free. Visitors have a wide choice of sporting activities such as darts, football, archery, billiards, snooker, crazy golf, table tennis and tennis. There is a heated pool, sauna, solarium and gym. The village runs a special football week with coaching by players from West Ham Football Club. There is nightly entertainment with visiting guest artists.
Prices available on request.
Discounts Children under 2 staying in full-board accommodation are free.

VAUXHALL HOLIDAY PARK
Acle Road, Great Yarmouth, Norfolk
NR30 1TB
Tel: 0493 857231

UK (Norfolk)

Self-catering caravans and chalets in Great Yarmouth. Each holiday home is fitted with a fully-equipped kitchen and all have a bathroom with hot and cold water, shower, WC, basin and shaver point. Towels and linen not supplied. There is a colour TV with a video and satellite link for films. Details of cot and linen hire are sent on receipt of your booking. The park, awarded four pennants by the AA, has a launderette, supermarket, hair-stylist, restaurant and take-away meals. The Jolly Roger Club, supervised by experienced staff, organizes sports days, Punch and Judy shows, cartoons and many other activities. For children under 5 there is the Jack and Jill nursery and play area, and a paddling pool. Other free facilities include an adventure playground, games room with pool and snooker and a heated swimming pool supervised by a lifeguard. In the evening there are magicians, jugglers, fancy dress parties, discos and competitions in the Family Club House. Most weeks there is a celebrity cabaret in the Holiday Inn (adults only). Vauxhall Holiday Park also has a touring and camping site.
Prices (per holiday home per week)
4-berth caravan: £84–£275
6-berth caravan or chalet: £90–£370
6-8 berth caravan: £152–£380

WARNER HOLIDAYS
Warner House, North Street, Havant,
Hants PO9 1SQ
Tel: 0705 478888

UK

Self-catering, full- and half-board
holidays in holiday villages and super-
centres. Accommodation is in comfortable rooms with private bathrooms, or
caravans, chalets and apartments.
Some luxury and family suites are available at certain centres. Village facilities
offer a choice of restaurants, with
special children's meals, picnic lunches
made on request, bars, coffee shops,
discos, cabaret, swimming pools and
sports facilities with qualified instruction at some centres. For babies there
are free meals, nurseries with qualified
staff, nappy-washing service and listening patrols. Under-5s playgroup with
games, toys and organized activities.
Other clubs for under-10s and 10–15s.
This company also offers short breaks
of 3 or 4 days.
Prices   (per week, full board)
£194–£236 (adult)
£95–£160 (11–15s)
£60–£118 (2–10s)
Discounts   On some holidays under 2s
go free. Children aged 2–15 receive substantial discounts on adult prices.

MARK WARNER HOLIDAYS

(see **Hotels***)*

Home-swapping

If you want a cheap way to take the whole family on holiday to a comfortable base in a faraway spot without breaking the bank, home-swapping must be the answer. The idea is that you supply details of your home and family to a company who list you in a yearly directory which is then circulated to all the people listed. You can browse through it at your leisure, choosing a country and a property that appeal to you. You then exchange photos and letters with as many people as you like before making your final decision. References may be taken up and a holiday agreement exchanged for added security.

One company listed here undertakes all the administration involved in setting up a home exchange, but they charge heavily for this service. However, it does remove the element of risk by verifying details of all properties, and it saves you a lot of work.

The advantages of home exchange are many. You have someone looking after your home, even feeding your pets, while you're away, so you have peace of mind. But most of all you can afford to visit faraway countries, living in comfortable accommodation, having the free use of a car if you want, and getting to know the area like a native. Families of all sizes, including one-parent families, can exchange homes and the savings to be made are enormous.

What about dishonesty and damage to your property? We are assured that complaints about these things are very rare. Your best security is to get to know your exchange family well by corresponding in some detail.

Prices

Unless otherwise stated 1990 prices have been quoted. These are intended only as a guide to the type of holiday offered and travellers should check with the company concerned for 1991 pricing details.

INTERVAC INTERNATIONAL HOUSE EXCHANGE SERVICE

Withey House, Withey Close West,
Stoke Bishop, Bristol BS9 3SX
Tel: 0272 687431

Worldwide

Long-established company which publishes 3 directories a year in January, March and May, listing thousands of home for exchange and rent in more than 40 countries. The registration fee covers the cost of your entry and copies of the 3 directories. You may include a photo of your property for a small extra charge. The company is happy to advise on any aspect of the exchange procedure. They also offer a 'last minute' phone service to members still looking for a holiday after publication of the third directory.

Cost Listing your home for exchange costs £34 a year (£39 to overseas members). Including a photo costs £5 extra. A second home listing costs £10.

WORLDWIDE HOME EXCHANGE CLUB

45 Hans Place, London SW1X 0JZ
Tel: 071-589 6055

Worldwide

An international home exchange directory with around 1000 listings from 34 countries. To list your home, you have to join by 5 January, although there is a supplement which comes out in April. You must supply a detailed description of your home; inclusion of a photograph is optional and costs extra. Making contacts and arrangements is left to you, but the directory contains guidelines on correspondence, sample home exchange agreements, notes about insurance and suggestions on how to prepare your home.

Cost The yearly membership fee is £20. Including a photograph of your property costs £5. First-class mail is £1 extra. Airmail £3.

Hotel Holidays

When you think about taking the family away for a hotel holiday, you will probably be thinking of a traditional package-style trip. This section contains many examples of companies offering holidays in Spain, Greece, Florida and other popular locations, but also includes companies that organise holidays in Britain and other spots far from the traditional package resorts.

We do not pretend to be comprehensive in this listing, but all the companies included either cater particularly for families or provide an interesting or unusual service. Many offer more than just hotel accommodation and you will also find examples of self-catering deals, themed holidays (such as golfing trips) and self-drive packages within this listing.

There are many fantastic deals for families on the market and, as the amount of disposable income per family diminishes, travel companies try harder and harder to make us part with our hard-earned cash. Keep your eyes open for special offers in the Sunday newspapers and take note of weekly updates on television and radio travel shows for advice and particular bargains.

Many brochures advertise free places for children but be sure that you read the small print carefully before becoming too enthusiastic. In general, if you don't mind sharing a room with your children (usually up to two) you are eligible for a substantial saving. In 1990, Kuoni, for example, were offering fantastic savings for children under 14 on their holidays to the Caribbean; these were reliant on several conditions of travel and if you are at all confused, you should contact the company direct and not rely totally on the advice of your travel agent where small print is confusing. Also, it would be worth your while to check the approximate size of the room you will all be sharing as a hotel's idea of how many beds can be fitted into a double room may differ considerably from yours.

One of the problems with free-holiday deals is that they may be offered outside normal school holidays. British parents are legally entitled to take their children away from school for two weeks holiday per year, but exam and revision times should be avoided at all cost when thinking about such an option.

One parent families are often eligible for discounts. It is always worth contacting the company concerned to enquire about special deals and group holidays. The head office of Gingerbread (for address, see Useful Addresses pp. 355–63) can provide you with further information about holidays arranged specifically for lone parents and their children both by them and other companies (eg Virgin) produce separate brochures listing the facilities available at each resort in detail. Before finalising your trip, you may also want to assess which airport is best suited to your travel requirements. Full details of the facilities available at British airports is given in our survey on pp. 267–77.

Prices

Unless otherwise stated 1990 prices have been quoted. These are intended only as a guide to the type of holiday offered and travellers should check with the company concerned for 1991 pricing details.

AER LINGUS HOLIDAYS
83 Staines Road, Hounslow Middx
TW3 3JB
Tel: 081-569 4001

Ire

Holidays in southern Ireland from 2–7 nights. Accommodation ranges from guest houses to luxurious hotels. Most have cots, and some provide children's menus. Fly/drive holidays, cottages, golfing holidays and coach tours are also available.
Prices Two nights, B+B in Dublin costs £115–£120 (guest house) or £140–£170 (comfortable hotel).
A 7-night motoring holiday (including car hire) costs £240–£270 (guest houses) or £295–£360 (hotels).
Discounts Children under 2 are charged 10% of air fare (cots and meals payable locally); 2–11s receive up to 50% discount if sharing with parents.

AIRLINK HOLIDAYS
9 Wilton Road, London SW1V 1LL
Tel: 071-828 7682

Gr   Por   Sp

Hotel and self-catering holidays on Greek mainland and islands, Menorca and the Algarve. Accommodation is in small hotels and pensions. Cots may be hired for £10 per week.
Prices (per adult per fortnight, B+B)
Corfu: £174–£350
Rhodes: £219–£490
Algarve: £215–£339
Deduct £30 for one-week holidays.
Discounts Children under 2 travel free (no seat, meals extra); 2–11s receive £20–£30 discount, and 12–18s receive £10–£20 discount, depending on season.

AIRTOURS PLC
Wavell House, Holcombe Rd,
Helmshore, Rossendale, Lancs
BB4 4NB
Tel: 0706 260000

Can.Is.　Cyp　Gr　Maj　Mal
Menorca　Por　Sp　Tun　US

Hotel and 'village' apartment holidays
in many locations, with special emphasis on the Greek and Spanish islands.
Most hotels have swimming pools, including a children's pool. Cots and
baby-sitting can usually be arranged on
request, payable locally. Airtours Getaway Gang – membership free to all
8–12 yr olds – at certain properties: 1
hour per day, 6 days a week, May to
October. Departures are only from most
UK airports.
Prices　(per adult per fortnight, self-
catering, including flights)
From £99
Discounts　Under-2s travel free (no
seat). Some hotels offer free places to
the first child per booking aged 2–11
(sometimes 2–15), provided they share
parents' room. Additional children sharing receive 20% discount on one-week
holidays, and 20% on two-week holidays. This applies to all destinations
(except the Canaries) throughout the
season. On apartment holidays the first
child per booking aged 2–19 receives a
free holiday subject to availability. If no
free child places available first child
goes for maximum £139, second child
goes for maximum £169.

ALBANY TRAVEL
211 Deansgate, Manchester M3 3NW
Tel: 061-833 0202

Aus　Can　Far East　Ind　NZ　US

Wide range of hotel holidays, fly/drive
and tours. Accommodation in 3–5 star
hotels, most with swimming pools,
some with play areas and baby-sitting
services. Most provide cots.
Prices　(per adult for duration specified)

Hong Kong: 7 nights, 3-star hotel (no
meals) £677–£1022
Australian cities: 14 nights, high-grade
hotels (no meals) £1100–£1300
American cities: 7 nights, 4-star hotel
averages £488–£829 (no meals)
Canada: 7 nights, 3-star hotel, averages
£573–£930
India: 9 nights/10 days tour £892–£2449
Discounts　90% for children under 2
on many holidays (details on booking),
and about 30% for 2–11s. A few hotels
offer discounts for children up to 18.

ALLSUN HOLIDAYS
c/o OLYMPIC AIRWAYS – *see* **Airlines**
Tel: 071-629 8870

Gr

Holiday specialists in the Greek islands.
Accommodation vouchers are included
in the price of the holiday. Cots and
baby-sitting are sometimes available.
Ask when booking.
Prices　(per week for 2 adults and a
child including flights and transfers)
Low　£550
High　£650
Discounts　Children under 11 receive a
10% discount if they share parents'
room.

AQUASUN HOLIDAYS
41 Crawford Street, London W1H 1HA
Tel:071 258 3555

Mal

Small company offering holidays in
penthouses, apartments and hotels in
Malta and Gozo. Most have swimming
pools. Cots are available either free of
charge or for £1 a day payable locally.
Prices　(per adult per week, including
flight and transfers)
Self-catering: from £175 (low), £187
(mid), £205 (high)
3-star hotel, half board: from £196
(low), £212 (mid), £229 (high)

Discounts Under-2s pay £25 (no seat on plane); meals payable locally. Children aged 2–13 receive a 33% discount.

ARCTIC EXPERIENCE LTD
29 Nork Way, Banstead, Surrey
SM7 1PB
Tel: 07373 62321
also at: The Flatt Lodge, Bewcastle,
Cumbria CA6 6PH
Tel: 06978 356

Ala Can Far Fin Grn Ice Nor
  Swe

Hotel holidays and tours (both independent and escorted) throughout Scandinavia, Iceland and Greenland. Accommodation ranges from tents and guest houses to high grade hotels. Some have swimming pools, saunas and gymnasiums. Sporting activities and 'adventure excursions' are available on most holidays. Most hotels provide cots. Travel by air or (on some holidays) by sea. Many activity holidays are also available, as well as fly/drive, self-catering, camping and cruises.
Prices (per adult)
Eight days' B+B in a medium-grade hotel, by air:
Iceland: (Low) from £430, (High) from £463
Norway: from £1276
Lapland: from £1147
Discounts Available on most holidays. Details on request.

ARIES HOLIDAYS
57 Joyce Road, Bungay, Suffolk
NR35 1LA
Tel: 0986 89 5552

Fr

Small company offering self-drive holidays in both inland and coastal France. Accommodation in 1–3 star hotels. Various sporting activities available. Most hotels provide cots for a small fee.

Prices Quotations are given on request as holidays are tailor-made. Examples: 2 weeks' half board in Languedoc region (June) costs around £385 per adult and £315 per child under 12. 1 week's half board in Normandy (July–August) costs about £220 per adult and £95 per small child.
Discounts Quotations on request.

AUSTRAVEL
50–51 Conduit Street, London W1
Tel: 071 734 7755 or 0272 77425
(*Bristol*)

Aus NZ

Tailor-made, deluxe or charter holidays, with option of unlimited and open-dated stopovers to Australia. Most hotels can supply cots.
Prices A round-the-world trip departing from Luton and returning to Gatwick costs from £749 per person. This includes one Singapore stop, various Australian destinations, plus stopovers in USA.
Discounts Children under 2 pay £150; 2–11 pay 75% of adult fare.

BALKAN HOLIDAYS
Sofia House, 19 Conduit Street,
London W1R 9TD
Tel: 071 491 4499

Bul Rom Tur

Hotel, villa and apartment holidays. Turkey may only be visited on two-centre holidays. Cots should be requested when booking. High chairs are occasionally available. Baby-sitting is available in 3 Bulgarian resorts.
Prices (per person, per week, half board)
From £145–£257
Discounts Under-2s pay £15 only (no seat on plane). Cots and meals are payable locally. Children aged 2–12 may receive a substantial discount (details available on request).

BELGIAN TRAVEL SERVICE

Bridge House, Ware, Herts SG12 9DG
Tel: 0920 461131

Bel

Weekend, short-break, 1- and 2-week holidays in a range of hotels, one with swimming pool, all by a beach. Cots are available for £2.50 per night.

Prices (per adult for 4 nights, including return ferry crossing and transfers)

Low   £59–£139
Mid   £71–£159
High   £73–£163

The lower prices are for a small hotel, the higher for a top-class hotel with pool.

Discounts   Under-2s are free; cots and meals payable locally. Children aged 2–13 sharing a room with 2 adults receive about 40–75% discount, depending on age. Those occupying own room receive a reduction of £25%. These discounts apply all year round.

BEST HOLIDAYS

31 Topsfield Parade, Tottenham Lane, London N8 8PT
Tel: 081 348 8211

Mal   Por   Sp   Yug

Summer holidays only. Accommodation is offered in hotels, villas and apartments. Most of the larger hotels can supply cots, high chairs and babysitting. Children's swimming pools are available in some locations.

Prices   A self-catering apartment sleeping 4 people for 2 weeks ranges from £159–£279 per adult.

Discounts   Under-2s go free on charter flights (no seat), and pay about 12% on scheduled flights. Children aged 2–12 receive a 15–40% discount, depending on date, accommodation and the number of adults in the party. A sixth person is entitled to a free place in a villa party on holidays in May and October.

BRITTANY FERRIES HOLIDAYS

(*see* **Ferries**)

Fr   It   Por   Sp   Swi

A wide range of holidays in hotels, gîte country cottages, villas, apartments, chambres d'hôtes and campsites.

Brittany Ferries has nearly 1500 self catering properties to choose from to suit every size of family ranging from cottages to flats, to attractively converted farm buildings or grand apartments within châteaux. These holiday homes offer real freedom and independence with many situated close to the beach and providing a wide range of sports and entertainments.

Hotel holidays are available with accommodation ranging from comfortable 1-star inns to deluxe Relais and Châteaux hotels. Many hotels have family rooms and can supply cots on request.

Holidays in Spain and Portugal offer accommodation in *paradors*, *pousadas*, hotels and apartments.

All Brittany Ferries' ships have children's rooms with video screens and a selection of toys. High chairs and special children's menus are available in the restaurant and there are special mother's rooms for changing babies. For disabled passengers Brittany Ferries has lifts from the car deck to the passenger deck.

Prices   (per adult per week, including ferry crossing with car)

Gîte: £60–£85 (low), £75–£105 (mid), £96–£140 (high)
Seaside hotel: £123–205
Manor house hotel: £120–£202
Seaside apartments (France): £62–£161
Relais & Châteaux (5 nights): £347–£387
Chambres d'hôtes (5 nights): £95–£135
Campsites: £65–£111
Parador/Pousada: £261–£347
Seaside apartments (Spain): £97–£165

Discounts   Children under 4 travel free on all inclusive holidays and ferry crossings, but cots, linen and meals are payable locally. No reductions available on Relais & Châteaux holidays. In gites

4–13's pay £13–£44, in a seaside hotel £85–£137, in chambres d'hôtes £60–£70, and in campsites £13–£23. In Spain children pay between £21 and £35 for accommodation in an apartment and £208–£252 for a *parador/pousada* holiday.

CAPRICE HOLIDAYS LTD
Market Place Chambers, No. 1 Market Place, Stevenage, Herts. SG1 1DD
Tel:(0438) 316622

Fr It Bel Hol Aus Ger

Hotel holidays to 11 European cities. Choice of method of travel (own car, coach, air) and hotel category (from budget to luxury). Multi-centre arrangements also available (travel by air/hovercraft/self-drive). The company can arrange restaurant bookings suitable for the type of group travelling (families, couples, etc.). Cots may be hired. The emphasis is on personal choice of the type and budget of holiday desired.
Prices (per adult, B+B, inc. flight)
Wide variety, depending on method of transport, length of stay and choice of hotel.
Paris: from £59 for 3 days
Italian cities, eg. Venice: from £199 for 3 days
Amsterdam: from £61 for 3 days
Brussels and Bruge: from £61 for 3 days
Discounts Cots and meals payable locally. There are some limited reductions for children aged 2–11, depending on choice of holiday.

CARIBBEAN CONNECTION
Concorde House, Forest Street, Chester CH1 1QR
Tel: 0244 341464

Bahamas Ber Crb US

The widest choice of islands and top quality hotels throughout the Caribbean. Tailor-made holidays combining more than one island are all part of an emphasis on personal service.

Children and infants are welcomed at most hotels. Especially suitable for infants, the luxury villas selection provides all the facilities you could wish for including housekeeper, cook, nanny, etc.

For children the 'All Inclusive' selection gives parents total freedom while the children are entertained by nannies all provided free.
Prices per adult
From £700 in summer, £1100 in winter for 7 nights on a room only basis
Fly Concorde, First Class or Club World
Quotation requests welcomed for tailor-made holidays
Discounts Children 2–12 from £299
Infants under 2 pay only £100
Full details on request

CASTAWAYS
2–10 Cross Road, Tadworth, Surrey KT20 5JU
Tel: 0737 812255

Sp

One- and two-week hotel holidays in the quieter areas of Majorca. Some hotels offer baby-sitting, special meals, organized games and excursions for older children.
Prices (per adult per fortnight, half board including flight)
2-star hotel: £401–£497
5-star hotel: £1178–£1619
Discounts Under-2s £15 (no seat); cots and meals payable locally. One or two children (2–12) sharing parents room receive 10%–65% discount depending on departure date. (Many hotels have 4-bedded rooms.)

CELEBRITY HOLIDAYS & TRAVEL
18 Frith Street, London W1V 5TS
Tel: 071 734 4386

Cyp Tur

Hotel, villa and bungalow holidays. The hotels are of good quality and all rooms have private facilities. The self-catering accommodation is very comfortably furnished and fully equipped. Cots may be hired for £2 per day. Fly/drive and 2 centre holidays can be arranged on request. Breakfast is provided for all accommodations.

Prices (per person per fortnight, B&B hotel accommodation, including flight and transfers)
High: £451
Low: £347

Discounts Under-2s travel free, but may pay around £20 for the flight. Children aged 2–12 pay 15% of adult fare.

CELTIK HOLIDAYS
Celtic Line Travel Ltd, 94 King Street, Maidstone, Kent ME14 1BH
Tel: 0622 690009

Sp

Hotel and villa holidays in Menorca. Accommodation ranges from rustic tavernas to luxurious beach houses. Cots, high chairs, pushchairs and babysitting can be arranged on request.

Prices (per adult per week, including B+B and flight)
Low   £143
High   £200

Discounts Children receive a 30–40% discount, except in peak season when they receive a standard £15 reduction. (Children do not have to share parents' room in order to qualify for these discounts.)

C.I.E. TOURS INTERNATIONAL
185 London Road, Croydon CR0 2RJ
Tel: 081 667 0011

Ire

Motoring holidays and weekend breaks in Southern Ireland. Accommodation ranges from guest houses to quality hotels. Most provide cots. Self-catering cottages are also available, as well as coach tours (no children under 12). Travel may be by air or sea.

Prices (per adult for 6 nights in a B+B, including flight and car-hire)
Guest houses: £219–£259
Hotels: £279–£349
(Deduct about £80 if taking your own car.)
Three nights' in Dublin (by air) costs £169–£239.

Discounts Under-2s usually go free; meals and cots payable locally. Reductions of between £33 and £82 are available for children aged 2–11 if sharing with parents.

CITALIA
Marco Polo House, 3–5 Lansdowne Road, Croydon CR9 1LL
Tel: 081 686 0677

It

Hotel, villa and apartment holidays in many beach resorts, plus cities and lakes throughout Italy. The company also offers some coach tours, self-drive and fly/drive options, plus a luxury cruise from Venice to Istanbul. Hotels are generally 2–5 star, the grander ones offering an impressive variety of sports facilities, plus air-conditioned rooms with colour TV and fridge as standard. The simpler hotels are still very pleasant, but offer fewer facilities. Some have children's pools, playgrounds and games rooms. Cots may be available on request. Self-catering holidays in villas and apartments offer a variety of accommodation, all comfortably furnished. Some offer a limited maid service and cots are supplied free.

Prices available on request, or phone 081 686 5533 for a brochure.

Discounts Under-2s are free in villas and apartments when there is maximum occupancy, otherwise they receive ordinary child reductions. Children aged 2–16 receive £25 discount throughout season.

In hotels, when sharing a room with 2 adults, under-2s receive 90% discount (no seat on plane). 2–11s receive 20% discount if sharing with 2 adults, 10% if sharing with one adult or another child.

CLUB CANTABRICA
Holiday House, 146–148 London Road,
St Albans, Herts AL1 1PQ
Tel: 0720 33141/66177

Fr   Gr   It   Maj   Sp

Hotel, apartment, camping and caravan
holidays, with a choice of travel by
coach/ferry, air or self-drive. Some
hotels have swimming pools and rooms
with private balconies. At all resorts a
wide variety of equipment may be
hired, including cots, pushchairs, sleeping bags, pillows, hairdryers, irons and
parasols. At selected sites a special children's club is available 6 days a week
for 3–12 year-olds, offering organized
games, competitions and entertainments. Childminding can be arranged in
the evenings for a small charge.
Prices   (per fortnight camping in Spain
for 2 adults and 1 child, including coach
travel and insurance)
Low   £333
High   £452
The same holiday with B+B in a hotel in
Spain costs:
Low   £361
High   £512
Discounts   Children under 2 travel free
(no seat); cots and meals payable
locally. On hotel holidays 2–10s (sometimes 2–12s) receive a 10–15% discount. On self-catering holidays 1 child
up to 17 years is eligible for 10–50%
discount on certain dates.

CLUB MEDITERRANEE
106–110 Brompton Road, London
SW3 1JJ
Tel: 071 581 1161

Worldwide

Large choice of resorts, mostly in warm
climates. Accommodation in hotels,
bungalows or straw huts. Most resorts
have swimming pools, bars, restaurants, nightclubs and many sporting
activities. Some clubs do not accept
children under 12, others have minimum age limits ranging from 4 months

to 8 years. Of these, most run children's
clubs (free), and the few which accept
babies also provide créches, cots, potties, sterilizers, bottle-warmers and
pushchairs.
Prices   (per adult per week, with
flights, full board, including entertainment, some drinks and most sports)
Spain: £538 (low), £641 (high)
Thailand: £1107–£1060
Tunisia: £400–£511
Greece: £471–£708
Club membership fee: £8 per adult, £4
per child over 4.
Discounts   Some clubs make no
charge for children under 6 except in
high season. Others give discounts of
90% for children under 2, 60% for 2–4s
and up to 30% for 5–11s. Reductions are
lower in high season.

CRESTA HOLIDAYS
Cresta House, 32 Victoria Street,
Altrincham, Cheshire WA14 1ET
Tel: 061 927 7000 or 0345 056511

Fr

Hotel, apartment, and cottage/gîte holidays with a choice of fly/drive, self-
drive or air travel. Several hotels have
rooms with air-conditioning, telephone
and colour TV. Swimming pools and
sports facilities are generally available.
Children are often free when sharing
parents' room. Cots are subject to availability, and are mostly free of charge.
Prices   (per adult, including short
Channel crossing)
Average apartment sleeping 4: £80
(low), £120 (mid), £160–£180 (high).
Prices for fly/drive and air travel holidays are available on request.
Discounts
BY CAR *Hotels* Children under 2 are free
unless cots are charged for. Children
aged 2–13 receive reduction of £30 but
are often free if sharing parents' room.
Apartments Under 4s are free. 4–13s
pay approx. £20.
BY AIR *Hotels* Children under 2 pay £30
for flight. Cots as above. Children 2–11

receive reduction of £30 or often nominal accommodation charge.
Apartments Reduction approximately £10 per child.

CYPRAIR HOLIDAYS
23 Hampstead Road, Euston Centre,
London NW1 3JA
Tel: 071 388 7515

Cyp

Hotel and apartment holidays offering accommodation usually with air-conditioning, central heating, private bathroom, balcony, telephone and radio. Swimming pools and tennis courts are available in many locations. Cots and highchairs are free and baby-sitting is available in larger hotels. At some hotels activities are organized for children, and most provide special food for children and babies.
Prices   (per adult per fortnight in high season, including flight)
2-star hotel: £314
4-star hotel: £625
Low season prices are about 10% less.
Discounts   These vary. It is best to consult the brochure or ring the company for details.

DAVIES AND NEWMAN TRAVEL LTD
Norway House, 21–24 Cockspur Street,
London SW1Y 5BN. Tel: 071 930 588

Au   Fr   Ger   Hol   Jer   Nor   Por
   Sp   Swi

Hotel holidays (mostly short-breaks) in Europe. Accommodation ranges from 3-star hotels to luxury French châteaux. Some have swimming pools, tennis courts, games rooms and other sports facilities. Fly/drive holidays are also available. Cot hire is free in some hotels (ask when booking).
Prices   (per adult)
2 nights, including accommodation and flight Paris £139.

Discounts   Children under 2 pay £20–£30, depending on destination; 2–11s receive up to 60% discount if sharing with parents.

EMBASSY HUSHAWAY BREAKS
PO Box 671, London SW7 5JQ
Linkline 0345 581811 *(brochure requests and bookings)*

UK

Over 95 hotel holidays in London and throughout Britain. Every hotel has a bar, restaurant, bedrooms with private bathrooms, colour TV, telephone and tea/coffee-making facilities. Cots can normally be supplied on request. Children's menus available.
Prices   (per adult per week)
Bottom of range: £170–£190
Towards top of range: £280–£350
Discounts   Depending on availability of large bedrooms, children under 16 stay free when sharing a room with 2 adults. This offer is valid for 1 child per adult. A 50% reduction is available on standard menu prices for children under 11 if special children's menus are not available. Children occupying their own room receive 25% discount on the full adult price.

ENTERPRISE SUMMERSUN
Groundstar House, London Road,
Crawley, West Sussex RH10 2TB
Tel: 0293 519151 *(Crawley)*
021 666 7000 *(Birmingham)*
061 832 7456 *(Manchester)*
041 204 2552 *(Glasgow)*

Gr   It   Ken   Mad   Mal   Por   Sp
   Tun   US

Part of the Owners Abroad group, Enterprise offers a vast range of holidays in accommodation ranging from small family-run hotels and pensions in unspoilt resorts to large lively hotels with many facilities. Some of the Enterprise hotels have a 'Family Floor' where there is a centre for children up to 4, as well as an evening baby patroller service, play-pens and a baby shop. Many hotels have a pool section for children, special menus, early meals, babysitting service and playground, with organized activities and a mini-club for children aged 4–12. Enterprise also offer Lake and Mountain holidays, details of which are in a separate brochure. Cots must be booked in advance and cost from nothing to £3 per day.

Prices (per adult per week, including flight, transfers and half board)
Low   £97–£355
High   £194–£384

Discounts Children under 2 travel for £15, provided they sit on an adult's lap. Meals are payable locally. Discounts are available to 1 child sharing with 2 full fare-paying passengers. One child aged 2–16 per booking is entitled to the child price specified for each holiday, dependent on sharing with 2 full fare-paying passengers. The discount on the prices quoted above is between £35–£50. Some hotel rooms have space for a fourth bed, in which case two children may qualify for the discount.

FALCON FAMILY HOLIDAYS

33 Notting Hill Gate, London W11 3JQ
Tel: 071 757 5544

Sp   Por   US(Florida)

Hotel and apartment holidays in a variety of resorts, including the Spanish islands. Hotels offer children's playgroups, free room patrol service and special swimming pools. Falcon also have their own free children's clubs for 4–11 year-olds, but older children are welcome. The nursery is also available 5 days a week for children under 4. Cots and pushchairs may be hired.

Prices 4-person (2 adults and 2 children) self-catering apartment in Portugal for 1 week (including flight): from £599
Half-board hotel, Majorca (4 people): from £529

Discounts Children under 2 pay £15 for flight (no seat); cots and meals are payable locally. In a family of 4, children up to 16 years are eligible for some kind of discount. First child discounts are quoted on request. A second child is free at all times.

FINLANDIA TRAVEL

2nd Floor, 223 Regent Street, London W1R 7DB
Tel: 071 409 7334/5

Den   Fin   Ice   Nor   Swe   USSR

As their name would suggest, Finlandia is particularly known for its knowledge of Finland, but the programme also includes holidays throughout Scandinavia and the USSR. The company offers flexible tour programmes including city breaks, multi-centre or combination tours from Helsinki to Stockholm, Leningrad and Moscow by air, rail, or sea. Tailor-made tours and activity holidays are also arranged. Special 4-day pre-Christmas programmes to 'Santa's Lapland' are particularly popular; these include reindeer driving, snow-mobile safaris and a meeting with Santa Claus on the Arctic Circle. There is also a 7-day 'Christmas in Lapland' programme. All necessary thermal clothing is provided. The company offers other unusual tours, including a tour on an ice-breaker in winter and, in summer, a 4-wheel-drive jeep safari in 'The Land of the Midnight Sun'.

Prices City Breaks (per person for 4 days including flights, accommodation and breakfast)
From: £328
Lapland Santa Claus Tours
From: £665

Discounts Low-cost flights to Helsinki are available
Winter: £235
Summer: £250
Special rates for families are available on Santa Claus tours.
Full details are available on request.

GOLDEN GATEWAYS
Kent Crusader Ltd, London Road,
Southborough, Tunbridge Wells, Kent
TN4 0PX
Tel: 0892 511808

UK (South East)   Bel   Fr

Hotel and self-catering holidays at seaside and inland locations in good quality accommodation. Many hotels have
babyminding services, and a few have
children's playgrounds and entertainment staff.
Prices   Hotels range from £32–£110 for
2 nights' bed and breakfast. Overseas
hotel prices include ferry travel. Rail and
coach travel can be arranged.
Discounts   All hotels have reductions
for children under 14 sharing parents'
room, ranging from no charge (except
meals) to half price.

GOZO HOLIDAYS LTD
Dunny Lane, Chipperfield, Kings
Langley, Herts WD4 9DQ
Tel: 0923 260919

Go

Hotel, farmhouse and apartment holidays on the relaxing island of Gozo,
near Malta. Some watersports are available. No children under 14 are accepted
on diving holidays.
Prices   (per adult per week, half board)
Low   from £315
Mid   from £367
High   from £413
Discounts   Children under 2 pay £35
(meals extra). Details of discounts available for children aged 2–12 on Hotel
holidays are available on request. Flight
reductions of up to £30 per child are
sometimes available (details on booking).

HIGHLIFE VALUE BREAKS
PO Box 139, Leeds LS2 7TE
Tel: 0800 700 400

UK

Short break holidays throughout the UK
in comfortable hotels, some with swimming pools and games rooms. Cots are
widely available. Travel is not included
but rail/air travel can be arranged to
most cities.
Prices   (per adult per night, B & B in 3
star hotels)
Keswick £25
Plymouth £25.50
London £25.50
Edinburgh £30
Discounts   Children under 16 stay free
in parents room subject to availability.
Meals extra. 25 per cent discount if
occupying own room, meals included.

HORIZON HOLIDAYS
Broadway, Five Ways, Edgbaston,
Birmingham B15 1BB
Tel: 021 632 6282, 081 200 8733,
061 236 3828

Alg	Can.Is	Cyp	Fr	Gam	Gr
Ib	It	Ken	Maj	Mal	Min
Mor	Por	Sp	Tun	Tur	Yug

OSL Villa holidays in the Mediterranean
to villas accommodating up to ten
people. Most have swimming pools,
and all include a free car. *HCI Club holidays* offer a choice of hotels, apartments and villas, from full board to self-
catering. Holidays include free sports
and entertainment, and Children's
Clubs. *Horizon Summer Sun* to Europe,
Africa and Florida; includes long haul,
villas and apartments, and lakes and
mountain holidays. Many hotels offer
playgrounds, kindergartens, baby-
sitting service, and the Hippo Club for
3–11 year olds, which includes games,
activities, bedtime stories and baby
patrolling.
Prices   available on request.

Discounts *OSL Villas*: child reductions available. *HCI Club*: child reductions available for first and second children sharing with 2 adults. *Summer Sun*: for first child sharing with 2 adults up to 70% in hotels, and for first and second child sharing up to 50% each in villas and apartments.

INGHAMS TRAVEL
10–18 Putney Hill, London SW15 6AX
Tel: 081 785 7777

Au Bul Fr It Swi Yug

Hotel holidays in the lakes and mountain regions, plus Austrian cities and tours throughout Austria, Bulgaria, French and Italian Alps, and Switzerland. Travel can be by air, coach, self-drive or rail. Some self-catering apartments are also available. Some of the hotels offer baby-sitting and cots are prebookable. Many of the resort villages have sports complexes which cater superbly for children and toddlers. Most sporting/activity-related events organized by the resort take place in the school holidays from early July to end August.

Prices (per adult per week, half board in Austrian mountains, including flight) From £191

Discounts Children under 2 travel free on charter flights (no seat), and pay £12 on scheduled flights. Cots and meals payable locally. Where hotels offer children's discounts, 2–11s receive 20–50% off. 70% discount is offered throughout the season in 6 hotels in Austria and 6 in Switzerland, depending on whether or not a room is shared.

INTASUN HOLIDAYS
Intasun House, Cromwell Avenue,
Bromley, Kent BR2 9AQ
Tel: 0274 760022

Bul Can.Is Gib Gr It Mal
  Mor Por Sp Tun Yug

Hotel and apartment holidays in a wide selection of resorts on the Mediterranean and the Algarve. Many hotels offer children's playgrounds, cots and highchairs, special children's menu, early supper and baby-sitting service. The company's club for children aged 3–16, offers a daily programme of activities and an evening listening patrol, which is free up to midnight.

Prices (per person per fortnight, including flight and airport transfers) Starting prices for a child in a self-catering apartment travelling with adults are:
Low: from £69
Mid: from £79
High: from £139
Starting prices for a child staying half-board in a hotel are:
Low: from £69
Mid: from £79
High: from £139

Discounts Children under 2 travel free on all flights except those from Heathrow, and to Cyprus from Gatwick, Manchester and Birmingham, where a charge of £28 is payable. Such children are not entitled to a seat. Cots and food are payable locally.

A limited number of free holidays are available in certain accommodation on specified dates. The age range for these places varies from 0–17 and only 1 free holiday or child price is available per 2 adults, except in apartments, where any number of children qualify for the child price. In hotels offering free places, a second child receives a 15–35% discount. In other hotels a second child receives a 10–20% discount. Full details of these and adult prices are available on request.

INTOURIST TRAVEL LTD
Intourist House, 219 Marsh Wall,
London E14
Tel: 071 538 8600

USSR

Hotel holidays, including winter sports and journeys on the Trans-Siberian Express. No cots available but wherever possible, children may use folding beds in parent's rooms.

Prices (per adult, including all travel and meals)
Moscow + Leningrad, 1 week: from £465
3 night break in Moscow: from £345
Discounts Children under 2 pay £10 for flight (no seat and food costs to be paid locally); meals payable locally. 2–11s sharing parents' room receive 25% discount (1 child per adult).

ISLAND HOLIDAYS
Victory House, Lower Trudiot, St Peter Port, Guernsey, C.I.
Tel: 0481 721897

Ch.Is (Guernsey, Herm, Sark)

Hotel, guest house and self-catering holidays. Some hotels offer children's swimming pools, games facilities and babysitting. Cots are usually available for hire.
Prices (per adult per week in Guernsey hotel, including flight from Southampton)
Low £135
High £345
Discounts *By air:* children under 3 travel free (no seat); 3–11s receive a 50% discount. *By sea:* similar discounts apply, but age limits vary with each carrier.

JERSEY GATEWAY
65 The Esplanade, St Helier, Jersey, Channel Islands
Tel: 0534 71196

UK (Jersey)

Wide-selection of hotels and guesthouses in Jersey and Guernsey. Many with indoor and outdoor swimming pools, games rooms, baby-listening service and some with their own 'Children's Club'. Cots/high chairs normally available at no extra cost, request when booking. Early teas can normally be arranged for small children.
Prices (per adult per week, half board, travelling by sea)

Low £100–£127
Mid £128–£214
High £140–£248
If flying, a supplement of £15–£67 is payable, depending on date.
Discounts Most hotels offer generous discounts for children when sharing with adults.

JETSAVE HOLIDAYS
(*see* **Fly/drive**)
Tel: 0342 312 033 (Inclusive holidays)
0342 327 711 (Flights only)

US Can SA

Hotel and self-catering villa and apartment holidays in Florida, California and Hawaii. All accommodation is geared towards families and most offer swimming pools, playgrounds, games rooms and sports facilities. Cots and babysitting can be arranged on request in some locations.
Discounts Details of discounts for children are available on request.

JET TOURS AND FRENCH TRAVEL SERVICE
69 Boston Manor Road, Brentford, Middlesex TW8 9JQ
Tel: 081 568 6981

Fr

Breaks and short holidays in France and the French Tropical Islands with travel by air, rail or self-drive. Accommodation is in hotels or apartments. Kindergartens, clubs and special facilities for children are available in some hotels, plus supervision for children aged 3–12 in some resorts.
Prices (per adult per week, self-catering)
By air: from £235
By rail: from £170
Discounts By air: children under 2 pay £20; cots and meals payable locally. Child discounts are available.
By ferry: children under 4 are free. Child discounts are available.

JUBILEE HOLIDAYS
391 Honeypot Lane, Stanmore, Middx
HA7 1JJ
Tel: 081 206 0188 *(London) or* 0345
581828 *(Scotland & Northern Ireland)*

UK (Ch.Is)

Hotel and guest house holidays on
Jersey and Guernsey, many with indoor
and/or outdoor swimming pools,
games rooms and baby-listening service. Cots/high chairs normally available at no extra cost. Request when
booking. Wide selection of hotels in
Paris and Amsterdam.
Prices (per adult per week, including
return ferry crossing from Weymouth or
Portsmouth)
Guest house: £106–£132
Second-register hotel (half board):
£141–£200
Discounts Most hotels and guest
houses offer generous discounts to children sharing a room with 2 adults.
Details for Paris and Amsterdam on
request.

LANCASTER HOLIDAYS
26 Elmfield Road, Bromley, Kent
BR1 1LR
Tel: 0274 760022

Can.Is Cyp Gre Mal Por Sp
  Tun Tur

Offers a wide choice of holidays,
appealing to all age groups – particularly families. Accommodation ranges
from tents and mobile homes to self-
catering and 4-star hotels. Many properties are specially selected for young
families and offer children's representatives, 'First Mates' club for 3–12 year
olds, room patrol service and bed-time
stories.
Prices Example: For 4 sharing apartment on Costa Brava in October from
£128
Discounts Generous reductions available for children up to age 16 where 1

child shares with 2 full fare-paying passengers on certain deals. Numerous self-
catering apartments offer 'fifth person
in apartment free'. Infants pay £29,
which covers the cost of a cot in resort.

MANOS HOLIDAYS
38–44 Gillingham Street, London
SW1V 1HU
Tel: 071 630 0311

Gr

Hotel and apartment holidays on the
Greek mainland and islands. Accommodation ranges from village rooms to
comfortable hotels. Many have sports
facilities and swimming pools, and
some of the larger hotels have children's pools and play areas. Cots are
available if requested when booking
and cost £2 per night.
Prices (per adult per week, B+B) from
£182–£300
Discounts Children under 2 travel for
£15 on most flights (no seat). Details of
other discounts available on request.

JENNY MAY HOLIDAYS
2/10 St John's Road, London
SW11 1PN
Tel: 071 228 0321

Gr

Small company offering villa and apartment holidays on the islands of Rhodes
and Symi. One or two centre holidays
can be arranged. All accommodation is
fully furnished and equipped, although
some of it is very simple. Cots may be
hired for £2.00 per night if booked in
advance. Baby-sitting can be arranged
locally.
Prices (per adult per property, including flight)
From £205
Discounts Children under 2 travel for
£15 (no seat); 2–11s receive £25–£70
discount.

MEDALLION HOLIDAYS
314–6 Upper Richmond Road, Putney,
London SW15 6TU
Tel: 081 785 3255

Go   Mal

Hotel and apartment holidays on Malta, Gozo and Comino. Nearly all hotels have swimming pools and sports facilities. Some have children's pools, play areas and baby-minding services. Cots may be supplied free or cost up to £1.60 per night.
Prices   (per adult per week, B+B in comfortable hotel)
Low: from £157
High: from £383
Discounts   Children under 2 pay £30 (no seat on plane); cots and meals are payable locally. Most hotels offer a reduction of about £5 per night for 2–11s, if sharing with parents.

MERIDIAN HOLIDAYS
12–26 Dering Street, London W1R 9AB
Tel: 071 493 2777

Can.ls   Fr   Gr   Por   Sp

Holidays in comfortable hotels and apartments, plus golfing holidays in France and Portugal. There are few children's facilities in France and Greece, but some of the hotels in Spain, Portugal and the Canary Islands have children's pools, clubs and play areas. Travel in own car to France, and by air to other destinations.
Prices   (per adult per week)
Greece: £175–£270 (no meals)
Portugal: £211–£395 (B+B)
Spain: £199–£389 (B+B)
Canary Islands: £275–£379 (half board)
Discounts   Under-2s £15 (no seat).

METAK HOLIDAYS
70 Welbeck Street, London W1M 7HA
Tel: 071 935 6961

N. Cyp   Tur

Hotel holidays, mainly in Turkey. Very few hotels have specific children's facilities, but many have swimming pools

and various sports on offer. Coach tours, fly/drive and a few apartments are also available.
Prices   (per adult per week)
Turkish coast B+B: £224 (April) £274 (August)
Istanbul: £250–£270 (budget hotel), £375–£425 (luxury hotel)
North Cyprus: £359–£399 (comfortable hotel, half board)
Discounts   Children under 2 £30 (no seat, meals extra). Most hotels offer 15–20% discount for 2–12s sharing with parents.

MULTITOURS
21 Sussex Street, London SW1V 4RR
Tel: 071 821 7000

Go   Mal

Hotel and apartment holidays mainly in 3- and 4-star hotels. The majority have swimming pools. A few have baby-listening services and play areas. Many have games rooms and water sports facilities.
Prices   (per adult per week, B+B)
Malta: £130
Gozo: £154
Discounts   Children under 2 pay maximum £25 on all Multitours products, including flights. If flights are not included, children under 2 travel free. Cots and meals payable locally. Children aged 2–12 are sometimes accommodated free (meals extra), otherwise they receive discounts ranging from £20–£100 (breakfast included in some hotels).
One-parent families   Some hotels offer special deals. Details on request.

DAVID NEWMAN'S EUROPEAN COLLECTION
(*see* **Cottages**)

Au   Bel   Fr   Hol   It   Swi

Hotel, chambre d'hôte and château holidays arranged for the independent motorist. Family facilities are frequently excellent, with ample sports and leisure amenities. Cots can often be provided on request, but you may be advised to take your own travel-cot. The proprietor offers lots of helpful, no-nonsense advice. This company also acts as an agent for Cuendet Italia (see CHAPTER TRAVEL in **Villas**).

Prices These vary greatly. A family of 4 staying in a 2-star hotel in Brittany during high season would pay a total of £690 for one week and £1150 for 2 weeks, including travel arrangements.

Discounts Children under 4 travel free and are usually accommodated free when sharing parents' room. Cots and meals payable locally. 4–13s receive around 20% discount.

NORTH SEA FERRIES HOLIDAYS
North Sea Ferries, King George Dock, Hedon Road, Hull HU9 5QA
Tel: 0482 795141

Au Bel Fr Ger Hol

Hotel and self-catering holidays with self-drive option. Accommodation varies from standard family hotels to de-luxe hotels, offering indoor pools, sauna, gymnasium and TV lounge. Self-catering accommodation is in bungalow parks which usually have ample shopping, sports and leisure facilities.

Prices (per adult per week, including ferry crossing)
A self-catering bungalow in Holland
Low: £93 to High: £137
(Price based on 6 people sharing 1 car and 1 bungalow)
A hotel in the Black Forest (4 night break)
Low: £131 to High: £190
(Price based on 6 people sharing 1 car)
Details of 'go-as-you-please' scheme are available on request.

Discounts Details of discounts for children are available on request. They vary from holiday to holiday.

NORWAY LINE HOLIDAYS
(*see* **Ferries**)

Nor

Touring and 1- or 2-centre holidays with accommodation in hotels, pensions, farmhouses or family hostels. Self-catering chalets are also available for self-drive holidays. Some hotels offer swimming pools, playrooms and entertainments.

Prices (per adult)
Chalet (10 days): £225–£375, including car ferry for 2 people.

Discounts Children under 16 receive a range of discounts, depending on holiday type.

NORWEGIAN STATE RAILWAYS TRAVEL BUREAU
(*see* **Rail Travel**)

Den Fin Nor Swe

Scandinavian holidays with a choice of travel by air or ferry. Escorted and unescorted tours are available, with accommodation in hotels, ranging from pensions to luxury lodges. Internal travel can be arranged by rail, coach or self-drive. Cots may be available – ask when booking.

Prices (per adult per week, B+B, including flight)
Oslo, good hotel: from £413 in summer.

Discounts Children under 12 receive about 50% discount, depending on tour chosen. Discounts for 12–16s are quoted on request.

OLAU HOLIDAYS
(*see* **Ferries**)

Bel Ger Hol

Hotels: A wide choice of holidays and short breaks in Holland, Belgium and Germany. Hotels are in the main small and cosy, and ideal for families. Bungalow parks: Holland only. The bungalows are self-contained and have fully-equipped kitchens.

Prices   Hotels: from £36 per person (including return passenger ferry crossing, berth in a 4-berth cabin and bed and breakfast for 1 night). Special rates for children are available on request.
Bungalow parks: from £46 per person for a 3–4 night stay for a family of 6 persons (including return ferry fare for passengers, car and accommodation).

FRED OLSEN TRAVEL
Europa House, 266 Upper Richmond Road, London SW15 6TQ
Tel: 081 780 1040

Den   Nor   Swe

One- and two-centre holidays, plus coach, bus or car tours. Accommodation is offered in hotels, pensions, inns, farmhouses and self-catering flats and cottages. Some offer swimming pools, games rooms, children's play areas and nurseries (usually in the larger hotels). Cots and high chairs are available in most hotels. Childminding is occasionally possible, but not readily available.
Prices   (per adult per fortnight)
Norway, self catering: £120 (low); £203 (high).
This includes a North Sea crossing with car plus 2-berth cabin. It also includes local car ferry crossing, if necessary to reach your destination.
Discounts   Children's reductions are complicated, so will be supplied on request.

OLYMPIC HOLIDAYS
Olympic House, 30–32 Cross Street, London N1 2BG
Tel: 071 359 3500

Cyp   Gr   Por

Hotel, pension and villa holidays in accommodation ranging from simple to luxurious. The majority of hotels offer children's pool and cots (often free of charge), and babysitting is available on request. Daytime flight departures to most destinations. Some hotels have facilities for disabled travellers.

Prices   (per adult per week, in Portugal, including flight)
Self-catering apartment: £165 (low), £205 (mid), £235 (high)
5-star hotel with B+B: £205 (low), £235 (mid), £319 (high).
Discounts   Children under 2 pay £15 on charter flights (no seat). Some free holidays are available for children aged 2–11 in low season. At other times discounts apply.

VIKKI OSBORNE
Nelson Road, Newport, Isle of Wight PO30 1RD
Tel: 0983 524221

UK (Isle of Wight)

Wide choice of hotels ranging from modest to luxurious. Many have baby-listening services and some have swimming pools, games rooms, paddling pools, play areas, cots, high chairs and special meals. Travel can be arranged by rail, coach or car.
Prices   (per adult per week, travelling by car)
£169–£205
Discounts   Children under 3 travel free (meals and cots extra) – hotels should be contacted direct regarding their accommodation. Children aged 3–4 receive slightly over 50% discount; 4–14s receive 50% discount.

P&O EUROPEAN FERRIES
Channel House, Channel View Road, Dover, Kent CT17 9TJ
Tel: 0304 214422

Europe

This company offers a range of short breaks for families, together with holidays tailored to your requirements through the 'Go-As-You-Please' scheme: hotels, chambres d'hôtes, and self-catering accommodation are available. Cots should be requested in advance.
Prices   One week's holiday (including ferry crossing) in self-catering apartment for 2 adults and 2 children starts

from £260. Five nights 'Go-As-You-Please' holiday (including ferry crossing) for 2 adults and 2 children with chambre d'hôtes accommodation starts from £378.

Discounts 'Go-As-You-Please' range of holidays using a selection of hotels including Novotel where children under 16 are free for shared accommodation. Small charge will be incurred for hire of cot. In hotels children under 4 are free (breakfast payable direct to hotel).

PAB TRAVEL
11 Dale End, Birmingham B4 7LN
Tel: 021 233 1252

Ire

'Go as you please' motoring holidays in southern Ireland with accommodation in hotels, farmhouses or guest houses. Book as you go along from a large list of places to stay. Connecting travel can be arranged by air or ferry. Coach tours are also available. Some hotels and guest houses may charge for cots.

Prices (per adult per 6 nights' B+B, with travel by car and ferry)
Guest house: £102 (low), £150 (high)
Hotel: £140–£225
Weekends in Dublin (by air) from around £110, and in Cork (by car and ferry) from around £65.

Discounts Children under 2 go free (meals extra); 2–15s pay about half adult price (slightly more if not sharing with parents).
Hotels: Children under 5 go free (meals extra); 5–11s (sharing) pay about one-third of adult price, and two-thirds in own room. 12–25s (sharing) also pay about two-thirds.

PACIFIC CONNECTION
Concorde House, Forest Street, Chester
CH1 1QR
Tel: 0244 329551

Aus   F.Eas   NZ   Pac.Is   US

Hotel, villa, apartment and cruising holidays. Free watersports are available at

many hotels. Most locations can provide cots, high chairs and baby-sitting – some even provide a full nanny service.

Prices All holidays are tailor-made. Guideline price: including hotels at 6 stop-overs around the world from about £2300.
Quotation requests welcomed.

Discounts Infant and child reductions are available, but vary dependent on destinations chosen.

PAGE & MOY LTD
136–140 London Road, Leicester
LE2 1EN
Tel: 0533 552521

Can   Far East   Eur   Haw   US
USSR

Hotel holidays and coach tours in many locations round the world. Accommodation is in comfortable hotels, some with swimming pools. Cots may usually be hired. A Mediterranean cruise is also available.

Prices (per adult per week, half board)
Greece: £260–£400
Tuscany: £350–£450
Hong Kong (no meals): £680–£700
Thailand (8 nights' B+B): £580–£650

Discounts Children under 2 are charged up to £15 (no seat); cots and meals payable locally. Reductions of up to 20% are offered to children aged 2–11 if sharing with parents.

PAN AM HOLIDAYS
Clipper House, Southern Perimeter Road, Heathrow Airport, Hounslow, Middlesex TW6 1YN
Tel: 081 759 4000 (reservations)

US

Scheduled flights from Heathrow to over 50 cities across the US. Accommodation throughout the USA, Central and South America, Hawaii, Bahamas and the Caribbean. Everything from Adventure Holidays to cruises. Car and motorhome hire is available.

Prices (per person per week with 2 adults sharing)
1 week hotel accommodation in Orlando from £99 (up to 2 children may share the same room free of charge). This package can be purchased in conjunction with any published Pan Am fare.

PANORAMA HOLIDAY GROUP LTD
29 Queens Road, Brighton, East Sussex BN1 3YN
Tel: 0273 206531

Ibiza Tun Tur

Hotel and apartment holidays, plus holidays in mobile homes in Ibiza. Most hotels offer children's swimming pools. Cots and high chairs can often be hired and baby-sitting is usually available on request. Fully-trained children's monitors organise special activities and will take children for 5 hours a day, 5 days a week. This facility is available in Ibiza and Tunisia (free of charge). The holiday programmes are called 'Ibiza Experience', 'Tunisia Experience', and Panorama also operate 'Rail Experience' and 'Ski Experience' (further details on request).
Prices (per adult per week, in self-catering apartment, including flight)
Low: from £139 (Ibiza)
High: up to £225 (Ibiza)
Discounts Under-2s travel free (no seat). Children aged 2–15 (apartment holidays) and 2–12 (hotel holidays) receive a wide variety of discounts usually quoted as a child price.

PORTLAND HOLIDAYS
218 Great Portland Street, London W1N 5HG
Tel: 071 388 5111

Au Cyp Gr Mad Maj Mal
Por Sp Tun US

This company offers a wide range of hotel, villa and apartment holidays.

Many hotels are geared to families, offering children's pools, play areas, cots, high chairs and early suppers. Baby-sitting is sometimes available.
Prices (per adult per week, as specified, including flight)
1 week self-catering in Majorca: from £164 (low) and from £205 (high).
1 week half board in Crete: from £224 in May, £296 in July.
Discounts Children under 2 pay £15 for flight (no seat); cots and meals payable locally. 2–11s receive 10–60% discount in certain hotels on specified dates. This applies to 1 child sharing with 2 adults. Elsewhere, including villas and apartments, 1 or 2 children sharing a room with 2 adults each receive a 10% discount.

POUNDSTRETCHER FLIGHTS – WORLDWIDE
(*see* **Fly/drive**)

At Aus Can Crb Far East Ind
Mid.East NZ S.Am US

Flights with British Airways to cover 80 destinations worldwide. Poundstretcher travel discounts available for use against travel options such as car hire, hotels and onward flights.
Prices return fares start at £329 for flights to New York or Boston (subject to change).
Discounts Under-2s usually pay 10% of the full fare. Discounts for children aged 2–11 vary depending on the destination.

POUNDSTRETCHER USA HOLIDAYS
(*see* **Fly/Drive**)

US

Tours to USA. Single centre stays, twin-centres, multi-centres, cruising, coach tours and fly-drives. Destinations featured include Florida, California, New York, Nevada, Texas, Louisiana, New England, Arizona and Hawaii.

Prices 7 nights in Orlando, including flights, accommodation and transfers. (Per person based on 2 adults sharing a room.)
Low: £435
Mid: £555
High: £595
Discounts Children under 12 – discounts of up to 70%. Further discounts for infants under 2. 3rd/4th adult discounts. All applicable when sharing a room with 2 full-paying adults.

PRESTON TRAVEL
4 Dollis Park, London N3 1JU
Tel: 081 349 0091

UK (Channel Islands)

Hotel and guest house holidays, mainly on Jersey. Most places have baby-listening facilities, and some have swimming pools, games rooms, children's pools and early meal-times. A few have play areas and special menus. Cots usually available. There are also a few apartment holidays (Guernsey) and a campsite (Jersey). Travel can be arranged by air or sea.
Prices (per adult per week, half board with travel by sea)
Guest house: from £130
Hotel (medium grade): from £160
Discounts Many free children's places are on offer at certain hotels. Otherwise, children's prices are from £40 per week.

PULLMAN HOLIDAYS
31 Belgrave Road, London SW1V 1RB
Tel: 071 630 5111

Egy Isr

Hotel, kibbutz, inn and self-catering apartment holidays, with fly/drive option. Some hotels offer children's pools and babysitting on request. Cots may be hired.

Prices (per adult per week, fly/drive kibbutz holiday)
£360–£410 (based on 4 sharing car)
Discounts Children under 2 travel free (no seat); cots and meals payable locally. 2–12s sharing room with 2 adults receive 10–30% discount.

QUO VADIS LTD
243 Euston Road, London NW1 2BT
Tel: 071 387 6122

Fr It

Short-break hotel holidays by air to Italian and French cities, with accommodation mostly in 3- or 4-star hotels. Cots are usually available for hire, but there are few specific children's facilities. Fly/drive holidays are also on offer.
Prices ('Special Breaks' prices per person for 4 nights including flights and coach transfer)
Venice: £219
Rome: £149
Florence:£199
Paris: £117 (two nights)
Discounts Children's discount of 50% on 'Special Breaks' programme for children sharing parents' room (between October and April). Children's discount of 30% on the flexible 'France Classique' programme.

THE RYAN TOURIST GROUP
200 Earls Court Road, London
SW5 9QX
Tel: 071 244 6355, 0800 181 143
(Reservations)

Ire

Hotel, farmhouse/town and country homes, touring and golf holidays in the company's own hotels. Choice of travel by sea or air. The holidays include Irish breakfast, with some offering a dinner supplement if required.
Prices (per person per 6 nights B+B in hotel, with return ferry crossing)
£179–£249

Discounts   There is a flat rate for under-12s and under-16s, representing 70–90% discount. Other excellent discounts are often available and travellers are advised to contact Ryan before booking.

SALLY HOLIDAYS
81 Piccadilly, London W1V 9HF
Tel: 071 355 2266

Au   Bel   Fr   Ger   Hol   It   Swi

Although better known for their package-type apartment and gîte holidays, Sally Holidays also offers motoring holidays with the option of pre-paid hotel vouchers on a 'go-as-you-please' scheme. The vouchers are valid in hundreds of hotels throughout the countries specified. Accommodation is 2–4 star and varies in style from traditional to modern. This scheme is perfect for those families who wish to travel independently.
Prices   Details of this scheme are available on request.
Discounts   Of the hotel chains featured in this package, one chain (with properties in France, Belgium, Germany and Switzerland) allows up 2 children (under 16 yrs) to share their parents'-room free of charge, while 2 other chains offer the same deal for 1 child.

SCANDINAVIAN SEAWAYS
Scandinavia House, Parkeston Quay, Harwich, Essex CO12 4QG
Tel: 0255 241234 *(Harwich)*,
091 96 0101*(Newcastle)*

Den   Ger   Nor   Swe

Touring or 'stayput' holidays with a choice of accommodation in hotels, inns, farmhouses, self-catering apartments or campsites. Facilities for children vary from place to place, but normally cots can be reserved on request.
Prices   A short break to Denmark involving 2 nights on ship and 2 nights in a hotel (B+B) costs around £99 per adult. A self-catering apartment with 2 nights on ship and 3 nights in apartment costs around £64 per adult (winter).
Discounts   Children under 4 travel free on ferry. Cots and meals are payable locally. On the prices quoted above, children aged 4–16 receive a reduction of £16 (winter).

SCANSCAPE HOLIDAYS
Hill Gate House, 13 Hillgate Street, London W8 7SP
Tel: 071 221 3244

Den   Fin   Ice   Nor   Swe

Holidays by air, sea with car, or coach to Denmark, Norway, Sweden, Finland and Iceland. Wide range of accommodation available from country farmhouses to self-catering summerhouses. Legoland in Denmark is popular, where hotels are geared to family needs, and include baby-sitting and child minding facilities. Cots for infants are included in the holiday price. Single parent families are also catered for, with generous reductions for the children. Some hotels provide special facilities for disabled travellers.
Prices
Low: Family of 2 adults and 2 children under 16 staying at a farmhouse near Legoland on a 4-night short break, travelling by sea with car, including breakfast: total £466, including entry to Legoland.
High: Details as above: £496.
Discounts   Children under 12 travelling by air to Legoland receive a 50% discount on the adult price. Infants on the same holiday travel for £30.

SCILLONIA HOLIDAYS LTD
72a Queen Street, Newton Abbot, Devon TQ12 2ES
Tel: 9626 62291/2

UK (Isles of Scilly)

Small company offering hotel and guest house holidays. Some have swimming pools, and a few have baby-listening facilities. Cots are usually provided (enquire when booking). Apartments are also available. Travel can be arranged by sea (from Penzance) or by air.

Prices (per adult per week, half board with travel by sea)
Low season: £250
High season: £280
Air supplements: £135 from Gatwick, £70 from Exeter, £20 from Penzance.

Discounts Children under 4 usually travel free by sea; cots and meals payable locally. Quotations on request for children aged 4–16.

SEALINK HOLIDAYS

Charter House, Park Street, Ashford, Kent TN24 8EX
Tel: 0233 647083 (Reservations)

Au   Bel   Fr   Ger   Hol   Ire   Sp
    Swi   UK

'Free-as-you-Please' is part of Sealink Holidays' extensive short-break programme which includes France (particularly North France and Paris), Amsterdam, Bruges and Ireland. They produce separate brochures for Continental self-catering and self-catering in Ireland. They also produce a brochure aimed at travellers from Northern Ireland offering Short Breaks in Scotland and Northern England, using the Larme/Stranraer ferry route.

Prices (per adult per week, B+B self-drive, including ferry)
Gîtes: from £80
Self catering: from £94

Discounts Children under 14 are free if booked before the end of March, otherwise they pay £15 each per holiday.

SEYMOUR HOTELS AND HOLIDAYS

15 Mulcaster Street, St Helier, Jersey, Channel Islands
Tel: 0534 73485

UK (Channel Islands)

Small company offering holidays in medium- to high-grade hotels. Some have swimming pools and games rooms, and one also has a paddling pool, children's club, special menus and early mealtimes. Cots are available in all but one hotel.

Prices (per adult per week, half board)
Medium-grade hotel: £178.50–£262.50
High-grade hotel: £315–£392

Discounts Children under 3 travel free. Under-12s receive discounts of 10% if in own room, or 50% if sharing with 2 adults.

SIMPLY SIMON HOLIDAYS

1/45 Nevern Square, London SW5 9PF
Tel: 071 373 1933

Gr   Sp

Small company offering holidays in Greece, the Greek Islands and Spain. Accommodation in small family-run hotels, pensions and tavernas. Most hotels are by the beach but there are no specific children's facilities, and cots are not always available.

Prices (per adult per week, B+B)
Greece: £170–£220 (pension)
£180–£240 (hotel)
Spain: £190–£260 (pension only)

Discounts Children under 2 usually travel free, with any accommodation charge payable locally. Reductions are available for a third person sharing, varying according to destination and season.

SKI ESPRIT

Austen House, Upper Street, Fleet, Hants. GU13 9PE
Tel: 0252 616789

Fr   Swi

Small company specializing in family holidays. Choice of 2 wo resorts, 1 coastal and 1 near the Swiss border, with hotel or self-catering accommodation. Facilities include babysitting, free crèches and children's picnics. Cots are free for children under 2. Travel by ferry and own car.

Prices (per adult per week, B+B)

Low £90
Mid £160
High £210

Discounts All children under 4 go free. Two children up to 14 are accommodated free if sharing with parents, otherwise they receive 50% discount.

SKYTOURS LTD

Greater London House, Hampstead Road, London NW1 7SD
Tel: 081 200 8733; 021 632 6282 (Birmingham); 061 236 3828 (Manchester)

Can.Is. Gr Ibiza Maj Mal Min Por Sp Tun

Large package company (part of Thomsons and sister company of Britannia Airways), offering summer holidays all around the Mediterranean. Some hotels have children's pools, playgrounds, cots, high chairs, early suppers and a free evening baby patrol up to midnight. There may be a charge per night for a cot (if available), which must be paid to the hotel, together with the cost of baby food. Sid's Kids Club offer daily activities for 3–11s.
Prices (per adult per fortnight, including return flight and transfers)
Starting prices for a self-catering apartment in Ibiza:
Low £109
Mid £160
High £209
Starting prices for full-board in a one-star hotel in Majorca:
Low £124
Mid £166
High £223
Discounts Children under 2 travel for £15 (no seat). A certain, unspecified number of 'free' places are offered to children up to 11. If the free places are allocated when you book, 2–11s receive up to 80% discount in April, May and October. Children not sharing a room with their parents receive 15% discount. On the Spanish holidays quoted above, children receive 38–73% discount (self-catering) and 35–80% (hotels).

STEEPWEST HOLIDAYS LTD.

130–132 Wardour Street, London W1V 3AU
Tel: 071 629 2879

N.Cyp Tur

Wide range of holidays in hotels and self-catering apartments. Fly/drive and flight-only deals are also available. Property throughout Turkey and North Cyprus. Two centre holidays are also offered. For details of facilities available for children in 1991 season, contact Steepwest Holidays.
Prices (per person for 14 nights self catering)
From £296
Discounts Details of discounts available for children in 1991 season are available on request.

SUN BLESSED HOLIDAYS

Victoria House, Princes Road, Ferndown, Dorset BH22 9JG
Tel: 0202 861616

UK (Channel Islands)

Tailor-made short- or long-stay holidays in Jersey, Guernsey and Alderney, by air from 26 UK airports, or by sea. Several grades of hotel and guest house are available. Many hotels have swimming pools, indoor leisure facilities, tennis courts or games room, and baby-listening service. Cots are provided on request and cost £3 a day on average.
Prices (per adult per week, including return flight or ferry crossing and half-board accommodation)
First-class hotel: £395 (low), £397 (mid), £428 (high).
Second-class hotel: £180 (low), £203 (mid), £267 (high).
Guest house: £173 (low), £175 (mid), £198 (high).
Discounts Under-2s pay a flat fee from nothing to £15. Meals are payable locally. Children aged 3–11 receive a 15–50% discount on accommodation. All discounts are based on a child sharing with two adults.

SUNMED HOLIDAYS

4–6 Manor Mount, London SE23 3PZ
Tel: 081 291 5000/7979 *or* 061 834 7011
(Manchester), 041 204 2552 *(Glasgow)*

Can.Is   Gam   Gr   Ken   Mor
Senegal   Tu   Tur   US

Hotels, villas and village rooms offered in many locations. In the more basic accommodation, the availability of private showers and WCs cannot be guaranteed. Six resorts offer a children's 'Sunbeam Club' supervised by nursery nurses for 6 hours a day, 6 days a week. Some of the larger hotels have children's pools and playgrounds. Cots cost about £1 per night.
Prices   Budgie Holidays (you choose the resort, Sunmed chooses the accommodation) from £125 (Low) and from £224 (High).
Thailand from £476
Florida: from £294
Discounts   For some destinations under-2s pay £65, with cots provided free. Children aged 2–12 sharing a room with 2 adults receive 25%–50% discount.

SUNSPOT TOURS LTD

96 Tooley Street, London SE1 2TH
Tel: 071 378 8111

Go   Mal   Tun

Hotel and apartment holidays in the Mediterranean. Most hotels have swimming pools and some have games rooms, tennis courts and watersport facilities, particularly those in Tunisia. A few provide children's pools, babysitting, high chairs and early meals. Cots are usually available free.
Prices   (per adult per week, half board in a medium-grade hotel)
Malta: £205
Tunisia: £220–£300
Discounts   Children under 2 pay £30 each, which includes cot hire. Meals extra. Discounts of £11–£140 are available in most hotels for 2–11s (2–5s or 2–8s in a few cases) if sharing with 2 adults.

SUNVIL TRAVEL

Sunvil House, Upper Square, Old Isleworth, Middx TW7 7BJ
Tel: 081 568 4499

Az   Cyp   Gr   Hun   It   Por

This company offers holidays in hotels, tavernas, villas and apartments, plus a fly/drive option. Some hotels have children's pools and play areas. Cots may be hired for about £2.50 per day.
Prices   (per adult, self-catering in Corfu, including flight)
1 week: £210–£289
2 weeks: £230–£340
Discounts   Under-2s pay either £15 or £25, depending on destination (no seat on flight). No discounts on fly/drive holidays. Children aged 2–11 receive up to 30% discount on the basis of 1 child per 2 full fare-paying adults. The child must occupy a third bed in adults' room.

SUPERBREAK MINI-HOLIDAYS LTD

305 Gray's Inn Road, London WC1X 8QF
Tel: 071-278 0383/9646/4211

Ire   UK

Short-break holidays offered in city and coastal locations throughout England, Scotland, Wales and Ireland. Travel is arranged on British Airways flights, or British Rail. A special fly/drive or rail/drive deal is offered in conjunction with Hertz. Accommodation is available in a wide variety of hotels, many offering a good selection of sports and leisure activities. Cots may be available – ask when booking.
Prices   (per adult per weekend B+B, including return flight or standard class rail travel)
London: £55–£234
East Anglia: £67–£168
Edinburgh: £79–£194
Discounts   Children under 2 are free; cots and meals payable locally. Where triple or quad rooms are available, up to 2 children under 16 can stay free when sharing with parents. Meals are payable

locally. Extra children, or children requiring their own accommodation, pay 50% and receive half adult meal portions. Free rail travel is offered to free children, but those paying the 50% for separate accommodation also pay 50% of the rail fare. These reductions do not apply to air packages.

One-parent families One child under 16 sharing a twin room with one adult may be free, depending on availability. Extra children, or children requiring their own accommodation are entitled to a 50% discount.

TABER HOLIDAYS

126 Sunbridge Road, Bradford,
W. Yorks BD1 2SX
Tel: 0274 735611 *or* 081 441 4010

Eur Cities   Ger   Nor

Specialist operator to Norway, Germany and many European cities offering travel by air or sea, with or without a car. Escorted holidays and self-catering are also available. Choose from bed and breakfast or half board in a wide range of hotels. Cots, high chairs, etc may be available in some hotels. Special food may be arranged for babies if requested in advance. Facilities for disabled travellers are usually available, but you are advised to discuss your requirements with the company in advance.
Prices (per adult, half board in Norway, including return flight)
1 week: £403–£581
2 weeks: £604–£906
10-day 2-centre holiday: £508–£741
(per adult, half board in Germany, including return flight)
1 week: £277–£1,059
2 weeks: £411–£2,079
10 day 2-centre holiday: £452–£619
('European Cities' programme, per adult for 2 night's bed & breakfast, including return flight, must include Saturday night).
2 nights: £140–£429

Discounts Children up to 11 receive 40% discount on travel-inclusive holidays when sharing a room with 2 adults. Children up to 15 are also entitled to a reduction on ferries. Sea travel reductions are often available.

THOMSON HOLIDAYS

Greater London House, Hampstead Road, London NW1 7SD
Tel: 081 200 8733 (London),021 326 6282 (Birmingham), 061 236 3828 (Manchester)

Worldwide

A very large package company with hotel, villa and pension holidays, as well as 'theme' holidays, such as 'Small and Friendly' and 'Lakes and Mountains'. In the large hotel/apartment resorts in Spain there are lots of facilities for children, including a special club with supervised play and games up to 3 hours a day, 6 days a week, children's pools, early meals, cots (payable locally) and a baby-listening service.
Prices (per adult per fortnight, half board/full board in a typical family resort on the Costa Brava including return flight and transfers)
Low   £150/£250
Mid   £250/£300
High   £300/£350
Discounts Every child qualifies for a reduction, ranging from £15–50% with some discounts available for children aged up to 16 years. Thousands of free places for children in the months of April, May, June, July and October.

TIME OFF LTD

2a Chester Close, Chester Street, London SW1X 7BQ
Tel: 071 235 8070

Au   Bel   Fr   Ire   It   Hol   Hun
  Por   Sp   Swi

Small company offering 2–7 night holidays in European cities. Accommodation ranges from basic to luxurious. Cots are available for hire at some

hotels (enquire when booking). Travel can be arranged by air or rail/coach and ferry.
Prices (per adult, as specified)
3 nights' B+B in a 2-star hotel, travelling by rail and ferry: Paris £135, Brussels £120, Amsterdam £160.
Add on about £30–£50 if flying.
Discounts When sharing accommodation, a discount of £10–£20 is granted to under-14s (overland) or under-12s (by air).

TJAEREBORG LTD
194 Campden Hill Road, London W8 7TH
Tel: 071 727 2680 *or* 061 236 9511 *(Manchester)*

Cors Cyp Gr Isr It Mal Por Sp Tur US Yug

Large, well-established company offering hotel and apartment holidays in a wide variety of resorts (including islands). There are special facilities at some resorts, such as clubs for 3–11s. Many hotels have special arrangements for children, including cots, high chairs, baby-sitting, children's menu, playground and pool.
Prices (per adult for 1 week in the Algarve, including flight)
Low   £140
Mid   £240
High £270
Discounts Children under 2 pay £15 for flight (no seat); cots and meals payable locally. All hotels offer 10–40% discounts for 2–15s; these apply to 1 or 2 children sharing with 2 adults, although not all hotel rooms have space for the second child. Children aged 13 and over receive the third or fourth adult discount when sharing with 2 adults. Children in own room receive a standard 20% discount throughout season.
One-parent families are offered a discount of 20% for the first child sharing a room with them. A second child receives the usual hotel discount of 10–40%.

TRAVELSCENE LTD
6 Travelscene House, 11/15 St. Ann's Road, Harrow HA1 1AS
Tel: 081 427 8800
Reservations: 081 274445

Eur N. Afr US

Short breaks to the cities of Europe. Travel can be arranged by air, train or coach and accommodation is offered in 2–5 star hotels. 35 departure points in UK.
Prices (per adult in high season, including flights)
Paris, 3 nights B+B: £123
Amsterdam: £155
Discounts Under-2s pay £15; cots and meals payable locally. Children aged 2–11 receive £20 discount each on rail and air, £10 on coach.

TRUST HOUSE FORTE PLC
Reservations Office: 24–30 New Street, Aylesbury, Bucks HP20 2NW
Tel: 081 567 3444 *or* 0345 500400 (from any UK destination, charged to cost of a local call only)

Ire UK

A long-established hotel company offering leisure breaks of 2–6 nights and holidays of 7 nights and more in hundreds of locations. Choose from ancient inns, elegant country houses or modern, purpose-built hotels, all well-placed for sightseeing. Most prices provide are half board in rooms with private bathroom, colour TV, telephone and tea/coffee-making facilities. Cots, high chairs, Heinz baby food and special children's menus are always available, A 'Bumper Funcase' of colouring books and games is also offered in some hotels. Baby-sitting can be arranged in advance for a small extra charge. Activities, such as golf, swimming, canoeing and historical tours can be arranged on request, usually for an extra charge. Trust House Forte have named five of their venues 'Family Favourite Hotels'. In addition to the provision of a 'Bumper Funcase' (see above) children have access to an indoor or outdoor swimming pool (dependent on time of year), a play area, games room and baby listening service. Check in advance for hotels featured.

Prices   (per adult per night, April '90 to April '91)

Stratford-upon-Avon: £47–£57 (breaks); £39–£49 (holidays).

York: £38–£45 (breaks); £33–£39 (holidays).

Edinburgh: £38 (breaks); £33 (holidays).

Dublin: from £130 for 2 nights including return air travel.

Discounts   Under-16s sharing a twin room with 2 adults, or a single room with 1 adult are accommodated free. There are special travel reductions on Rail/Coach Inclusive Breaks, and in some cases under 16s travel free. Meals are payable locally, but there is 50% discount on those chosen from adult menus. Trust House Forte also provide special children's meals on their 'Hungry Bear' menu. Children under 5 eat free at Carverys and at breakfast. If occupying own room, under-16s receive 25% discount on the adult price and pay half fare on rail travel (where applicable). This may differ in Ireland. Anchor hotels offer guests free or discounted entry to selected local places of interest.

One-parent families with more than one child are accommodated, where possible, in a room suitable for the size of their party. Details should be checked in advance.

TWELVE ISLANDS

Angel Way, Romford, Essex RM1 1AB
Tel: 0708 752653

Gr

Family hotels, apartments and villas in the Dodecanese (translated as 'Twelve Islands'). Some hotels and apartments have children's pools. Cots may be hired for £2.50 per night.

Prices   (per adult, as specified, including flight)

Average: £300

Discounts   Under-2s travel free (no seat). On certain dates in hotels 1 child aged 2–14 sharing a room with 2 adults receives £20–£50 discount. On certain dates in self-catering accommodation these children receive £10–£30 discount.

UK EXPRESS

Third Floor, Whitehall House,
41 Whitehall, London SW1A 2BY
Tel: 071 839 3303

Tur

Package holidays and coach tours to coastal and city destinations in a wide range of accommodation. Larger hotels may have children's swimming pools. Cots may be available – ask when booking.

Prices   (per adult per week, B+B in Istanbul, including flight)

Low   from £290
High   from £295

Discounts   Under-2s pay £39; 2–11s sharing a room with 2 full fare-paying adults receive 10% discount on all holidays.

VFB HOLIDAYS LTD.

(*see* **Cottages**)

Fr

Auberge holidays in rural areas of France, such as Alsace/Jura, Aquitaine, Auvergne, Brittany, Burgundy, Languedoc, Loire Valley, Midi/Pyrenees, Normandy and Provence. The company will suggest suitable hotels for children, which provide recreational facilities, early suppers, special menus or babysitters. They can also organize a tour of France arranging 3–4 night stays in any of their 50–60 'Stay Put' hotels.

Prices   (per adult, including return Dover/Calais ferry crossing with car and 3 nights' accommodation with half board)

Hotels vary widely, but average £110–£140.

Discounts These depend on the individual hotel. Children sharing parents' room may receive a discount of 20–30%.

VIRGIN HOLIDAYS LTD
3rd Floor, Sussex House, High Street, Crawley, West Sussex RH10 1BZ
Tel: 0293 562944

Can Mex US W.Ind.

Hotel holidays in the US (Florida, New York, Atlantic City), Jamaica, the Bahamas and the Cayman Islands. Hotels are of a high standard and most have swimming pools, games rooms and sports facilities. Some also provide children's pools, special menus, play areas and cots. (Some hotels may charge for cots.) Apartments, fly/drive and cruising holidays are also available. Virgin produce an excellent range of holidays that are suitable for disabled travellers. They are listed in a separate brochure, available from the number listed above.
Prices (per adult per week, accommodation only)
Flydrive Ski: from £359
California Flydrive: from £349
Discounts Under-2s pay £40 on all holidays; 3–11s sharing with 2 adults receive 25–35% discount.

MARK WARNER HOLIDAYS
20 Kensington Church Street, London W8 4EP
Tel: 071 938 1851

Cors Gr It Sar Tur

Small friendly company with holiday clubs in the Mediterranean, offering comfortable hotel-type accommodation. Many sporting activities available, especially watersports. Supervision of 4–9 year-olds, including games and watersports lessons during high season, plus early mealtimes and special menus. Cots are provided free where available (no linen).
Prices (per adult per week, full board including flight, entertainment, some drinks and most sports)

Crete: £397–£558
Turkey: £389–£570
Corsica: £372–£540
Discounts Discounts for children under 12.

WAVES HOLIDAYS
61c Seymour Road, Westbourne BH4 9AE
Tel: 0202 751700

UK

Specialists in holidays by the sea with a choice of popular resorts. Accommodation is available in a wide selection of hotels, self-catering apartments and chalets. Travel can be arranged by self-drive or rail. Many hotels provide a baby-listening service, supervised children's meals, entertainments and indoor leisure facilities.
Prices (per adult on half board)
Self-drive: 2 nights – from £28–£120, weekly – from £93–£420.
Rail inclusive: 2 nights – from £37.50, weekly – from £102.50.
Discounts Under-2s are free. Special reductions are offered to children aged 2–14 or 15, some as high as 50%.

WINTER-INN, INNTRAVEL
The Old Station, Helmsley, York YO6 5BZ
Tel: 0439 71111

Bel Fr

Small, friendly company specializing in short break holidays, mostly out of season, in rural Belgium and France. Accommodation is in small, family-run hotels. Cots are generally available. Travel is by ferry and own car, or fly-drive to the South of France.
Prices (per adult for 3 nights' half board)
Bruges: £75–£125
Normandy: £70–£122
Discounts Children under 4 go free (meals extra). Reductions of £15 per

holiday are offered to children aged 4–14. For Self-drive and Fly/drive holidays, children under 2 go free, 2–11 have a reduction of £50.

YUGOTOURS LTD

150 Regent Street, London W1R 6BB
Tel: 071-734 7321 *or*
071 439 7233 *(London)*,
021 233 3001/2466 *(Birmingham)*,
061 236 8700 *(Manchester)*,
041 221 3752 *or*
041 226 5525 *(Glasgow)*

It   USSR   Yug

Large company offering a wide variety of packages, plus cruise, self-catering and naturist holidays. Where available, children's facilities are listed separately under each hotel or apartment in easily readable form. Playgrounds, high chairs, special meals and baby-sitting are all available at various destinations. Cot hire is £2–£7 per day.

Prices   (per adult per fortnight, half board in Yugoslavia, including flight)
Low   from £270
High   from £416

Discounts   There are some free places available for children aged 2–11 throughout the season in some hotels. Otherwise reductions are based on a child sharing a room with a full-fare adult on 1 child to 1 adult basis. Discounts of 60% are applicable in April and early May, the rest of the season a 30% reduction applies. Self-catering holidays carry a 20% reduction throughout the season.

Rail Travel

Rail travel has been around a long time and many people tend to think that this must make it cheap. In some instances this can be perfectly true, but in others it can be quite wrong – even horrifyingly expensive. For example, travelling from New York to San Francisco by trains costs more than travelling by air; it also takes two days longer! However, speed isn't everything. Perhaps you want to take things at a more leisurely pace and see the countryside rather than zoom above it hidden in cloud.

Whatever reasons you have for choosing to travel by train (and despite the few practical incentives that train companies offer), there are some good value tickets to be had, and 'family cards' often allow very generous discounts. It is well worth taking a small amount of food and an ample supply of cartoned drinks on such a journey. The buffet car may be non-existent or only serve drinks unsuitable for young children. You are advised to read the articles on avoiding boredom (pp. 000 and 000) and Sheila Sang's advice to travellers (pp. 000). A flat-pack of toilet paper is often a godsend!

Certain discount tickets or rail passes may be bought in the UK, usually through tourist offices. If you're committed to train travel, do buy them as the savings can be substantial.

A word of warning about rail travel: in some countries, such as Turkey and Italy, it can be tediously slow, with trains stopping at every small station and taking literally hours to cover a distance that could be bicycled more quickly. Rapid or Express trains do exist, but in our experience they can still be unbelievably slow. In some countries, too, rolling stock can be very old. It might look picturesque, but it can also be pretty uncomfortable, so take something soft to sit on. If you can book seats, do so. It's maddening and frustrating to queue for hours on the morning of your departure to find that the train was booked solid the day before.

If you have a long journey planned, it is always advisable to book a couchette or sleeper. Children find this exciting, but the main reason is to get some comfortable sleep and help keep up the children's normal routine. It also gives you a little peace and quiet. *Note:* It is not unusual for a baggage allowance to be specified by the rail company and for it to vary, depending on what class you travel. Children's baggage allowance is usually half that of adults'. Check with the company concerned or the National Tourist Office of the country concerned before travelling.

Prices

Unless otherwise stated 1990 prices have been quoted. These are intended only as a guide to the type of holiday offered and travellers should check with the company concerned for 1991 pricing details.

The entries in this section are arranged alphabetically by country rather than by railway name.

RAILWAYS OF AUSTRALIA
c/o Compass Travel, GSA Department, 9–11 Grosvenor Gardens, London SW1W 0BH
Tel: 071 828 4111

Railways of Australia operate a network of air-conditioned rail services linking coast to coast of this vast country. Itineraries of up to 5 or 6 days on trains such as the Ghan or the Prospector allow you to travel in comfort through the sometimes fierce heat, but still get a real insight to Australia. Some states, such as Queensland and New South Wales, operate their own rail tours. Hot and cold showers are standard on most trains, as are dining cars, lounge club cars or buffet cars. Sleeping accommodation is in several categories, ranging from private bedrooms with day lounge to reclining seats. On long-haul journeys, sitting cars are not usually available – you must occupy a sleeping berth, and this often means that meal charges are compulsory. Video TV and recorded music are available on some trains.
Discounts Children under 4 travel free provided they do not occupy a separate seat or berth. Bassinets are available if requested at time of booking. Children aged 4–15 pay half fare, unless occupying a sleeping berth and having meals, when they pay full fare.

The best value for continuous travel is the *Economy Austrailpass*. A 14-day pass costs A$415 and provides seated accommodation. Economy berths are only available on a limited number of services and the economy pass does not allow you to pay additional fare and travel first class. Holders of an Austrailpass are entitled to a 20% discount on Hertz car hire.

Note: If you plan to stay several days in various cities and resorts, point-to-point rail travel may be more economical. *CAPER* tickets, which must be booked and paid for at least 7 days in advance, can save you up to 30% on some journeys.

AUSTRIAN FEDERAL RAILWAYS
c/o Austrian National Tourist Office, 30 St George Street, London W1R 0AL
Tel: 071 629 0461

Austrian Federal Railways cover 5800 km and have direct connections with all European countries. A small extra charge is payable for reserving a seat, and for travel on express trains. Motorail links are available between Vienna, Italy and Yugoslavia.
Discounts Children up to the age of 6 travel free provided they do not occupy a separate seat; 6–15s pay 50% of the adult fare.

Nationwide Area Tickets entitle you to travel on any train in Austria and include a 50% discount on tickets with private rail companies and Lake Constance shipping companies.

Province Tickets, for travel in the 8 provinces of Austria, entitle you to similar discounts.

Group tickets for 4–9 people travelling on same route in same class are entitled to 30% reduction, and children travel at half the reduced price.

BELGIAN NATIONAL RAILWAYS
Premier House, 10 Greycoat Place, London SW1P 1SB
Tel: 071 233 0360

Belgian trains offer no special facilities either for children or overnight travellers. However, many types of ticket are available and some may be purchased at Victoria in London. On internal tickets journeys cannot be broken, but international tickets are more flexible. Bicycles can be hired from main Belgian railway stations all year round. A list of participating stations is available on request. Children under 6 must not occupy a seat on crowded trains – however, trains are rarely crowded.

Discounts Children under 6 travel free on internal tickets, provided they do not occupy a separate seat on crowded trains; 6–11s pay 50% of adult fare. On international journeys travellers aged 12–25 receive a discount. At weekends a first person receives 40% discount, and up to 5 others (if travelling in a group) receive 60%. The first person does not have to be in a group to qualify for this discount.

Runabout tickets, valid for 16 days, allow you to travel freely on the whole Belgian rail network. They can also be used to travel to and from adjoining countries.

B-Tourrail tickets, valid for 5 days, must be used within a 17-day period. The *TTB Card* (train, tram, bus) is also valid for 5

out of 17 days, but can be used on several forms of transport. On both the *B-Tourrail* and *TTB* tickets there are reductions for people under 26. The *50% Reduction Card*, costing 500 francs and valid for one month on the whole network, allows you to buy an unlimited number of single tickets at half fare.

Details of other reductions for young people and families are available on request.

BRITISH RAIL (BR)
Administration Head Office, Euston House, 24 Eversholt Street, London NW1 1DZ
Tel: 071 928 5151

An extensive and efficient rail system covering all parts of the UK, with an Inter-City link to Ireland. Details of services and fares are best requested from the nearest local station or BR-appointed travel agent. Sleepers may be booked in advance. A buffet/restaurant car is available on many services.

Discounts   On ordinary single and return tickets children aged 5–15 pay half the reduced adult fare. Further reductions are available for children aged 4 and under. Ask at the ticket office.

The *Family Railcard* costs £20 and is valid for one year. It allows adults a discount of between 25–33% on standard class tickets, and up to 4 children under 16 years to pay £1 each. There are no discounts on sleepers. You may not use this card during rush hours and on certain busy services (apply to BR for details). This card is only available to people aged 18 and over who are resident in the UK.

All-Line or *Regional Rover* tickets offer unlimited rail travel within specified areas, with certain ferry sailings included. The standard class All-Line Rover costs £160 for 7 days and £255 for 14 days. Under-5s travel free. Children aged 5–15 receive one-third discount.

CHINESE RAILWAYS

c/o China Tourist Office, 4 Glentworth
Street, London NW1
Tel: 071 935 9427

Over 50,000 km of track linking nearly
every part of China. Although electrifi-
cation is taking place, many of the trains
still have steam locomotives. This is the
main form of transport in China, second
only to the bicycle. Express services run
four times a week between Beijing and
Ulan Bator, twice a week between
Beijing and Moscow, and five times a
day between Guangzhou and Kowloon
(more often in high season). There are
three categories of travel: regular, express and sleeper. Sleeper cars and
refreshment cars are available on all
long-distance trains. To ensure a
sleeper you should reserve it about
three days in advance. Tickets must be
bought from station to station, and in
the peak season must be booked five
days in advance. Bookings can be made
at local travel agencies.
Discounts Under-2s travel free. Children
of 2 upwards, who measure less than
1 m (3 ft 4 in) tall pay half price. There
are no special passes.

DANISH STATE RAILWAYS (DSB)

c/o SCANDINAVIAN SEAWAYS *(see
Ferries)*
Tel: 0255 240240

DSB and a few private companies cover
the country with a dense network of rail
services supplemented with buses on
quieter stretches. Refreshments are
available on most trains.
Discounts Under-4s travel free.
Children aged 4–11 pay half fare. An
adult accompanied by a child aged 4–11
can travel together on two children's
fares on a DSB train. Large discounts
are available for groups of three or
more.

FRENCH RAILWAYS (SNCF)

179 Piccadilly, London W1V 0BA
Tel: 071 493 9731

Air-conditioned and sound-proofed carriages with reclining seats, bar, restaurant or snack bar. Couchettes of 6 and 4
berths are available on overnight trains.
Special facilities include a mother and
baby room with a changing table, play
room with games and toys, special children's menu and special restraints for
couchettes to prevent children falling
out. Family compartments are available
for two adults with at least one child
under 12 and one under 4. Further information available from British Rail
offices.
Discounts Children under 4 travel
free, provided they do not occupy a separate seat or berth. If you prefer you can
purchase a *Billet bambin* at a percentage of the adult fare which entitles your
child to a separate place. Children aged
4–12 pay half the adult fare.

HELLENIC RAILWAYS
ORGANIZATION (OSE)

c/o National Tourist Office of Greece,
4 Conduit Street, London W1
Tel: 071 734 5997

Limited and slow railway network on
the Greek mainland only. While trains
are cheaper than buses, they can be old-
fashioned and rather spartan. A popular
misconception is that they are much
slower than buses. This is untrue, and
over long distances may be preferred as
less crowded, and equipped with toilets. It is advisable to book seats.
Sleeper cars are available on long-
distance trains and may be booked in
advance.
Discounts Under-4s travel free; 4–12s
pay half fare.
Season tickets, both first and second
class, are available at reduced rates.
They allow unlimited travel for the duration of the ticket.

INDIA RAIL
c/o Government of India Tourist Office,
7 Cork Street, London W1X 2AB
Tel: 071 437 3677

Some 37,850 miles of track, over 7000 stations and over 11,000 locomotives, many of them steam trains. Travel is relatively inexpensive. Buses connect with trains to serve parts of the country not on the rail network. Advance reservations of 2–3 months are essential, particularly for overnight journeys. Reservations can be made up to 360 days in advance; it's best to do this through travel agents.
Discounts Generally, children under 5 travel free and 5–12s pay half the adult fare. An *Indrail Pass* offers unlimited travel for a period of 7–90 days and must be paid for in £UK or $US. Holders are exempt from reservation fees and sleeping car charges. Child Indrail passes are half the adult price.

IRISH RAIL
CIE, 185 London Road, Croydon,
Surrey CRO 2RJ
Tel: 081 686 0994

An extensive service covering all parts of the country, offering Inter-city and suburban connections. As no journey is very long, there are no sleeping cars.
Discounts Children under 5 travel free. Other children under 16 pay half fare up to a maximum of £9 on scheduled services.
The *Family Ticket* allows discounted travel for two adults travelling with up to three children. Details from CIE.

ISRAEL RAILWAYS
c/o Israel Government Tourist Office,
18 Great Marlborough Street, London
W1V 1AF
Tel: 071 434 3651

Not an extensive network, but cheaper than buses, which are very cheap. Trains run from Nahariya in the north, and from Tel Aviv to Haifa. Seats may be reserved in advance for a small extra charge. All trains have a buffet car. No trains run on the Sabbath or on Jewish holy days.
Discounts Children under 3 travel free; 3–12s travel at half fare.

ITALIAN STATE RAILWAYS (CIT)
Marco Polo House, 3/5 Lansdown
Road, Croydon CR1 1LL
Tel: 081 686 0677

An extensive and efficient network covering most of the country. There are several classifications of train, from very slow 'locale' trains that stop at every station, to first-class 'super-rapidos' which offer a fast service between the main cities. Rail travel is a good (and cheap) way of seeing Italy.
The CIT office in Croydon can only sell tickets from England to Italy and rail passes within Italy, not tickets to and from specific places in Italy or timetable information.
Discounts Children under 4, not occupying a seat, travel free; 4–11s pay 50%. *Biglietto turistico* allows non-Italian tourists unlimited travel on any train and may be purchased in the UK or at major railway stations in Italy. They are valid for 8–30 days and cost from £65–£112 (second class), depending on duration.
Chilometrico tickets are valid for 3000 km and may be used by up to five people at the same time for a maximum of twenty separate journeys. These cost £68 (second class).
Family tickets for four people allow adults 30% discount and children 65%. They must be bought in Italy.

JAPAN RAILWAYS (JR)
c/o Japan National Tourist
Organization, 167 Regent Street,
London W1R 7FD
Tel: 071 734 9638 *or*
4296 2029/4296 0794 *(Paris)*

General information on fares and timetables is available from the tourist office. For more specific information contact the Paris office. JR operates an efficient and complex network of rail services. There are play areas on some of the modern express services.

Discounts Children under 6 travel free; 6–12s travel at half fare.

A *Japan Rail Pass* is available to foreign tourists and costs 27,800 yen for 7 days. This must be purchased outside Japan. It is available from Japan Airlines, if you are flying with JAL, but there are several other agencies where it may be purchased independently. Details from the tourist office. The rail pass also allows travel on bus and ferry services.

MALAYAN RAILWAYS (KTM)

c/o Tourist Development Corporation (Malaysia), 57 Trafalgar Square, London WC2N 5DU
Tel: 071 930 7932

The Tourist Development Corporation can only give information, and does not provide a booking service. Two main lines operate: one runs along the west coast to Singapore then turns north to Kuala Lumpur and Butterworth, meeting Thai Railways at the border; the other line runs to the north-east near Kota Bharu. Express or normal services are available. Some trains are air-conditioned, and overnight trains have sleepers, which must be reserved in advance.

Discounts A *KTM Railpass* entitles the holder to unlimited travel in any class and to any destination for a period of 10 or 30 days and costs 85 or 175 Malaysian dollars. Sleepers are extra.

MOROCCAN RAILWAYS

c/o Moroccan Tourist Office, 205 Regent Street, London W1R 7DE
Tel: 071 437 0073

Tangier, Rabat, Casablanca, Meknes, Fez, Marrakesh, Taza and Oujda are linked by modern, air-conditioned

trains. Timetables are available from the tourist office. Fares are very low.

Discounts Children under 4 travel free; 4–12s receive 50% discount. Groups of six or more receive a 20–50% discount.

NETHERLANDS RAILWAYS

25/28 Buckingham Gate, London SW1E 6LD
Tel: 071 630 1735

Holland is relatively small – about the size of East Anglia – so no train journey takes very long. It operates a railway system which is generally regarded as one of the most modern and efficient in the world. A large number of stations have bicycle depots from which bicycles may be hired by the day or week. It is advisable to reserve the bike in advance to avoid disappointment. For travellers arriving at Schiphol airport there is a fast direct train link to Amsterdam.

Discounts Children under 4 are carried free on all journeys within the Netherlands. On international rail journeys children aged 4–11 pay 50% of the adult fare on the Dutch rail section.

Further savings can be made with the *Railrunner* tickets, available to children aged 4–11 who are accompanied by a fare-paying adult (aged 19 and over). This flat-rate ticket (about 35p) entitles a child to the same (first or second-class) journey as the accompanying adult, regardless of distance. Up to 3 children can travel on Railrunners with any 1 fare-paying adult.

Family Rover tickets are available in June, July and August to families with children under the age of 19. They are entitled to unlimited travel on any 4 days within a 10-day span.

Note All tickets allow you to break your journey as often as you like, provided the stops are on your route and within the period of validity of your ticket (usually one day).

NEW ZEALAND RAILWAYS CORPORATION
c/o Compass Travel, GSA Department, 9–11 Grosvenor Gardens, London SW1W 0BH
Tel: 071 828 4111

Some long-haul trains have air-conditioning, snack bar and restaurant. Other trains have no refreshment facilities. Seats are guaranteed if booked up to 72 hours in advance. Sleeping accommodation is in 2-berth sleepers with washing and shaving facilities, or in a reclining seat with pillow. Take your own carrycot for babies.
Discounts Children under 4 travel free; 4–14s pay half fare.
The *Travelpass*, valid for 8, 15 or 22 days, offers similar child discounts and allows unlimited travel by train, coach and ferry. The cost of a pass is £138, £173 and £213 for each duration.

NORWEGIAN STATE RAILWAYS
21–24 Cockspur Street, London SW1 5DA
Tel: 071 930 6666

A fairly small railway system with no connections to the extreme north of the country. Bus and air routes cover the gaps. Special compartments with washing and nappy-changing facilities are available on long-distance trains. *(Also see NORWEGIAN STATE RAILWAYS entry – Hotels)*
Discounts Children up to 4 travel free; 4–15s travel at half fare. A discount of 10% is available for 2–10 people travelling as a 'mini-group'.
A *Nordic Railpass* allows 21 days' unlimited travel in Norway, Denmark, Finland and Sweden. The 1987 cost of this pass was £151 (second-class) and children aged 4–12 pay half price.

PERUVIAN RAILWAYS
c/o Peruvian Tourist Office, 10 Grosvenor Gardens, London SW1 0BD
Tel: 071 824 8693

Peru has three separate rail lines – the central, southern and Cusco–Machupicchu lines. Tickets for the central line must be bought from the main station in Lima, tickets for the Cusco–Machupicchu line bought in Cusco, and tickets for the southern route bought at the point of departure.
Discounts Children under 12 pay half fare. There are no special passes.

PHILIPPINE RAILWAYS
c/o Philippine Department of Tourism, 199 Piccadilly, London W1V 9LE
Tel: 071 734 6358

A railway system exists only on the largest of the Luzon Islands, connecting San Fernando in the north with Manila, and Legazpi to the south. Refreshment cars are usually available, but sleeper cars are not. We were advised that most people prefer to travel by bus. Within Manila the Light Rail Transit System (LRT) is an elevated railway covering 16 stations over 15 km. The fare is fixed to and from any one point. Travel time from end to end is 30 minutes.
Discounts None. Children pay the same fare as adults.

ROMANIAN RAILWAYS
c/o Romanian National Tourist Office, 17 Nottingham Place, London W1
Tel: 071 224 3692

11,000 km of rail within Romania, and links to all European countries are maintained by Romanian Railways. Tickets may be booked in advance and refreshment cars are available on Rapid trains.
Discounts Children under 5 travel free; 5–10s travel at half fare.

SPANISH RAILWAYS (RENFE)

c/o Spanish National Tourist Office,
57/58 St James's Street, London
SW1A 1LD
Tel: 071 499 0901

An extensive network of railways. Only general information is available from the tourist office. Specific information and tickets are obtainable from the European Rail Travel Centre at Victoria Station in London. Couchettes and sleeper reservations through France may be made with SNCF (q.v.)

Discounts Children under 4 travel free; 4–12s pay 50%.

Tourist cards, valid for 10, 20 or 30 days, are available to individuals, families and groups of up to five people. They entitle the holder to make an unlimited number of second-class journeys throughout the network.

Chequetren tickets offer a 15% discount to individuals and families if purchased in advance.

Group tickets allow a 30% discount to groups of at least 10 people. A 25% discount is available on individual return tickets on journeys of over 100 km in each direction on 'Blue Days'. A calendar of these dates is available from the tourist office. On the motor-rail service, a ticket holder with a sleeper or couchette may transport a car on the same train, or one up to 10 days earlier or later. This service is free on Blue Days if the car has 4 or more passengers.

SWEDISH STATE RAILWAYS (SJ)

c/o NORWEGIAN STATE RAILWAYS (q.v.)

An efficient, mostly electrified, rail network covering the whole country. Restaurant car or buffet available on all long distance trains. First- and second-class sleepers and couchettes available on overnight journeys. On trains where it is essential to reserve seats, reservations can be made in advance for a small extra charge. On some long-distance trains special compartments marked 'Bk' are available for nursing mothers. Fares are among the cheapest in Europe.

Discounts Under-4s travel free (no seat). Children aged 4–15 pay half fare. *Group fares* (for 2–5 people) also apply to families, allowing substantial discounts.

The *Nordic Railpass* is valid in Sweden (see Norwegian State Railways for details).

A 'Go-as-you-please' ticket for 14 or 21 days' travel on the Inlandsbanan (Inland Railway) represents good value and also entitles you to certain discounts on accommodation, restaurants and sightseeing. This is only available from June—end August. For rest of year an *Inlandsbanen Pass* is available, but offers fewer discounts.

SWISS FEDERAL RAILWAYS

c/o Swiss National Tourist Office, New Coventry Street, London W1V 8EE
Tel: 071 734 1921

Most trains run in each direction at least once per hour. Meals, drinks and snacks are available on many services. Tickets and sleeper reservations must be bought before travelling. If you travel without a valid ticket you will be obliged to buy a single ticket with a surcharge which works out more expensive than buying the appropriate return fare. Bicycles can be hired from every station, but advance booking is essential.

Discounts Children under 6 travel free.

The *Swiss Family Card* offers a reduction on Swiss railways, postal coaches, boats and most mountain railways. Parents pay full fare (or half fare if they also hold the *Swiss Half Fare Travel Card)*, children up to the age of 16 travel free and unmarried children up to 25 years pay half fare.

STATE RAILWAY OF THAILAND
Hua Lam Phong (Bangkok), Station
Rama IV Road, Bangkok 10500
Tel: (Bangkok) 223 7010, 223 7020

Rail connections to most parts of the country. Sleeping accommodation is in couchettes, or reclining seats that convert to berths (second-class only). Tickets may be purchased up to 30 days in advance. General information may be obtained from the Tourism Authority of Thailand, Tel: 071 499 7679.
Discounts Children under 4 who are less than 100 cm (3 ft 4 in) tall travel free provided they do not occupy a separate seat; 4–12s who do not exceed 150 cm (5 ft) in height, pay 50% of adult fare.

TUNISIAN RAILWAYS
c/o Tunisian National Tourist Office, 77a Wigmore Street, London W1
Tel: 071 224 5561

An efficient system of trains connect most parts of the country, and travel on them is very cheap. No refreshment or sleeper cars available. Tickets must be purchased in Tunisia.
Discounts Children pay the same fare as adults, but the price is very low.

US RAIL (AMTRAK)
c/o Compass Travel, GSA Department, 9–11 Grosvenor Gardens, London SW1W 0BH
Tel: 071 828 4111

America is a vast country, and given the distances, perhaps it's not surprising that train fares are frequently more expensive than air fares. All trains have reclining seats and a food service car. Many are air-conditioned. Sleeping accommodation is available in various grades of bedrooms and 'roomettes', where seats convert to bunks at night.
Discounts Children under 2 travel free if accompanied by an adult; 2–11s pay 50%.
There are some *Special Fares* which must be purchased outside the US, which could be cheaper on certain routes. Details on request.

YUGOSLAV RAILWAYS
c/o Yugoslavia Tourist Office, 143 Regent Street, London W1
Tel: 071 734 5243 *or* 071 439 0399

Yugoslav Railways have an extensive network linking most points in the country, and connecting with all countries in Europe. Express and fast trains have couchettes and sleeping cars, a bar and dining car. There are buffet cars on domestic routes. Tickets for domestic routes can only be bought in Yugoslavia. Car transport can be arranged on many routes.
Discounts Children under 4 travel free provided they do not occupy a separate seat; 4–12s travel at half fare.

Safaris, Treks & Exotic Tours

For holidays with a difference and, it must be admitted, not too much thought for expense, this section is essential reading. If you want to get away from the well-trodden tourist track, but still ensure that you don't miss anything, the following agents/operators can arrange the holiday of a lifetime – a real adventure for you and your children.

First of all we must point out that there are many more safari and trek operators than listed here, but research showed that the majority either refused to take children, or did their utmost to discourage them. The nature of these holidays means that they appeal most to independent travellers, usually aged between 18 and 45. Travel may be in anything from converted lorries to air-conditioned coaches, but it is always on dusty, pot-holed roads and it can be exhausting even for a healthy, active adult. Several agents expressed the fear that children's crying or chattering might frighten away the animals that everyone has come especially to see. Concern is currently being expressed that, in their eagerness to live up to the promises of their brochures, safari operators may encourage their drivers to try to get as close as possible to any available wildlife. It is certainly true that they try to pack as much viewing time into the holidays as possible. Travellers are advised to consult the company concerned if they are at all worried about the character of the holiday they are booking.

As these adventure holidays are not geared to children you must go well equipped. Take your own travelling carrycot and baby-sling plus adequate supplies of nappies, baby food, milk and medicines. Although some treks include a doctor on the team, the majority do not, so it is best to go prepared. It's worth remembering that children are very resilient and adaptable, but you know your own child best, so think hard before making a commitment to this type of holiday.

The holidays to exotic locations – China, India, Malaysia and so on – allow you to travel in more comfort but, unless they're beach holidays, still contrive to pack in as much as possible. Sightseeing in cities can be as arduous as clambering over ancient monuments and a pushchair could be very useful, but will it be practical? All the companies we list will give specific advice on request.

Prices

Unless otherwise stated 1990 prices have been quoted. These are intended only as a guide to the type of holiday offered and travellers should check with the company concerned for 1991 pricing details.

A.A.T. KINGS AND AUSTRALIAN PACIFIC TOURS

2nd Floor, William House, 14 Worple Road, Wimbledon, London SW19 4DD
Tel: 081 879 7769

Aus

Luxury coach tours, camping safaris and wilderness expeditions in most parts of Australia. Children may be taken on short tours of 2–3 days, but the company generally discourages taking them on longer tours. No children under 8 are allowed on hotel tours, and children under 11 are discouraged from joining camping tours.
Prices   (per adult per week approx.)
Camping: £400
Accommodation tours: £550
Prices vary a great deal.
Discounts   Children under 15 receive a 15% discount.

ABERCROMBIE & KENT TRAVEL

Sloane Square House, Holbein Place, London SW1W 8NS
Tel: 071 730 9600

Af Bur Ch Egy Ind Indo Isr
  Jor Mau Mly Mor Nep PNG
Sey Sng Th UAE

Up-market and tailor-made holidays in a wide variety of exotic places. The company offers many safaris and treks, but does not encourage children on these trips as they are generally arduous and offer no special facilities for children. However, specific advice will be given on request. On beach-centred holidays, many hotels are geared towards families and offer children's play areas, swimming pools and cots.
Prices   (per adult)
Thailand (7 nights): £794–£2737
Kenya (7 nights): £975–£2050
Mauritius (7 nights): £990–£1519
Discounts   As these holidays are expensive and many considered unsuitable for children, the company offers specific advice and information on request.

AFRICA BOUND HOLIDAYS

93 Chiswick High Road, London W4 2EF
Tel: 081 994 9247

Af

Safaris to Botswana, The Gambia, Mauritius, Rwanda, Tanzania, Zaire, Zambia, Malawi and Zimbabwe, and beach holidays in Kenya. Personalized itineraries to suit your requirements. Accommodation is mainly in lodges situated in national parks. All safaris have their own tour guide. Riding and walking excursions are optional extras. From 1991, Africa Bound will be offering a 'Gorilla Safari' in Rwanda and Zaire. For this, and other walking safaris, no children under 14 will be accepted. This is due to the 3-hour walk expected of participants each day. However, children are welcomed at all lodges and, provided they are under their parents' supervision, may take part in game drives. There are no specific children's facilities.
Prices   (per adult)
£1404–£1528

(These prices do not vary from season to season but from 1991, holidays will be priced according to the time of travel. Full details are available on request) **Discounts**   Children under 2 pay 10% of adult fare; 2–11s pay 50%, provided they share parents' room.

BALES TOURS LTD
Bales House, Barrington Road,
Dorking, Surrey RH4 3EJ
Tel: 0306 885991

Af   Asia   Aus   Can   Far East
   Middle East   S.Am   US

Escorted tours to many exotic locations. Choice of tours, from budget to 'top market'. All tours allow for free time, but as itineraries can be demanding, travellers are advised against bringing children under 8. Hotel holidays are offered in Aswan, Rio and Hong Kong.
Prices   Tours range from £455 (8 days in Egypt) to £2800 (23 days in South America). High season supplements of £20–£295 are charged on certain tours.

BUTTERFIELD'S INDIAN RAILWAY TOURS
Burton Fleming, Driffield, East Yorkshire
Tel: 026287 230

Ind

Railway tours of central and southern India, living and travelling in specially converted carriages attached to scheduled trains. Hotel accommodation is provided at some stops, and guided tours at many. Much travelling and very limited space, so not recommended for children. Because sleeping space is so precious, children are charged at full rate unless they share parents' beds. The South India Railway Tour, which includes return flights from London, is more leisurely, with comfortable sleeping facilities on the trains.
Prices   (per adult, including meals and snacks aboard train, hotel accommodation at two stops and services of two guides)

Great Indian Railway Tour (no flights included)
18 days: £575
25 days: £595
South India Railway Tour (inc. return flight from London)
23 days: £1495
Discounts   May be negotiable for children.

THOMAS COOK FARAWAY HOLIDAYS
PO Box 36, Thorpe Wood,
Peterborough PE3 6SB
Tel: 0733 502801

Can   Crb   Egy   Far East

Thomas Cook specializes in upmarket long haul destinations.
Discounts   Children under 2 pay a flat rate of £85 to all destinations. Air Canada gives 90% discount to children under 2, and 25% discount to children aged 2–11, and while in Canada children pay £15 per night in the hotel. Children aged 2–11 pay 50% of adult price to the Caribbean, Indian Ocean and Bermuda if sharing a room with 2 adults.

ECOSAFARIS
146 Gloucester Road, London SW7 4SZ
Tel: 071 370 5032/3

Worldwide

Special interest tours and safaris to East and Central Africa, India, Tibet, Turkey Nepal, South America and France. The tours take in almost everything from local culture to conservation. The company discourages taking children under 12 on safaris and the more rigorous expeditions, but special arrangements can be made and specific advice is given on request. On easier trips that are hotel-based, children of any age may travel. Tailor-made holidays to anywhere in the world can be arranged on request.
Prices   (per adult)

A Kenya safari with one week's full board camping and one week B+B in a coastal hotel starts from £678 (including flight).

Discounts   As these holidays tend to be rather expensive and children something of a rarity, discounts will be calculated on application.

EGYPTIAN ENCOUNTER

5 Station Street, Lymington, Hants
SO4 19BA
Tel: 0590 676922

Egy

Tours of Egypt lasting 8 and 12 days, including a Nile cruise for 5 or 8 days. Accommodation is in luxury hotels or cruise boats. Cots are available on request when booking. The company will also arrange visa renewal.

Prices   (per adult per 8 night tour, B+B, including flights and transfers)
From: £780
Discounts   Details of child discounts are available on request.

GLOBEPOST TRAVEL SERVICES

324 Kennington Park Road, London
SE11 4PD
Tel: 081 587 0303

Ch

Guided tours to different areas of China by air, bus and train. Also motorbike tours. Emphasis on scenery and culture. Accommodation in the best available hotels. Full sightseeing programmes with bilingual guides. Children welcome. School tours also available.

Prices   (per adult, including flights, accommodation, internal travel, guides and sightseeing fees)
10 days: £1199
17 days: £2241

JALTOUR

Portland House, 4 Great Portland Street, London W1R 5AA
Tel: 071 637 3330

Ch   HK   Jap   Kor   Phi   Sng   Th

This company is part of Japan Airlines and specializes in escorted and independent tours of Japan, with stopovers in Hong Kong, the Philippines, Korea, Singapore and Thailand. Hotel accommodation is not described, but pictures of some of the hotels may be found on the back of the brochure. All are either first class, deluxe or super deluxe; details sent on request.

Prices   from
Low   £899
High   £929
Discounts   Children under 2 pay 10% of the full adult price; 2–12s pay 50%. These discounts may vary, depending on the hotel.

JASMIN TOURS LTD

23 High Street, Chalfont St. Peter, Bucks SL9 9QE
Tel: 0753 889577

Mid East   Far East

Escorted tours, some with guest lecturer. Most itineraries are quite demanding as there is a lot of sightseeing involved. Accommodation is in comfortable, well-appointed hotels. The availability of childminding varies; it is best to enquire at the hotel. People are advised against bringing children under 5.

Prices   Tours (all durations) range from £449–£2500 per person.
Discounts   Children up to 12 are entitled to a discount between 10–30%, depending on the hotel and provided they share a room with 2 adults.

JETSET TOURS
Jetset House, 74 New Oxford Street,
London WC1A 1EU
Tel: 071 631 0501

Aus   Crb   E.Af   Ind   Ind.Oc   NZ
S.Pac   S.Am   S-E.Asia   US

Tailor-made hotel holidays in Australia
and New Zealand, plus stopover tours
in California and other areas specified
above. Hotels and facilities vary from
basic to grand, the cheapest being
around £12 a night. Cots and high chairs
are usually available, and some hotels
arrange babysitting and activities for
children. Facilities are available for disabled travellers.
Prices   Quoted on request as all holidays are tailor-made. A return flight to
Perth starts from £747.
Discounts   Children receive a 15–50%
discount, depending on flight, hotel,
number of people sharing room and
age of child. Specific quotations given
on request.

KUONI TRAVEL
Kuoni House, Dorking, Surrey RH5 4AZ
Tel: 0306 740500 (reservations)

Worldwide

Long-established company offering
safaris and escorted tours to exotic
places, such as Africa, Australia, the
Caribbean, China, the Far East, India,
South America and the US. Holidays are
in comfortable hotels, with camping
during some parts of safaris. Cots can
be arranged in advance. Some tours are
not suitable for young children. Ask the
company's advice before booking.
Although formerly associated exclus-
ively with high-class (and very expensive) holidays, Kuoni have in recent
years extended their service to include
lower-priced packages.
Prices
Low: from £349
High: from £5,000
Discounts   The first child under 12
who travels with 2 adults and shares
their room receives 50% discount. Any

additional children (or first child if in
own room) receive 15% discount. In the
1991 season, Kuoni are offering several
attractive deals for families. These include Caribbean trips in which one child
under 12 sharing a room with 2 adults
pays only £149 for the entire holiday
(regardless of length of stay). This offer
is, of course, dependent on several conditions of travel. It is advisable to contact Kuoni for details of special offers.

MELIA TRAVEL
12 Dover Street, London W1X 4NS
Tel: 071 491 3881

Cub   S.Am

Hotels holidays and sightseeing tours
which can be tailored to your needs and
interests.
Prices   (per adult per week in Rio, B+B
in 3-star hotel)
From £729
Discounts   Children under 2 pay 10%
for flight (no seat); 2–12s receive 20%
discount, but must each be accompanied by an adult.

P & O TRAVEL
77 New Oxford Street, London
WC1A 1PP
Tel: 071 831 1441
1 Derby Square, Liverpool L2 9QR
Tel: 051 235 5464
1–2 East Street, Southampton, Hants
SO9 2GQ
Tel: 0703 227341

Worldwide

The Down Under Club specializes in
holidays to Australia and New Zealand
via the Far East or USA. Package holidays, flights only, ferries and cruises to
other destinations.
Prices   per adult
Down Under Club £755 return to
Australia or New Zealand via Far East or
USA
£925 return Round-the-World ticket to
Australia or New Zealand

Discounts Down Under Club – infants pay 10% of adult fare; children pay 67%. Children 1–11 get 50% reduction on P & O cruises.

REGENT HOLIDAYS (UK) LTD
Regent House, Regent Street, Shanklin, Isle of Wight PO37 7AE
Tel: 098386 4212/4225 *or* 0272 211711 (Bristol)

Alb   Ch   Cub   Cze   Grn   Hun
Ice   Laos   N.Cyp   N.Kor   Tur
USSR   Vie   Yem

Packages to some familiar, as well as some highly unusual, destinations. Accommodation is in 2–5 star hotels and facilities for children vary enormously. The company is happy to advise.
Prices (per adult in low season, including flight)
Weekend in Turkey, B+B: from £160
1 week in Albania, half board: from £499
Discounts On flights under-12s receive 10–40% discount, depending on destination and carrier. In accommodation under-2s are often free, while 2–5s generally receive 50% discount, and 6–11s receive 25%. However, most hotels operate a 50% reduction on the single room charge for under-12s if sharing a room with two adults.

SILK CUT FARAWAY HOLIDAYS
Meon House, Petersfield, Hants GU32 3JN
Tel: 0730 65211

Af   Ala   Bor   Brz   Can   Ch   Crb
Egy   Far East   Mau   Mly   NZ
Sey

Safaris to Kenya, Tanzania and Borneo, beach holidays in the Caribbean, Kenya, Malaysia, Mauritius and the Seychelles, and escorted tours to most destinations above. Accommodation is in moderate to superior hotels. Cots can be provided on request.

Prices (per adult)
Mauritius (beach holiday, 7 nights half board):
From: £1149
Borneo (14 night tour, incl accommodation and some meals):
From: 1594
Discounts Under-2s occupying a cot in a room with two full-fare adults, pay 10%; meals payable locally; 2–11s sharing with two adults usually pay 60%, but this varies, depending on hotel.

SPEEDBIRD HOLIDAYS
Pacific House, Three Bridges, Hazelwick Avenue, Crawley RH10 1NP
Tel: 0293 611611

Af   Aus   Can   Ch   Crb   Gulf   Ind
Ind.Oc   Jap   NZ   S.Am
S.E. Asia   S.Pac   US

Speedbird, a subsidiary of British Airways, offers a large choice of faraway holidays. Selected hotels in St. Lucia, Jessica and Barbados provide family offers and facilities such as free accommodation for children on certain dates and a children's club which organizes activities. Particularly recommended for families are Phuket, Thailand and Mauritius. Children's reductions are available on special stopover fares to Australia and New Zealand.
Prices Available on request
Discounts All discounts apply to children sharing a room with 2 full fare paying adults. Children under 2 pay £75 only (no seat on plane); 2–11s receive 50% discount; 12–15s receive 10% discount.

TRAVELBAG
12 High Street, Alton, Hants GU34 1BN
Tel: 0420 88724

Aus   Can   Far East   Ind   Mly   NZ
S.Pac   Th   US

Touring and resort holidays in Australia, New Zealand and Thailand,

with the option of stopovers in India, US, Canada, Malaysia, the Far East and South Pacific. Most accommodation is in 3–4 star hotels. This company also sells flights only.
Prices   (flights only)
Perth: £539–£899
Auckland: £699–£959
Round-the-World: from £1079
Hotel prices will be quoted on request.
Discounts   On flights children under 2 pay 10%; 2–12s pay 50%. Accommodation discounts will be quoted on request.

TWICKERS WORLD
22 Church Street, Twickenham, Middx TW1 3NW
Tel: 081 892 8164/7606

Af   Aus   Ch   Far East   Mid. East
  N.Am   NZ   S.Am   S.Pac.Is

Children are not allowed on the cultural tours and wilderness journeys that this company offers, but may join beach holidays. Accommodation is in hotels, lodges and apartments, some of which have suites large enough for two adults and three children. Cots can be provided if requested when booking.
Prices   (per adult per week, including flight)
Seychelles, self-catering: from £681 (based on four people sharing)
Discounts   Details of child discounts available on request.

UK CHINA TRAVEL SERVICE
24 Cambridge Circus, London WC2H 8HD
Tel: 071 836 9911

Ch

Guided tours to various parts of China, lasting from 8–26 days. Options via Korea, Nepal, USSR or Thailand. Itineraries can be hectic and are not recommended for children. Accommodation is in twin-bedded hotel rooms, which can be very basic. Children are generally expected to share adults' room (bed provided if necessary).
Prices   (per adult)
£499 for 8 days
£1998 for 21 days
Discounts   Details of child discounts available on request.

VOYAGES JULES VERNE
Travel Promotions Ltd, 10 Glentworth Street, London NW1
Tel: 071 486 8080/8571

Af   Alb   Asia   Aus   Can   Ch   Far East   Ind   S.Am   USSR   W.Ind

Guided tours to many destinations, with accommodation in the best available hotels (sometimes basic). Internal travel by bus, train and boat. Itineraries are tiring and not recommended for children under 8, but the company is prepared to negotiate.
Prices   (per adult)
From £300 upwards.
Discounts   Details of child discounts available on requests.

Sailing

Many of the holidays in this section tend to be instructional, offering you the opportunity to learn how to sail a wide variety of craft. This type of holiday is not generally suited to children under 9, and some companies have even more rigorous age limits. However, family needs are catered for by some, and several companies offer junior courses for children as young as 5 (more often 9 or 10) where they can learn to sail dinghies. Crèche and baby-sitting facilities are offered by a few companies.

Charter boats (skippered or independent) will often accept children of any age, providing safety harnesses for toddlers and buoyancy aids for all children apart from babies. For families flotilla sailing seems to be the best bet. It allows you the freedom to skipper your own yacht, but gives you the security of travelling in a small convoy following the lead boat which has a trained captain and crew to navigate and help you out en route if necessary. For this sort of holiday at least one adult on your boat must have some sailing experience or have taken a short flotilla sailing course prior to, or at the beginning of, the holiday. A second adult is necessary on each boat to help with ropes and mooring. Single parents with young children would need to team up with another group or family in order to manage the yacht safely. It is worth contacting your local Gingerbread group, who may be able to put you in touch with like-minded one-parent groups (see Useful Addresses pp. 355–63 for the address of Gingerbread's head office).

If you're an experienced sailor there's nothing to stop you chartering a boat and taking it where you please – but bear in mind that rough seas (particularly in British coastal waters) will necessitate keeping the children below and this can lead to frayed tempers all round. From our research on this section we would recommend that novice sailors start with an easy voyage in safe and calm waters – probably somewhere in the Mediterranean. Proficiency is acquired fairly quickly and you'll soon be able to move on to more adventurous sailing.

Prices

Unless otherwise stated 1990 prices have been quoted. These are intended only as a guide to the type of holiday offered and travellers should check with the company concerned for 1991 pricing details.

BOSHAM SAILING

Bosham Lane, Bosham, Chichester,
West Sussex PO18 8HP
Tel: 0243 572555

UK (S. Coast)

Dinghy sailing classes of 5, 7 or 12 days' duration. Two age groups: Junior (9–14 years) and adult (over 14). Optional test for Royal Yacht Association at end of course. Half board accommodation in private homes in Bosham. There is also a 4-berth caravan available, or you can choose a hotel. No childminding facilities are provided.
Prices   A 5-day course, including all equipment, instruction and packed lunches: £138–£165 (adults), £129–£149 (children).
Accommodation per night: B+B £10; half board £13.50; caravan £13.50 (or £75 per week).

GREEK ISLANDS SAILING CLUB

66 High Street, Walton-on-Thames,
Surrey KT12 1BU
Tel: 0932 220416

Gr

Shore-based dinghy-sailing and wind-surfing holidays on the 'unspoilt' islands of Paxos, Zakynthos, Ithaca and Cephalonia, for both beginner and expert. The company offers a wide range of craft plus expert tuition by RYA-qualified instructors, with special instruction for children. Full safety cover and buoyancy aids provided. Accommodation is either in studios, shared apartments or villas (*see* entry in **Villas**). Cots, high chairs and baby-sitters are available. Premier Class travel is available as an option.

Prices   (per adult per fortnight, including return flight, transfers, airport tax, accommodation, craft and tuition)
Low   £430
Mid   £530
High   £640
Discounts   On two-week holidays children aged 2–12 receive 5–10% discount, depending on season.

LORNE LEADER

Dan & Gillian Hind, Lorne Leader,
Ardfern, By Lochgilphead, Argyll
PA31 8QN
Tel: 08525 212

UK (Western Scotland)

Lorne Leader is a refurbished Brixham trawler with 12 passenger berths, hot and cold running water, heating, WCs and showers. From May–September, skipper and crew take her on 6- and 11-day cruises around the Hebrides. There are different themes, such as birdwatching, art, and folk music, and special family holidays with childminding and more trips ashore.
Prices   (per berth, including all meals and sailing instruction)
6 days: £250–£350
12 days: £680
Discounts   10% for children under 11.

MADE TO MEASURE HOLIDAYS

Conwell House, 43 East Street,
Chichester, Sussex PO19 1HX
Tel: 0243 533333 *or* 0904 37502 (York)

Med

Tailor-made sailing holidays of a very high standard in the Mediterranean. Details available from the company on request.
Prices   available on request

MINORCA SAILING HOLIDAYS
265 Green Lanes, London N13 4XE
Tel: 081 886 7193 *or* 081 882 3925

Sp

Dinghy-sailing and windsurfing holidays in Minorca, with expert tuition from RYA instructors at whatever level is required. Accommodation is in self-catering apartments and villas which sleep 4–8 people, or a small, family-run hotel. Some villas have private gardens and swimming pools. Cots are supplied free on request. Childminding can be arranged at certain times of the year; at the moment May and June are most popular.
Prices   (per adult per week, including flight)
Low   £275–£450 (based on 2 people sharing)
High   £448–£650 (based on 4 people sharing)
Discounts   There are no reductions for children between early July and mid-September. At other times under-2s pay £25, 2–5s pay 50% of adult rate, and 6–11s pay 80%.

ROCKLEY POINT SAILING SCHOOL
Rockley Sands, Poole, Dorset BH15 4LZ
Tel: 0202 677272

UK (S. Coast)

A range of sailing courses lasting 2–13 days for beginners, intermediate and advanced. Also wind-surfing courses and various watersports, such as canoeing. Children aged 8–12 are specially catered for, and there are also courses for unaccompanied 10–17 year-olds. Accommodation is in guest houses, caravans or campsites (bring your own tent).
Prices   (excluding lunches, waterproofs and wetsuits)
6-day sailing course: Adults (over 13) £113–£130, Juniors (8–12) £105–£135.

Accommodation: 6-berth caravan from £160 per week; guest house (half board) £12 per night.
Discounts   5% off course fee for 3 members of the same family; 10% discount for 4 members.

SUNDOWN MARINE YACHT CHARTER LTD
Sundown House, Rectory Lane, Woodmansterne, Surrey SM7 3PP
Tel: 07375 51271

Aus   Crb   Far East   Fr   Gr   It   Pac   Tur   Yug

Selection of sailing holidays. Choose from sail-yourself yachts, flotilla holidays, crewed sailing/motor yachts and crewed Turkish caiques. Yachts have 4–10 berths and range from comfortable to luxurious. Children and babies welcome. Cotsides can be arranged, but sometimes you have to provide your own buoyancy aids.
Prices   (per yacht/boat, excluding flight)
6-berth yacht (sail-yourself for 2 weeks in Greece): £1090–£1690 (£45 per day extra for captain).
12-berth Turkish caique, including captain, crew and diesel: £200–£450 per day.

SUNSAIL
The Port House, Port Solent, Portsmouth, Hants. PO6 4TH
Tel: 0705 210345

Cor   Gr   Sar   Tur   Yug

Sailing, cruising and Sunsail Club holidays in the Mediterranean with expert tuition.

Sunsail also offers skippered holidays for those who prefer not to 'do-it-yourself'. Accommodation is either on board or in shore-based club rooms. Older children can learn to sail and windsurf. A crèche run by qualified staff is available at some of the Clubs for children aged 1–12 years. Cots, high chairs, potties, specially designated play areas, sandpits, children's dinghies, windsurfing rigs, a baby listening service and children's pools are among the facilities on offer at some of the Clubs.

Prices   (per adult per fortnight including flight and accommodation at Sunsail Clubs)
Low from £350
Mid from £440
High from £580

Discounts   Seasonal percentage reduction off adult price for children 2–12 years sharing room with parents in cot or Z-bed.

YACHTCLUB CHARTER COMPANY LTD
307 New Kings Road, London SW6 4RF
Tel: 071 731 0826

Crb   Gr   Tur

Variety of holidays for beginners and more experienced sailors alike, based at Bodrum and Gocek. Sail-yourself, skippered charter or crewed yachts with 6–12 berths, galley, shower and WC. Also Turkish 'gulets' for hire. Children and babies welcome.

Prices   (per adult per fortnight, in MAXI 84 yacht, including flight and transfers)
£348–£472 (4 people sharing)
£381–£592 (3 people sharing)

Skiing

Skiing must surely be one of the fastest growing markets for family holidays. While skiing's up-market image still exists in resorts such as Gstaad and St Moritz, a growing demand for winter holidays that don't break the bank has spawned many companies and many new resorts. In fact, fierce competition among tour operators has brought benefit to all skiers. This is reflected in the discounts offered to families.

Children aged 2–12 (some companies say 2–15) are eligible for all sorts of discounts, which are dependent on their sharing a room with two full-price adults. These discounts may be offered as a flat fee, a specific monetary reduction or a percentage discount. It really does pay to compare; some companies use the same accommodation but charge wildly different amounts.

Of course, the expense of a skiing holiday isn't just the travel and accommodation. You have to have equipment and ski passes, and to be honest, the proper (waterproof) clothing is a great advantage. It's not very comfortable skiing in wet jeans. If you don't want to splash out on clothing until you know that you're committed to skiing, it's possible to hire it from many ski shops.

But to get back to families – how can parents go on skiing holidays without taking it in turns to mind the children? It is both amazing and gratifying how many resorts offer excellent childminding facilities. Nurseries often take babies, some as young as one month, more often 6–9 months. They are staffed by qualified nurses or nannies who organize fun and games for toddlers, as well as supervising meals. Older children, usually from 3-12, may attend kindergarten, a play-group that also offers ski instruction for an hour or so a day. Babysitting may usually be arranged through the company representative or the local tourist office. All these childminding facilities are normally paid for at the resort, and the number of hours per day that they are available varies from 5–14. Some companies offer these services free and have their own English-speaking nannies.

A lot of people believe that starting children on the slippery slope is best done around the age of 3, and the consensus of opinion is that they love it. Skis come in all sizes and there are generous discounts on equipment hire and ski passes in virtually every resort. Do note, however, that some resorts do not supply separate instruction for children; they are expected to join adult groups. As far as we can see, the main drawback to this is that the children usually outshine the adults.

If the company you travel with offers children's ski schools organized in the resort, do make careful enquiries as to exactly what care they provide.

Prices
Unless otherwise stated 1990 prices have been quoted. These are intended only as a guide to the type of holiday offered and travellers should check with the company concerned for 1991 pricing details.

ACTIVITY TRAVEL
19 Castle Street, Edinburgh EH2 3AH
Tel: 031 225 9457 *or* 081 541 5115

Au   Fr   Swi   US

Ski holidays in 8 resorts with a choice of accommodation in hotels, chalets or self-catering studios and apartments. Chalets vary in size, sleeping from 6–28 people, and the company stresses that they also vary enormously in terms of location and facilities. Most are furnished functionally rather than luxuriously. Certain chalets are deemed particularly suitable for families, although no special provision is made for children. The same applies to self-catering accommodation. Nurseries for children aged up to 2 and kindergartens for 3–7s are available in all resorts.
Prices   Depending on location and date, one week costs from £249–£539 in a chalet, from £134–£336 in an apartment, and from £355–£647 in a hotel. All these prices include return travel. If you make your own travel arrangements, deduct about £80 from chalets and £60 from apartments and hotels.
Discounts   Free and half-price (1-week) holidays are available to one child under 14 per family on certain dates if they share parents' room. Child discounts are available. Cots and meals are payable locally.

ALPINE TOURS
16A High Street, Ashford, Kent
TN24 8JG
Tel: 0233 34382

Au

A medium-sized company offering both winter and summer skiing holidays in various high altitude resorts in Austria's Tirol. All-year skiing at the Stubai Glacier and Hintertux Glacier. The summer season runs from May to November. Accommodation varies from B+B pensions to hotels with half-board and self-catering apartments. A staffed kindergarten is available in Neustift and at the top station of the Stubai Glacial ski area. Special ski school for children including lunch with full supervision available. Most of the hotels offer hire of cots and high chairs together with special food for babies and small children.
Travel by air from Gatwick and Manchester to Innsbruck (also departures from regional airports), luxury coach or self-drive.
Prices   (per adult per week)
B+B in a pension: £229–£254
Half-board in a hotel: £274–£369
Apartment: £249–£349
For coach travel deduct £70 and self-drive £114 from the above air prices.
Discounts   Children under 2 travel at a nominal fee of £10 (no seat). Cots and

meals are payable locally. If sharing parents' room children aged 2–5 years 40%, 6–10 years 25% and 11–15 years 10%.

At the Stubai Glacial ski area children under 15 pay half price for liftpasses, while those under 10 are free if one parent purchases a lift pass.

BALKAN HOLIDAYS

Sofia House, 19 Conduit Street,
London W1R 9TD
Tel: 071 491 4499

Bul   Rom   Yug

Ski holidays in the resorts of Borovets and Pamporovo from December to April. Accommodation is in hotels, purpose-built wooden chalets or apartments. Ski instruction, equipment hire and passes are available at reduced rates if ordered when booking. A nursery in Borovets takes children from 4 months–4 years and is open from 9.00 a.m.–11.00 p.m. (Prices vary). Children's ski schools are available in both resorts and take children from 3–7 or 4–8 years.
Prices   (per adult per week, half board, including flight)
From £171
Discounts   Children under 2 travel free; cots and meals payable locally. 2–12s sharing parents' room receive a 25–50% discount, depending on location. In both resorts children receive substantial discounts on all excursions, and may sometimes be free.

BLADON LINES

56–58 Putney High Street, London SW15 1SF
Tel: 081 785 3131

Au   Fr   It   Swi

Ski holidays in many reputable resorts, including the quaintly-named Obergurgl. Accommodation is offered in various grades of hotel, pensions and self-catering apartments. The availability of crèches and kindergartens

varies from resort to resort, but many operate from around 9.30 a.m. to 4.00 p.m. In the evenings, the company representative can usually arrange a babysitter (payable locally) if given a few days' notice. Where available, cots may cost up to £30 per week. Small ski pack discounts are offered to children (usually under 14), and some resorts offer free ski passes to children under 6. Bladon also offers a free nursery-booking service.
Prices   (per week, including return flight)
Hotel in France: half-board in twin room with bath ranges from £300–£500 per adult. (A supplement is payable in high season.)
Pension in Austria: B+B in a twin room ranges from £245–£300 per adult. (A supplement is payable in high season.)
Chalet: £198–£500
Self-catering apartment in Meribel: £154–£300, depending on date and number of occupants.
Train or self-drive travel come cheaper.
Discounts   Hotel and pension: Bladon will quote children's discounts on request. Chalet: Children under 2 pay £30 per week, provided they share parents' room and do not occupy a seat on the plane; 2–6s receive a discount of £10 per week, and 7–12s receive £5 per week.

ENFANTS CORDIALES

Beach House, 8 Barnfield Wood Road,
Beckenham, Kent BR3 2SR
Tel: 081 658 6541

Fr

A company recommended by the Ski Club of Great Britain for its experience in dealing with children. Holidays are based in the resort of Megève, which offers easy access to slopes for all skiing abilities. The resort also offers a 'palais des sports' with a wide variety of activities, including a children's pool. Accommodation is in catered chalets. A free baby-sitting/childminding service for children aged 3 months and over is

available every day until 1.00 p.m. An hourly charge is made for any additional time. Outings and activities are organized for older children. Children's meals are served when required in order to keep up your normal routine. Facilities for children include cots, high chairs, potties, changing mats, linen, duvets, baby baths, mugs, feeding bowls, videos and games.
Prices (per week, including flight)
Adults: £260–£450
Children: £210–£337 (own room)
Children: £160–£262 (sharing parents' room)
Children under 2 pay £60 for the flight, food and accommodation, which includes cot and bedding.
Discounts Children under 13 are eligible for prices specified above. They may also receive discounts on equipment hire and ski passes.

ENTERPRISE
(see **Hotels**)
Tel: 0293 517733

And Au Bul Fr It Rom Swi Yug

Ski holidays in 82 resorts. Accommodation is either in self-catering apartments or hotels, with travel by train, air or self-drive. Facilities vary, but most resorts have a children's ski school and a kindergarten, although the minimum age varies. There are special prices for children's lift passes and equipment hire. Cots must be booked in advance and are either free or cost up to £5 per day.
Prices (per adult per week, including flight and transfers)
Self-catering apartment for 4 in Arinsal: £125–£217
Half board in a hotel in Kitzbuhel: £219–£299
Discounts Under-2s travel for £15 (no seat). Two children aged 2–11 sharing a room or apartment with two full fare-

paying adults qualify for discounts. The first child receives 15–50% (60% on 2-week holidays), and the second child receives 10–40%, depending on season.

HORIZON HOLIDAYS
(*see* **Hotels**)

Au Fr Swi

Ski holidays in 24 resorts with accommodation in hotels, pensions and apartments. Creches are available in some resorts, and nurseries and kindergartens are available in most resorts for children over 2. 'Beginners' Weeks' for those new to skiing include equipment hire, lift passes and ski school with English speaking instructors.
Prices available on request
Discounts Child reductions for first and second children sharing with 2 adults. Up to 60% for first child and up to 40% for second.

INGHAMS TRAVEL
10–18 Putney Hill, London SW15 6AX
Tel: 081 785 7777

Au Bul Fr It Rom Swi US

Ski holidays with choice of travel by air, rail or self-drive, and accommodation in hotels or self-catering apartments. Cots may be hired. Children's ski schools and kindergartens are available in most resorts, but the age range accepted varies.
Prices (per adult per week, half board)
From £61 (self-drive)
From £146 (by air)
Discounts Under-2s travel free on charter flights (no seat), and pay £12 on scheduled flights; cots and meals payable locally. Children aged 2–11 (maximum of 2 per 2 adults) receive a discount of 10–30% each. No discounts on self-catering holidays. Various discounts available on children's ski packs.

INTASUN SKISCENE
(*see* **Fly/drive**)
Tel: 0274 736403 *(Bradford)* or
021 454 6677 *(Birmingham)*,
041 332 4466 *(Glasgow)*,
0232 320340 *(Belfast)*

And Au Fr It Rom Sp Swi US

Large company offering ski holidays with travel by coach/ferry, train and air. Accommodation is in hotels and self-catering apartments. Nurseries and ski schools are available for babies and children in most resorts, but the minimum ages vary. Ski hire, tuition, lift passes and ski passes are extra.
Prices (per adult per week, including return flight and transfers)
Starting prices for a self-catering apartment are:
Low £144
Mid £187
High £237
Starting prices for half-board in a hotel are:
Low £187
Mid £219
High £248
Discounts Children under 2 travel free, except on long-haul flights. Children receive a £10–£15 discount on apartment holidays, and £15–£50 on hotel holidays when sharing a room with two adults. All children receive discounts on ski hire, tuition, lift passes and ski passes.

INTERHOME
383 Richmond Road, Twickenham, Middx
Tel: 081 891 1294

Au Bel Can.Is Fr Ger Gr Hol It Swi Por Yug

Ski holidays in a wide variety of resorts. No travel is included but ferry arrangements can be made on request. Accommodation is in apartments and hotels. Childminding and children's ski schools are available in some resorts, but the company takes no responsibility for this and their availability should be checked with the tourist office for the relevant country. Arrangements for cot hire can 'possibly' be made – ask when booking.
Prices (per 4-person apartment in Switzerland)
£115–£400 (late January)
Discounts On hotel holidays children aged 3–12 receive 50% discount if sharing parents' room. On short ferry crossings under-3s travel free; 3–13s pay £25 each. No child discounts on self-catering accommodation.

MADE TO MEASURE HOLIDAYS
(*see* **Sailing**)
Tel: 0243 533333

Au Fr Nor Swi US

This company offers a wide range of flights, ferries, hotels and self-catering apartments, so you can make up your package to suit your needs. The brochure gives quite detailed descriptions of all properties (all personally researched) with star ratings for après ski provision. Some 'Happy Family Swiss Hotels' have facilities which include free care of children aged 3 upwards (younger children by arrangement), a playroom, cooking facilities for the preparation of baby food, children's meals, early suppers, high chairs and cots at no extra charge. Kindergartens and nurseries are available at all destinations, with one resort taking babies as young as 6 weeks. A special children's brochure detailing all the relevant facilities cross-references with the main ski brochures so that parents can tell at a glance which resorts and hotels are most suitable.
Prices On application
Discounts Under-2s usually pay 10% of the air fare; cots and meals are payable locally. Discounts for children aged 2–12 vary greatly from hotel to hotel, so the company will make a specific quote on your selection.

NEILSON SKI
Arndale House, Otley Road,
Headingley, Leeds LS6 2UU
Tel: 0532 744422

Au Can Fr It Nor Swi Yug
US

This company prides itself on well-organized ski tuition, but other activities, such as walking, skating and tobogganing are also available. Accommodation is offered in hotels and self-catering apartments and the brochure describes the provision for children at each resort. A 'Neilsonettes' baby patrol is offered in some hotels, and certain resorts organize free children's parties. 'Garderies' for children aged 3 months–3 years operate in many resorts, and ski kindergartens or local childminders are organized for older children. These services vary in cost and are not included in the holiday price.
Prices   (per adult per week, including return travel)
Half-board in a hotel in Italy: £219–£759
Self-catering apartment in France: £89–259
Ski hire, tuition and lift passes are all extra.
Discounts   Under-2s travel free (no seat on plane); they are not allowed to travel by coach. Cots and food are payable locally. Children aged 2–11 who share a room with two full fare-paying adults receive 10–50% discount. This applies to the youngest child in each party. Second and successive children receive 10% discount regardless of room arrangements. Free children's places are available on certain dates.

SCOTTISH SKIING
Hi-Line, Dingwall, Ross-shire IV15 9JE
Tel: 0349 65000

UK (Scotland)

Ski holidays in a wide choice of resorts in the Cairngorms, Glenshee, Aonach Mor, the Lecht and Glencoe. Travel can be arranged by air, coach or self-drive

and you have a choice of hotels, guest houses and a variety of self-catering accommodation. Children's ski classes are normally available for 7s upwards, but younger ones can be included by special arrangement. A crèche for 2–8s is available at the Lecht, offering trained nannies, play areas and organized activities.
Prices   (per adult, 5 nights mid-week)
Cairngorm: £85–£250 (hotel, half board)
The Lecht: £80–£180 (hotel, half board)
Discounts   These are available for under-18s in Cairngorm and under-16s at Glenshee and the Lecht. Specific quotations are given on request.

SKI CHAMOIS
18 Lawn Road, Doncaster, S.Yorks
DN1 2JF
Tel: 0302 369006

Fr

Ski holidays in 5 resorts, with a choice of hotel, 2 jumbo chalets or self-catering accommodation. Travel options include plane, sleeper-coach and self-drive.
Prices   (per adult for 10 days)
Self-catering apartment in Courchevel: £109–£199 (seasonal supplement payable).
Catered chalet Courchevel Morzine: £129–£319
Discounts   All under-2s are free and all children under 13 qualify for discounts. The first child receives a 10% discount on all dates. A second child may receive a free holiday on certain low-season dates, provided 2 adults and a first child pay the full brochure price. At other times a second child receives 10–50% discount. Early booking discounts are also available.

SKI ESPRIT
Austen House, Upper Street, Fleet,
Hants GU13 9PE
Tel: 0252 625175

Fr Swi

Small tour operator specializing in family skiing holidays. Choice of 20 chalets in eight resorts in the north-western alps. Facilities include full day crèches, free baby-sitting, supervised lunches for older children at ski school. Cots are free for children under 2. Travel by air, car or independently.

Prices (per adult per week, half board)
Low: £228
Mid: £368
High: £438

Discounts 33% off one in five adults. Children's discounts: all children under two, £38; Xmas and New Year, children (2–15) 60% off; Jan. and Apr. departure, children (2–15) 50% off; Feb. and Mar. deps, discounts between 30%–15%.

SKI FALCON
(*see* FALCON FAMILY HOLIDAYS –
Hotels)
Tel: 071 757 5400 *or* 061 831 7000
(Manchester), 041 248 6008 *(Glasgow)*

And Au Bul Fr It US

Ski holidays with choice of travel by air, train or self-drive (accommodation only). Accommodation is in 2- to 4-star hotels, pensions and apartments. 5 resorts in Austria and France; 2 resorts in Andorra; 3 resorts in Bulgaria, Italy and Colorado. Bulgaria and France are particularly recommended for children.

Prices (per week half board in Bulgaria for a family of 4)
£681.50 (including insurance)
Ski packs cost £85 per adult and £58 per child, and include ski and boot hire, lift passes and 4 hours' tuition per day.

Discounts Under-2s are charged £15. Children aged 2–12 receive up to 50% discount on some properties.

SKI RED GUIDE HOLIDAYS
18–20 Clifton Street, Blackpool, Lancs
FY1 1JP
Tel: 0253 23939

Fr Sco

Ski holidays with choice of travel by coach, plane or self-drive. Accommodation is in chalets, hotels and apartments and you may choose bed and breakfast, half board, full board or self-catering in some locations. Kindergartens are specified in all resorts (except Scotland) and offer skiing tuition for children aged 4–8 on 5 afternoons a week. Babysitting can be arranged with chalet staff, payable locally. Picnics are arranged one day a week, weather permitting.

Prices (per adult per week, half board)
Meribel, chalet: £179–£289
Flaine, hotel: £215–£309
Cairngorms, hotel (weekend): £49–56

Discounts Under 2's travel free on coach, but pay a nominal sum for flight; cots and meals payable locally. Children aged 2 or 3–11 who share a room with two adults receive various discounts depending on accommodation and date from between 5%–30% with a limited number of free places. Substantial reductions are available for children on equipment hire and ski passes in some resorts. A 5% early booking discount is also available.

SKI SUPERTRAVEL
22 Hans Place, London SW1X 0EP
Tel: 071 589 5060

Au Fr Swi US

Ski holidays with accommodation in hotels, chalets and a variety of hotels. Childminding is available in certain resorts, but the minimum age varies. Where available, cots in chalets are free, but hotels usually charge and the cost is payable locally.

Prices   (per adult per week)
Chalets: from £324 (low), from £394 (mid), from £529 (high)
Hotels: from £529 (low), from £554 (mid), from £604 (high)
Discounts   On chalet holidays, children under 2 pay £21 (cots and meals payable locally). Discounts for 2–15s vary, depending on departure date and whether they have a main bed or an extra bed. They may pay a flat fee from £199 depending on season, or receive a reduction of £20. On hotel holidays under-12s receive a 25% discount if they share parents' room. Substantial discounts available on ski passes.

SKI THOMSON
(see **Hotels***)*
Tel:081 200 8733 *(London)*; 021 632 6282 *(Birmingham)*; 061 236 3828 *(Manchester)*

And   Au   Fr   It   Sp   Swi   Yug
    US

Ski holidays with travel by air or self-drive. Accommodation is in hotels, chalets and self-catering apartments, but children under 17 are not allowed on chalet holidays unless you book the whole chalet for your party's exclusive use. Cots and children's meals are available in most resorts. Kindergartens and ski schools are available at most resorts. The minimum age varies, but some do take young babies. New for 1990/91, Ski Thomson Children's Clubs are available at St Johann in Tyrol, Austria and Risoul in the French Alps. In this free service for non-skiing 3–8 year olds, children are looked after by a specially trained Ski Thomson children's rep.
Prices   (per adult per week, including return flight and transfers)
Self-catering apartment from £111
Half board in hotel accommodation from £149

Discounts   On air holidays under-2s pay £15 (no seat); cots and meals are hirable locally. Children aged 2–11 receive a 10–55% discount, depending on departure date. Substantial discounts on ski passes and equipment hire are available in most resorts.

SKI-VAL LTD
91 Wembley Park Drive, Wembley Park, Middx HA9 8HF
Tel: 081 903 4444 *or* 081 903 0888

Fr   US

Ski holidays in Val-d'Isere and Colorado, with travel by air, coach/ferry or self-drive. Accommodation is in hotels, clubs, chalets and apartments. Nurseries, kindergartens, children's ski schools and clubs are available in some resorts, and baby-sitting can usually be arranged with chalet staff on request.
Prices   (per adult per week, including coach travel outwards, flight return)
Club chalet: from £195
Discounts   On family breaks children under 17 receive 10% discount in addition to child reductions as follows: 7–10s receive £10 per week discount and 11–14s receive £5. Children under 2 pay £20, which includes cot hire; meals are payable locally. 2–7s sharing a room with 2 adults pay £20 plus the cost of a plane or coach seat. No reductions available for children in hotels or self-catering accommodation.

SKI WEST
1 Belmont, Lansdown Road, Bath BA1 5DZ
Tel: 0225 444516

Au   Fr   It   Swi

Ski holidays in a wide variety of resorts, with choice of travel by charter flight, coach/ferry, self-drive or fly/drive. Accommodation is in chalet parties, hotels and pensions, and self-catering flats. Cots may be hired and cost

£10–£40 per week. Nurseries and baby-sitting facilities are available in most resorts.
Prices (per adult per week, half board, including flight)
France, chalet hotel: £374
This price applies at Christmas and is typical of the mid-range offered by this company.
Discounts Children under 2 travel free on flights, but pay airport tax. They must pay full fare on coach travel. No charge for under-2s' accommodation, but cots and meals are payable locally. In chalets under-18s may receive up to 50% discount if accompanied by one full fare-paying adult. Hotels usually offer 15–20% discount for 2–12s. No discounts available on self-catering flats.

SKI WHIZZ LTD
Hillgate House, 13 Hillgate Street, London W8 7SP
Tel: 071 221 1121

Aus   Fr   It   Swi   US

This company is an affiliated member of the Ski Club of Great Britain. It offers holidays in 16 resorts and a choice of accommodation in chalets (sleeping 6–25), a ski lodge (sleeping 80) and crèche chalets (with childminding service). Travel can be arranged by air, self-drive or train.
Prices (per person per week in catered chalet including flight and transfers)
£350 (mid season)
Discounts 1 free holiday for every 10 booked. Group discounts available on groups larger than 6 of between £10 and £12 per person. Child discounts – details on request.

SKIWORLD
Skiworld House, 39a–41 North End Road, London W14 8SZ
Tel: 071 602 4826

And   Au   Fr   It

Ski holidays with accommodation in hotels, pensions, chalets and self-catering apartments and travel by air, train, coach/ferry and self-drive. Certain resorts are particularly geared to children, with kindergartens and crèches where English is spoken, and baby-sitting can be arranged. Cots are available in all resorts. Children's clubs and ski schools with English-speaking instructors are also available. Baby-sitting can be arranged.
Prices (per adult per week, including travel)
Self-catering apartment in Autrans, France: £135–£249
Hotel with half board: £299 (by air)
Discounts Children under 2 are free. Generally hotels and self-catering apartments do not have large discounts for children unless they are specifically trying to attract them. Half price insurance for children aged 2–15.

SUNMED
(*see* **Hotels**)
c/o Redwing, Groundstar House, London Road, Crawley RH10 2TB
Tel: 0293 519151

Fr   It

At certain hotels pre-bookable childcare for children aged between 18 months and 8 years with 'Aunty Snowflake' service. The Clubs are open 6 days a week (Sunday to Friday). Cots are available in most accommodation and the charge for this, and infant food, is payable locally.
Prices available on request
Child discounts Infants under two years of age on the date of their return flight pay only £15 provided they sit on

an adult's lap during the flight and transfer, unless a seat is available. Up to 60% off for children aged between 2 and 16.

SUPERTRAVEL LTD
22 Hans Place, London SW1X OEP
Tel: 071 584 5060

Au   Can   Fr   Swi   US

Ski holidays with accommodation in hotels, chalets, luxury mountain lodges and a tailor-made ski holiday department. Where available, cots in chalets are free, but hotels usually charge, with the cost payable locally.
Prices   (per adult per week)
Chalets: £229 (low), £309 (mid), £449 (high)
Hotels: £389 (low), £494 (mid), £629 (high)
Mountain Lodges: £579 (low), £759 (mid), £859 (high)
Discounts   On chalet holidays children under 2 pay £21 (meals payable locally). Discounts for the 2–10s and the 11–15s vary, depending upon departure date, but are generally between 35–60%.
On hotel holidays under 12s receive a 25% discount if they share a room with parents. No discounts on mountain lodges. A La Carte holidays are subject to individual costings and any children's discount will be offered wherever possible. Substantial discounts available on lift passes in those resorts offering family passes.

SWISS SKI
Swiss Travel Service, Bridge House, Ware, Herts SG12 9DE
Tel: 0920 463971

Swi

Ski holidays in hotels or self-catering studios, with the option of air travel or self-drive. Some hotels classified as 'Ideal for Family' have extensive reductions and special facilities, such as a free kindergarten. However, virtually all resorts have a supervised kindergarten, but none appears to take children under 2 years.
Prices   (per adult per week, half board, including flight and transfers)
3-star hotel: from £306
4-star hotel: from £420
5-star hotel: from £500
Discounts   On air holidays, under-2s travel free (no seat); cots and meals are payable locally. Children aged 2–11 receive a 50% discount all season, provided they share parents' room. When not sharing there is a £70 discount per child. Children aged 12–15 each receive a £25 discount. On self-drive holidays the discounts for children under 12 are as above, but those occupying their own room receive no reduction. Substantial discounts are available for children on ski passes and equipment hire.

WINTERWORLD
8 Deanwood House, Stockcross, Newbury, Berkshire RG16 8JP
Tel: 0653 30621/35434

Swi

Family skiing holidays in Villars, Switzerland. Fly/drive or self-drive, with accommodation in catered or self-catered chalets or luxury hotel. Company minibus service in and around Villars. In catered chalets childminding is provided for children under 5 on alternate days from 10am–4pm. Additional hours can be arranged at local prices. A daytime kindergarten is available for children up to the age of 10, costing approximately 70sf per day. Cots can be rented at approximately £10 per week.
Prices   (per adult per week, including flight and transfer)
Self-catering: £209 (low), £239 (mid), £295 (high)
Catered chalet: £259 (low), £329 (mid), £399 (high)
Hotel: £389 (low), £475 (mid), £475 (high)
Discounts   Children under 2 sleeping in parents' room pay £50 per week in a

catered chalet. This includes cot, linen and food (but not special baby food). On self-catered holidays children under 2 pay £20 per week. In both cases infants do not have a seat on the plane, nor a baggage allowance. Children 2–12 years, staying parents' room, get £75 off brochure price, £20 off if in own room.

Special Interest and Activity Holidays

Whether you're a steam train enthusiast, aspiring circus performer, devoted horse-rider or musician, you'll find your special-interest holiday to suit your likes. If an activity holiday is up your street, we list many centres offering a wide variety of physical and cerebral pursuits. You don't have to be a hearty, outdoor type to enjoy one of these holidays, and if you prefer not to participate at all, you're at liberty to do so.

For families who dislike beach holidays and have a sense of adventure, activity holidays are ideal. But what if your children are mad about archery and badminton, while you're keen on photography and abseiling? No problem. Most centres have flexible arrangements to cater for different interests within a family and can create a holiday to encompass all your special interests. And if you have no special interests and don't know what you might like, you can opt for a multi-activity holiday which gives you a taste of everything on offer. Most activities are graded for difficulty, and qualified instructors are always in attendance.

It's worth noting that some centres operate all year round and employ permanent, qualified staff. Others simply take over a school for a couple of weeks during the summer, so the choice of dates is limited, even if the activities aren't.

Children are often not allowed to participate in adult activities, such as rafting or hiking, but the minimum age tends to vary from centre to centre. Around 10 is the general rule, but special programmes are available for children aged 6 upwards. Children under 6 are often allowed on site but facilities vary. Usually they are accepted on the understanding that parents take full responsibility for them.

Prices
Unless otherwise stated 1990 prices have been quoted. These are intended only as a guide to the type of holiday offered and travellers should check with the company concerned for 1991 pricing details.

BEARSPORTS OUTDOOR CENTRES

Windy Gyles, Belford, Northumberland
NE70 7QE
Tel: 0668 213289

UK (Northumberland)

Activity holidays close to the Scottish border. Programmes can be quite strenuous and include rock climbing, canoeing and cross country walking. Children under 5 are not allowed to participate, but are welcome at the centre (no crèche facilities). Accommodation is in twin rooms which have hot and cold running water, but shared showers and WCs. The programmes last a weekend, 5 days or 7 days.

Prices (including full board, instruction and use of equipment)
Residential courses: weekend £45, 5 days £95, 7 days £135.
Use of centre only (per day): £13.50 (full board), £8 (B+B).

Discounts Babies free; 50% off for under-9s accompanied by both parents.

COUNTRYWIDE HOLIDAYS

The Countrywide Holidays Association, Birch Heys, Cromwell Range, Manchester M14 6HU
Tel: 061 225 1000

UK (Cornwall, Cumbria, Derbyshire, Gwynedd, Hampshire, Isle of Wight, Norfolk, Perthshire, Somerset, Yorkshire)

Activity holidays for children of 6 and over based in the same centre as their parents. Adventure weeks, Family fortnights, Multi-action holidays, Youngsters' Fun weeks, include such activities as sailing, canoeing, rock climbing, orienteering, archery, abseiling, underground exploration, gorge walking and many others under the supervision of professional guides and instructors. Play leaders organize games in the evening. Some centres have videos and games rooms. There are no crèche facilities for very young children, but cots are provided free of charge and

bottles can be warmed up. Accommodation with full board is in a series of guest houses, including a castle, an Elizabethan manor and many mansions in beautiful grounds.

Prices (per adult)
From £80–£299, depending on centre and holiday chosen.

Discounts Children under 2 sharing parent's room are free. Non-participating children staying in the centre and sharing a room with each other pay 25% if aged 2–6, 50% if aged 7–13 and 75% if aged 14–17.

Adults booking 2 consecutive weeks receive a discount of £20 each off the cost of the second week.

Non-participating families staying in the centre receive a discount of £10 (1 or 2 adults and 1 child) or £20 (2 adults and 2 children).

COURTLANDS CENTRE

Kingsbridge, South Devon TQ7 4BN
Tel: 0548 550227

UK (South Devon)

Activity holidays in a converted manor farm set in 4 acres close to the sea and Dartmoor. Accommodation is in dormitories and twin-bedded rooms. One wing of the house can be rented weekly on a self-catering basis and is ideal for families. A separate bathroom for adults only is available with dormitory accommodation; children use communal showers and washrooms. The price includes 3 meals a day, special equipment for certain sports and evening entertainments, such as discos, games, videos and barbecues. Children must bring sleeping bags and pillow cases; adults are supplied with linen, blankets and duvets. Activities include canoeing, sailing, riding, surfing, waterskiing, archery, orienteering, assault course, hikes, climbing, abseiling, sea fishing and yacht cruising. All cater for different abilities. Children aged 6–8 may participate in young children's adventure holidays. Unaccompanied holidays (Adventure Run) are open to anyone aged 9 years upwards. You can opt for one activity or a multi-activity programme, and the centre will try to accommodate differing interests within families if you give prior notice when booking. Adults pay only for accommodation if they choose not to participate. An indoor sports hall is available for evenings or use in foul weather.

Prices   Multi-adventure holidays start from £208 per week.

Discounts   Children under 6 are charged by arrangement. Small children sleeping in a cot and sharing their parents' room go free.

INSIDE TRACK
1 Castle Street, Berkhamsted, Herts HP4 2BQ
Tel: 0442 866957

Hol   UK

Seventeen different holidays in picturesque areas where there are preserved railway lines. Travel by steam train, with optional excursions by bus. Half board accommodation is in first-class and family-run hotels. Cots may be available; ask when booking.

Prices   (per adult)
Devon (4 days): £169–£179
Scotland (7 days): £375–£395

Discounts   Nominal charge for under-4s. Children aged 4–14, sharing with parents, pay approximately half adult price. Children's discounts are available on British Rail fare to departure point – usually of around 60%; under 3s travel free.

LAKELAND EXPERIENCE HOLIDAYS
Green Lodge, Eskdale Green, Eskdale, Cumbria
Tel: 09403 382

UK (Lake District)

Guided or instructed activities include abseiling, rock climbing and canoeing. Daily, weekend or week-long programmes. Full board accommodation in

good hotels or guest houses. Instruction and use of equipment included in price. Small children are welcome to join in activities; baby facilities might be arranged on request.

Prices   (per adult)
One night £50, weekend £115, one week £250; £110 per week/£20 per day if organizing own accommodation.

Discounts   Children get a 10% reduction.

LANCASTER UNIVERSITY SUMMER PROGRAMME
Summer Programme Office, University of Lancaster, Cartmel College, Lancaster LA1 4YL
Tel: 0524 382118

UK (Lancashire)

One-week programmes involving sports, outdoor activities, arts, crafts and study courses. Accommodation on campus. Children aged 5–17 are fully catered for, with own courses and social programme. Free access to sports facilities and social events. Dates 1991: July 21–August 10.

Prices   (including full board and tuition fees)
Adults: £170–£300 (depending on courses taken)
14–17 year-olds: £160–£185
5–13 year-olds: £145–£165

Discounts   £35 off adult price for 2-week stay. Discounts on request for groups of 10 or more.

MILL ON THE BRUE
Trendle Farm, Bruton, Somerset BA10 0BA
Tel: 0749 813589/812307

UK (Somerset)

Family adventure holidays, including archery, assault course, canoeing, ropes course, grass skiing, problem solving activities, climbing wall, abseil tower and rifle shooting. All activities are suitable for children over 8. Family

rooms sleep 2–8 people. Sheets and pillowcases provided but bring your own sleeping bag or duvet.
Prices (per person per day)
Activities: £15
Accommodation: £15
Alternative bed and breakfast accommodation can be arranged.

MILLFIELD VILLAGE OF EDUCATION
Millfield School, Street, Somerset
Tel: 0458 45823

UK (Somerset)

Five-day activity holidays from late July to late August. Choice of 113 different courses, including sports, arts, crafts and academic studies. Children of all ages are welcomed. Free crèche and babysitting facilities. Children over 8 may stay unaccompanied. Accommodation is in the school's boarding houses (room with shared bathroom). Children under 10 share parents' room; older children share together.
Prices (per 5 days' full board)
Adults: approx. £108 (depending on number of courses taken)
Accompanied children: £98 (under 12) or £88 (under 8)
Unaccompanied children: £108
Tuition fees are £51 per course (swimming £13 upwards).
Discounts Early booking discount of 10% for previous applicants.

NATURIST HOLIDAYS
Peng Travel Ltd, 86 Station Road, Gidea Park, Essex RM2 6DB
Tel: 04024 71832

Crb Fr Gr Sp US Yug

Nudist holidays in many locations, including Corsica and Florida. Accommodation is situated in nudist villages or nudist areas and campsites in studios, villas, hotels, apartments and bungalows. Naturist cruises are also available in Yugoslavia and Turkey, but do not take children under 16.

Prices (per family of 4 per fortnight, camping, tent provided)
France, self-drive, including ferry: £436 plus insurance.
Discounts Children under 2 pay £15 on air holidays; cot hire and meals payable locally. Under-4s are free on self-drive holidays. On other holidays children up to 17 are eligible for various discounts, quoted on request.

NORTHUMBRIA HORSE HOLIDAYS
East Castle, Annfield Plain, Stanley, Co. Durham
Tel: 0207 235354/230555

UK (N.E. England, Norfolk)

Europe's largest equestrian holiday company catering for all ages, from complete beginners to seasoned riders. Holidays last 7 and 14 days and may be based in one place from which you ride out and back daily, or you can go post trail riding, following a progressive route across country and stopping somewhere different every night. Horse-drawn caravan holidays are available in Norfolk. Accommodation is full board in comfortable twin-bedded rooms in licensed premises. There are no age restrictions, but young children must be accompanied and attended to by parents.
Prices (per adult per week, full board)
A 'learn to ride' holiday ranges from £169.
A post trail riding holiday ranges from £239.
Discounts Children up to 14 receive a 10% discount if they share a room with 2 adults.

PGL FAMILY ADVENTURE
Hilton Court, Penyard Lane, Ross-on-Wye HR9 5NR
Tel: 0989 768768

Aus Fr Hol Ire UK

Family activity holidays at over a dozen different centres. Accommodation is in hotels, colleges and schools with single/twin/family rooms and dormitories, university apartments, caravan leisure homes or luxury bungalow tents, depending on location. All self-catering accommodation is fully equipped. A few non-residential places are available for families who bring their own caravans and stay in the sites nearby. Activities include sailing, archery, tennis, climbing, swimming, fencing, riding, canoeing, windsurfing, skiing, cycling, squash, arts and crafts. Single or multiple activity holidays can be arranged. At catered centres the minimum age is 7, but there are 2 where the minimum age is 4. A Babar Playscheme is available for 4–6s at these 2 centres. There are no age restrictions on self-catering holidays. Minimum ages apply to certain activities.

Prices   At a centre in Wales, which has the Babar Playscheme, one week's full board, including activities, costs from £199 per person.

Discounts   The general rule is that children of participating age pay the same as adults. Travel discounts may be available to them at centres abroad. Children aged 4–6 who participate in the Babar Playscheme are entitled to about 45% discount.

TAUNTON SUMMER SCHOOL

Taunton School, Taunton, Somerset
TA2 6AD
Tel: 0823 276543

UK (Somerset)

One-week activity programmes between mid-July and early August. Courses include arts and crafts, studies, games, sports and local tours. Accommodation is in double or family rooms in school boarding-houses. Children may sleep in dormitories, if preferred. Courses for all ages from 7 to 70 plus. There is no crèche and cots are not provided.

Prices   One week's accommodation in a family room (3–4 beds), including tuition, basic materials and evening activities costs £165 per person.

Discounts   For families and small groups.

VARMLAND HOLIDAYS

c/o Holiday Scandinavia Ltd. (*see* *Cottages*)

Swe

The company called Holiday Scandinavia acts as an agent for holidays offered by the Värmland Tourist Board — a beautiful area between Sweden and Norway around Lake Vänern. Accommodation is available in cottages, chalets and hotels and a wide variety of activities is available: survival courses, riding, prairie wagon trails, mineral hunting, fishing, walking, skiing, cycling, rafting, elk and beaver safaris and even cycle trolley riding along disused railways.

Prices   The 'Family Dream Holiday', which offers a variety of adventurous activities costs 3275 Kroner for a family of 2 adults and 2 children in a 4-bed apartment.

VFB HOLIDAYS

Normany House, High Street,
Cheltenham GL50 3HW
Tel: 0242 235515
(*see* **Cottages**)

Fr

Alp Activ activity holidays in the French Alps in July and August, self-catering or family-run hotels: tennis, horseriding, swimming, archery, mountain biking, ice-skating, grass-skiing, climbing, mountain walking among others.

Prices   (per person for 14 nights in small apartment, including car ferry and insurance)

Low from £207
High from £229
Discounts Reductions from 5% to 40%
in hotels, and even more substantial reductions in apartments.

YMCA NATIONAL CENTRE
Lakeside, Ulverston, Cumbria
LA12 8BD
Tel: 05395 31758

UK (Lake District)

Week-long programmes in July and
August. Activities include rock-climbing, archery, crafts and local visits.

Accommodation is in either twin rooms
with own facilities, 2–4 bed rooms with
shared facilities, or chalets with separate facilities. A daytime playscheme is
provided for 4–6 year-olds, but no
crèche or cots.
Prices (per adult, including all activities and excluding VAT)
One week: Twin room £165, 2–4 bed
room £140, chalet £140
Discounts Under-6s receive discounts
of £6 (weekend) and £25 (one week);
6–11s receive discounts of £5 (weekend)
and £12 (one week)

Villas & Apartments

For many people self-catering accommodation in the form of villas and apartments is the solution to taking a family holiday. You have privacy, comfort and all mod cons, but are rarely far from shops and restaurants, so you can self-cater as much or as little as you like.

What constitutes a villa? Usually they are detached properties standing in their own grounds, but increasingly they may be terraced properties in purpose-built 'villages'. The standard of furnishing and equipment varies, but at the very least it is reasonably comfortable. If the properties are privately owned, as many are, the surroundings can be quite luxurious – but so can the price. If, for example, you'd like to rent Rex Harrison's villa in the south of France, you'll have to pay more than a small fortune!

The accommodation on apartment holidays is equally variable, ranging from multi-storey blocks to maisonettes in historic châteaux. Most claim to be reasonably comfortable and to supply enough facilities to cook a meal. However, from reports we have received, it is evident that some companies may provide facilities that are less than ideal.

If you want a place with character you might have to forgo your own private balcony and the use of a swimming pool, but there may be bonuses in the shape of local farmhouse produce and perhaps a landlady willing to baby-sit. On the other hand several large villa companies have representatives who can organize baby-sitting for you. Always enquire before booking about the availability (and cost!) of cots, bunk beds, high chairs, playpens and so on. You may be pleasantly surprised by how much companies offer for families.

Prices

Unless otherwise stated 1990 prices have been quoted. These are intended only as a guide to the type of holiday offered and travellers should check with the company concerned for 1991 pricing details.

AUTO PLAN HOLIDAYS LTD
Energy House, Lombard Street,
Lichfield, Staffs WS13 6DP
Tel: 0543 257777

Au Den Fr Ger It Nor Swi

Self-drive holidays with accommodation in apartments, villas, chalets,
bungalows and small hotels. All self-
catering accommodation is fully
equipped, but no linen is supplied. On
travel-inclusive holidays the prices include ferries, 2 hotel stops en route, AA
5-star insurance and your
accommodation.
Prices (per adult per week)
A travel-inclusive holiday in a self-
catering chalet is from £164 (low), £206
(high).
Discounts On inclusive holidays,
when minimum occupancy has been
paid, children under 4 go free. In other
circumstances under-4s receive £15 discount and 4–13s receive £10 discount.
On hotel holidays under-4s go free;
4–13s who share parents' room receive
15% discount for first child and 10%
discount for second child. No child discounts on villa rental only.

BEACH VILLAS
8 Market Passage, Cambridge CB2 3QR
Tel: 0223 311113

Bar Ber Crb Cors Cyp Fr Gr
It Por Sar Sp Tur US Yug

Villas for rent in many mainland and
island locations, including Antigua and
Elba. All accommodation is fully furnished and equipped, including linen.
At some locations maid service is available. Car hire discounts are offered with
local companies if booked in advance.
Cot hire is £12 per week.
Prices (per person per week, including flight)
Costa Blanca, self-catering family 'unit'
for 4: £169–£250
Discounts Children under 2 travel for
£15. A minimum discount of £35 applies
at all times for 2–11s, but on specified

dates they may receive £35–£80 discount. Those aged 12–15 receive £15
discount at all times, except in July and
August.

BLAKES VILLAS
Wroxham, Norwich, Norfolk NR12 8DH
Tel: 0603 784141

Fr It Sp

Self-catering holidays with many
properties ranging from luxurious
accommodation with pools to holiday
villages and simple country gîtes. All
accommodation is fully furnished and
equipped, except for linen and towels.
In Italy, linen and towels are included. In
Spain, they are either included or available at extra cost. Each villa is listed
with a photograph, usually a floor plan,
description of the rooms and kitchen
(many with dishwasher and washing
machine), a list of local amenities and
the level of comfort to be expected.
Prices (per property per week, including short Channel crossing for car and 2
adults)
Low: £195–£1895
High: £325–£2260

BRIDGEWAY TRAVEL SERVICES LTD
Algarve Select Emerson House, Heyes
Lane, Alderley Edge, Cheshire SK9 7LF
Tel: 0625 585196

Por

Small company offering 1–3 bedroom
beach-front apartments on the Algarve,
ranging from comfortable to luxurious.
Daily maid service, linen, towels, sun
beds and starter food pack included.
Cots and cot linen/blankets provided at
no charge. Baby-sitting available.
Prices (per person per week)
1-bedroom apartment for 2–4 people:
from £234 to £367, depending on number sharing.
2-bedroom apartment for 3–5 sharing:
from £224 to £426.

3-bedroom apartment for 5–7 sharing: from £224 to £426.
Children over 2 count towards the total occupancy of the property.
Discounts   Under-2s pay £15 (no seat on plane); 2–14s receive 10–50% discount, depending on season.

BRITTANY VILLAS
2 Monson Road, Tunbridge Wells, Kent TN1 1RU
Tel: 0892 36616

Fr

An extensive selection of villas, all fully equipped. Blankets and bolsters supplied. Cot hire is available.
Prices   (villa for 6 per week)
June: from £160
July: £250
Aug: £297
Discounts   Children receive various discounts, according to ferry service.

CARIBBEAN VILLAS
53 St Owen Street, Hereford HR1 2JQ
Tel: 0432 263333

Crb

Villa specialists with properties in Antigua, Barbados and St Lucia, some overlooking white sandy beaches, others set among tropical greenery. All villas are fully furnished and equipped, including linen and towels. Most have daily maid service, some have a cook and laundress (even a butler). Cots can be provided, but cost extra as do food starter packs. Car hire is available.
Prices   (per adult per fortnight, including return flight and transfers)
£585–£1128
Most villas cost between £600 and £700.
Discounts   Under-2s sharing parents' room pay £157–£162; 2–12s sharing parents' room pay £388–£421. Under-2s in own room receive a discount of £333–£378, and 2–12s receive a discount of £122–£139.

CHAPTER TRAVEL
International Chapter, 102 St John's Wood Terrace, London NW8 6PL
Tel: 071 722 9560

Gr   It   Mex   Mor   Por   Sp
  W.Ind

Beautifully restored historic properties in Italy, a wide selection of châteaux, villas and farmhouses in France, and villas in the West Indies, Mexico, Morocco, Portugal, Greece and Spain. Villas and apartments are very well furnished and fully equipped, including linen. Most have swimming pools. Cots can be provided if requested in advance. Maid service is provided in the Caribbean and Morocco, and elsewhere is available on request. Travel arrangements can be organized if you wish. This company also acts as an agent for Tuscan Enterprises and Cuendet Italia.
Prices   (per property per week)
Villas: £200–£1500 (low); £350–£6000 (high)

CHATEAU WELCOME
PO Box 66, 94 Bell Street, Henley-on-Thames, Oxon RG9 1XS
Tel: 0491 578803

Fr

Over 70 privately owned châteaux all over France offering the opportunity to stay with top professional and noble families. Children are welcome and there are many opportunities to join the family in their favourite sports and pastimes, such as tennis, golf, riding, hunting, shooting and fishing, etc. An excellent opportunity to make friends and practise your French. Most hosts can provide dinner for their guests. You will be received as a privileged guest and as a friend of the family.
Prices   Room with breakfast (double occupancy with private bathroom) from £30–£230. Suites and family rooms are also available.

CORFU A LA CARTE

8 Deanwood House, Stockcross,
Newbury, Berks RG16 8JP
Tel: 0635 30621

Gr

Villa, apartment and cottage holidays on Corfu, Paxos and Skiathos. Accommodation ranges from the basic to the luxurious, but all is fully furnished and equipped, including linen, hand towels and maid service. Baby equipment, high chairs, cots and playpens may be hired when booking. Cots cost £20 for two weeks. This company is experienced in dealing with family holidays involving babies and young children.
Prices (per adult per week, including flights)
£190–£489
Discounts Under-2s pay £20 per flight (no seat). Children aged 2–16 receive up to £60 discount in June and £35 in August.

CV TRAVEL

43 Cadogan Street, Chelsea, London
SW3 2PR
Tel: 071 581 0851 *or* 071 584 8803

Gr It Por Sp Tur

Villas in the unspoilt areas of Corfu, Paxos, southern Italy, Tuscany, Majorca and the Algarve; also crewed boats in Turkey. Properties range from simple Greek village houses to Italian palazzi. All villas are comfortably furnished and fully equipped, including maid service and some have cooks. Gas, electricity and water are included and linen is provided and changed weekly. Cots cost £11 per week in Greece, Italy and Portugal; £17 per week in Spain. High chairs and playpens can also be hired in many villas. CV Travel can arrange baby-sitting at most villas. Food hampers can be provided on arrival at the villa and cost between £18–£24. Windsurfers, small boats and cars can also be booked in advance in the UK. The brochure has a useful information section with details of airport hotels and parking and CV Travel also provide all clients with a copy of their holiday booklet with detailed information and advice on the holiday areas, what to take on holiday, national tourist offices and suggested guide books and other reading.
Prices £225–£995 per adult per fortnight, including flights.
Discounts Under 2s pay £25 for flight (no seat, meals or luggage allowance); children aged 2–12 receive discounts of £10–£40.

CORONA HOLIDAYS

73 High Road, London E18 2QP
Tel: 081 530 3747

Can.Is

Winter and summer holidays in luxury villas and apartments. Most properties are in 'complexes' with half board option. Facilities for children vary; some offer playgrounds, parties, free day-nursery and baby-sitting service. Cots and pushchairs are available for hire. UK flights (charter and scheduled), can be arranged from your nearest local airport on request.
Prices (per person per week, 4 sharing)
Apartment in Tenerife: £83.30
Flights extra.
Discounts Under-2s pay £15 for flight (no seat), cots and meals payable locally. Children aged 2–11 from £20 reduction per week on most holidays, and up to 50% discount all season at one popular family resort.

CUENDET ITALIA

c/o CHAPTER TRAVEL (q.v.) *and* DAVID NEWMAN *(see* **Cottages** and **Hotels***)*

It

Extensive directory (£3.50) of villas, apartments, castles and farmhouses to let in Tuscany and Umbria. Properties range from simple rural accommodation to luxury villas by the sea. All are

fully furnished and equipped, including linen. Some have access to nearby sports facilities and farmhouse produce, depending on location. Minimum let in July and August is 2 weeks. Garden furniture is supplied in many locations. Cots on request.
Prices   (per property per week)
Villas: £200–£1950 (low); £250–£2550 (high). Most villas are between £300–£600 in the summer.

DOMINIQUE'S VILLAS
13 Park House, 140 Battersea Park Road, London SW11 4NB
Tel: 071 738 8772

Fr

A selection of beautiful villas, farmhouses, manor houses, even châteaux in secluded countryside, some in spectacular settings. The villas are situated in the Loire, the Dordogne, Lot et Garonne, Provence and the Côte d'Azur. All are fully furnished and equipped, most with a swimming pool, washing machine and dishwasher. Gas, electricity and water are free, but heating is extra. Linen is sometimes included in the cost of the property, and can always be hired if requested in advance. Cots are provided free of charge, but must also be requested in advance. The inventory deposit, which varies from villa to villa, can be paid by Eurocheque. Clients are asked to water the garden and maintain any pool. Each villa is listed with a photograph, details of the accommodation and local amenities.
Prices   (per villa per fortnight, including short Channel crossing for car and 2 adults)
Villas: from £600
Additional adults pay £26 for the ferry crossing and children aged 4–13 pay £14. Children under 4 travel free.

ENTERPRISE
(see **Hotels**)

Gr   It   Mal   Por   Sp

Self-catering holidays in studios and apartments mostly set in complexes with use of swimming pool, bar and restaurant. All accommodation is fully equipped, including linen and towels. Maid service is provided and there is a welcome pack of groceries on arrival. Some of the complexes have either a separate shallow section or a children's pool. Some have a games room, mini-golf and organized activities for children. Cots must be requested on booking and are either free or cost up to £3 per week. Babysitting can be arranged in some resorts.
Prices   (per adult per week, including flight and transfers)
4-person apartment on Algarve: £99 (low), £179 (high).
Discounts   Under-2s travel for £15 (no seat). There are discounts for children aged 2–16, ranging from 10% to 50%, dependent on children sharing with 2 full-fare paying passengers. Some apartments have space for a fourth bed, in which case 2 children may qualify for a discount.

FLORIDA HOME OWNERS' ASSOCIATION
Lyndale, Dayseys Hill, Outwood, nr Redhill, Surrey RH1 5QY
Tel: 034 284 2623/4155

US (Florida)

Luxury villas and apartments for rent throughout Florida. All accommodation is fully furnished and equipped, including air-conditioning, colour TV, linen and towels. Some properties have their own private swimming pool; others have access to a pool, but there may sometimes be a charge. Cots are generally available for hire. Most properties are within reach of Disneyworld. The

company also make fly/drive travel arrangements.
Prices (per property per week) from £235

FRENCH VILLA CENTRE
175 Selsdon Park Road, South Croydon, Surrey CR2 8JJ
Tel: 081 651 1231

Fr

Villa specialists with properties in coastal and rural locations. Some apartments, gîtes and luxury cottages are also available in certain areas. All accommodation is fully furnished and equipped, the gîtes being the cheapest and simplest. Travel arrangements can be made on request, but if you prefer to make your own, you simply pay for the accommodation. Cots can be supplied for a small fee, normally around £5 per week.
Prices (per property per week)
Low   £130
Mid   £250
High   £450–£650
Discounts Children receive the standard discounts on ferries and flights.

GLOBAL HOLIDAYS
26 Elmfield Road, Bromley, Kent BR1 1LR
Tel: 081 464 7515

And   Au   Bar   Bul   Cyp   Fr   Gr
It   Jam   Mal   Nor   Por   Sp
Swi   Tun   Tur   US

Specializes in family self-catering holidays in studio or apartment accommodation. The Global 'Wizzy Club' provides a qualified children's representative to look after children up to 12 years old, and a baby minding service is also available. Cots are free of charge, and there are single parent family offers.
Prices (per adult per 14 nights)
Air: £127–£869

Coach: £92–£256
Discounts All children (ages 2–17) travelling with 2 adults receive a discount, and free places are available.

GREEK ISLANDS CLUB
(see **Sailing**)
Tel: 0932 220477

Gr

Ionian villa and apartment specialists on the 'unspoilt' islands of Paxos, Zakynthos, Cephalonia, Lefkas, Ithaca and Kythira. All properties are well furnished and close to beaches and small villages. A daily maid service operates, except on Sundays. Car hire and private boat hire available. Cots, high chairs and baby-sitters can be provided.
Prices range from £416–£608
Discounts Children under 2 pay £50, which includes cot and linen. Other child discounts available on request.

HALSEY VILLAS
22 Boston Place, Dorset Square, London NW1 6HZ
Tel: 071 723 6043

Fr   It   Por   Sp   W.Ind

Luxurious, privately-owned villas, many in exotic locations, such as Barbados, Jamaica, the Grenadines and the Virgin Islands. All are beautifully furnished and equipped, most with resident staff and nearly all with private swimming pools. Cots, high chairs and baby-sitting can be arranged, and provision can be made if special food for children or babies is required. The company will make travel arrangements on request and are happy to advise which properties are most suitable for disabled people.
Prices In high season villa rental ranges from £500–£5000 per week.

Discounts Only available on children's air fares. The company will quote on request.

HORIZON VILLAS AND APARTMENTS
(see **Hotels***)*

Alg   Cyp   Fr   Gr   Ib   It   Mal
Mor   Por   Sp

Large selection of villas and apartments, from *OSL Villa Holidays* in the Mediterranean to villas accommodating up to 10 people. Most have swimming pools, and all include a free car. *HCL Club Holidays* offer a choice of hotels, apartments and villas, from full-board to self-catering. Holidays include free sports and entertainment, and children's clubs. *Horizon Summer Fun* to Europe, Africa and Florida; includes long-haul, villas and apartments. Hippo Club for 3–11 year olds includes games, activities, bedtime stories and baby patrolling.
Prices   available on request.
Discounts   *OSL Villas:* child reductions available.
HCL Club: child reductions for first and second children sharing with 2 adults.
Summer Fun: For first and second children sharing up to 50% in villas.

ILIOS ISLAND HOLIDAYS LTD
18 Market Square, Horsham,
W. Sussex RH12 1EU
Tel: 0403 59788

Gr   Tur

Villa and apartment holidays in the quieter parts of the Greek islands: Cephalonia, Laskada, Naxos, Skiathos, Skopelos and Zakynthos. All are comfortably furnished (some more so than others), and are fully equipped, including linen. Cots and high chairs may be hired for £10 and £5 per week respectively if requested when booking. Cot linen is limited, so you are advised to take your own.
Prices   (per adult per fortnight in a villa, including return flight and transfers)
Low   £276–£350
High   £369–£495

Discounts   Under-2s pay a flat fee of £25 (no seat on plane). Some free child places are available in early and late season in all locations.

INTERHOME
(see **Skiing***)*

Au   Fr   It   Sp   Swi

Villas, apartments, houses and hotel holidays. All self-catering accommodation is comfortably furnished and fully equipped. Extra charges may be made for electricity, gas, linen, towels and final cleaning, depending on location. The availability of cots is uncertain; ask when booking.
Prices   (per apartment per week)
A good quality apartment for 4 people in high season costs £200.
Discounts   None available on accommodation. Under-4s travel free on ferry; 4–13s pay £30 each, which includes insurance.

KOSMAR VILLA HOLIDAYS
358 Bowes Road, Arnos Grove, London
N11 1AN
Tel: 081 323 4705

Gr

An Anglo-Greek company specializing in villas, apartments and studios in Crete, the Cyclades, the Peloponnese and Poros. Accommodation is fairly basic, often with the third and fourth beds in the living room. All kitchens have a fridge, 2 or 3 gas burners, (rarely an oven), some cutlery, crockery and bed linen. Towels are not provided. Gas, electricity and water are free. Cots may be hired for £10 per week. All villas are listed with details of the accommodation and distance from the beach. Car hire is included in the price of some villa holidays, but can be arranged elsewhere on request.
Prices   (per adult per fortnight, including flight and transfers)
Villas: £150–£299

Discounts   Children under 2 are free. A few holidays for children aged 2–12 with a discount of £100 or more are available throughout the year. Otherwise 2–15s receive a discount of 5–20%.

LA FRANCE DES VILLAGES
(*see* **Cottages**)

Fr

Riding holidays suitable for families in Burgundy, Auvergne, Tarn, Pyrenees (including northern Spain). 3–7 day treks with about 4 hours rising per day. Basic riding competence necessary. Choice of accommodation includes gîtes, auberges and château-hotels. Also canoe treks and 4-wheel-drive treks.

Prices   From £159 per person per week

LASKARINA HOLIDAYS
St Mary's Gate, Wirksworth,
Derbyshire DE4 3DG
Tel: 062 982 2203/4

Gr

Villas, apartments, studios and hotels in 'unspoilt' resorts on ten Greek islands. All self-catering accommodation is fully furnished and equipped – some rather more luxuriously than others. A maid service for light cleaning only is available at least once a week. Cot hire, including linen, is £50 per week.

Prices   (per adult per fortnight)
Low   £211–219
Mid   £239–£249
High   £289–£299

Discounts   Children under 2 travel free (no seat). Free places are available in specified accommodation for 2–12s on 2-week holidays from early May to mid-June and during most of October. These free places are limited to one child per 2 adults. At other times reductions are offered to one child per adult. Children aged 2–12 receive a £20–£40 discount, and 13–18s receive a £10–£40 discount, all depending on season and accommodation.

LUNIGIANA HOLIDAYS
71 Busbridge Lane, Godalming, Surrey GU7 1QQ
Tel: 04868 21218

It

Small, family-run company offering villas, apartments and cottages for rent in northern Tuscany and a flat available in Florence. Accommodation ranges from the rustic to the luxurious, but all is fully furnished and equipped, including linen. Cots may be hired in all properties. Swimming pool available at Villa Castagnet.

Prices   (per mid-range property per week)
Low   £165
Peak   £280

MAGIC OF ITALY
(*see* **Fly/Drive**)

It

Villa, apartment and hotel holidays throughout Italy. Accommodation ranges from the simple to the luxurious, but all self-catering accommodation is fully furnished and equipped, including linen. Cots are usually provided free, but at some villas and hotels a fee is charged. Car hire is available at £155 per week.

Prices   (per adult per fortnight in self-catering accommodation, and per adult per week in a hotel)
Villas: £279–£307 (low); £349–£399 (high)
Hotels: £249–£388 (low); £349–£409 (high)

Discounts   Children under 2 travel for a flat fee of £20 (no seat). On villa, apartment and hotel holidays 2–11s receive a £20 discount. These reductions apply to one child per 2 full fare-paying passengers sharing a twin room in hotels.

MAGIC OF SPAIN
(*see* **Magic of Italy, Fly/drive**)

Sp

Villa, apartment, paradores and hotel holidays throughout Spain. Accommodation ranges from the simple to the luxurious, but all self-catering accommodation is fully furnished and equipped, including linen. Cots are usually provided free, but at some villas and hotels a fee is charged. Car hire is available from £109 per week.

Prices (per adult per fortnight in self-catering accommodation, and per adult per week in a hotel)
Villas: from £289 (low); from £395 (high)
Hotels: from £329 (low); from £389 (high)

Discounts Children under 2 travel for a flat fee of £20 (no seat). On villa and apartment holidays 2–11s receive a £20 discount, and on hotel holidays a 20%–25% discount, depending on season and accommodation. These reductions apply to one child per 2 full fare-paying passengers.

MEON VILLA HOLIDAYS
Meon House, Petersfield, Hants
GU32 3JN
Tel: 0730 68411

Fr (including Corsica)   Go   Gr   It
Mal   Por   Sp

Very wide selection of villa and apartment holidays, some with car included. According to the brochure, the properties range 'from 3-star comfort to 5-star luxury'. All accommodation is fully furnished and equipped, including linen, hand towels and maid service. Many of the properties have their own private swimming pool.

Meon also offer self-drive holidays to France, Portugal and Spain, organizing ferry crossings and the accommodation of your choice: villa, cottage, farmhouse or apartment. Cottages and farmhouses do not supply linen and towels. Cot hire can be arranged on request.

Prices (per adult per fortnight, including flight, in a 4-person villa with private pool on Algarve)
Low   £456
High   £657

Discounts Children under 2 pay a flat fee of £30 for 2 weeks, £15 for one week, and this includes cost of cot hire. 2–11s receive a reduction of £10–£40, depending on season.

PALMER & PARKER
63 Grosvenor Street, London W1X 0AJ
Tel: 071 493 5725

Crb   Fr   Por   Sp   US

Up-market villas furnished and equipped to a very high standard. All have maid service, private swimming pool and car hire. Cots and high chairs may be hired weekly for £15 each.

Prices A 4-bedroom villa sleeping 8 in Portugal in August costs around £609 per person

Discounts Under-2s pay a flat fee of £30. Children aged 2–11 receive a reduction of £40 in Spain and Portugal. In France there are no accommodation discounts, but children are entitled to a 20% discount on the fly/drive part of the holiday. In the US and Caribbean under-2s pay 10% of adult price; 2–11s receive a reduction of about £150 each.

PERRYMEAD PROPERTIES
55 Perrymead Street, London SW6 3SN
Tel: 071 736 4592/5331

It

A selection of villas and apartments for rent throughout Italy. The properties range from converted sixteenth-century abbeys to modern apartment blocks. All are fully furnished and equipped. Linen and maid service provided in certain locations. Cots are available free. This company also acts as an agent for Cuendet Italia.

Prices (per property per week)
£150–£4000
Discounts Only available on children's travel. Details on request.

THE PORTUGUESE PROPERTY BUREAU LTD
3–6 The Colonnade, Maidenhead,
Berkshire SL6 1QL
Tel: 0628 770220

Por

Spacious self-catering 2-, 3- and 4-bedroom detached, terraced and cluster villas in and around Carvoeiro on the Algarve. Most properties are set in a garden and have a private or shared pool. All the villas are fully furnished and well equipped, including linen and towels. Maid service is included in the price, as is water, electricity, gas and water heating. The company looks after the garden and pool. Cots are available for £15 per week, high chairs for £15 per week. A free welcome food pack is provided on arrival. There is a breakage deposit of £50 refunded within 3 weeks after departure. Hire of a 5-seater car with roof rack, unlimited mileage and full insurance is included in the price.
Prices (per adult per fortnight, including flight, airport tax, insurance and car hire)
2-bedroom cluster or terraced villa with shared pool: £272–£530
2-bedroom villa with own pool: £300–£632
Discounts Under-2s are charged £40, which includes hire of cot. Children aged 2–12 receive a discount of £20 each.

SALLY HOLIDAYS
81 Piccadilly, London W1V 9HF
Tel: 071 355 2266

Bel Fr

Although operating ski, short-break and 'go-as-you-please' motoring packages, Sally Holidays is best known for self-drive holidays featuring apartments and gîtes throughout France and Belgium. These represent good value to families due to the company's 'free children' policy, where up to 2 children are accommodated free of charge in a vast number of the apartments included. In addition to properties in major resort areas, the company offers more rustic accommodation in central France.
Prices (per person per week, based on 2 adults sharing apartment in France, including return ferry crossing)
Low: £60–£150
High: £80–£250
Discounts Up to 2 children are accommodated free of charge in the majority of properties featured. Further details are available on request.

SELECT HOLIDAYS
Centurion House, Bircherley Street,
Hertford SG14 1BH
Tel: 0992 553711

Cyp Gam Fr Isr It Ken Mad Mal Mau Por Sp Sey

Villa, apartment and hotel holidays in mainland and island destinations. All self-catering accommodation is fully furnished and equipped, including maid service. Cots may be hired for about £5 a week, but sometimes they are free. Many properties have their own private pools; apartment complexes have access to communal pools and sports facilities. Some hotels offer cots, high chairs and a baby-sitting service. Two-centre holidays can be arranged on request.
Prices available on request
Discounts Under-2s travel free on charter flights and pay £50 on scheduled flights. Children under 12 normally pay 30–50% of adult price, provided they share parents' room. Some hotels give no discounts during peak periods.

SIMPLY TURKEY
8 Chiswick Terrace, Acton Lane,
London W4 5LY
Tel: 081 747 1011

Tur

Several privately-owned villas and studios available for rent, all comfortably furnished and equipped, including maid service. Cots can be provided by arrangement. High chairs can be hired for £10 per week. Hotels are small, usually family-run and in resorts with plenty to do throughout the day. Babysitting can be arranged.
Prices (per adult per week, B+B, including flights and transfers)
From £209
Discounts Children under 2 travel free; 2–16s receive £20–£50 discount, depending on season and length of stay.

SLIPAWAY HOLIDAYS
90 Newland Road, Worthing,
W. Sussex BN11 1LB
Tel: 0903 821000

Fr

A wide selection of villa and apartment holidays throughout France. All accommodation is comfortably furnished and fully equipped, apart from linen and towels. In some properties an extra charge may be made for electricity, gas and hot water. Cots can sometimes be hired locally by prior arrangement.
Prices (per fortnight for 2 adults with car, including Dover–Calais ferry)
Mid-range villa in Brittany: from £349–£950
Discounts Children under 4 travel free, and the company can arrange discounts for under-14s on ferries.

SKIATHOS TRAVEL
4 Holmesdale Road, Kew, Richmond,
Surrey TW9 3JZ
Tel: 081 940 5157

Gr

Villas, apartments and hotels on the Greek islands of Skiathos, Skopelos and Alonissos. All accommodation is close to sea and the company particularly recommends Skiathos for children, as it has safe, sandy beaches. All self-catering accommodation is 'adequately' furnished and equipped, including linen and hand towels. Maid service available in some locations. Cots may be hired for £13 per week.
Prices (per adult per fortnight, including flight)
3-bedroom villa: £339–£476
Discounts Children under 2 travel free (no seat); 2–11s are eligible for £10–£20 discounts, depending on season and length of stay.

STARVILLAS LTD
25 High Street, Chesterton, Cambridge
CB4 1ND
Tel: 0223 311990

Fr   Gr   Por   Sp

Extensive selection of villas and apartments. All accommodation is fully furnished and equipped, and most supply linen and maid service. Cots and cot linen are available in most locations for a fee of £12 per week.
Prices (per adult per fortnight, including flights)
Portugal, 2-bedroom villa with pool: £350.
The weekly rental for this villa in peak season, exclusive of travel, is £432.
Discounts On flight-inclusive holidays, under-2s pay £10 (no seat); 2–16s receive a £35–£50 discount. This normally applies to one child per adult, but the company claims to be very flexible about this, even in peak season.

SUNSELECT VILLAS
60 Crow Hill North, Middleton,
Manchester M24 1FB
Tel: 061 655 3055

Fr

Self-catering villas and cottages in northern and southern Brittany. Most villas have their own gardens with garden furniture and are a short walk or drive from the nearest beach. All are fully furnished and equipped. Linen and towels are not provided, but can be hired locally. Cots are supplied free in southern Brittany and can be hired in the north. A returnable deposit of £60 is payable with the final invoice. Gas, electricity (except for heating), water, and cleaning before arrival are free. This company also offers canal and river cruising holidays in Brittany and Maine/Anjou. If ferry crossings are at night the cost of a cabin is extra. For disabled travellers a suitable villa can always be recommended.

Prices (per villa per 2 weeks, including ferry for car and 2 adults)
Low £495–£785
High £735–£1305
Return fares are payable separately for additional passengers: children aged 4–13 pay £15; adults pay £32 or £39, according to season. Single week bookings are possible.

Discounts Children under 4 are free. A reduction of £25 is offered on all one-week holidays taken before 13 July and after 3 September.

SUN TOTAL
Total Holidays Ltd, 10 Hill Street,
Richmond, Surrey TW9 1TN
Tel: 081 948 6922

Au Fr Gr Tur

Small, privately-owned company which specializes in villa, apartment and pension holidays in the Greek Islands, and winter skiing holidays in France and Austria. Cots can be hired for £20 per week. Childminding can be arranged locally on request.

Prices (per adult per week in summer self-catering accommodation, including flight)
Low £209
High £319
(per adult per week in winter catered accommodation, including flight)
Low £169
High £350

Discounts Children under 2 pay £20, which includes the cot. Discounts of 50% are offered to any child aged 2–5 in winter, and 2–10 in summer when you book early and the children share with 2 full fare-paying adults. The 50% discount does not apply during peak periods. The ordinary discount is a flat rate which works out at between 20% off the adult rate up to 14 years.

THOMSON HOLIDAYS
(*see* **Hotels**)
Tel: 081 200 8733 *(London)*, 021 632 6282 *(Birmingham)*, 061 236 3828 *(Manchester)*

Cyp Gr Ibiza It Maj Mal Min Por Sp

Large selection of good quality private villas with pools and small apartment complexes offering excellent value holidays for families. All accommodation is fully furnished and equipped, including linen, hand towels and maid service. Cots are available in most places, some provided free, others costing around £2 per night.

Prices (per adult per fortnight, including return flight and transfers)
Low £150–£365
Mid £200–£430
High £280–£480

Discounts Children under 2 pay £15 (no seat on plane). Children aged 2–16 all receive discounts. First child sharing with 2 adults qualifies for reduction of 10%–40%. All additional children receive discount of between £25–£45.

VILLA MATCH
(*see* WORLDWIDE CARS, **Car rental**)
Tel: 0273 739100

And   Crb   Fr   Gr   It   Mal   Por
Sp   Swi   US

Large computer listing of privately-owned villas all over the world. Prospective clients are given details of villas matching their requirements, make their selection and then book directly with the owners. The company acts only as a matching agency and does not charge a fee to enquirers. Its lists also note the availability of cots and high chairs (cots are free in most villas). Linen is supplied and changed once a week. Villa Match also operates a small car hire company – see **Car rental**.
Prices   (per property per week)
From:
Peak season: 2-bedroom villa in Ibiza
£80
To:
Peak season: luxury house in Algarve with private pool   £1695

VILLAS ITALIA
13 Hillgate Street, London W8 7SP
Tel: 071 221 4432

It   Sar

Large selection of quality villas and apartments and family-run hotels in Tuscany, Liguria, Umbria, Venice, Neapolitan Riviera and Sardinia. Accommodation ranges from rural farmhouses to luxury beachside villas, many with pools. Tailor-made travel arrangements by car/ferry or flights from Gatwick, Heathrow, Manchester and Glasgow.
Prices   (per person for one week in Tuscany, low season, based on four sharing apartment with pool, including flight from Gatwick)
£200
Discounts   Generous child reductions available.

PATRICIA WILDBLOOD
Calne, Wilts SN11 0LP
Tel: 0249 817023 *or* 081 658 6722

It   Por   Sp   Tun

A wide selection of comfortable private holiday homes in Menorca, plus some holidays in the Menorca Country Club. Villas range from simple beach-side accommodation to a large house set in its own grounds with private pool. Most villas have a pool and barbecue. All are fully furnished and equipped, including linen. Maid service can be arranged. Cots are available and must be paid for locally. Gas, electricity and water are free. A welcome food pack is provided on arrival. Windsurfing facilities can be arranged. Car hire is available on request.

In a separate brochure, the company offers a selection of luxurious villas in Tuscany (car hire included), the Algarve and the Marine Holiday Village in Tunisia. Those on the Algarve are near various clubs which allow full use of their facilities for tennis, swimming, squash, windsurfing and sailing. However there is an extra rental supplement of £25 per week on some villas with pools, plus £55 if you want the water heated and £24 per week to keep the water warm.
Prices   available on request.
Discounts   Children under 2 pay £35 (exclusive of cot hire). Outside high season children aged under 7 are entitled to a reduction of £40 on the basis of one adult per child. Otherwise 2–7 year olds receive a discount of £40, 7–12 year olds £30, and 12–16 year olds £20.

WINTERWORLD
(see **Skiing Holidays**)

Swi

Self-catering, self-drive summer holidays for families interested in exploring the art, history and scenery of western Switzerland and the Rhône Valley.

Apartments and chalets in Villars sleeping 4–6 people have fully-equipped kitchens and south-facing balconies. They are cleaned every other day. Travel is by ferry, and the company minibus is on hand in and around Villars. Free childminding available on alternate days, and at other times at local prices.

Prices   (per adult per fortnight, self-drive, including ferry crossing)
Low: £220
Mid: £245
High: £295
Discounts   Children under 2 go free, provided they share parents' room.

Walking Holidays

Don't disregard this section in the belief that these holidays will only appeal to seasoned walkers. The companies listed grade their walks for difficulty and will advise you which to take if you are in doubt. Some of the people we spoke to said that young children, even babes in arms (or slings) were commonplace on their tours, while others had experienced none younger than eight. Ultimately it's down to you. If *you* are fit and healthy and can tolerate carrying a baby or toddler for several hours, these companies won't turn you away, but they will have a few words of caution for you.

Can you guarantee that your child won't impede the progress of the tour? Unscheduled stops for feeds and nappy changes are not really fair on the other walkers. Also pushchairs are out of the question on all but the most level and simple of walks.

Some larger companies claim that other guests muck in and help look after and entertain children. The same cannot be promised with all groups. The success of the walk boils down to your sensibility and your child's adaptability, so be honest with yourself before making a commitment to this type of holiday. It could be great, and indeed many children love it. On the other hand the fear of your child delaying or upsetting the rest of the party may be too offputting.

Prices
Unless otherwise stated 1990 prices have been quoted. These are intended only as a guide to the type of holiday offered and travellers should check with the company concerned for 1991 pricing details.

HF HOLIDAYS LTD
Imperial House, Edgware Road,
London NW9 5AL
Tel: 081 905 9556

Aus Fr It Maj Mal Sp Swi
UK

Independent and accompanied walking holidays. Walks are graded from gentle rambles to full-scale mountaineering and include discovery and theme walks for those with special interests in such things as archaeology and birdwatching. The more arduous tours are not suitable for young children. Family walking holidays bear children in mind, so there are organized social events and entertainments in the evening. There are also crèche facilities for very young children, leaving parents free to enjoy a day's walking. Entertainments and children's facilities are not necessarily available abroad; ask when booking. Accommodation in the UK is mainly in HF's own 'characterful' houses, with small, family-run hotels in some locations. Abroad, accommodation tends to be in guest houses. Rooms are single, twin or multi-bedded with tea and coffee-making facilities in each. Cots and high chairs can be provided on request, and there are facilities for washing and drying clothes. Potties and pushchairs may also be provided if requested when booking. Some baby foods and disposable nappies are on sale at HF centres.
Prices A family holiday with one week's full board in UK ranges from £129–£214 per adult.
Discounts These are available only on family holidays: under-5s are free, 5–9s receive 70% discount, 10–13s receive 55% discount and 14–16s receive 35% discount.

RAMBLERS HOLIDAYS LTD
Box 43, Welwyn Garden City, Herts
AL8 6PG
Tel: 0707 331133

And Au Az Bor Can Ch Cyp
Egy Fr Gr Him It Jap Jor
Mad Mex Mor NZ PNG
Peru Phi Por Sp Swi Th
Tur UK W.Ind Yug

This company offers escorted walking tours, graded for difficulty, in an astonishing variety of destinations. Some holidays, which involve extensive travelling, are essentially coach tours.- with a walking ingredient, although air, rail and local transport may also be used. Some tours are not suitable for children; advice given on request. Those which are suitable will need your assurance that your child(ren) will not impede the progress of the party. No children under 10 years.
Prices (per adult per tour, including flights and transfers)
Austria, 1 week half board: £270–£330; 2 weeks £390–£460.
Canada from £1200.
Both these tours are considered suitable for children.
Discounts These are available for children sharing parents' room, but can vary greatly, depending on location. Details on request.

WELSH WAYFARING HOLIDAYS
Neuadd Arms Hotel, Llanwrtyd Wells,
Powys LD5 4RD
Tel: 05913 236

UK (Wales)

Guided walks in the Cambrian mountains, Brecon Beacons and Elan Valley. On a 7-day holiday, walking is done on 5 days, and on a 4-day break, walking is done on 3 days. Accommodation is in the family-run Neuadd Arms Hotel. Some en suite rooms are available and are considered particularly suitable for families. Cots can be provided if requested when booking. A launderette and drying-room are available. If you opt out of walking (which you are free to do), arrangements can be made for riding, birdwatching, mountain cycling, fishing and car touring. Details on request.

Prices (per adult per week, including full board with packed lunch and afternoon tea)

From £165

Discounts   On accommodation only, under-5s are free. Children aged 5–12 receive 75% discount when sharing parents' room; 13–16s receive 40% discount. Small children are entitled to reduced rates on restaurant meals, and there is a special children's menu at the bar's snack counter.

Section 3

Holiday transport

Facilities for families at British airports

This is a survey of the facilities available at airports throughout Britain. We have tried to make each entry as comprehensive as possible, but we would welcome further information, personal experiences or advice from readers.

In this age of long airport delays, it is well worth the travelling family's while to read this section carefully before booking a flight. Although the larger airports may have more lavish facilities, it is worth remembering that they also have to deal with a greater volume of passengers. Smaller airports often have a shorter clearance time for customs and baggage control and this fact alone might mean the difference between a hassled journey and relaxing trip.

It is always advisable to contact the airport information desk before you set off. The staff will be able to give you details of the facilities available and advise you on any special needs or requests.

In general, children love the thought of travelling by plane. You can encourage them to look forward to their time at the airport by helping them to draw pictures and write stories. These might be about what they are expecting to see, or what they think planes and airport buildings of the future will be like. Most airports have viewing terraces where, usually for a small fee, you and your children can have a grandstand view of the planes landing and taking off (contact the airport information desk in advance to check availability). Games involving making plane noises and running around with arms outstretched may be great fun in your garden or front room, but remember that an over-excited child hurtling through a crowded concourse will drive you (and other passengers) to distraction.

There are several colourful children's books on the market about children's visits to an airport and these can be successfully used when calming an anxious child's fears. If adults show fear of flying, children will quickly assume that aeroplanes are frightening things. Try to keep your own misgivings to yourself. Above all, it is important to make children feel from an early age that flying is fun.

By giving this part of your holiday as much advance planning as possible, you may even manage to view your time at the airport as an enjoyable part of your holiday.

Aberdeen

Aberdeen Airport
Dyce
Aberdeen
AB2 0DU
Tel: (0224) 722331

Eur   UK

7 miles from city centre, 35 minutes by express bus service (exact fare required on boarding). Aberdeen station is nearest rail connection point. Car parking available adjacent to the terminal.
Mother and baby room in main terminal; facilities available on request from information desk.
Disposable nappies available.
Children's meals and snacks available, but no baby food.
Medical facilities in main terminal building, with qualified nurses on duty at the information desk.
Books and toys for sale in terminal.
Allow 20 minutes to clear baggage and customs.
Child seats available with car-rental.

Belfast

Belfast Airport
Belfast
BT29 4AB
Tel: (08494) 22888

Can   Eur   UK   USA

16 miles from Belfast, 30 minutes by shuttle-coach from city centre.
Mother and baby room in main departure lounge.
Disposable nappies are available.
Children's meals, snacks, and baby food available.
Play area available from September 1990.

Books and toys for sale in terminal, also audio and video cassettes.
Allow 40 minutes to clear baggage and customs.
Child seats available with car-rental.

Birmingham

Birmingham International Airport
Birmingham
B26 3QJ
Tel: (021) 767 7145/6

Worldwide

Excellent bus, coach and British Rail connections; 10 minutes by rail from Birmingham New Street Station.
Both short-term and long-term parking available. Disabled travellers should contact the airport manager in advance to confirm details of facilities available.
Mother and baby rooms are situated adjacent to the Birmingham Bar, and in the international departure lounge.
Disposable nappies available.
Children's meals and snacks available, but not baby food.
Playcare centre, with trained staff, will take without charge 2–8 year olds for 30-minute periods. This facility is situated opposite the American Express office.
Spectators' viewing gallery, with shop and buffet facilities, is open from early morning to early evening all year round. There is a small charge made for admission.
Allow 30 minutes to clear baggage and customs.
Books and toys for sale in terminal.
Child seats available with car-rental.

Bournemouth
Bournemouth Airport
Christchurch
Dorset
BH23 6DB
Tel: (0202) 593939

Ch. Is   Cyp   Gr   It   Sp   UK   Yug

6 miles from Bournemouth. No public transport connections.
Mother and baby room in main terminal.
Disposable nappies are available.
Children's meals and snacks, but no baby food.
Books and toys for sale in terminal.
Allow 30 minutes to clear baggage and customs.
Child seats available with car-rental.

Bristol
Bristol Airport
Bristol
BS19 3DY
Tel: (0275) 874441

*Can   Ch   Ch. Is   Cub   Eur   Ind
Mor   Nicaragua   Tun   Tur   UAE
UK*

8 miles from city centre. A service bus runs to the airport from Bristol Marlborough Street bus and coach station and Bristol Temple Meads railway station (journey time approx 40 minutes).
Both short-term and long-term parking facilities are available.
Mother and baby room situated on ground floor of main terminal.
Disposable nappies available.
Children's meals available, but not baby food.
Books and toys for sale in terminal.
Allow 20 minutes to clear baggage and customs.
Child seats available with car-rental.

Cardiff
Cardiff-Wales Airport
Nr. Cardiff
South Glamorgan
CF6 9BD
Tel: (0446) 711111

Can   Eur   Tur   UK

12 miles from city centre. Express bus service runs from Cardiff bus station, which is adjacent to Cardiff main line railway station (journey time approximately 40 minutes).
Good car parking facilities available.
Disabled travellers should contact airport security in advance for information.
Mother and baby room in female toilet area.
Disposable nappies available.
Children's meals and snacks and baby food are available.
Books and toys for sale in terminal.
Spectator roof-top terrace available to all visiting public and passengers.
Allow 20 minutes to clear baggage and customs.
Child seats available with car-rental.

Coventry
Coventry Airport
Warwickshire
CV8 3AZ
Tel: (0203) 301717

Eur   Ire

2 miles from Coventry city centre, 20 minutes by bus from city centre.
No mother and baby room.
Children's meals and snacks, but no baby food.
No books and toys for sale in airport.
Allow 10 minutes to clear baggage and customs.
Child seats available with car-rental.

Derby: *see* **East Midlands**

East Midlands
East Midlands Airport
Castle Donnington
Derby
DE7 2SA
Tel: (0332) 810621

*Bel Ch. Is Fr Gr Hol Sp UK
Yug*

8 miles from Loughborough, approximate journey time 30 minutes by coach.
Parent and baby rooms situated in main terminal and airside.
Disposable nappies are available.
Children's meals, snacks, and baby food are available.
Soft play area situated opposite airport information desk.
Books and toys for sale in terminal.
Cartoon booths and TV booths are sited both landside and airside.
A selection of games is available from the information desk.
In the event of delays, children's entertainment is organized, and children's play-packs are available from the information desk.
Allow 30 minutes to clear baggage and customs.
Child seats available with car-rental.

Edinburgh
Edinburgh Airport
Edinburgh
EH12 9DN
Tel: (031) 333 1000

Can Eur UK

25 minutes by express bus from Waverley Bridge rail terminus in city centre (approximate journey time 25 minutes).
Mother and baby room situated on ground floor of main building near to gate 6, between the bar/buffet and the international arrivals area.
Disposable nappies available.
Children's meals and snacks available, but no baby food.
Medical facilities available in main terminal building and a trained nurse is usually on duty at the information desk.

Books and toys for sale in terminal.
Spectators' gallery available during daylight hours.
Allow 20 minutes to clear baggage and customs.
Child seats available with car-rental.

Exeter
Exeter Airport
Exeter
Devon
EX5 2BD
Tel: (0392) 67433

Can Eur UK

5 miles from city centre.
Short-term and long-term parking available. Disabled travellers are advised to contact the airport prior to arrival. An express bus service links the airport with Exeter mainline railway and coach stations.
Mother and baby rooms situated on first floor of main terminal building and in the international departures lounge.
Disposable nappies are not available.
Children's meals and snacks available, but no baby food.
No books or toys available in terminal.
Video lounge in international departures lounge.
Allow 20 minutes to clear baggage and customs.
Child seats available with car-rental.

Gatwick
Gatwick Airport
West Sussex
RH6 0NP
Tel: (0293) 28822

Worldwide

Good public transport connections. British Rail Gatwick Express service runs from Victoria every 15 minutes (journey time varies from 30 to 45 minutes depending on time of journey). Luggage for British Airways flights (and for airlines which they handle) may be checked in at the air terminal in Victoria Station.

Short-term and long-term parking available. Disabled travellers are advised to contact airport staff in advance to confirm facilities available. Babycare rooms (equipped with nappy dispensers) are provided in both terminals. There are two in the North Terminal – The Avenue (first floor, central toilet block) and international departures lounge (second floor, opposite skyshop); and three in the South Terminal – Gatwick Village (third floor, near Country Table buffet), in female toilet block (near Post Office), international departures lounge (second floor) and in female toilet (ground floor). Parents with pushchairs may use the disabled toilet facility in the lounge. Another room is provided in the Satellite (near to the rapid transit station).

Disposable nappies available.

Showers are available in North and South Terminals for a small fee. Towels and soap may be hired nearby.

Children's meals, snacks and baby food available both landside and departure-side.

Medical facilities (including doctors on call 24 hours a day) available in both North and South Terminals.

Books and toys for sale in terminal.

Soft play area for children aged five and under in Gatwick Village (third floor). Children must be supervised by a parent or guardian.

TV lounge (showing satellite television) is situated in Gatwick Village (third floor, South Terminal).

Spectators' viewing gallery (small charge made for admission).

In the event of long delays, children's entertainment may be provided.

Travel-Care office situated in South Terminal (third floor). Staff offer help to anyone at the airport who has a problem, whether travel related or not.

Allow 40 minutes to clear baggage and customs.

Child seats available with car-rental.

Glasgow
Glasgow Airport
Paisley
PA3 2ST
Tel: (041) 887 1111/1807

Worldwide

30 minutes from city centre on M8. Nearest railway station is Paisley Gilmour Street (2 miles from airport). Regular bus service from Glasgow city centre (Central and Queen Street stations and Anderston Cross and Buchanan bus station) to airport forecourt.

Short-term car-parking facilities are available near to the terminal building.

Mother and baby room on first floor.

Disposable nappies available.

Children's food and snacks but no baby food. Airport catering services will microwave your own food on request.

Medical unit situated on ground floor of domestic arrivals hall.

Books and toys for sale in terminal.

Allow 30 minutes to clear baggage and customs.

Child seats available with car-rental.

Teeside
Teeside Airport
Darlington
Co. Durham
DL2 1LU
Tel: (0325) 332811

Ch. Is.   Hol   Sp   UK   Yug

Located 6 miles from Darlington. Bus and train connections.

Mother and baby room in main concourse.

Nappies not available.

Children's meals and snacks, but no baby food.

Books and toys for sale in terminal.

Allow 20 minutes to clear baggage and customs.

Child seats available with car-rental.

Wales: *see* **Cardiff**

Guernsey
Guernsey Airport
La Villiaze
Forest
Guernsey
Tel: (0481) 37766

Fr   Swi   UK

5 miles from St Peter Port town centre.
Regular bus service to town centre. Taxi
rank in airport forecourt.
Car parking for 280 cars.
Mother and baby room. Disposable
nappies are available from information
desk in emergencies only. Nappies,
baby food and other supplies may be
obtained from shop ten minutes walk
away (turn left outside airport
entrance).
Buffet open all day for lunches, snacks
and drinks.
No books and toys on sale in airport. No
duty-free shop.
Allow 15 minutes to clear baggage and
customs.
Child seats available with car-rental.

Heathrow
Heathrow Airport
Hounslow
Middx
TW6 1JH
Tel: (Terminal 1): 081 745 7702/4
(Terminal 2): 081 745 7115/7
(Terminal 3): 081 745 7412/4
(Terminal 4): 081 745 4540

Worldwide

Good transport connections. Central
London to Heathrow (approximate journey time 50 minutes) by London
Underground (Piccadilly Line, every 3–7
minutes). Coach services from all over
Britain call at Heathrow (check arrival
and departure points with operator in
advance). London Transport's Airbus
operates a regular service to and from
central London (all buses are equipped
to carry disabled passengers).
Short-term and long-term car parks
available. Disabled travellers are advised to contact airport information
desk for further details.
Parent and child rooms are available in
each terminal. They may be locked very
late at night or early in the morning and
at these times, passengers are advised
to contact the terminal's information
desk.
Disposable nappies available.
Children's food, snacks and baby food
available.
Medical centre, staffed 24 hours a day,
is situated in Queen's Building.
Playcare Centre, staffed by qualified
nursery nurses, is available free of
charge for 2–8 year-olds. It is situated in
the airside departures concourse of
Terminal 4.
Spectator viewing facilities are available for a small charge on the roof of
Terminal 2 (disabled visitors are admitted free, but dogs are not permitted).
Travel-Care unit, situated in the Queen's
Building, is staffed by professional
social workers. A confidential advice
service is offered to passengers during
office hours.
Books and toys for sale in terminal.
Allow 30 minutes to clear baggage and
customs.
Child seats available with car-rental.

Humberside
Humberside Airport
Kirmington
South Humberside
DN39 6YH
Tel: (0652) 688456

Ch. Is.   Den   Hol   Nor   UK

13 miles from Scunthorpe. No public
transport connections.
No mother and baby room.
No special children's or baby food.
Books and toys for sale in terminal.

Allow 15 minutes to clear baggage and customs.
Child seats available with car-rental.

Jersey
Jersey Airport
St Peters
Jersey
JE1 1BY
Tel: (0534) 46111

Fr   UK

5 miles from St Helier. Regular bus service to town centre (journey time approximately 20 minutes). Taxi rank outside arrivals hall.
Car park adjacent to airport.
Mother and baby room in departure lounge.
Nappies not available.
Children's food, snacks and baby food available.
Medical facilities are available on site.
Disabled travellers are advised to contact information desk for details of facilities available.
No books or toys for sale at airport.
Spectators may gain access to terminal roof, but best views are from the NW side of the airfield.
Allow 15 minutes to clear baggage and customs.

Kent
Kent International Airport
P.O. Box 500
Manston
Kent
CT12 5BP
Tel: (0843) 823333

Ch. Is.   Sp   Yug

2 miles from Ramsgate. No public transport connections. Taxis from Ramsgate town centre.
Parking facilities are good, with some packages providing free parking.
Children's play area and televised films.

Disabled travellers are advised to contact airport staff before travelling for information about the facilities available and to make any particular requests.
Mother and baby room situated in central concourse.
Disposable nappies are available.
Children's meals and snacks, but no baby food.
Books and toys on sale in terminal.
Allow 15 minutes to clear baggage and customs.
Child seats available with car-rental.

Leeds-Bradford
Leeds-Bradford Airport
Yeadon
Leeds
Tel: (0532) 509696

Can   Eur   UK

8 miles north-west of Leeds. 6 miles north of Bradford. 11 miles south of Harrogate. No direct rail connection to the airport. Regular bus service from Leeds and Bradford. Taxis available outside terminal during operational hours. Short-term and long-term car parking available for 1,000 cars.
Mother and baby room situated on ground floor.
Disposable nappies available.
Children's food and snacks, but no baby food.
Books and toys for sale in terminal.
Disabled travellers are advised to contact the airport duty office before departure for details of facilities available.
Allow 30 minutes to clear baggage and customs.
Child seats available with car-rental.

Liverpool
Liverpool Airport
Liverpool
L24 1YD
Tel: (051) 486 8877

Eur   UK

8 miles from city centre. Regular train service from city centre to Garston

Station (10 minutes by bus from airport terminal). Runcorn Station is 10 minutes away by taxi, available from airport terminal entrance.

Car parking available adjacent to airport terminal.

Disabled travellers are advised to contact airport information desk in advance for details of facilities available.

Mother and baby room in main concourse. The key is available from the information desk.

Nappies not available.

Children's food and snacks, but no baby food.

Medical aid should be sought at the information desk or from any security officer.

Books and toys for sale in terminal.

Allow 30 minutes to clear baggage and customs.

Child seats available with car-rental.

London

London City Airport
King George V Dock
Silvertown
London
E16 2PX
Tel: (071) 474 5555

Bel   Fr   Hol

Easily accessible by public transport from central London. A regular riverbus service (approximate journey time 35 minutes) from Charing Cross Pier or Swan Lane Pier. London City Airport/Silvertown Station is on the North London Line and is within walking distance of the airport terminal. The airport is five minutes by taxi from Plaistow Underground Station (District & Metropolitan lines).

Long-term and short-term car parks adjacent to airport entrance.

Mother and baby room situated on ground floor, near to female toilet.

Nappies not available.

Children's meals and baby food not available.

Toys available in terminal.

Good facilities for disabled passengers. Check with airport staff before travelling.

Allow 10 minutes to clear baggage and customs.

Child seats available with car-rental.

Luton

Luton International Airport
Luton
Bedfordshire
LU2 9LY
Tel: (0582) 405100

Ch. Is.   Eur   Ire   UK

Excellent coach, rail and road connections. Regular service from Central London by British Rail *Luton Flyer Railair Link* (journey time as little as 43 minutes). Regular connections from Luton Station with Intercity trains to the Midlands and beyond. Direct coach services to many destinations in UK, Heathrow and Gatwick airports.

Both long-term and short-term parking is available. Disabled drivers are strongly advised to write to the Airport Director in advance for allocation of suitable spaces.

Mother and baby rooms are situated in the landside concourse and departure lounge.

Disposable nappies available.

Children's meals, snacks and baby food available.

Medical centre in landside concourse (open 24 hours).

Playcare centre staffed by qualified nursery nurses where children aged 2–8 years may be left for short periods free of charge.

Books and toys for sale in terminal.

Children's entertainments may be organized, in the event of long delays.

New domestic terminal due for completion autumn 1990. This will contain refurbished spectator facilities.

Good facilities for disabled visitors. Check with airport staff for details of availability.

Allow 40 minutes to clear baggage and customs.
Child seats available with car-rental.

Manchester
Manchester Airport
Manchester
M22 5PA
Tel: (061) 489 3000

Worldwide

Good transport connections by bus, rail and car. A regular shuttle bus service calls at Manchester Victoria railway station and Piccadilly bus and railway stations. A rail link to the airport terminal is currently under construction and is due for completion in 1992.
Long-term and short-term parking facilities available. Disabled travellers should contact airport staff in advance for further details of the facilities available to them.
Changing facilities are available in the female toilet areas in both terminal A (domestic arrivals hall) and terminal B (main concourse and international pier C satellite).
A nursery is provided in the international check-in hall (opposite desks 80–87) where babies and young children can be attended to in privacy and comfort. The key is available from the information desks in the main concourse and the international arrivals hall.
Children's meals, snacks and baby food available. Ice-cream parlour.
Playcare centre staffed by qualified nursery nurses where children aged 2–8 years may be left for short periods free of charge. This is situated opposite the duty-free shop in terminal B.
Books and toys for sale in terminal.
Chemist's shop in main concourse.
Spectator terrace available during daylight hours.
Allow 30 minutes to clear baggage and customs.
Child seats available with car-rental.

Newcastle
Newcastle International Airport
Woolsington
Newcastle
NE13 8BZ
Tel: (091) 286 0966

Eur   UK   USA

Good rail, bus and coach connections. Regular bus service runs from Newcastle Central railway station and Eldon Square bus concourse direct to airport terminal (approximate journey time of 25 minutes). Coach service to and from major cities in England and Scotland. The nearest station in the Tyne & Wear Metro system is Kenton Bankfoot, from which a regular bus service runs to the airport terminal (approximate journey time of 10 minutes). Work will soon begin on an extension of the Metro line direct to the airport buildings.
Short-term and long-term parking facilities.
Mother and baby room in main concourse.
Disposable nappies available.
Children's meals and snacks available, but no baby food.
Books and toys for sale in terminal.
Roof terrace is open to spectators during daylight hours.
Disabled travellers are advised to contact the airport prior to arrival to confirm facilities available.
Allow 30 minutes to clear baggage and customs.
Child seats available with car-rental.

Norwich
Norwich Airport
Norfolk
NN6 6JA
Tel: (0603) 411923

Ch. Is   Hol   Sp   UK   Yug

3 miles from Norwich city centre. Regular bus service (approximate journey time 15 minutes).

Parent and child room in main concourse.
Disposable nappies available.
Children's meals and snacks, but no baby food.
Books and toys for sale in terminal.
Allow 30 minutes to clear baggage and customs.
Child seats available with car-rental.

Prestwick
Prestwick Airport
Prestwick
Ayrshire
KA9 2PL
Tel: (0292) 79822

Can   USA

Rail, coach and road connections. A courtesy coach service operates from Prestwick Station, which is on the main line from Glasgow to Ayr (approximate journey time from Glasgow 45 minutes). A regular coach link runs from Glasgow city centre (Buchanan Street bus station) and Edinburgh (St Andrews Square bus station).
Short-term and long-term parking facilities. Disabled travellers are advised to contact the airport information desk in advance for details of the facilities available.
Mother and baby rooms are situated in the main terminal (landside) and the international departure lounge.
Disposable nappies available.
Children's food and snacks available, but no baby food.
For medical services, contact the information desk.
Books and toys on sale in terminal.
Spectator's terrace situated on the second floor, overlooking the aircraft parking area. Terrace contains an amusement arcade.
Allow 30 minutes to clear baggage and customs.
Child seats available with car-rental.

Southampton
Southampton Airport
Southampton
SO9 1RH
Tel: (0703) 629600

Ch. Is   Fr   Hol   UK

Situated 5 miles from Eastleigh. 7 miles from Southampton town centre by train.
Parent and child room in main concourse.
Nappies not available.
Children's meals and snacks, but no baby food.
Books and toys for sale in terminal.
Allow 15 minutes to clear baggage and customs.
Child seats are available with car-rental.

Southend
Southend Airport
Southend
Essex
SS2 6YF
Tel: (0702) 340201

Ch.Is   Eur

3 miles from Southend, 18 miles from M25 (junction 29), with bus and British Rail connections. 60 minutes by rail from London (Fenchurch Street and Liverpool Street stations).
Short-term and long-term parking available.
Good facilities for disabled travellers but passengers are advised to contact airport staff for further details before travelling.
Parent and baby room in main concourse.
Nappies not available.
Children's meals and snacks available, but no baby food.
No first-aid room, but airport fire-service staff are trained to give medical attention for minor ailments.
Books and toys for sale in terminal.
Allow 15 minutes to clear baggage and customs.
Child seats available with car-rental.

Stansted

Stansted Airport Ltd
Stansted
Essex
CM24 8QW
Tel: (0279) 502379/502520

*Can   Crb   Eur   Mex   Tun   Tur
USA*

Situated 35 miles north east of London. Trains to Bishop's Stortford on electrified London/Cambridge line from Liverpool Street (approximate journey time 50 minutes). Bus service between Bishop's Stortford station and airport. Direct train service due for completion in 1991.
Short-term and long-term car parking

available. Disabled travellers are advised to contact the airport information desk for further details of the facilities available.
Mother and baby room is situated in the main concourse. A parent and child room (for use by parents of either gender) is located halfway between the arrivals and departure halls.
Disposable nappies are available.
Children's meals and snacks available, and baby food is complimentary.
Books and toys for sale in terminal.
Children's entertainment may be organized in the event of long delays.
Allow 30 minutes to clear baggage and customs.
Child seats available with car-rental.

Airlines

Whether you're planning a short hop across the Channel or a long-haul flight to Australia, air travel can be a bit of an ordeal if you have children in tow. However, airlines do try to help, and many of them have excellent facilities for those needing to feed and change babies, or to amuse toddlers and small children.

Major airlines will obviously have a greater range of services than smaller carriers, but you can expect to find any of the following: bassinets, cots, changing facilities, baby food, milk, bottle-sterilizing and warming facilities, disposable nappies, children's meals, toys, games and books, seatbelt extensions. In addition you will often find you can take the push chair right up to the aircraft rather than having to carry your child, and many airlines allow people with children to board early.

It is essential to request everything you might need when reserving your seats. If you book through a travel agent, do ask for confirmation of your requirements. Airlines are usually willing to supply almost anything, if properly requested, but all too often the tour operator fails to make the request, or does not make it clearly enough. For peace of mind it's worth phoning the airline yourself about twenty-four hours before departure and reiterating your needs.

To find out exactly which childrens' facilities particular airlines offer, it's best to contact them direct. Below you will find the addresses and phone numbers of 63 major airlines.

Aer Lingus
223 Regent Street, London W1
Tel: 081 569 5555

Aeroflot Soviet Airlines
70 Piccadilly, London W1V 9HH
Tel: 071 355 2233 or 071 491 1756

Air Canada
7/8 Conduit Street
London W1R 9TQ
Tel: 071 759 2636 (Reservations)

Air France
158 New Bond Street, London W1Y 0AY
Tel: 071 499 9511

Air India
17–18 New Bond Street, London W1Y 0BD
Tel: 071 491 7979

Air Malta
23 Pall Mall, London SW1Y 5LP
Tel: 071 839 5872

Air Mauritius
49 Conduit Street, London W1R 9FB
Tel: 071 434 4375/9

Air New Zealand
New Zealand House, Haymarket,
London SW1Y 4TE
Tel: 071 930 3434

Air Zimbabwe
52 Piccadilly, London W1V 9AA
Tel: 071 499 8947

Alitalia
205 Holland Park Avenue, London W11 4XB
Tel: 071 602 7111

American Airlines
15 Berkeley Street, London W1X 6ND
Tel: 081 834 5151

Austrian Air
50–51 Conduit Street, London W1R 0NP
Tel: 071 439 0741

Britannia Airways Ltd
Luton Airport, Luton, Beds LU2 9ND
Tel: 0582 424155

British Air Ferries
Viscount House, Southend Airport,
Essex SS2 6YL
Tel: 0702 354435

British Airways
Speedbird House, PO Box 10,
Heathrow Airport, Hounslow,
Middlesex TW6 2JA
Tel: 081 897 4000

British Midland Airways
East Midlands Airport, Castle
Donnington, Derby DE7 2SA
Tel: 0332 812469

BWIA (British West Indian Airways)
48 Leicester Square, London WC2H 7LT
Tel: 071 839 9333

Caledonian Airways
Caledonian House, Gatwick Airport,
Sussex RH6 0LF
Tel: 0293 36321

Canadian Airlines International
Rothschild House, First Floor, Whitgift
Centre, Croydon, Surrey CR9 3HL
Tel: 081 667 0666

Cathay Pacific
52 Berkeley Street, London W1X 5FP
Tel: 071 930 7878 or 0345 581581

Continental Airlines
Beulah Court, Albert Road, Horley,
Surrey RH6 7HZ
Tel: 0293 776464

Cyprus Airways
29 Hampstead Road, London NW1 3JA
Tel: 071 388 5411

Dan Air Services Ltd
Newman House, 45 Victoria Road,
Horley, Surrey RH6 7QG
Tel: 0345 100200

Delta Airlines Inc
Victoria Place, 115 Buckingham Palace
Road, London SW1
Tel: Freephone 0800 414767

Egyptair
29–31 Piccadilly, London W1V 0PT
Tel: 071 734 2395/6 or 071 437 6426

El Al (Israel Airlines)
185 Regent Street, London W1R 8BS
Tel: 071 437 9255

Emirates
125 Pall Mall, London SW1Y 5EA
Tel: 071 930 3711

Finnair
14 Clifford Street, London W1X 1RD
Tel: 071 408 1222

Garuda Indonesia
35 Duke Street, London W1M 5DF
Tel: 071 486 3011

Gulf Air
10 Albemarle Street, London W1X 3HE
Tel: 071 409 0191

Iberia
29 Glasshouse Street, London W1R 5RG
Tel: 071 437 5622

Icelandair
Third Floor, 172 Tottenham Court Road, London W1P 9LG
Tel: 071 388 5599

JAL (Japan Airlines)
5 Hanover Square, London W1R 0DR
Tel: 071 408 1000

Kenya Airways
16 Conduit Street, London W1R 9TD
Tel: 071 409 0277

KLM (Royal Dutch Airlines)
8 Hanover Street, London W1R 9HF
Tel: 081 750 9000

Korean Air
Greener House, 66–68 Haymarket, London SW1
Tel: 071 930 6513

LOT (Polish Airlines)
313 Regent Street, London W1R 7PE
Tel: 071 580 5037

Lufthansa
23–26 Piccadilly, London W1N 0EJ
Tel: 071 408 0442

MAS (Malaysian Airline System)
61 Piccadilly, London W1V 9HL
Tel: 071 872 8444

MEA (Middle East Airlines)
48 Park Street, London W1Y 4AS
Tel: 071 493 5681

Monarch
Luton Airport, Beds LU2 9NU
Tel: 0582 424211

Northwest Airlines
8–9 Berkeley Street, London W1X 5AD
Tel: 0345 747800

Olympic Airways
Commonwealth House, 2 Chalkhill Road, London W6 8SB
Tel: 081 846 9080

Pan Am
193 Piccadilly, London W1V 0AD
Tel: 071 409 0688

Philippine Airlines
Centrepoint, 103 New Oxford Street, London WC1
Tel: 071 836 5508

PIA (Pakistan International Airways)
45 Piccadilly, London W1V 0DY
Tel: 071 734 5544

Qantas
Qantas House, 395–403 King Street, London W6 9NJ
Tel: 0345 747767

Royal Air Maroc
205 Regent Street, London W1R 7DE
Tel: 071 439 4631

Royal Jordanian Airlines
177 Regent Street, London W1R 9FB
Tel: 071 734 2557

Royal Nepal Airlines
114–115 Tottenham Court Road, London W1P 9HN
Tel: 071 387 1541

Ryanair
Barkat House, 116/118 Finchley Road, London NW3 5HT
Tel: 071 435 7101

Sabena
Geminii House, 10–18 Putney Hill, London SW15 6AA
Tel: 081 780 1444

SAS (Scandinavian Airlines System)
52 Conduit Street, London W1R 0AY
Tel: 071 734 6777

TAP (Air Portugal)
38–44 Gillingham House, Gillingham Street, London SW1V 1JW
Tel: 071 828 0262

Thai Air
41 Albemarle Street, London W1X 3FE
Tel: 071 499 9113

TWA (Trans World Airlines)
200 Piccadilly, London W1V 0DH
Tel: 071 439 0707

Saudi Arabian Airlines
171 Regent Street, London W1 5RG
Tel: 081 995 7777

Singapore Airlines
143 Regent Street, London W1R 7LB
Tel: 071 747 0007

Sudan Airlines
12 Grosvenor Street, London W1X 9FB
Tel: 071 499 8101

Swissair
Swiss Centre, 10 Wardour Street,
London W1V 4BJ
Tel: 071 439 4144

US Air
Piccadilly House, 33–37 Regent Street,
London SW1Y 4NB
Tel: *Linkline* 0800 777333

Varig
16/17 Hanover Street, London
W1R 0HG
Tel: 071 629 5824

Virgin Atlantic Airways
Ashdown House, High Street, Crawley,
Sussex RH10 1DQ
Tel: 0293 562000/562345

Zambia Airways
163 Piccadilly, London W1V 9DE
Tel: 071 491 0650/8/9

Ferries

A short crossing, such as Dover–Calais, which takes $1\frac{1}{4}$ hours, is not really long enough for children to get bored or seasick. However, longer crossings such as Plymouth–Santander, which lasts 24 hours, can be quite gruelling, even if the sea is calm.

Many of the major ferry companies realize that boredom can be a problem for people of any age, and for those not wanting to prop up the bar for the duration, there may be entertainments, such as cinemas, TV, swimming pools and amusement arcades. For children there are often play areas, electronic games, supervised activities and special menus at reduced prices. For nursing mothers there are often quiet rooms where babies can be fed and changed in private. Cots are available on many ships but they should always be booked in advance.

If you have a long crossing ahead of you, it is wise to travel at night so that your children's routine is changed as little as possible. A cabin is a sound investment, not a luxury.

B+I LINE
Reliance House, Water Street,
Liverpool
Tel: 051 227 3131 or 071 734 4681
(London)

Regular sailings between Holyhead and
Dublin, and between Pembroke and
Rosslare. Children's facilities include a
special children's menu. (Also see B+I
LINE entries – **Cottages** and **Hotels**)
Prices   (per family of 4 with car)
Holyhead – Dublin return: £140 (low)
Discounts   Children under 5 travel
free. Children aged 5–16 pay 50% of
adult fare.

BRITISH CHANNEL ISLAND FERRIES
PO Box 315, Poole, Dorset BH15 4DB
Tel: 0202 681155

Year-round overnight sailings from
Poole, plus day sailings from April to
October. Overnight accommodation is
offered in comfortable cabins. Ships
have many facilities, including chil-
dren's playrooms.
Prices   (depending on date)
Car (any length): £33–£46
Adult: £26–£32
Discounts   Under-5s travel free; 5–16s
pay 50% of the adult fare.

BRITTANY FERRIES
1 Battersea Church Road, London
SW11 3LY
Tel: 071 836 5885

Regular sailings between several ports:
Portsmouth to Caen and St Malo;
Plymouth to Roscoff and Santander;
Cork and Roscoff (March – October
only). 'Truckline' Les Routiers service
between Poole and Cherbourg available
during summer only. Special facilities
on board include a nursing mothers'
room, children's play area, TV, and high
chairs in the restaurants. (Also see
BRITTANY FERRIES – **Cottages, Hotels**)
Prices   (Portsmouth–Caen return, car
only)

Low   £38
Mid   £68
High   £98
Each adult pays £20–£32.
Discounts   Children under 4 travel
free; 4–13s pay 50% of adult fare.

HOVERSPEED
Maybrook House, Queen's Gardens,
Dover CT17 9UQ
Tel: 0304 240202/240241 or 081 554
7061 (London)

Regular hovercraft flights between
Dover, Calais and Boulogne. The company also runs a Seacat catamaran be-
tween Portsmouth and Cherbourg.
Crossings are more frequent during
summer months, and fares are highest
during July and August. There are no
special child facilities on board the
hovercraft, but there is a nursing
mothers' room in the hoverport.
Prices   (per medium-sized car with a
family of 4 from Dover return)
Low   £146 (Dec)
High   £278 (Aug)
A 60-hour Fly-away Special costs £87.
Seacat prices available on request.
Discounts   Under-4s travel free.
Children aged 4–14 pay around 50% of
the adult fare.

ISLE OF MAN STEAM PACKET COMPANY LTD
Imperial Buildings, Douglas, Isle of
Man
Tel: 0624 661661

Daily sailings from Heysham to
Douglas, with many additional sailings
between Heysham and Liverpool from
April to September. The crossing takes
about 4 hours. Day trips and weekend
excursions are also available. Special
facilities include a room off the ladies'
lavatory where nappies can be changed
and a mothers' room where babies can
be fed in peace.
Prices   (per adult per single journey)
Mid   £19 (child 5–15 £9.50; car (4.5m)
£45)

High   £23 (child 5–15 £11.50; car
(4.5m) £54)
Discounts   Children under 5 travel
free.

NORTH SEA FERRIES
King George Dock, Hedon Road, Hull
HU9 5QA
Tel: 0482 795141; Reservations: 0482
77177

Nightly sailings from Hull to Rotterdam
and Zeebrugge. Child facilities include
cots, if requested when booking, and a
children's playroom.
Prices   (per car under 6 metres long)
Low   £49
High   £60
Each adult pays £8–£22, depending on
sleeping arrangements (*NB* on top of
reclining seat price)
Discounts   Under-4s travel free, provided they share a berth with their
parents. Children aged 2–13 pay 50% of
the adult fare, and must occupy a cabin
berth. A special 'Family Cabin Fare' is
available, based on 4-berth inside
special cabins, 4-berth economy cabins
or 4-berth outside special cabins.

NORWAY LINE
Tyne Commission Quay, Albert Edward
Dock, North Shields NE29 6EA
Tel: 091 296 1313

Sailings twice or three times weekly,
depending on time of year, between
Newcastle, Stavanger and Bergen. Rail
connections to Newcastle from all parts
of the UK can be arranged on request.
Children under 16 pay half adult rail
fare. There are no special on-board
facilities for children. (*Also see* NOR-
WAY LINE *entry* – **Hotels**)
Prices   (single journey)
Car: £28
Adult: £25–£155 (depending on accommodation and date).
When a car is carrying four paying passengers, the car is free.
Discounts   Children under 4 travel free
if sharing berth with parents. Under-16s

receive 50% discount. Other reductions
include 10% off passenger fare for
members of the YHA and 25% off for
students.

OLAU-LINE
Sheerness, Kent ME12 1SN
Tel: 0795 666666

Two daily sailings between Sheerness
and Vlissingen in Holland. On-board
facilities for children include a playroom
(unsupervised) and a swimming pool.
Midweek during summer holidays,
there is a children's entertainment programme. (*Also see* OLAU-LINE *entry* –
Hotels)
Prices   (per single journey)
Special Tariff for 1 car and up to 5 passengers from £65.
53-Hour return – adults £26, children
(4–13 years) £16.
Under-4s: Free
Discounts   A special family fare is
available on day sailings: up to three
children travel free if accompanied by
two adults paying £45 (without car).

P & O EUROPEAN FERRIES
Channel House, Channel View Road,
Dover, Kent CT17 9TJ
Tel: 0304 203388

Daily sailings on the following routes:
Dover to Calais/Boulogne/Zeebrugge/
Ostend; Felixstowe to Zeebrugge;
Portsmouth to Cherbourg/Le Havre;
Cairnryan to Larne. Special facilities on
board for the family include: children's
play areas; video lounges showing free
films; mother and baby changing facilities. Children's menus/portions are
available from waiter and self service
restaurants. Cabins are available on
Portsmouth–Le Havre/Cherbourg and
Felixstowe–Zeebrugge routes.
Prices   Please note fares are dependent on route and date of travel. Fares
for a fortnight's holiday start from £129
(low season) to £286 (peak season)
based on a car plus 2 adults and 2 children (4–14 years).

Discounts Reduced fares for students, and children (4–14). Children under 4 travel free.

P & O SCOTTISH FERRIES
PO Box 5, Jamieson's Quay, Aberdeen AB9 8DL
Tel: 0224 572615

Daily, and some weekday only, sailings from Aberdeen and Scrabster on the Scottish mainland to the Orkneys and Shetlands. From end May–early September connections from Lerwick to the Faroes, Iceland, Norway and Denmark are offered in conjunction with the Smyril Line. P&O does not specify any particular facilities for children or nursing mothers.
Prices (Aberdeen–Lerwick) June–September prices
Car (under 4.3 m): £123 (return)
Adult: £36–£74 (single), depending on accommodation.
Discounts Under-4s travel free; 4–13s pay half adult fare.

SALLY LINE
Argyle Centre, York Street, Ramsgate, Kent CT11 9DS
Tel: 0843 595522 *(Ramsgate)*, 071 409 2240 *(London)*

Regular sailings between Ramsgate and Dunkirk. Motorail link from Lille (53 miles from Dunkirk) to Bordeaux, St Raphael and Narbonne. All boats have a supervised crèche and special play areas for children, including a 'Sea of balls' – an enclosed room filled with plastic balls which provides hours of fun – video games, TV, children's meals at reduced prices and a room for nursing mothers. *(Also see SALLY TOURS –* **Hotels***)*
Prices (return crossing per car with 2 adults and 2 children)
Low £112
High £228
A car with five passengers is eligible for an unlimited return ticket costing from £122. Many other deals are available, including 60-hour returns and special day-trip rates.
Discounts Children under 4 travel free. If motoring, the first child under 14 always travels free.

SEALINK
Platform 2, Victoria Station, London (Personal callers only).

Regular sailings to Holland, France, Ireland and the Isle of Wight. Sealink has special arrangements with other ferries, so you can book a connecting ferry from Marseilles to Corsica and get a 10% discount on the total fare. Connections can also be arranged from Italy to Greece, Yugoslavia and Egypt. On-board special facilities include a children's room with games section and videos, and there is a mother and baby room. *(Also see SEALINK HOLIDAYS –* **Holiday centres, Hotels** and **Villas***)*
Prices (per single journey, Dover–Calais)
Car: £41–£102
Adult: £13.50
4–13s: £8.50
Under-4s: Free
Discounts Up to two children under 14 with motorists travel free on day sailings. This does not apply to foot passengers or cyclists. All other children under 14 pay 50% of adult fare.

SCANDINAVIAN SEAWAYS
Scandinavia House, Parkeston Quay, Harwich, Essex CO12 4QG
Tel: 0255 241234

Regular sailings between UK, Denmark, Sweden and northern Germany, with connections to Norway. Special on-board facilities for children include cots, playroom (unsupervised), organized games and cinema. *(Also see SCANDINAVIAN SEAWAYS entry –* **Hotels***)*
Prices Supersaver return fare per adult from: £66 sharing a 4-berth couchette Harwich–Hamburg.

Discounts   Children under 4 travel free if sharing parents' accommodation; 4–16s pay 50% of adult fare and are given separate berths. A 10% discount is available on the Scandinavian Seaways fare if you book a connecting crossing with the Larvik Line from Denmark to Norway. There is a 30% discount on the Larvik crossing if you travel midweek.

SWANSEA CORK FERRIES

Ferry Port, Kings Dock, Swansea
SA1 8RU
Tel: 0792 456116

Crossings between Swansea and Cork between May and September. Four sailings in each direction in low season and six between mid-June and mid-September. In high season the outward journeys are at night, returns during the day. In low season all but one are at night. The crossing takes 10 hours. Cabins, berths and pullman seats can be booked, but cost extra. There is a snack bar, restaurant and a swimming pool. Cots are not available in the cabins.

Prices   (per return journey per car with up to 4 adults)
£150–£318

Discounts   Children under 5 travel free at all times, 5–15s are half price as foot passengers. In a car, two children = one adult.

Section 4

Getting there

Keeping the Kids Amused . . . and Keeping your Sanity

One parent's solution to the problems of travelling with children

Sheila Sang

You've picked your destination, holiday fever is upon you all, but there's the journey to face. Anyone who's ever travelled with children will know: kids and travel don't mix. If they're not squabbling or wanting something to eat, they're being sick or thinking of new ways of asking 'how much longer?' Use our guide to make sure you have all the essentials to keep your brood happy and amused. Who knows, you might even have a good trip.

Tool kit for travel

There are some basic things which no travelling parent should be without – tailor them to suit your children and your journey.

- **A favourite toy** You may find that your child will play with only one or two things, however long the journey. Take a firm favourite that you know has long-playing power.
- **A new toy** If there's something your child has been longing for, consider making a present of it before or during a tedious journey.
- **Food** fills their mouths and minds at the same time – fewer complaints! Avoid anything messy, like yoghurt, chocolate or bananas and steer clear of pastry which is at best messy and may bring on travel sickness. Bring along plenty of fresh and healthy nibbles like carrot sticks, cubes of cheese or apple slices rubbed in lemon and kept in a polythene bag. Crisps and individual packets of raisins are an easy option and always popular. If you're providing a picnic you'll obviously need to expand on this – but keep it simple and stick to finger foods.

- **Drink** Throwaway cartons of fruit juice and squash are great when travelling. Bring plenty – it could save you a fortune. Cans, on the other hand, are a downright nuisance – few young children can drink the lot in one go, and they spill easily. You can now buy snap-on sealers for ring-pull cans and these will make canned drinks more practical when travelling and, hopefully, will keep the liquid fizzy. If your child is too young to use a straw, fill a bottle with drink and take a beaker to avoid spills.
- **Clothes** Bring a change of the basics for everyone who might need them (this might mean a spare tee-shirt for your eight-year-old, but three complete wardrobes for your three-month-old baby).
- **Baby wipes** for all ages. They're an easy and gentle way of keeping hands and faces clean. Many are available in travel packs; save money by refilling from the larger size.
- **Tissues** They're invaluable for everything from a runny nose to an inadequate public loo, and take up less space than toilet roll. And of course they'll mop up accidental spills too.
- **Books** Invaluable. For a baby or toddler three or four slim paperbacks should get you through most journeys (on a long journey they'll bear repeating), for older children a new book in a favourite series (Dr Who? Famous Five?) should be a winner. See our chapter on books on p 000.
- **Personal stereo** These are a very useful investment, particularly if you're travelling a long distance. They allow children to listen to absorbing story or song tapes, and will give you a few minutes hard-earned peace and quiet – particularly important if you're travelling alone, or you're outnumbered by your kids. For children under the age of about four you can get specially designed cassette players with easy-to-use controls and, more importantly, a device that allows you to set a maximum volume, to protect your child's ears. Some players have sockets for more than one pair of headphones, allowing two children to listen at the same time. This may save you from noisy arguments!
- **Children's backpack** How you carry the rest of your essential en-route supplies will vary depending on how you're travelling, but it's a good idea to let each child take care of at least some of their own things in an easy-to-carry backpack. It'll keep their belongings where they can find them (in principle, at least!) and lighten your own load a bit. But beware of leaving children in charge of anything that's expensive or irreplaceable.

Baby on Board

If you've got a baby, you already know that they need more than their own weight in paraphernalia. You'll need all the usuals – nappies, wipes and so on – and more. If you've got a good changing bag that will help, if not, consider buying one. Go for one with a detachable changing mat, lots of separate pockets for small items and a zipped and lined pocket for dirties. If you're still breast feeding then food and drink is laid on, otherwise use disposable bottles – they're cheap and easy to use. If you want to heat them, or heat baby food in jars, think about buying a travel bottle warmer – go for the type that doesn't need plugging in. It's also worth using disposable bibs – no yukky dirties to store all journey.

Toys and Games

However you're travelling, toys and games are no luxury. Take a reasonable supply – but avoid games with lots of easily-lost small parts, and don't bring anything that makes a lot of noise – a talking doll or bleeping computer game will drive you all mad.

For babies bring along a selection of teethers and rattles, soft toys or cloth books to look at and suck, and some building beakers if you'll have access to a table.

Board jigsaws are great for toddlers (you can often find puzzles that relate to travelling); pencil and paper are essentials for all ages. A wipe-clean magic slate will be fun to use, and handy for scoring games. Once children are older special travel versions of popular board games, such as Connect 4 or draughts will be popular.

But you're likely to find that it's your company and powers of invention that are most in demand. Try some of these 'eye spy' type games to cheer flagging spirits.

Granny went to market and she bought . . . A memory game where each of you adds a new (and preferably irrelevant) item after repeating her shopping list so far.

Yes/no game Take turns at answering questions without saying yes or no.

What is it? Describe an everyday object to someone who must guess what it is.

Animal, mineral or vegetable One of you picks an object and tells the others whether it's animal, mineral or vegetable. The rest of you try to guess what it is by asking questions that can be answered by yes or no.

Watch this space Before you go, make up a list of things you're likely
to see on your journey and cross them off as you spot them. For non-
readers, draw pictures (of a cow, horse, bus, lorry, etc).

Travel sickness

Travel sickness can make long journeys a problem for the whole
family. Train travel is the least likely to induce it, while coach journeys
and choppy ferry crossings are most likely to bring on an attack.
Plenty of fresh air can help, and travelling later in the day is generally
better than first thing in the morning. Try to make sure the child has
eaten, but avoid greasy foods and fizzy drinks. Apples, barley sugar,
and dry biscuits make good snacks.

Be prepared for the worst. Keep a stock of disposable nappy sacks
handy for your child to be sick in. They're scented and easy to dispose
of. A damp cloth sprinkled with bicarbonate of soda will remove the
worst of the smell in case of accidents.

Try your child with 'Sea Bands'. They're stretchy cloth bracelets
with a firm plastic bobble that you place over acupuncture pressure
points in the wrist to prevent nausea. Trials indicate that they do help
adults, although it's hard to get exactly the right point in a child's
wrist.

By car

Chances are your children will be quite familiar with travelling by car,
so you don't have any of the benefits that the novelty of a voyage can
bring. They're going to need entertaining from hour one.

On the plus side, you're not so restricted in what you can take with
you, you can stop whenever you like (or whenever you need to), and
your children will be comfortably seated, albeit irritable and restrained. With a bit of luck they may even doze off.

- Do pack as much as possible in the boot, to keep the car clear and
  uncluttered. If you restrict the children's leg room they'll get
  uncomfortable sooner, and then you'll all suffer.
- Do keep food and drinks to hand – but not within reach of the
  children.
- Do stop regularly if you can. Plan for an unhurried journey and
  encourage the children to go to the loo when you stop, to cut down
  on irritating unscheduled breaks.

- Do encourage each child to use a bag for rubbish – otherwise their playthings could soon disappear under a mound of crisp wrappers, drinks cartons etc, and they'll become uncomfortably cluttered.
- Do use motorways where you can. They're faster, less likely to cause travel sickness, and the kids are more likely to doze off. Most motorway service areas have baby changing and feeding rooms.
- Do make long journeys late in the evening or at night if possible, so that the children can spend most of their journey asleep. Make sure the children are comfortable, safely strapped in with their heads supported by spare clothing or an inflatable neck rest. But if you're the only driver, this is often not an option, as you could easily become too tired to drive safely.
- Do be patient. It's very likely you'll have to spend at least some of the journey playing games with, and generally trying to amuse, the children.
- Don't encourage children to read in the back of the car. It can cause headaches or make children feel sick.

By train

This is probably the easiest and most comfortable way of travelling with children. You'll usually have a table for games or drawing on, which can double as a changing mat at a pinch (the loos in most trains are too small, though some trains do now have baby changing facilities). Your children will also be free to wriggle in their seats to their hearts' content, and wander up and down the train (with a supervising adult if need be). They may even make friends with other children in the carriage.

- Do use a good shoulder bag with a wide strap to carry all the clutter you're likely to want at hand.
- Do make use of the excellent mother and baby facilities at most major stations.
- Do reserve your seats, even when you're travelling at off-peak times. You could consider asking to be near the buffet, which has the advantage that food and drinks are at hand, but buffet prices are often high and these carriages are usually crowded and have a lot of through traffic. If you're waiting for a train to stop at your station ask a guard whereabouts the carriage you'll be travelling in will stop – no panic as you try to get your luggage and your children on.

- Do travel off-peak whenever possible. Tickets are often cheaper, and trains less crowded. You're also more likely to find sympathetic fellow-travellers.
- Do try to break up a long journey for your child – even if it's just by going to the end of the carriage to stand by an open window.
- Do take a rubbish bag. The amount of rubbish generated by a family picnic won't fit in the train's bins.
- Don't rely on the buffet. They're sometimes closed for parts of the journey, and sometimes not open at all.

By air

Air travel's fast, but the journey to get to the airport and long waits once you get there often mean that's not the way it feels. Many charter flights require that you turn up two hours before take off – and that's assuming the flight's not delayed. And children quickly become fractious once they've got over the excitement of being on a plane, because they're confined in a small space and have little to look at.

- Do make sure the airline knows if you're travelling with a baby. You can often book a small cot in advance and order baby food. But most under-twos will be expected to spend the journey on your lap – trying for both of you.
- Do arrive in time to get seats together, preferably at the front of the plane or behind the safety exits, where there will be more leg room and space to store your belongings. This also has the advantage that your child won't annoy the person in front by raising and lowering their table and kicking and jogging the seat back. A window seat will give you more privacy if you want to breastfeed.
- Do bear in mind that you're allowed only one piece of handluggage each, and that most of your things will go in an overhead locker that will be hard to get at unless you sit at the aisle. Try to keep the things you *know* you'll need in one small bag that you can keep by your feet.
- Do pick a good spot in the departure lounge, near a window that looks out onto the planes, if possible. Some airports have supervised play areas for children – ask when you check in (*see* Airport Facilities p. 000).
- Do use mother and baby facilities at the airport – they're usually comfortable and it'll be easier than trying to feed or change your baby on the flight. See the section on airport facilities on p. 000.

- Do make sure the children use the toilet at the airport before boarding. They won't be allowed to use the one on the plane until after take-off.
- Do be prepared for the pressure changes at take-off and landing to hurt your children's ears. Sucking and swallowing can help, so have some boiled sweets ready for older children, and offer babies the breast or bottle. Yawning also helps – you could encourage your child to do so by yawning yourself.
- Do check with the airline if you're relying on a personal stereo as in-flight entertainment for your child. Some airlines don't allow their use in case they interfere with radio frequencies. In the light of recent terrorist attacks, all personal stereos, radios etc. must be declared before boarding.
- Don't check in your buggy or carrycot before you need to. Many airlines will take them from you just as you get on the plane. Make sure they're clearly labelled.
- Don't count on children eating airplane food – if you're travelling at a time they need to eat, bring something you know they like. And don't count on getting fed in the plane if you're travelling single-handed with an under-two. It's a physical impossibility with a toddler on your lap in a crowded plane.

By ferry

Travelling by ferry can be great fun for the kids – what other type of transport lets them explore level by level, then run around and let off steam on the deck? Many ferries now boast children's playrooms and video rooms, where you can sit and relax with your kids, or even leave reliable older children while you do a bit of exploring yourself. But again, long waits and long journeys can dull the novelty, and at peak times overcrowding can lead to far from pleasant journeys.

- Do check out how long you're likely to wait to get your car on the ferry. If you've got a long wait you'll do better to go to the ferry terminal, even if it's very crowded, particularly after a long journey.
- Do take some toys and games to the ferry terminal or be prepared to play with your children. They're often crowded and there's little specially laid on.
- Do make sure you have a small bag packed with everything you're likely to want on the trip, because you probably won't be allowed to go back to your car during the crossing.

- Do use the mother and baby facilities on the ferry. They're usually a cut above the usual ladies' loos, and fairly spacious.
- Do travel overnight and book a cabin if you're taking a long sea crossing. Put your children in pyjamas before you leave home so they can sleep in the car as well.
- Do bring some drinks and snacks with you. Ferry facilities can be expensive, there may be queues, and on night crossings bars and restaurants may shut.
- Don't let young children explore unattended. They could easily get lost or get excited and climb up on the rails on deck.
- Don't let older children discover the many tempting slot machines unless you can face the arguments about disappearing holiday spending money.

By coach

Travelling by coach is the least attractive option if you have children, even in a modern and luxurious coach. Indeed, some companies refuse to take reservations for children under twelve. The problem is that your child will be expected to sit still for what is often quite a long journey – there simply isn't anywhere for them to go, and any undue restlessness or wandering is going to disturb other passengers. On top of that, rest stops are likely to be fairly few and far between, and certainly not at the intervals that a child would like.

- Do go by luxury coach if you can afford it. These provide refreshments and videos that will help distract your child.
- Do check in advance that there's a toilet on the coach to avoid disasters. (There usually is).
- Do arrive early, to get good seats. If your child is prone to travel sickness the middle of the coach is far better than the back.
- Do try to keep your essential travel kit in one big bag, which you can then store in the luggage rack overhead, or under your seat. You won't want to be cluttered up with loads of bags.
- Do travel by night if possible. Your child should then sleep for most of the journey.
- Don't leave anything you'll want on the journey in your luggage. It will be packed away in the hold under the coach.

Holiday Reading for Kids

Wayne Jackman

If you are about to embark on a family holiday then it is essential to consider entertainment for the children, particularly on the journey. Remember the old Latin saying, 'bored and restless children cause *parentus nervosa breakdownum*' (I'll leave you to work that out). So, before you set off clutching your road map and insect repellent, arm yourself with pens, pencils, drawing paper, activity books, puzzles and story books for the children. The books recommended on the following pages are organized into four age groups and are available as lightweight paperbacks.

Another useful distraction is a selection of story tapes which can be played on the car cassette or on a personal stereo. There are hundreds of stories, rhymes and songs available on tape and Roald Dahl story tapes never fail to amuse. With a little careful planning the journey will seem like part of the holiday! Bon vacances.

Books For The Under Fives

The Snowman, by Raymond Briggs (Picture Puffins, 1980).
This is a timeless classic already familiar to many children through the beautiful film based on Raymond Briggs' drawings. No words, just beautiful illustrations that any young child can follow on their own.

Each Peach Pear Plum, by Janet and Allan Ahlberg (Picture Puffins, 1989).
Written by the well-known husband and wife team, this is a simple but ingenious book. The charming, detailed illustrations combine perfectly with the rhyme on each page. One of my family's favourites, which is read again and again.

What's The Time Mr. Wolf?, by Colin Hawkins (Fontana Picture Lions, 1986).

The bright and bold illustrations in this book are both humourous and occasionally deliciously scary. With a clock face on each page and a cleverly repetitive text this is a brilliant introduction to learning to tell the time.

Alfie Gives a Hand, by Shirley Hughes (Fontana Picture Lions, 1985).

Shirley Hughes is one of the most popular authors for younger children and the reason is obvious. Each of her books relates directly to a child's experiences and is beautifully illustrated. In this one, Alfie has been invited to a birthday party, but should he take his comfort blanket?

The Very Hungry Caterpillar, by Eric Carle (Picture Puffins, 1974).

This book is popular with children between the ages two and five year after year. A clever folding-page arrangement, with a text that is easy to remember and shout out, creates another book that bears constant re-reading. It also helps a child to count and learn the days of the week.

Pre-Reading Activity Book, developed by Oxford University Press for The Early Learning Centre (1987).

Terrific value for money, this activity book contains stacks of line drawings to colour in and is thick enough to last any holiday bar an expedition up the Zambezi river. As one young critic said, '*It's got great "colouring-in" things and matching-up stuff and it's brilliant*'. Enough said!

Hand Rhymes, collected and illustrated by Marc Brown (Picture Lions, 1987).

A wonderful collection of poems with simple hand-actions to accompany them. Illustrations that are simple to follow; a delightful introduction to poetry which will provide hours of entertainment.

Books For Children Aged 6 – 8

Dirty Beasts, by Roald Dahl (Picture Puffins, 1986).

Brilliant irreverent and absurd comic verse about a menagerie of dirty beasts doing extraordinary things. Lively cartoon illustrations by Quentin Blake.

The Magic of the Mummy, by Terry Deary (Simon & Schuster, 1990).

Here's a funny, jokey story about a very spooky subject. Children will love it and it's perfect for them to read alone.

Amazing Mazes by R Heimann (Hippo Books, 1990)
The Great Puffin Joke Dictionary by Brough Girling (Puffin, 1990)

Two activity books stuffed full with the sort of quizzes and jokes that children of this age love. These will keep them occupied for hours but be prepared to lend a hand occasionally and suffer endless repetition of their favourite jokes, most of which are actually funny – the first time round!

Now we are Six, by A.A. Milne (Magnet Paperback Editions, 1979).

Go on – you read this when you were young, now pass on the delights of Christopher Robin and Pooh Bear. Learn them by heart and have a family recitation whilst waiting at Gatwick for Flight 216 to Majorca!

You Can't Catch Me, by Michael Rosen and illustrated by Quentin Blake (Picture Puffins, 1982).

Very funny poems and quite brilliant cartoon drawings make this a sure-fire winner.

Jimmy Tag-Along, by Brian Patten (Puffin Books, 1989).

Here are plenty of fun-filled stories with marvellous characters such as Mrs. Battyhats. Ideal for those who have developed reading fluency.

The Boy who Turned into a Goat (and other stories of magical changes), by James Riordan (Piper Books, 1988).

This is a wonderfully imaginitive collection of magical folk tales from around the world. It's ideal for reading aloud or for the reader who is progressing from picture books to longer stories.

Books for Children Aged 9 – 11

Matilda, by Roald Dahl (Puffin Books, 1989).

This is the tale of Matilda, a genius with gormless parents, who discovers that she can make trouble for the uncaring grown-ups in her life. Illustrated by Quentin Blake, this is Roald Dahl at his best and it is a funny and delightful book to read.

The Castle of Adventure, by Enid Blyton (Piper Books, 1988).

What are those flashing lights coming from the castle on the hill? A gang of children set out exploring and uncover a sinister plot. Bags of adventure here in this classic yarn.

Little Sir Nicholas, by David Benedictus (BBC Books, 1990).

This is a classic story of mistaken identity, jealousy, romance and intrigue in an historical setting. Don't be surprised to find kids reading this one under the sheets with a torch.

Why the Whales Came, by Michael Morpurgo (Magnet-Mandarin, 1987).

Here's a mysterious and captivating tale of an old eccentric called the Birdman and his relationship with two children on a small island community. The Birdman has a secret which is revealed when a whale is washed ashore.

Writing Jokes and Riddles, by Bill Howard (Armada Original, 1988).

This is a must for any child who enjoys making people laugh – or trying to! With plenty of examples, this book actually tries to explain the principles behind making jokes and will provide hours of distraction on long journeys.

Charlie and the Chocolate Factory, by Roald Dahl (Puffin Books, 1985).

Here is the ultimate Dahl book about the adventures of a group of children let loose in Willy Wonka's chocolate factory. It is fast-moving and humourous, exciting and unputdownable.

The Lion, The Witch and the Wardrobe, by C.S. Lewis (Lions, 1988).

This has to be one of the most exciting and enchanting adventure stories ever written. Follow Peter, Susan, Edmund and Lucy as they go through the wardrobe into the magical land of Narnia. Compulsory reading for every child.

Books For Children Aged 12 – 14

Courage Mountain – The Further Adventures of Heidi, by Fred and Mark Brogger (Puffin Books, 1990).

This is a thrilling and nail-biting war-time adventure full of suspense. A group of children must flee for their lives across the mountains.

Finders, Losers, by Jan Mark (Orchard Books, 1990).

Here's a very clever book containing six separate stories that are connected to each other in some way. Each story poses a puzzle that will only be understood once all six stories have been read. Well, that's one way to make sure you finish the book I suppose!

The Young Person's Guide to Saving the Planet, by Debbie Silver and Bernadette Vallely (Virago Press, 1990).

Nearly all young people are concerned about the environment and this book answers all their questions from acid rain to CFCs. It is full of positive actions young people can take, including certain holiday souvenirs which should be avoided!

Byker Grove, by Adele Rose (BBC Books, 1989).

Based on the BBC TV series of the same name, this is the story of a teenagers' dream hideout where they can do anything they want (within reason!). Good, 'street cred' language and a story full of pertinent teenage issues and characters such as 'good-looking but moody Martin Gillespie'!

Perhaps You Should Talk to Someone and other stories, edited by Julia Eccleshare (Viking, 1990).

Here's a great collection of short stories to appeal to all tastes. It's entertaining and perceptive, containing work by a sparkling list of top contemporary writers such as Graham Greene and Alice Walker.

Just William, by Richmal Crompton (Macmillan's Childrens Books, 1990).

This is the very first 'William' book ever written and this new paperback edition reproduces the original cover and illustrations beautifully. William's pranks are the scrapes of every healthy youngster and very, very funny. Buy it for yourself, never mind the children!

Odysseus II – The Journey Through Hell, by Tony Robinson and Richard Curtis (BBC/KNIGHT, 1987).

Don't be put off by the title, this is a fabulous book by two members of the Blackadder TV team. It's a very clever and funny adaptation of the old Greek myth – a sort of Junior Hitchhiker's Guide To The Galaxy.

Wayne Jackman has been a children's TV presenter for ten years on such programmes as Playschool, Allsorts *and* Saturday Starts Here. *He has written numerous children's books and for many of the children's TV programmes. He has three children himself and knows full well the relief that a good book can bring to a child on a long journey.*

Renting Somewhere to Stay

Kathy Rooney

If taking the family to a hotel seems too much hassle, then renting, whether a cottage, villa or apartment, is a practical and flexible option. You don't have to get organized for set mealtimes, and often the cost of a holiday is much reduced. The disadvantage of renting is that meals still have to be cooked, so parents don't escape from the daily chores of life at home.

When you are booking, whether through a travel company or privately, make sure you check out **exactly** what you are getting for your money.

Many brochures are well laid out and informative, but it is always worth trying to find out what may have been omitted from the details – is there a noisy, busy road nearby, for example? The recommendations of reliable friends and relatives are very useful.

Here are some suggestions for what you should check out:

Accommodation

- How big is the accommodation? (How many bedrooms? Will children have to share rooms?)
- Are cots supplied? Is there an additional charge? Does the children's room contain bunk beds and if so, are they fitted with safety rails?
- Is the kitchen big enough to cook comfortably in? (In many villas and apartments kitchens are minimal and it is not easy to cook a family meal.)
- Is linen supplied? Does 'linen' include towels? What about tea-towels? (It is well worth taking your own efficient drying-up cloth rather than relying on what you might find.) How often are the sheets changed?

Cleaning

- Does the rent include cleaning? If so, how often is the property cleaned? If cleaning is not included, can this be arranged for an additional fee?

Fuel and heating

- Are there gas and electricity? Are they included in the rent? If not, how are they paid for? If electricity and gas are metered how much is charged per unit? What sort of coin should you use to feed the meter? (Remember, surprising amounts of holiday spending money can disappear into gas and electricity meters.)

Facilities

- What equipment is there? Do you need to take a tin opener, corkscrew or sharp knife? (It's probably a good idea to take those essentials anyway.)
- Is there are washing machine and/or tumble drier? Are they coin operated?
- What drying facilities are there? This is especially important if you are holidaying in the UK or northern Europe where the weather is unreliable, and there is nothing worse than taking the smell of slowly drying sweaters home with you as your main holiday memory.

Swimming Pool

- If there is a pool, check how big it is. Also ask whether there is a shallow end or special children's pool for young non-swimmers. Check if the pool is filtered and how often the filter is examined. (Be wary if the pool is not filtered.) If the pool is shared, check how many people share it (approximately). Peak summer-time use can strain even the most efficient filtration unit.

Safety

- Is the property near a busy road? Check exactly how far away the road is – 20 metres or 200 metres can make all the difference to your holiday relaxation.
- Is there a garden? Does it have a fence or hedge? Is the back garden a safe place for children to play in unsupervised?
- Is there a river or stream near the property?
- If the property is near the sea, how far away is the beach? Do you have to cross the road to get there? How far away are any cliffs?

Transport

- Is a car essential? Question carefully to make sure your idea of 'essential' equates with that of the person trying to sell you the holiday. A couple of miles walk may be fine for an adult but is less practical with a baby in a buggy and a toddler trailing along behind.
- Is public transport available? How often do buses/trams/trains run, and to where? What is the time of the first and last bus etc each day? How expensive and easily available are local taxis?

Shopping

- Hw far away are the nearest shops? How near is a big supermarket? Do you need a car to get there?
- Are the local shops open on a Sunday? This is important if you are travelling on the Saturday and get delayed.
- Does the travel company supply a 'welcome pack' of tea/coffee, bread, eggs etc to tide you over the first evening/breakfast?

Eating out

- The chance to eat out *en famille* is a great plus of renting your own accommodation. Abroad, restaurants are by and large very tolerant of children, and even in the British Isles restaurants and pubs are beginning to cater for families.

- Before you book the accommodation check how far away the nearest eating places are. Are they within walking distance – even for young legs?

Special requirements

- Do you and your family have any special requirements? Always check what facilities are available before you confirm your booking.

Insurance

- Insurance is usually available when you book through a travel company. However, it is worth considering even if you book privately, as cancellations can still occur and it is best to be on the safe side. See pp. 306–10 for more information on insurance.

Baby-sitting

- Can baby-sitting be arranged locally? How much does it cost?

Change-overs

- What is the change-over date and time? There is no point in driving hell for leather all night to arrive in the morning only to find that you can't get access to the property before 5.30 pm.

Getting there

- Check directions very carefully, especially if you are driving. Some of the most interesting holiday properties gain their charm from being off the beaten track. That charm wears rather thin if it is late at night and you have a weary and fractious family that has been travelling all day in the back of a hot and stuffy car.

- If you are flying and hiring a car from the airport, check what will happen if your flight is delayed. Where will the hire company leave your key and documents?

Don't be put off by this list – when travelling with a family it is worth checking out as much as possible in advance, so you know what to expect (and what to pack) and can enjoy the holiday even more once you get there.

Whether a caravan in Scotland or a villa in the West Indies, renting your own accommodation can give you a terrific family holiday. Make sure you enjoy it!

Holiday Insurance

Ernest R. Jones

Have you ever been bitten by a camel? Or had a head-on collision with a llama whilst riding a bike? No? Well some people have, and all in the name of a 'good holiday'. There is an old idiom that says 'it will never happen to me'. However, such calamities happen frequently to all manner of travellers and unexpected incidents can range across the whole spectrum covered by a Comprehensive Travel Insurance Policy. They may include personal accidents, all manner of minor and major medical problems, losses and thefts of all baggage, personal effects and money, personal liability (where you cause injury or damage to a third person or their property), delayed baggage (where the airline in their wisdom deliver it to the airport at Corfu when you happen to be staying in Tenerife), delay of your plane or ship, cancellation of your holiday due to events beyond your control such as family illness, bereavement or redundancy, curtailment where you need to return home early from your holiday due to illness of one of the travellers or illness at home of a close relation, and hi-jack compensation.

It is a fact that one in every fifteen persons travelling abroad will make a claim on their policy from the very minor and mundane type of incident such as Spanish Tummy (perhaps requiring a Doctor's visit and a prescription costing perhaps £45 in all) to multiple accidents, heart attacks, hepatitis, which may cost scores of thousands of pounds in some cases for treatment, surgery and repatriation.

Believe it or not, the UK Travel Insurance market is probably the most sophisticated in the world, possibly due in some part to the earnest desire of the British public to escape from the English weather. As a result, the market has diversified to include tailor-made travel policies. People travelling on business can have their own policy which, while covering most holiday eventualities, may also cover the cost of replacing that person at an important conference or meeting if he or she became ill, or covering the value of goods or samples which are not normally covered by holiday Travel Insurance. Perhaps the baggage limit should be increased as he or she would need to carry several suits and extra luggage which would need to be adequately insured.

Single parent families or indeed any family with young children should look around for policies which may give free cover to children under a certain age (such as Extrasure Travel Policy) or at least reduced premiums for children. Groups of physically or mentally disabled children or adults may require different types of cover, although very often the supervision of these groups is so efficient that claims are kept to a minimum. Nevertheless, a policy should be sought which will cover unforeseen illnesses, or events that may well stem from their disability.

Different types of holiday require different cover. Holidays can vary from teenage lager-drinking contests in Benidorm to an exotic Kenyan safari, scuba diving off the Florida Keys, or indeed a coach tour of Italy for Senior Citizens. Many policies are designed for particular types of holiday such as special winter-sports insurance. Long-haul holidays, such as those to Africa or Australia, may last for several months at a time and will therefore require greater baggage and personal-effects cover.

Specific holiday activities, such as scuba diving, caving, canoeing etc. attract many young people, but most of these activities are excluded from normal insurance cover. As a result Activitysure has brought out a policy designed specifically to cover such otherwise excluded sports. Motorists' needs while travelling are different, not least as there is a greater exposure of the risk of theft from their vehicles, but also a greater risk of personal accident. When hiring a car abroad, you will also need collision-damage insurance for the rented vehicle. Americasure has combined all these aspects into one policy at a considerable saving to the traveller.

Claims on all types of policy and for all types of traveller vary enormously. Contrary to some opinions, insurers do actually *want* to settle valid claims – efficiently handled claims are their best form of advertising. Many claims are handled by third party Administrators. However, it is necessary to supply to the Claims Handlers all the information, documentary or otherwise, which will enable them to settle the claim quickly. It is not in the Claims Handlers' interest to prolong a claim by protracted correspondence – it costs money, and holds up the settlement of a claim. Therefore, for example, if a traveller is robbed or loses items of value, they should report the incident to the local Police Station and obtain a report if possible. Some Police will not give a written report, and in such cases it would be useful to obtain a report from the hotel manager or courier to confirm that the Police were contacted. (Some companies will not meet a claim for theft or loss of valuables if there has been no attempt to contact the local Police.)

The *It will never happen to me* philosophy is a myth. Something *will* happen to you sometime, somewhere, but travellers can increase their chances of a trouble-free holiday by following a few pieces of common-sense advice.

- Be careful with your goods. Use hotel safes and never leave items unattended in vehicles, locked or otherwise. Some policies will not reimburse you at all for goods stolen from cars, while others insist that they should always be hidden under blankets or in a locked boot. However, it is safer *never* to leave your possessions unattended than to gamble with your policy.
- Drink only bottled water and soft drinks when there is any doubt as to the safety of the local water supply. This is essential when travelling with young children and many travellers advise giving babies and toddlers only boiled water.
- Do not over indulge in food or drink that your stomach may not be used to. The effects of rich or spicy food when combined with too much alcohol and sun can ruin your holiday.
- Carry a basic first aid kit to deal with minor problems. (A useful addition to such a kit is a flat pack of soft toilet paper!)

Medical claims generally require immediate treatment and a traveller will normally obtain that treatment locally and be reimbursed on their return home. Such compensation depends on the production of a medical invoice and a fully completed claim form.

However, almost all Travel Policies also include the services of a specialist Emergency Assistance Company. Their job is to help the traveller when faced with an emergency they cannot handle on their own. Serious accidents and illnesses account for most calls to such services. In cases which require hospitalization and evacuation to the home country, the Emergency Assistance Company can help. They must be contacted immediately a problem arises in order that the company's Doctor can discuss with local medical staff the details and diagnosis of an illness and decide when a patient will be fit to travel back to their home. In most cases, bills from Medical Centres can be settled direct by the Assistance and Claims Company without the patient having the added worry of having to find the cost of treatment in advance of compensation.

Many travellers who receive medical treatment are able to continue their holiday. However, some unfortunate holiday makers have to return home due to illness. Some are well enough to travel in a wheelchair, with perhaps another member of the family escorting them, but others need to travel on a stretcher, and will usually require a medical escort. Air ambulances are available but are only used when no other means of transport can be used, perhaps in a life-saving situation or where an immediate operation is required that is not available in the country of travel and the patient cannot wait for airline availability. Air ambulances are generally small aircraft, and therefore subject to slower flying times and air turbulence. They will have very little room, with space only for a stretcher, medical team and medical equipment. They are used only when absolutely necessary but are nevertheless essential in certain circumstances.

The Assistance Company is there to help in any situation and their emergency number should be used to seek positive help and guidance. In certain circumstances the British Consulate can help a traveller with advice or emergency passports but they are not usually able to help with financial assistance to pay bills or replace lost cash, tickets or personal effects.

Medical Insurance claims frequently exceed £25,000 and sometimes can exceed £100,000. Even claims under other sections of the Travel Policy can be expensive. Recently a man lit and threw a firework at a celebration which exploded in the face of another man, partially but permanently impairing his sight. The liability claim for the third party injury was £14,000.

It is essential therefore that the potential traveller does his homework when it comes to choosing travel insurance. He should look for a policy:

1. Underwritten by a well known insurance company or Lloyd's of London.
2. With medical benefits of not less than £100,000 for Europe and £250,000 for the rest of the world.
3. With adequate benefits for baggage and personal effects.
4. With cancellation limits that will cover the cost of most holiday purchases.
5. That includes an Emergency Assistance Company. The services of this company should be available 24 hours a day and it should employ bi-lingual staff to cope efficiently with any emergency.

Without doubt, the travel insurance premium is the best investment a traveller can make in deciding his holiday arrangements. Astonishingly, about one-third of the travelling public are not insured at all. These people take the enormous and unacceptable risk of jeopardising their and their families' future by being responsible for enormous medical bills and repatriation expenses. Holiday insurance is not expensive, especially when compared with the whole cost of the holiday.

So go away and enjoy yourself and forget about claims and losses, secure in the knowledge that your travel insurance premiums provide you with the peace of mind that if you do get bitten by a camel, dive into an empty swimming pool, or simply drink too much Sangria, your treatment costs will be taken care of. An old advertising slogan advised viewers to 'Get the strength of Insurance around you' – nowhere is that more relevant today than in holiday insurance.

June 1990
Ernest R. Jones,
Chairman and Chief Executive,
Mercury Insurance Services Ltd.

Section 5

Family Travel Know-how

Air Travel

We're all familiar with the speed and efficiency of air travel, but having children in tow presents a number of different considerations. In this entry we have compiled a quick checklist of airline services you can request when booking, plus various tips gleaned from parents who have hard-won experience of travelling by air with children.

Checking in   Allow ample time for this procedure and remember that babies do not have a separate baggage allowance, although a pushchair, carrycot and flight bag are permitted. Ask at the check-in desk about any special request that you have made.

Pushchairs   Some airlines allow pushchairs to be used until you board the plane, with some even stowing it in the passenger cabin if space permits. This might not seem a priority, but airports often have miles of corridors which can be an arm-aching distance to carry a squirming toddler.

Boarding   Most airlines allow families with young children to board before other passengers. They may also automatically give you seats near a bulkhead (the partition dividing the cabin) so that you have more room. Be sure to request this position if it's not offered; it also has the added advantage of giving adults more legroom.

Carrycots/skycots/bassinets   If you take your own carrycot it will be stowed with the luggage in the hold. Note that airlines prefer the collapsible variety. Most airlines will supply a cradle, skycot or bassinet, but you must request this when booking. They are normally suitable for babies up to nine months old with a maximum weight of 24 lb/11 kg.

Nappies   The thought of changing nappies in a confined space at 25,000 feet is not an appealing one, but some airlines now have changing tables in toilets and may even supply disposable nappies. Most stress that these are for emergency use, i.e. when your own supply runs out, and they are usually the smallest size, suitable only for very young babies.

Breastfeeding Altitude has no effect on the flow of breast milk. Some airlines (usually Oriental ones) will supply a screen or curtain if you want privacy during feeding.

Bottle-feeding If your child is bottle-fed it's a good idea to take several prepared (plastic) bottles with you which the crew will store and heat up as required. If necessary, the crew will also sterilize bottles and teats, usually in boiling water from the coffee-making facility rather than a special sterilizing unit. Many airlines keep a stock of bottles, milk and powdered feeds, but check in advance that the food they carry is suitable for your child.

Food A selection of prepared baby foods is available on many airlines so you don't need to carry heavy bags full of tins and bottles. Ask in advance for any specific dietary needs and most airlines will try to meet them or offer suitable alternatives. Older children may be offered children's meals, usually of the burgers, beans and chips variety. Again, these must be requested when booking. Vegetarian food must always be booked in advance, both for children and adults.

Help On every flight there will be at least one attendant designated to offer particular help with children. With any luck, he or she will seek you out and hold the fort with toddlers if you have to change the baby.

In-flight entertainment This can take many forms: toys, colouring books, games, stories, puzzles, comics, films, recorded music, computer games and nursery rhymes. Most are offered free of charge and, as a rule, the longer the flight, the greater variety of things to do. However, it's a good idea to bring your child's favourite toy or game.

Take-off and Landing All modern aircraft are pressurized for passengers' comfort, which means that we can breathe and function normally at high altitudes. During take-off and landing, however, it's not unusual to experience discomfort from pressure on the ears – a popping sensation sometimes leaving a temporary deafness. Children, particularly young babies, can find this very distressing. Their normal reaction is to cry and this, in fact, is the best thing they can do, as it relieves the pressure on the ears. Alternatively you can try to pre-empt their distress by bottle or breastfeeding them during take-off and landing, as the swallowing action can also provide relief.

For toddlers, sucking a dummy or a boiled sweet can help relieve the pressure, while for other children coping with popping ears can be turned into a game by yawning and blowing their noses.

If your child has a cold it would be wise to seek your doctor's advice before flying as catarrh can increase the discomfort of pressure on the ears and even lead to ear infections.

In-Flight If you are worried about keeping your baby or young child quiet during the flight, mild sedatives such as Phenergan can be purchased from the chemist, but do speak to your doctor first. Phenergan reduces the chance of travel sickness and will help your child to sleep. If you have not had time to request a special seat earlier you can always ask at the airport when you check in if there is a spare seat you could have next to you; on the plane you can ask the flight attendant to move you if you spot any spare seats. Another tip is to ask for flight meals to be served separately if there are two adults. That way you can take it in turns to enjoy your meal. If the flight is relatively short it is probably worth giving your baby a double nappy to avoid the need to change – space is short on airplanes. But by and large the range of facilities provided for mothers and babies can be quite impressive, even on smaller airlines. (Full details are given under **Airlines**, Section 3.) Although games and toys are supplied, it's wise to take a few favourite things for children under three as the toys provided by most airlines are only suitable for children over four. See also **Nappies**.

Disembarking Usually airlines that allow early boarding allow you to get off first – a boon in getting through customs and immigration quickly!

The Air Traveller's Code In April 1990 the Civil Aviation Authority published a leaflet giving advice on safety and security for air passengers. *The Air Traveller's Code* will tell you how much baggage you can take into the cabin, what you can and cannot carry by air, what security precautions you should take with your luggage, and how you can help to make security checks as quick and painless as possible.

Copies of *The Air Traveller's Code* can be obtained free of charge from: Air Traveller's Code, Freepost (GL1776), Cheltenham, Glos. GL50 2BR. Tel: (0293) 573 924 (24 hour answerphone service).

Airports

Thousands of families pass through airports every year, and the growth of family travel has provoked an excellent response from airport authorities and architects. Facilities for families can now be quite impressive. We have carried out a survey of British airports and have listed all those features a travelling family might find useful (you will find this section on pp. 267–77).

Mother and Baby rooms are becoming more and more common. My only gripe is that very few airports provide *Parent and Child* rooms, with the result that lone males travelling with children are forced either to struggle in a cubicle in the men's toilet or boldly to march into the women's toilet to use the Mother and Baby room. It seems a shame that so many airport designers have ignored the fact that children will not *always* be looked after by their mothers. However, things are changing and several airports have changed their policy. Another solution is to try the disabled toilet as these are mostly unisex.

Airport information desks are generally staffed by very helpful people. It is always worthwhile phoning the airport in advance to find out about the facilities available and to make any special requests. During the summer, when there are extensive delays, some airports organize entertainment for children, but you must never rely on this to avoid infant boredom. Always take a small selection of books and toys with you and be prepared to launch into your best comedy act when things seem at their most dire (*see* **Holiday Reading for Kids** pp. 295–300 and **Keeping the Kids Amused . . . And your Sanity** pp. 287–94).

A pair of reins can be useful when you are trying to keep hold of a mischievous youngster and watch your cases while monitoring the departure board. Try to arrange in advance a point in the airport where you can meet up with any of your children (and other adults!) should you get separated – with any luck, this might minimize your headache should disaster strike.

Flight delays mean delays with everything else, so if you suspect that your departure might be delayed it is well worth taking emergency supplies of food and drink that you can ration out. Extra nappies and a roll of soft toilet paper should also be packed. It is also important to warn the children not to be frightened of the numerous armed security guards they will see at the airport – they might be necessary, but they don't always add to the holiday atmosphere!

See also **Facilities for Families at British Airports** pp. 267–77.

Baby-sitting

Some parents (especially if they both have jobs outside the home) may look forward to a holiday as the time they can spend devoted to being with their children. But for most people a holiday is the time to relax and enjoy yourself – and this will often mean without the children's company! For this reason baby-sitting facilities or children's entertainment are features which many parents look for in making their holiday choice.

The most extensive facilities are offered at large hotels in popular resorts. Although the hotel may not be your ideal choice, if there is plenty for the children to do it may just mean you really can have a holiday yourself. Some of the smaller hotels may also say that a baby-sitting service is available on request. 'Baby-listening' services are often available in hotels of all sizes. Although this means you have to eat either in the hotel or very close by, it does offer the option of eating something other than that supplied by room service. In practice we have found that hotels can often provide you with a babysitter whom you pay directly and by the hour. Although you can ask about qualifications, this is largely irrelevant as it is likely that the sitter is the doorman's cousin or sister anyway. In Paris and Wiesbaden we found three very suitable women who turned up to look after our son. One was an exquisitely dressed postgraduate student who came with her own toys, another was a grandmother in jeans who had planned a ride in her brother's taxi as the entertainment for the day, and another, the trainee-receptionist in the hotel who spoke English and taught our child some German. All you can realistically do is make up your mind when you meet the sitters whether you will trust them or not. We did in each case and had no complaints. The rule of thumb is that even if the hotel does not mention baby-sitting, ask whether it is available.

Some of the tourist boards were helpful when we asked if they had information about particularly suitable hotels for families. The Swiss Tourist Office produces a very useful brochure which is free on request called 'Special Hotels for Families'.

Boredom

It's impossible to say whether travelling before the advent of the jumbo jet and package holidays really was more leisurely and pleasurable, but it is certainly almost always the opposite of that now. Boredom is a problem to be dealt with when travelling with children and we offer a few suggestions below.

Airports/airlines   If you are delayed in boarding your plane (all too likely these days) at least you still have freedom of movement and can go for walks around the airport. A lot of the airport shops have inexpensive toys on sale and this may be the moment to splash out. If you're not already seated near a window looking out at the planes, find one. Most children are fascinated by what they can see and this should pass the time fairly pleasantly. Once you're on the plane and it's delayed in taking off, you will have to be a bit more imaginative. Several parents suggested taking along small presents (new books or toys) to give to the children at intervals, possibly wrapped up so that they have the excitement of tearing off the paper. A lot of the airlines have special children's packs which include drawing books and crayons. On long-haul flights they often have a children's station on the in-flight audio entertainment which could save the day.

Car travel   If your children do not sleep in the car you will have to entertain them if the journey is long. To save your voice bring along their favourite tapes and books. You can always play 'the first one to spot ten blue cars' kind of games as well. Be prepared to stop to allow everyone a breath of fresh air, so build extra time into your journey.

Rail Bring games, but not the sort with too many small pieces which could roll away and get lost. Card games work well, though they can be noisy, and there is the continuing interest of watching the scenery as you whizz through the countryside. In some of the more exotic places trains go slower and there is so much new to see that boredom is lessened.

Coach Although coach travel can never be ideal for children, the advent of the modern coach journey is a great improvement on what came before. Fares are kept low, but in order to compete the companies have to offer at least what is available from the other services. Often video is on offer and that should keep most children happy. For smaller ones you may have to sit and read quietly to them while the film is on. Looking out of the window should take up at least some time. If you have a Walkman or personal cassette player, bring it. It will be worth the extra weight. The same thing applies to coach journeys as for cars and planes – make sure you bring some books, old favourites and new ones.

If you've tried everything and the children still complain of being bored, remind them you are too and you're all just going to have to live through it. After all, the aim is to reach the place where you are going when all boredom will be banished and the fun begins!

Breastfeeding

If you are breastfeeding already you will be aware of the benefits of this transportable method of nourishment. It is positively tailor-made for travel with babies. If you are travelling a long way, try and rest if you can to ensure there is no interruption to the milk flow. Most major airports, railway stations and ferries have mother and baby rooms for changing and feeding (ask staff for their location). Often they have bottle-warming facilities too. People do seem to respect these facilities so you will mostly find you are alone in the room and can feed in peace. The changing facilities are a godsend and useful for all children in nappies.

In hot climates and underdeveloped countries breastfeeding has the advantages of avoiding dehydration and conferring immunity. In the countries of southern Europe, and indeed in most countries with warm climates, it is normal to breastfeed, but this does not mean you are at liberty to be indiscreet. In Greece, for example, while no one would be surprised at your breastfeeding, they would not expect to see it in a restaurant. In Italy women have moved away from breast-feeding to such an extent that you are almost congratulated if you breastfeed. In France, of course, you can be very open about it. Nobody minds anything. Breastfeeding is very common in Spain, but is done in private. Spaniards would not be surprised to see tourists breastfeeding in public, but they would not do it themselves. In Saudi Arabia nobody minds you breastfeeding as long as your face is covered!

If you are travelling through hot countries and will be feeding in the car it is a good idea to bring a white sheet to put up over the window – not for modesty's sake but to keep out the glaring sun. A few muslin nappies will provide you with instant cover-up or some privacy if required.

If you want more information about breastfeeding or have very specific questions, you can contact the Association of Breastfeeding Mothers or the La Leche League (see **Useful Addresses**).

Clothing

Always adopt the layer approach to clothes when travelling with children regardless of the time of year or where you're going. The temperature inside aircraft varies from cool to very warm. Airports are often air-conditioned, but remember that the night temperature in some countries at certain times of year can be very different from the daytime temperature. On top of all that it is always possible that the weather will change at your destination. It is best to be prepared, although we don't suggest taking skiwear to Jamaica just in case!

Natural fibres are best, but some synthetics do have the distinct advantage of drying quickly. If you're going to a place where the washing facilities are likely to be non-existent, you should consider taking a travelling clothes line, pegs and washing powder or liquid.

Don't overpack: remember if you're going to a sun and beach holiday the children will spend a lot of time either in their swimming things or in teeshirts and shorts. Most European resorts will be happy to sell you teeshirts, plastic sandals, hats, toys and so on if you want to buy them there. We do suggest hats for children if you're going to spend a lot of time in the sun.

The layer approach to clothes has been the standard recommendation to skiers for decades. For a winter holiday waterproof or water-resistant clothes are a must. If you are going skiing and don't want to fork out for the very expensive children's clothing, you can hire them from ski shops in the UK or possibly at the resort.

You don't want to be prevented from going for a walk with the children just because there happens to be an unseasonal downpour; having experienced this in New York in July we were glad to have brought along waterproof over-trousers and a hat which kept out the worst of the weather.

Coach Travel

This is not one of the most popular modes of transport for travel with young children. In fact, a few operators do not allow children under 12 on their coaches. The problems of boredom and frustration tend to be greater in coaches because there's little room to move around and work off pent-up energy.

Coping in Cold Weather

In **Clothing** we advise dressing the children in layers and this particularly applies in cold weather and for winter sports. It is the air trapped between the layers of clothes that keeps you warm. Your child should wear a hat, gloves and water-repellent clothing whether you are actually going to ski or not. Glare on the ski slopes can be great so children (and adults) should wear goggles. Do not expose babies' eyes to this harsh light.

You will have to invest in proper footwear, unless you can hire warm, lined boots at the resort.

A barrier cream and moisturizer are essentials for all children, especially babies, to protect them from the wind.

Coping in Hot Weather

Although most children love the sun and heat, it is necessary to protect them against its potential dangers. Unless your children are very used to being out in the hot sun, you should limit the time they spend in direct sunlight in the first week of your holiday to the early morning and late afternoon. They should always be protected by covering them in sun screen lotion, and wearing a hat and sandals in case the sand or pavements are baking. You may also want them to keep a teeshirt on for a while. It's worth taking a clip-on sun cover for the buggy as hats can be hot and don't always stay on.

If you are not near a café or shop, take along bottled mineral water or juice to protect against dehydration. One mother wrote to us suggesting that you take a lot of the individual juice cartons to your destination as they are a) portable, b) you can mix them with mineral water to last longer, c) they are expensive (if available at all) at most resort areas. You should see that your children get salt in their diet to replace that which is lost very rapidly through sweating.

Prevent heat rash by making sure that your child's clothes are loose and made of cotton. Rubbing him or her with baby powder can help. If a heat rash does appear, don't panic – wash the child frequently with cool water, drying him thoroughly and put on some soothing calamine lotion.

A tip for breastfeeding mothers: if it is very hot and the last thing you feel like doing is clasping a sweaty body to yours (even the baby's!) insert a nappy between you and the baby. It will end up soaked in sweat but at least the two of you will be less clammy.

Mosquitoes can be real pests in hot climates, particularly at night when there are ample opportunities to bite unconscious bodies. Mosquitoes have a preference for female flesh but it's wise to protect both sexes and all ages. You can, of course, take your own mosquito nets but these can be tricky to set up. A sheet of muslin draped over a cot affords some protection, but could be stuffy on a hot night. There are some excellent repellents on the market. 'Autan' is available in sticks or sprays and we have found both very effective. Mosquito coils can be bought in camping stores. Once lit they burn very slowly and give off a vapour which repels mosquitoes. A more modern version of this is an electric device which resembles a two-pin plug. It has an indentation on one side in which you place a tablet of repellent. When the device is plugged in, the tablet warms up and gives off an odourless vapour – very effective we're told in keeping insects at bay. You can buy these devices in most chemist's shops abroad. Beware of complacency about mosquitoes nearer to home. We know of a child who was very badly bitten in Paris.

Ferries

People have conflicting opinions about ferries: some have unfailingly enjoyed their crossings, while others have loathed them. It does seem to depend on whom you travel with. We have heard good reports of Sally Lines, but it's obviously a matter of personal choice.

When you plan your crossing, choose a route which will make your car journey shorter when you have reached land. If you are already wincing at the amount of driving your journey involves, consider taking a longer ferry trip, e.g. to Spain direct. Children are easier to occupy on a boat and there is space to walk them around. The less time spent in the close confines of a car, the better.

British ferry companies are trying hard to improve their services, and it is now standard to find video lounges, bars, self-service restaurants and shops on board. Several companies offer special children's clubs, however, facilities for young children are pretty thin on the ground.

Once on the ferry, it can be very stuffy inside and on a rough crossing it's the worst place to be. If you think you or your child may be seasick, sit quietly on deck; most ferries have partially covered seating outside. A pair of reins can be useful to keep an active toddler under control.

There are always ample toilet facilities on board, but it can be hard to find peaceful and congenial surroundings to feed or change your baby. On a journey of more than two hours where no mother's room is available, it's worth booking a cabin as a retreat from the hordes.

Getting Lost

Being involuntarily separated from your child is the ultimate night-mare, and it is an even more uncomfortable experience in an unfam-iliar place. Since it is impossible to legislate against it, and since no amount of instruction or physical restraint will necessarily prevent it, here are the sorts of things to keep in mind so that when it happens, it is as painless as possible.

When you go on holiday always make sure that each child carries an identity badge with your local address and telephone number in the local language. An identity bracelet such as those used at swimming pools would be the most sensible device. Always try and teach your children your name and address, with as much information as they can sensibly absorb. Do not be afraid to talk to your children about getting lost and above all teach them not to panic. If children get lost in public places there are only two rules to remember, and to impart. Tell children, if lost, to stay in the same place and wait to be found. Do not walk around. Getting lost is no fun, but it comes to an end.

Homoeopathic Medicine

There are many proprietary medicines for dealing with common holiday ailments. However, if you prefer to use 'natural' remedies, there are many homoeopathic preparations that can provide effective relief without fear of side-effects or overdoses. Many high street chemists have free leaflets listing remedies for common afflictions, from colds to travel sickness. If you want specific advice, go to a homoeopathic chemist where the pharmacist will suggest some holi-day standbys.

Insurance *see* **Holiday Insurance** pp. 306–10.

Long-haul Travel

If you're determined to get off the beaten track and go somewhere outside Europe you will more than likely go on a holiday which is known in the travel trade as 'long-haul'. Unfortunately when travelling with children this description is all too apt! The keys to successful or at least sane, long-haul travel are:

1 Allow yourself plenty of time to get to the airport, to check in and make connecting flights.
2 Adopt an easy-going, or what one experienced traveller called 'laid-back', attitude. There are bound to be delays, frustrations and worse, but if you're relaxed everything will be easier to cope with – an obvious point perhaps, but worth remembering.
3 Cut down drastically on hand luggage.

A few golden tips were passed on to us by a very experienced travelling mother: ask other people to help you if you need it. Most will be glad to do so, but probably wouldn't 'bother' you to offer first. Carry a bag of drinks, nibbles and hard fruit (apples are best) to tide the children over in case of delay, or if the food is long in coming on the plane. Don't take soft fruit – the pressure inside the cabin once you are in the air will cause it to bruise at three or four times the rate it would on the ground. We found this out when the pears we brought turned into a soggy mess an hour or so into the flight. Also bring a change of clothes, either to allow for accidents or just to have something clean to change the children into when you arrive. You might convince yourself that way that you and they feel fresh.

We explained in **Air Travel** that it is very important a few days before travelling to book the bulkhead seats on the aircraft. They are the only seats where you can have a bassinet for the baby. Because they have more legroom and are just the other side of the service station you have the added benefits of more space and quick service for meals and drinks. The drawback is that you are smack in front of the screen and cannot watch the movie but this is not important for young children. If you are a family of four you'll have the whole row to yourself which allows you to feel you have your own little area.

In **Clothing** we advise you to dress the children in layers for travelling and this certainly applies to long-haul flights. The temperature inside the aircraft alternates between cold and very hot and you will want to be prepared. The airlines provide little blankets and pillows which are useful.

You will need one nappy per hour for the young ones and it is best to bring your own despite the bulk. Even if the right size is available from the flight attendants they may not be free to give it to you when you need it. Changing a baby of up to about one year works well enough in the bassinet. If your child can stand up, then changing him or her in the loo is not too bad given that the sink is near at hand. Some planes have a nappy-changing table in one of the toilets. The flight attendants will tell you which.

If you have more than one child it is a good idea to put labels on them with their name and address. The older ones are more than likely to explore the airport and getting lost is a possibility. (See **Getting Lost**.) Also using reins for toddlers and attaching them to the pushchair or trolley can save a lot of chasing around.

Generally, it is easier travelling west than east in coping with time changes and consequent jet lag. We talked to many parents and there is no overall recommendation to make about when children should sleep and when they should not. It is best to let them drop off as and when they feel like it. It would be counterproductive to impose a schedule. A useful tip if you are returning to the UK from the east coast of the US: take the daytime flight if possible. It means you arrive at 7 or 8 p.m. here having 'missed' the day but as you'll be tired from travelling anyway you'll probably find everyone goes to sleep normally and wakes up feeling fine.

Medical Emergencies

An emergency is by its very nature something for which you cannot prepare. You can however, with a few precautions, ensure that you are in the best possible position should your child fall ill or have an accident.

If you are visiting an EEC country you will need a certificate called an E111 to benefit from the reciprocal medical arrangements available. The EEC countries are: Belgium, Denmark, France, West Germany, Gibraltar, Greece, Irish Republic, Italy, Luxembourg, Netherlands, Portugal and Spain. You obtain the E111 by applying to your local social security office. It is valid in most cases for two years and only applies for urgently needed treatment. What is free and what you pay for in each country can be discovered by reading the leaflet SA30 available from the DHSS.

There are countries outside the EEC where some kind of reciprocal medical treatment arrangements are also in force, but often the cover given is not as comprehensive as in the UK.

The E111 is not a substitute for good travel insurance. Several things, such as repatriation, are not covered in any of the reciprocal arrangements, and in some countries injury from motor accidents may not be. Also, of course, in countries such as USA and Canada where all medical treatment has to be paid for you will need comprehensive insurance in any case. If you are in any doubt about what you need ask your travel agent, insurance company or insurance broker for advice.

Some parents we spoke to suggested that you take along your child's medical records just in case. You may feel happier doing this, but it is probably only really necessary if your child has a congenital condition or is taking a course of treatment.

Motorail

Driving across the Continent with baby and toddler in the back can be an exhausting experience, yet many families are understandably loth to dispense with the freedom and advantages of having their own car on the other side of the Channel. One compromise is to put the car on a train. From the Channel ports you can get as far south as Biarritz, Nice and Milan. From Paris you can reach Madrid or Lisbon; services through Belgium will take you south-east through West Germany to Salzburg, Villach or Ljubljana while from Gothenburg you can go north through Sweden to the Gulf of Bothnia. Norwegian state railways also run limited services.

Motorail isn't cheap. If you take only immediate and tangible costs into account it will certainly be cheaper to drive yourself. However, Motorail undoubtedly gets you there quicker and in a more relaxed frame of mind.

Motoring

There is no doubt that self-drive holidays are among the most popular. You have independence to travel as little or as much as you like, and you can stop whenever it takes your fancy. As with other holidays, the secret of success is in the planning and you must be certain to comply with international regulations.

Essential documents are a valid driving licence and/or International Driving Permit (available from the AA), vehicle registration and proof of insurance. The latter can be in the form of an insurance certificate or a Green Card which is obtainable from your insurers. It is also essential to display a sticker on your car denoting nationality, to carry a warning triangle in case of breakdown, and to adjust your headlights to dip to the right (except for Ireland). Requirements about such things as seatbelts, wing mirrors, fire extinguishers and first-aid kits vary from country to country, but it is your responsibility to ensure that your vehicle complies with local laws. Note too that children under certain ages are not allowed to travel in front seats. The AA can provide details about this and all other requirements.

Before you set off, make sure your car is safe with good brakes and tyres (including the spare), and efficient windscreen wipers. It's also wise to carry a spare fan-belt and some bulbs. The AA offer excellent breakdown insurance throughout Europe – worth the expense for peace of mind. In many Eastern European countries there are cars which patrol the roads to assist motorists if they break down. The AA and RAC have all sorts of useful information about motoring in different countries, and some of the national tourist offices have special leaflets available.

There is much debate about the best way to organize a Continental motoring holiday from the UK, particularly if you have a long drive to make after your ferry crossing. Is it best to travel in daylight hours or overnight? Should you drive direct to your destination or make several stops en route? Each method has its advocates and we outline here those recommended to us by seasoned travellers with children.

Travel during daylight hours means that your children are awake and in need of distraction or entertainment for a big part of the day. This is fine if you have lots of energy and your children don't suffer from travel sickness. You'll also see more of the countryside and perhaps your children will find this adequate diversion. Frankly, we doubt it and can only recommend daylight travelling if your journey is fairly short.

Overnight travel has many champions. Those we know keep their children up late, allow them to 'help' with packing and then set off to the port with the children tucked up in sleeping bags. With any luck, they fall asleep in the car and sleep through the crossing. Normally the parents can have a snooze too. When the boat docks, the children can be carried to the car in their sleeping bags and get the rest of their ten hours. By the time they wake, it's possible to have driven several hundred miles. In order for this to work it's really essential to have two drivers.

To stop or not to stop – this depends on the length of your journey. If it's only a few hours to your destination then it's probably all right to drive direct. If it's more, then it's advisable to stop a few times en route. You and your co-driver need the rest, your children appreciate the break from the car and if you choose your stops carefully, they can be highlights of the holiday rather than hardships.

Nappies

The invention of the disposable nappy has made every parent's life easier, and this is especially so when travelling. Despite the inconvenience of bulk, it is worth carrying enough to see you through your journey as nothing can be worse than running out at a crucial moment. Although the airlines may have nappies, you can't count on it. Railway stations, ferry ports and coach stations are unlikely to stock them. A rule of thumb is one nappy per hour of your journey plus a few to allow for delays. Take a roll of nappy sacks (plastic bags) to dispose of the soiled nappies. Nothing is more unpleasant in toilet cubicles than used nappies just thrown in with the paper towels. Also the bags are useful for uneaten food.

Disposable nappies can be bought almost anywhere now, judging by what our writers tell us in Section 2 (**Choosing Your Destination**) but they may be pricey.

One parent wrote to us to suggest that if you take a large pack of nappies with you, treat it as a piece of luggage. Put a label on the nappy pack (sixty–seventy should last a fortnight) and throw into the aircraft hold. Remember that although on beach holidays the children will probably go without nappies by day, because of the amount they drink they will consequently be changed more in the evenings.

Necessities

Parents will have their own views on what is essential to take on a journey and what we offer below are only suggestions gleaned from our experience and research.

For babies: A large bag with outside pockets is the best sort. Put the baby's toys in the pockets. Those made of canvas or nylon are strong and can stand up to the rugged treatment they will receive. The cotton bags lined with plastic for nappy-changing are very useful, but small, so you should bring this packed into the larger bag. It is not always possible, but try to repack the bag in the same order so you don't have to rummage through the whole thing every time you want a tissue. Plastic bags of the small binliner sort are a must. You can put soiled nappies, food or bottles in them. If you are bottle-feeding the baby and travelling by air, it is best to bring the bottles already made up as the flight attendants can warm them for you. If travelling by rail or car it may be better to bring the separate ingredients and count on getting boiled water in the restaurant car or when you stop on the road. Always bring several teats, two pairs of plastic pants and a couple of muslin or towelling nappies. You should also take washing things, a wet flannel, a small towel, kitchen roll, tissues or toilet roll and perhaps also moist towelettes in individual packets. Sterilizing tablets, baby wipes, lotion, cotton wool, several bibs and a supply of nappies should see you through.

Some companies charge an exorbitant price for hiring cots, in which case you may like to consider taking a travel cot with you.

For toddlers: If you bought a strong bag when the baby was small it should still be with you for this stage and can hold the following: jars of food (preferably something the child can eat cold if need be, such as fruit), several plastic spoons, bibs, cartons of juice with the straw attached (they all seem to love these), plastic cup with spout, plastic bags, a few favourite (small) toys and books. If the child is in nappies you will still have your nappy-changing bag and this is a must. We found the kind of collapsible seat which you screw on to any table top invaluable for children up to the age of 2. It lies flat in your case so takes up little space and its versatility means you can go out and eat with your child almost anywhere. A potty could be useful, depending on what stage of training your child has reached. At least one change of clothes should be brought for each child in nappies, and don't forget the socks!

Open Spaces, Parks and Shopping

Wherever you travel to you will be interested in what facilities the country provides for children. These vary enormously. Most cities and towns have parks of some sort or other and a lot of them have play areas reserved for children. We were surprised to find in Paris that there were lots of little parks with swings, slides and sandpits, often in a small area of the churchyard.

Parents become adept at sniffing out areas where they will be welcome with their children and where they can sit for a relaxing half-hour. In that ultimate consumer society, Japan, it is made easy for you to shop in their department stores because you can often leave your child under surpervised care while you go and spend money!

If you are in a city and the weather is inclement, it's worth knowing that many museums have 'hands on' exhibitions where the whole idea is for children to touch and handle the displays. This is a welcome development and could pass many a happy hour.

Passports

It's probably a good idea to get your children their own passports rather than adding them to yours or your partner's; if one of you has to fly home with an injured child this could cause chaos. Acquire a passport for your child as soon as you can to avoid last-minute panics. But if you have left things to the last minute you can always get a British Visitor's Passport over the counter at the post office on production of two photographs. The snag with this is that under-8s can't have their own – if travelling solo they have to have a proper passport.

Preparation

There are two schools of thought on this subject. One has it that you should all go to bed early, with the children relaxed and calmly ready for their journey. The other has it that you should keep them up later than usual, packing and getting excited. Set off early and don't let them sleep until you are on your way – in the plane, car or train. This may work with the over-3s if you are driving from say, the UK to the south of France, but if you are going by air it is probably best to be as rested as possible when you start your day. There is normally delay, lots of walking with hand luggage and standing in queues.

The more you can explain and involve your children in the holiday the more they will enjoy it and get from it – and you likewise. For the child who can read a bit lots of *Junior Guides* and so on are available for foreign countries. You can also buy delightful picture book foreign dictionaries. Even if your child isn't at the reading stage, you can still teach a few basic words in the appropriate foreign language – please, thank you, hello, good-bye. The locals will love it and your children will feel wonderfully clever.

In general, we cannot overstress the importance of research. It may have been fun going to new places trusting to serendipity and your initiative when you were childless; with a baby it really isn't on. Write to the embassy and the tourist office of the places you're going to; read the books listed at the end of the country descriptions; browse through the travel section of your local bookshop or library; ask the AA or RAC for motoring advice.

Rail Travel

Depending on which country you're in, rail travel can have a lot or a little to recommend it. The network and rolling stock may hark back to the 'golden days' of steam – a positive inducement to some travellers – while some countries boast a futuristic monorail system. The older systems can be pleasant to travel on, but sometimes painfully slow. The modern system can be astonishingly fast, but painfully crowded.

Most countries operate electrified systems that cannot be described as old-fashioned, but are hardly the latest word in comfort and pleasure either. Of course, there are exceptions, such as the French TGV (Train à grande vitesse) which travels at great speed and has superb facilities. In the summer SNCF operate ten routes for families with children, and amenities include play areas equipped with toys and games, special menus, a nappy-changing area and an electric point for a bottle warmer. (Make sure you have one with continental voltage.)

On most railways it's best to assume that nothing special will be offered to families with children, so always take your own supplies of food, drinks and amusements, even if restaurant cars are specified. The variety and quality of some railway food leaves a great deal to be desired.

Make the rail journey as pleasant as possible, for you and your fellow passengers, by travelling at off-peak times. You will save money, have more space and experience shorter queues for the toilets (sometimes pretty unsavoury places). It's not a good idea to let children play on the floor for reasons of safety and hygiene. However, children do contrive to get sticky and dirty on any journey, so don't dress them in their best clothes, and be sure to take a damp facecloth or refresher pads for sprucing up.

On long journeys it's always a good idea to book a couchette and travel overnight, so you will arrive reasonably refreshed. Children who travel free (usually those small enough to sit on a lap), must share a parent's berth. Cots are rarely provided.

Sightseeing

The most important point to bear in mind about sightseeing is not to overdo it and put your children off for life. Make the most of the baby stage; it gets harder later. It ought to go without saying that you are asking for trouble if your haul your 3-year old round St Peter's or the Uffizi for hours on end – or get resentful if you find you can't. It can be frustrating for adults in a foreign country where they've never been before to find they can't go off and see the sights as they used to; if this applies to you then one solution is to organize a holiday with another family so that you can take it in turns child-minding. You and your partner can always take it in turns too.

This is not to say that you can't get away with a limited amount of sightseeing – with appropriate promises of ice creams or treats and some common sense. Don't drag the children round a city on a blazing hot day when they would rather be on the beach or in the pool. On the other hand, in reasonable weather conditions, most children will enjoy ruins – though it may be difficult if they're not allowed to climb on them. If your child is old enough you can get him or her involved with suitably modified explanations of what you're going to look at and why – though don't be too surprised if your child's enthusiasm wanes when you get to your destination. Above all, keep it short; it's much better to finish the experience on a high when you're all enjoying yourselves.

But even if you decide sightseeing is not for your family you will want your children to get something more out of a holiday abroad than a suntan/ sunburn. With a little help and guidance from you older children will get a lot of interest and fun out of noticing the differences between abroad and back home – differences ranging from houses, streets, dress, shops, vegetation to language, food, ways of behaving etc. Learning to notice such things will be of a great deal more educational value to your child than a formal museum, as well as being part of what 'going abroad' is all about.

Skiing

Ski holidays are becoming increasingly popular with families. As a result, many resorts throughout Europe are adding services especially for young children.

Most resorts now have plenty of self-catering accommodation close to the ski slopes and many companies offer baby-sitting and child-minding services so that parents are able to ski alone for at least a few hours. It is very common to find child-minding in the form of kindergartens. They offer organized activities, supervised lunches and children's ski schools, usually for those aged four and above. The under-4s are normally looked after in nurseries, but where this service is not available, the local tourist office will help you find a baby-sitter.

For those worried about the expense of kitting out the children, it's possible to hire ski wear from shops like Moss Bros. The smallest sizes fit children around four years old. Organizing a skiing holiday with children under five can be very difficult. It may be possible to arrange for supervision with a local family via your holiday company and some travel companies are beginning to organize full-time supervision for infants while adults ski (eg *see* Thomson entry in Skiing section pp. 231–41). Ask your travel agent's advice before booking.

Travel-cots

If you plan to travel widely with your small children to places where cots may not be provided, or are very expensive, it may be worth buying a travel-cot. A wide variety is available, the lightest weighing about 5kg and ranging upwards in price from about £50. They all fold into reasonably compact bundles and will fit into a car boot (or behind the back seat). Some are sturdy enough to take a child up to four and all will accommodate a 20-month-old. For some families a travel-cot might even be a more sensible buy than an ordinary one – particularly as some have mesh sides and can double as a playpen (another plus on holiday).

Before you splash out, though, you need to decide how often you're going to use the cot and what your priorities are. The sturdier ones that will last your child until he or she goes into a normal bed are, of course, heavier and more expensive than the lighter, flimsier ones which are basically a piece of material suspended on a frame. Some mattresses are more substantial than others and you might want to choose a travel-cot that would take a normal cot mattress for everyday use.

Walking

Walking is fun, healthy and a perfect way to spend a holiday for all the family. There are several companies offering walking holidays, but some do not permit very young children. However, there's nothing to stop you organizing your own rambles. Just make sure they're within your children's ability or you'll end up carrying them. About two miles is usually manageable. Make sure you have a good map, preferably one prepared by Ordnance Survey, as paths are not always clearly signposted. Try to make frequent stops on the route – not only for food and drink breaks – but to look at the flowers, animals and trees. Take some books along to help identify flora and fauna. Children love to keep records, so get them to note down what they see and perhaps draw some pictures. If you can, pick a route that has a hill, or better yet, a stile or two to climb. Some farms in Britain have 'farm trails' – walks around the farm where you and your children can see the animals.

Remember that stout shoes and sensible clothing are necessary for a serious ramble, but don't make it hard work or you'll put your children off walking for life. A good backpack with well-padded hip belt is essential for carrying toddlers; it's worth paying more to get a good one as the cheap ones are very uncomfortable to wear.

Section 6

Medical
Know-how

Introduction

The illnesses and health problems that occur most often on holiday tend mainly to be minor ones. Every effort to prevent and anticipate them is well worthwhile; however a minor illness affecting just one family member – especially if that member is a child – can spoil enjoyment quite effectively for the whole family. More serious illnesses also occur, and good medical treatment is sometimes difficult to find.

Almost all of the likely problems are preventable, and here is a quick guide to some of them.

Accidents

Accidents are by far the most common cause of death or serious injury in travellers of all ages. Much of the problem is that most people lower their guard on holiday, taking risks they would never consider at home. Most accidents occur on the roads, and there are almost always important preventable factors. Common sense precautions that are usually observed at home are often ignored abroad. These include wearing seatbelts, observing speed limits (and not driving too fast when there aren't any), not drinking and driving, avoiding driving at night or when you are tired or suffering from jet lag, and looking both ways before crossing the road! Child seats and restraints should also be used, and children kept on the rear seat, even in countries where there is no legal compulsion to do so.

In an accident that results in injury to anyone else, prison custody for the driver is the rule in many countries, until the case is eventually heard – no way to begin a family holiday. Always make sure that you are adequately insured for driving abroad. Car insurance, and insurance for rented cars, should cover bail bonds, fines and legal costs. It can be difficult to raise the money for such expenses at short notice from the inside of a prison cell. The risk of illness in prison may also be high.

Not the least reason for doing everything possible to prevent accidents abroad is that emergency services and medical care of a good standard may be difficult to find, especially if you are in an island resort, or in a remote place.

Important potential hazards to children abroad include insecure balconies and balustrades; hotel lifts of the continental type, in which the lift cage has only three sides – enabling hands and clothing to become trapped against the lift shaft; and unsafe electrical and gas appliances in rented accommodation.

Air Travel

Travel sickness should be prevented in advance, especially if you know that your children are prone to it (see Travel Sickness). Pressure changes make the ears 'pop' during ascent, and may cause earache during descent. Babies who cry on descent should be fed, or given a dummy to suck, and older children in discomfort should be told to pinch their noses and blow, or to suck sweets. Small babies usually tolerate air travel well, and are easiest to look after when breastfed; toddlers do not like being restrained, and easily become restless and irritable; on the longest journeys it may be worth travelling with a mild sedative like Phenergan in reserve (see Antihistamines). Older children may get bored – so travel prepared.

Allergy

Anyone who has had a serious allergic reaction in the past should travel with everything they might need in an emergency, as well as appropriate identification (such as a Medic-Alert necklace or bracelet, available from the Medic-Alert Foundation, 17 Bridge Wharf, 156 Caledonian Road, London N1 9UU. Tel: (071) 833 3034.

Animal Bites

Worldwide, dogs are the worst culprits. In the USA, over a million people are bitten each year, badly enough to need hospital treatment; in the UK there are about 250,000 cases, and abroad, on holiday, the risks are much higher. Rabies is a hazard in many countries, and prompt medical treatment may be more difficult to obtain.

All animal bites – and human bites – carry a high risk of infection. Bites should therefore be scrubbed with soap or detergent in running water for at least five minutes, and any dirt or debris carefully removed. An antiseptic capable of killing viruses – such as iodine or alcohol (whisky and gin are also suitable for this purpose!) – should then be applied. Mercurochrome and other brightly coloured antiseptic dyes, popular in some countries, and hydrogen peroxide, are not suitable. At hospital, a medical attendant should further cleanse the wound; stitches are best avoided if possible, and antibiotics are often a valuable precaution. Children who have received their routine immunizations will be immune to tetanus; adults need a booster dose every ten years to maintain immunity. A booster dose of tetanus toxoid should be given after injury; severe wounds in a previously unimmunized person require additional treatment with tetanus immunoglobulin, which may not be readily available in smaller hospitals. Precautions against rabies may also need to be considered (see Rabies).

Antibiotics

If you are prescribed antibiotics abroad, make sure that the full course is completed. If your child is allergic to penicillin (or any other drug) make sure that any doctor consulted abroad understands this. Tetracycline antibiotics should never be given to children, and should not be taken by pregnant women.

Antihistamines

Antihistamines are used to treat mild allergy and itching from widespread insect bites or stings. Antihistamine creams and ointments should be avoided – sensitivity to them can occur following exposure to strong sunlight. Tablets are preferable; Piriton is suitable for children and adults, but tends to cause drowsiness; newer antihistamines like Triludan do not, and can be used by adults and children over six. Another antihistamine, Phenergan, is often used solely for its soporific effect, as a mild sedative for small children, and is occasionally useful for fractious children on long and tedious journeys.

Bee Stings

Stings should always be scraped out; grasping them with tweezers will inject more venom. Ice provides valuable relief for pain and swelling, with paracetamol for pain, if necessary.

Blisters

Blisters are a common problem on holiday, especially on an activity holiday. It is best to break in any new footwear gradually, well before going away. Protect the skin of the feet with talcum powder, especially if long walks are planned. Clean and tape over smaller blisters; larger blisters should be snipped open to drain, cleaned with antiseptic, and covered with a non-adherent dressing such as Melolin.

Blood Transfusion

The AIDS risks have received much publicity, but are not the only hazard of blood transfusion abroad. Other risks include hepatitis A, hepatitis B, syphilis and malaria. Furthermore, transfusion with badly matched blood causes severe reactions and can sometimes be fatal; it also has important long-term consequences in girls and women, leading to serious antibody reactions between mother and foetus in a future pregnancy; allergic reactions and febrile reactions may also occur, and the risk of these is greater when storage conditions are poor.

In most of western Europe, North America, Japan and Australasia, all donated blood is now screened for HIV antibodies and prospective blood donors are questioned carefully about their lifestyle and risk factors for AIDS. Elsewhere, however, adequate facilities for screening donated blood and selecting donors are the exception rather than the rule, and the risks from blood transfusion may be high.

Blood transfusion should be given only when medically essential. The risks from an unscreened blood transfusion must, however, be put in perspective, and balanced against the more immediate risks of not having a transfusion when there has been serious blood loss and there is a clear medical need. It is foolhardy to risk death from blood loss by refusing transfusion; most people who need transfusion in an emergency may find they in fact have little choice in the matter.

Accidents are the commonest reason for travellers to need a blood transfusion, and avoiding accidents is the most effective measure that any traveller can take to avoid a blood transfusion.

Breastfeeding

Breastfeeding on the move is in many ways more convenient than bottle feeding. In a hot climate, nursing mothers should make sure that they have plenty of extra fluid to drink. Additional fluid is not generally necessary for the baby, unless there is fluid loss from diarrhoea, vomiting, or a fever; but it is safest to travel with a bottle for use if needed, and to have already introduced a bottle for occasional feeds at home before travel.

Cold Climates

Children lose heat relatively much faster than adults, and need to be wrapped up well in cold climates. Clothing should be well-fitting, and in several layers. Gloves and footwear in particular should be of good quality. It is not possible to acclimatize to cold in the same way as it is to heat.

Colds

This is one of the commonest ailments abroad. The usual symptomatic remedies are helpful, and a decongestant nasal spray should be used to prevent discomfort from pressure changes during air travel, though anyone with a really severe cold should not fly.

Contraception

This is a subject that is almost always neglected both by travellers themselves and by their doctors. Diarrhoea reduces the absorption of the Pill. Long flights across time zones often result in doses that are missed or much delayed. The margin of safety, especially with low dose Pills, is small, and protection is easily lost. An alternative method should be taken in reserve.

Constipation

Dehydration, readjustment of bowel habits after crossing time zones, a change of diet and initial reluctance to use dirty toilets, can each contribute to this problem, which is surprisingly common. Plenty to drink, and a high fibre diet, are preferable to medication; it may be worth travelling with a small supply of natural bran, or a child's favourite variety of breakfast cereal.

Creeping Eruption

Creeping eruption is caused by hookworm larvae of dogs, cats, and other animals, which burrow into human skin by mistake. The larvae migrate aimlessly under the skin, producing a painful, raised, itchy, linear reaction. The condition is acquired by contact with soil or sand contaminated with animal excrement. Beaches in Africa, Asia and the Caribbean are often contaminated; also North America, along the Atlantic and Gulf coasts, as I recently discovered to my own cost . . . Sand below the high water mark is safe; everywhere else wear shoes or sandals and make sure children do the same. If the rash occurs, freezing the skin with ethyl chloride is a simple and effective remedy, but medical advice should be sought.

Dehydration

Dehydration can occur rapidly in small children, especially in extreme heat, or if there is diarrhoea, vomiting, or a fever. Almost all cases respond promptly to treatment with oral rehydration solutions (see below); dehydration can be prevented by ensuring an adequate fluid intake in the heat.

Diarrhoea

Although diarrhoea is the commonest of all holiday ailments and is the medical problem most clearly associated with travel in most people's minds, it is not inevitable and can be prevented by careful selection and preparation of food and drink (see Food Safety and Water).

If diarrhoea occurs, the most important aspect of treatment is replacement of lost fluid and salt – especially in children, and especially in warm climates. The best way of doing this is by drinking as much as possible of a solution containing salt and sugar (sugar promotes rapid absorption of the salt). The ingredients are available in correct proportion in sachets (such as Dioralyte, from any pharmacy) that can be made up with water. A child who is vomiting should still be given sips of this solution – and will usually absorb most of it.

Most cases of diarrhoea clear up without specific treatment within three days, though that is sometimes of little consolation. One suitable symptomatic remedy for adults and older children is Arret, available without a prescription in both capsule and liquid form. Diarrhoea with fever or blood (see Dysentery) requires skilled medical attention.

Antibiotics are often prescribed inappropriately for diarrhoea; antibiotics can themselves cause diarrhoea, and many cases persisting on return home are due to just this. Antibiotics should generally be reserved for cases in which fever is present, or a serious infection is suspected.

Dogs

Strange dogs should *never* be handled abroad. In many countries, they are in any case not used to being treated as pets, and dogs should never be left alone with small children. Apart from the risk of rabies that is present in many countries, dogs are able to transmit around eighty different diseases to human beings, all of which are more common in hot countries.

Drugs and Medicines Abroad

Take with you an ample supply of any medication anyone in your family is already using, or is likely to need. Keep all medicines out of reach of children, and preferably in childproof containers. To avoid possible customs problems, it is best if all medicines are kept in their original containers and are clearly labelled. Carry a prescription for anything unusual. Prescribing habits vary widely between different countries, especially within Europe. These variations apply to the form in which a drug is used – injections and suppositories are used in many countries in preference to oral treatment; and also to the particular choice of drug or preparation. In many countries, for example, steroid medications (cortisone-like drugs) are liberally over-used – in tablets, eye-drops and creams. These are powerful drugs that should not be abused, and it is not always easy for a lay person to identify them easily from their names alone. It is best to be cautious of any medication you are given, especially if it contains numerous different active ingredients; always ask for a detailed explanation of anything you are prescribed, if you are worried. Drugs that have been incorrectly stored, or have simply expired, may lose their effectiveness; some drugs, like tetracyclines, actually become toxic when out-of-date. All medications produced by reputable manufacturers carry an expiry date, and this should always be checked before use.

Dysentery

Dysentery is diarrhoea with blood and/or a fever, and always requires skilled medical attention. Until skilled attention is found, take careful steps to prevent dehydration.

Earache

Ear infections are relatively more frequent on holiday – perhaps from more frequent swimming. Ears should be towel-dried after swimming – not probed with cotton buds. Antibiotic treatment is usually necessary if it is prolonged or associated with fever, and swimming should then be avoided until after recovery.

Fever

Most of the causes of fever abroad are the usual causes of fever at home, such as colds, respiratory infections and tonsilitis. When travelling in any country with malaria, the possibility of malaria should be considered in any case of fever. Fever with diarrhoea suggests dysentery, and fever with neck stiffness, headache and inability to tolerate bright light, suggests the possibility of meningitis.

First-aid Kits

Consider including the following items:
- diarrhoea remedy, such as Arret
- oral rehydration sachets, such as Dioralyte
- travel-sickness remedy, such as Kwells or Stugeron
- painkiller, such as paracetamol
- mild sedative, such as Phenergan syrup
- antimalarial medication as appropriate
- calamine lotion and antihistamines for insect bites
- insect repellents
- sun screen
- lip cream
- cold remedy
- antiseptic for cuts and grazes
- sticky plasters, steri-strips and wound dressings, bandages
- thermometer

- sterile needles/syringes, if appropriate
- water purification supplies

Food Safety

Diarrhoea may cause anything from embarrassment and inconvenience to misery that may wreak havoc on your travel and business plans; other diseases spread by poor hygiene – and prevented by similar precautions – include dysentery, giardiasis, hepatitis A, typhoid, polio and parasitic infestations.

Careful choice and preparation of food offer the best protection; unfortunately, contaminated food can seem most appetizing, and the urge to eat what's available and what you have paid for when you are hungry can be irresistible. High risk foods include:

- raw or inadequately cooked shellfish or seafood
- raw salads and fruit that have not been thoroughly washed in clean water, or that you cannot peel yourself
- food that has required intricate preparation with much handling
- food that has been stored and reheated after cooking
- food left out in warm temperatures – such as hotel buffet lunches in most Mediterranean resorts – bacteria multiply fast under such conditions
- food on which flies may have settled

Eating safely means that you won't always be able to eat when, where and what you want. Food that has been freshly and thoroughly cooked is safe.

Heat Stroke

Children generally adapt well to the heat. Adaptation is improved by drinking plenty, well beyond the point of thirst-quenching; it is important to drink enough to keep the urine a consistently pale colour. Heat stroke results in failure of the body's heat control mechanisms; sweating diminishes, and body temperature rises; headache and delirium also occur; in this situation, prompt treatment is essential. The priority is to lower body temperature; remove clothing and cover the victim with a wet bed-sheet, while arranging transfer to hospital.

Hepatitis

Hepatitis is a viral infection of the liver. The illness itself consists of fever, chills, headache, followed by nausea, vomiting and jaundice; the liver becomes acutely inflamed with tenderness or pain in the upper-right portion of the abdomen. The illness can be relatively minor in some cases; in others, it may lead to liver failure, coma and death.

Hepatitis A is a disease of poor hygiene. It is commonest outside northern Europe, North America, Australasia and Japan, in warm climates. It is spread mainly by contaminated food and water; some foods, such as prawns and shellfish, are particularly likely to harbour the virus, so careful attention to food hygiene reduces the risk of catching the disease. Gammaglobulin injection provides protection for four to six months. Anyone who has spent long periods abroad may have acquired natural immunity to hepatitis A, and therefore may not need repeated injections of gammaglobulin for travel; a simple blood test for this can now spare those already immune from further unnecessary gammaglobulin injections.

Hepatitis B is spread in almost exactly the same ways as AIDS – sexually, by blood, and contaminated needles and medical or dental instruments. A safe vaccine is available, though it is an expensive one. It is currently used mainly to protect those at some special occupational risk, and people going abroad to live in high-risk areas.

Ice

Ice is only as safe as the water it is made from, and freezing itself does not kill germs. In places where the water supply is unsafe, don't use ice.

Injections

Hepatitis and AIDS are important hazards that are referred to elsewhere. Hepatitis B has occurred in numerous travellers who have received injections with contaminated needles and syringes, and the AIDS risk from this route of infection is also high. Disposable pre-sterilized needles and syringes are not widely available in many poor countries. If you are going abroad to live in one, or expect that you will need any other medication by injection (including dental anaesthesia) while you are away, you should either satisfy yourself that any needle or syringe used has been adequately sterilized (i.e. boiled for at least ten minutes) or you should take your own supply. Remember that if you have an accident when driving abroad, a blood test for alcohol may be compulsory – in Turkey, for example.

In the UK, needles and syringes are available without prescription at the discretion of a pharmacist. They are also available in kits that include other medical items, from MASTA, London School of Hygiene & Tropical Medicine, Keppel St, London WC1E 7HT Tel: (071) 631 4408; and from SAFA, 59 Hill St, Liverpool L8 5SA Tel: 051-708 0397. In the USA and most other countries, a prescription is necessary and a prescription should always be carried when travelling.

Insects

The sheer nuisance value of mosquito bites should alone be incentive enough to take careful precautions against them, but mosquitoes also spread disease: growing drug-resistance of the malarial parasite has lead to increased awareness of the importance of precautions against insect bites in preventing malaria, and careful precautions reduce the likelihood of insect-borne disease by a factor of ten.

Speculation about mosquitoes bearing AIDS is ill-founded, but malaria is by no means the only risk; there are many unpleasant insect-borne viral diseases for which there is neither a vaccine nor drug treatment, such as dengue fever, which occurs in Southeast Asia, Africa, the Caribbean and Latin America.

Mosquitoes bite especially around dusk, when it is important to wear long sleeves, trousers and socks. Apply a chemical repellent to clothes and exposed skin; diethyl-toluamide (DEET), hexane-diol and citronella are active ingredients to look for, available in sticks, sprays and gels. DEET can be used to impregnate clothing. In your hotel room use a spray insecticide early in the evening; if the room is not screened or air-conditioned, a smouldering mosquito coil, or a 'vaporizing mat' – its electronic equivalent – will release an otherwise harmless insecticidal vapour through the night.

Insurance

British travellers off to EEC countries should use leaflet SA30 (from the DHSS) to apply for form E111, giving proof of entitlement to free or reduced cost medical care; apply at least one month before you intend to travel. Additional medical insurance is always advisable, however, and should cover the cost of emergency repatriation by air ambulance if necessary. See the Holiday Insurance section on pp. 306–10.

Jellyfish

Jellyfish are common in the Mediterranean, and it is always worth asking local people if there are jellyfish about when you arrive at a resort. The sting produces a prickly sensation at first, going on to a raised, itchy, red rash that lasts four or five days. Fragments of tentacles should be removed promptly, and vinegar or lemon juice applied to inactivate any of the stinging capsules that may be left. Ice, calamine lotion, antihistamine tablets and paracetamol can be used to provide relief. Some types of jellyfish are dangerous and all should be treated with extreme caution whenever possible.

Jet Lag

Children generally adjust much faster than adults, and jet lag is not usually a problem for them. A mild sedative such as Phenergan may help re-establish sleep patterns.

Malaria

Last year over 2,250 people came back to Britain with malaria, the disease that kills more people worldwide than any other. Malaria occurs in over 100 countries and is spreading; so is resistance of the malarial parasite to conventional preventive drugs – chloroquine in particular. Increasing experience with alternative drugs revealed unacceptably high risks of toxic effects, so in countries with chloroquine-resistant malaria the most effective drugs now cannot be used.

All travellers to countries with malaria should take antimalarial tablets for the duration of their trip and for at least four weeks after leaving a malarial area; antimalarial drugs are not foolproof, and precautions against insect bites are also important to reduce the risk (see Insects). Malaria causes rapid deterioration and is potentially fatal; travellers to areas with resistant malaria should also now carry a treatment dose of antimalarial tablets with them at all times and take it if they develop a fever in circumstances where prompt medical care is not available. Advice on appropriate antimalarial drugs for the country you intend to visit is available from immunization centres; the Malaria Reference Laboratory (Tel: (071) 636 7921) can advise in case of particular difficulty.

Prickly Heat

True prickly heat is a sweat rash occurring on the sweatier parts of the body. The rash consists of tiny blisters on sore, reddened, mildly inflamed skin; prevent with frequent showers and keeping the skin clean and dry. Treat with calamine lotion.

Rabies

Dog bites are common even in the UK; abroad, the risks are higher. Rabies occurs in most parts of the world and is uniformly fatal. Only the following areas are free of rabies at present: Britain and Ireland, Scandinavian countries (including Iceland and Finland but excluding Denmark), peninsular Malaysia, Taiwan, Japan, the Pacific Islands, Antarctica, Australia and New Zealand. It is spread by licks and scratches from infected animals, not just bites, so never handle a stray or strange dog abroad.

In the event of a bite, prompt and thorough cleansing of the wound is most important; if rabies is a risk, make sure that safe new Human Diploid Cell vaccine is given – it is expensive and not always widely available; some British and US embassies abroad hold stocks, or may help you obtain it. Otherwise, return home at once – most insurance companies accept this as a valid reason for curtailing a holiday. Anyone travelling to remote places in countries with rabies should consider prior vaccination, which is safe and effective.

Return Home

A feature of malaria is a delay in onset of symptoms. In the UK many tragic deaths of returning travellers have occurred because the early symptoms of malaria – fever and headache – have been mistaken with those of 'flu; it is common for symptoms of malaria to be delayed perhaps for several weeks after return home. Symptoms of many other infectious and tropical diseases may also be much delayed, making diagnosis out of context much more difficult. If you or your children become unwell on return home, make sure your doctor knows that you have been abroad.

Stitches

Make sure that all needles to be used are sterile. Clean, gaping wounds can sometimes be held together with Steristrips, or similar adhesive tapes.

Sun

The British lobster look abroad is a familiar sight, but those who are more at home with the sun treat it with greater respect. Acute sunburn not only adds to the long term risk of cancer and premature ageing, but is a miserable way to begin a holiday and results in a blotchy, uneven tan. Anyone not interested in a tan should cover up and use a high protection factor sunscreen; if you want a tan, achieve it very slowly. Sunburn is especially cruel for children, whose skin is easily damaged, and to whom a tan is anyway of little interest; water-proof sunscreens, now produced by almost all of the leading manu-facturers, are more likely to provide effective protection.

Sunburn

Calamine lotion soothes affected areas and mild painkillers are often helpful. Stay out of the sun, or use a total block sunscreen, until the skin has healed.

Teeth

Make sure that all current dental problems have been attended to before departure with a dental check-up for all the family. Sugary drinks, sweets and ices become all the more tempting on holiday and in the heat. This temptation should be resisted – teeth are as vulner-able to decay abroad as they are at home. Make sure that water used for brushing teeth is safe – use bottled, boiled, or purified water if there is any doubt as to the safety of the local tap water.

Travel Sickness

Many different brands of travel sickness remedy are available, includ-ing Kwells and Stugeron, the latter causing less drowsiness than most other brands. The important thing with any remedy is to take it *before* travel – once vomiting starts, it will be useless.

Vaccinations

These fall into two categories, those that are an essential requirement of entry – usually to protect the country you intend to visit – and those recommended for your own personal protection. The full DHSS recommendations are given in DHSS leaflet SA35 (available free from social security offices and some travel agents; GPs and immunization centres can also provide this information, as well as the vaccinations themselves, although GPs do not provide vaccination against yellow fever). A full course of vaccinations for travel outside Europe may take up to two months, so it is as well to plan ahead.

Most European countries have no formal vaccination requirements. Protection against typhoid, polio, and possibly hepatitis, is often advised for travellers to the Mediterranean. And all travellers should be immunized against tetanus.

Vaccinations provide valuable protection against important diseases, but are no substitute for other health precautions and are never enough on their own.

Vomiting

Specific treatment of vomiting in food-poisoning is not generally advised or considered necessary unless symptoms are so severe that skilled medical treatment is required.

Water

When there is the least doubt about hygiene, only drink water that you know is safe. Don't drink tap water or brush your teeth with it, stick to bottled or canned drinks – well-known brands are safe, but have bottled mineral waters opened in your presence and regard all ice as unsafe. Alcohol does not sterilize a drink!

Purify water by boiling, or with chlorine or iodine. For the latter, add four drops of 2 per cent tincture of iodine (a standard solution, available from any pharmacy) to each litre of water and allow to stand for 20 minutes before drinking.

Section 7

Useful Addresses & Phone Numbers

AA: *see* Automobile Association

Aberdeen Airport
Dyce
Aberdeen
AB2 0DU
Tel: (0224) 722331

ABTA: *see* Association of British
Travel Agents

**Ainsworth's Homoeopathic
Pharmacy**
(Mail-order service available)
38 New Cavendish Street
London
W1M 7LH
Tel: (071) 935 5330

Air Travel Advisory Bureau
Morley House
320 Regent Street
London
W1R 5AE
Tel: (071) 636 5000
(*See also* Civil Aviation Authority)

Allergy Identification Tags: *see*
Medic-Alert Foundation

**Association of Breastfeeding
Mothers**
26 Homeshore Close
London
SE26 4TH
Tel: (081) 778 4769
(*See also* La Leche League)

**Association of British Travel
Agents** (ABTA)
55–57 Newman Street
London
W1P 4AH
Tel: (071) 637 2444
(*See also* Civil Aviation Authority)

**Association of Pleasure Craft
Operators**
35a High Street
Newport
Shropshire
TF10 8JW
Tel: (0952) 813572

**Association Régionale de Tourisme
Equestre** (Riding in France)
Domaine du Volcelest
33830 Joué Belin–Beliet
Tel: 010 33 56 88 02 68

Automobile Association (AA)
Fanum House
Basingstoke
Hants
RG21 2EA
Tel: (0256) 20123

Belfast Airport
Belfast
BT29 4AB
Tel: (08494) 22888

Birmingham International Airport
Birmingham
B26 3QJ
Tel: (021) 767 7145/6

Boats and Cruisers: *see* Association
of Pleasure Craft Operators; British
Waterways Board; Inland
Waterways Association

Books, cassettes and videos: *see*
CFL; Books for Children; The Red
House; Stanfords; Tapeworm;
Travel Bookshop Ltd

Books for Children
(Children's Bookshop)
97 Wandsworth Bridge Road
Fulham
London
SW6
Tel: (071) 384 1821

Bournemouth Airport
Christchurch
Dorset
BH23 6DB
Tel: (0202) 593939

Breastfeeding: *see* Association of
Breastfeeding Mothers; and La
Leche League

Bristol Airport
Bristol
BS19 3DY
Tel: (0275) 874441

British Airways Immunisation Unit
156 Regent Street
London
W1R 7HG
Tel: (071) 439 9584
(*See also* Thomas Cook Vaccination
Centre)

British Consulates *see* CFL.

**British Rail (Motorail
Reservations)**
Tel: (0345) 090700
Fax: (031) 557 4795

British Waterways Board
Melbury House
Melbury Terrace
London
NW1 6JX
Tel: (071) 262 6711
(*See also* Inland Waterways
Association)

Bus and Coach Services (UK): *see*
National Express

CAA: *see* Civil Aviation Authority

Cadw Welsh Historic Monuments
(For information on historic
monuments of Wales)
Admissions Officer
Brunel House
2 Fitzalan Road
Cardiff
Tel: (0222) 465511

Camping and Caravanning Club
Greenfields House
Westwood Way
Coventry
CV4 8JH
Tel: (0203) 694 995
(*See also* National Caravan Council)

Cardiff–Wales Airport
Nr Cardiff
South Glamorgan
CF6 9BD
Tel: (0446) 711111

CFL Vision
PO Box 35
Wetherby
West Yorkshire
LS23 7EX
Tel: (0937) 541010
('Get it right before you go . . . and
while you're there'. Catalogue
number UK 6178. Central Office of
Information produced VHS or
Betamax video, available on free
loan, giving information for
travellers on consular protection
overseas)

Civil Aviation Authority (CAA)
CAA House
45–59 Kingsway
London
WC2B 6TE
Tel: (071) 379 7311

Comité National de Sentiers de Grande Randonée
(Walking in France)
92 rue Clignancourt
75883 Paris
Cedéx 15
France

Consumers' Association
2 Marylebone Road
London
NW1 4DX
Tel: (071) 486 5544

Cork Airport
Kinsale Road
Cork
Eire
Tel: 010 353 21313131

Corona Society: *see* Women's Corona Society

Countryside Commission
John Dower House
Crescent Place
Cheltenham
Glos
GL50 3RA
Tel: (0242) 521381

Countryside Commission for Scotland
Battleby
Redgorton
Perth
PH1 3EW
Tel: (0738) 27921

Coventry Airport
Warwickshire
CV8 3AZ
Tel: (0203) 301717

Cyclists Touring Club
Cotteroll House
69 Meadrow
Godalming
Surrey
GU7 5HS
Tel: (04868) 7217

DER Travel Service
(Motorail bookings for Germany, Belgium and Austria)
18 Conduit Street
London
W1
Tel: (071) 408 0111

Dublin Airport
Co. Dublin
Eire
Tel: 010 353 1379900

East Midlands Airport
Castle Donnington
Derby
DE7 2SA
Tel: (0332) 810621

Edinburgh Airport
Edinburgh
EH12 9DN
Tel: (031) 333 1000

English Heritage
(For information on historic monuments in England)
Marketing Department
Keysign House
429 Oxford Street
London
W1R 2HD
Tel: (071) 973 3000

English Tourist Board
Thames Tower
Black's Road
Hammersmith
London
W6 9EL
Tel: (071) 846 9000

Europ Assistance
(Insurance)
Europ Assistance House
252 High Street
Croydon
Surrey
CR0 1NF
Tel: (081) 680 1234

Exeter Airport
Exeter
Devon
EX5 2BD
Tel: (0392) 67433

Gatwick Airport
West Sussex
RH6 0NP
Tel: (0293) 28822

Gingerbread
(Association for one-parent families;
groups nationwide)
35 Wellington Street
London
WC2E 7BN
Tel: (071) 240 0953

Gingerbread Services Ltd.
35 Wellington Street
London
WC2E 7BN
(Send S.A.E. for details of two
group holidays organized each year)
Tel: (071) 240 0953

Glasgow Airport
Paisley
PA3 2ST
Tel: (041) 887 1111/1807

Glasgow/Prestwick: *see* Prestwick

Guernsey Airport
La Villiaze
Forest
Guernsey
CI
Tel: (0481) 37766

Heathrow Airport
Hounslow
Middx
TW6 1JH
Tel: (081) 745 7702/4 (Terminal 1)
     (081) 745 7115/7 (Terminal 2)
     (081) 745 7412/4 (Terminal 3)
     (081) 745 4540 (Terminal 4)

**Historic buildings, monuments and
gardens:** *see* Cadw Welsh Historic
Monuments; English Heritage;
Historic Scotland; National Trust;
National Trust for Scotland

Historic Scotland
(Information on historic
monuments in Scotland)
Marketing and Visitor Services
20 Brandon Street
Edinburgh
EH3 5RA
Tel: (031) 244 3101

Holiday Care Service
(Holidays for single and lone
parents)
2 Old Bank Chambers
Station Road
Horley
Surrey
RH6 9HW
Tel: (0293) 774535

Homoeopathic Chemists with mail-
order service; *see* Ainsworth's
Homoeopathic Pharmacy

Horse Riding: *see* Association
Régionale de Tourisme Equestre

Humberside Airport
Kirmington
South Humberside
DN39 6YH
Tel: (0652) 688456

Immunisation: *see* British Airways Immunisation Unit; and Thomas Cook Vaccination Centre

Inland Waterways Association
114 Regent's Park Road
London
NW1 8UG
Tel: (071) 586 2510/2556
(*See also* Boats and Cruisers)

Insurance: *see* Europ Assistance

Intolerance to drugs: *see* Medic-Alert Foundation

Jersey Airport
St Peters
Jersey
JE1 1BY
Tel: (0534) 46111

Kent International Airport
PO Box 500
Manston
Kent
CT12 5BP
Tel: (0843) 823333

La Leche League
(Advice on breastfeeding)
BM 3424
London
WC1N 3XX
Tel: (071) 404 5011
(*See also* Association of Breastfeeding Mothers)

Leeds-Bradford Airport
Yeadon
Leeds
Tel: (0532) 509696

Liverpool Airport
Liverpool
L24 1YD
Tel: (051) 486 8877

London: *see* Gatwick, Heathrow, London City Airport & Stansted

London City Airport
King George V Dock
Silvertown
London
E16 2PX
Tel: (071) 474 5555

Luton International Airport
Luton
Bedfordshire
LU2 9LY
Tel: (0582) 405100

Medic-Alert Foundation
(Allergy identification bracelets and necklaces)
17 Bridge Wharf
156 Caledonian Road
London
N1 9UU
Tel: (071) 833 3034

Manchester Airport
Manchester
M22 5PA
Tel: (061) 489 3000

Motorail: *see* British Rail (Motorail Reservations); DER Travel Service

National Caravan Council
Catherine House
Victoria Road
Aldershot
Hants
GU11 1SS
Tel: (0252) 318251
(*See also* Camping and Caravanning Club)

National Express (Central East)
24 Manasty Road
Orton Southgate
Peterborough
PE2 0UP
Tel: (0733) 237141

National Express (Central West)
Spencer House
Digbeth
Birmingham
B5 6DQ
Tel: (021) 622 4373

National Express (North East)
Wellington Plaza
Wellington Street
Leeds 1
Tel: (0532) 460011

National Express (North West)
Coach Station
Chorlton Street
Manchester
M1 3JR
Tel: (061) 228 3881

National Express (South East)
164 Buckingham Palace Road
London
SW1
Tel: (071) 730 0202

National Trust
(Details for properties in England,
Wales & Ireland)
36 Queen Anne's Gate
London
SW1H 9AS
Tel: (071) 222 9251

National Trust for Scotland
5 Charlotte Square
Edinburgh
EH2 4DU
Tel: (031) 226 5922

Newcastle International Airport
Woolsington
Newcastle
NE13 8BZ
Tel: (091) 286 0966

Norwich Airport
Norwich
Norfolk
NR6 6JA
Tel: (0603) 411923

One-parent families: *see* SPLASH;
Gingerbread; Gingerbread Services
Ltd.; Holiday Care Service

Ordnance Survey
Romsey Road
Southampton
SO9 4DH
Tel: (0703) 792765

Prestwick Airport
Prestwick
Ayrshire
KA9 2PL
Tel: (0292) 79822

RAC: *see* Royal Automobile Club

Ramblers' Association
1–5 Wandsworth Road
London
SW8 2XX
Tel: (071) 582 6878

The Red House
(Children's Bookclub)
Red House Books Ltd
Cotswold Business Park
Witney
Oxford
OX8 5YF
Tel: (0993) 774171

Royal Automobile Club
Royal Automobile House
PO Box 100
7 Brighton Road
South Croydon
CR2 6XW
Tel: (081) 686 2525

Scottish Travel Centre
Scottish Tourist Board
23 Ravelston Terrace
Edinburgh
EH4 3EU
Tel: (031) 332 2433

Scottish Youth Hostels Association
7 Glebe Crescent
Stirling
FK8 2JA
Tel: (0786) 51181

Shannon Airport
Co. Clare
Eire
Tel: 010 353 6145556

Single Parents: *see* SPLASH;
Gingerbread; Gingerbread Services
Ltd.; Holiday Care Service

Ski Club of Great Britain
118 Eaton Square
London
SW1 W9AF
Tel: (071) 245 1033

Southampton Airport
Southampton
SO9 1RH
Tel: (0703) 629600

Southend Airport
Southend
Essex
SS2 6YF
Tel: (0702) 340201

SPLASH
(Holidays for single parents)
Empire House
Clarence Street
Swindon
Wilts
Tel: (0752) 674067

Stanfords
(Bookshop specializing in travel
books & atlases)
12–14 Long Acre
London
WC2E 9LP
Tel: (071) 836 1321

Stansted Airport
Stansted
Essex
CM24 8QW
Tel: (0279) 502379/502520

Tapeworm
(Stories on cassette)
32 Kingsway
London
SW14 7HS
Tel: (081) 878 9532

Teesside Airport
Darlington
Co. Durham
DL2 1LU
Tel: (0325) 332811

Thomas Cook Vaccination Centre
45 Berkeley Street
London
W1A 1EB
Tel: (071) 408 4157
(*See also* British Airways
Immunisation Unit)

Travel Bookshop Ltd
(Specialist bookshop)
13 Blenheim Crescent
London
W11 2EE
Tel: (071) 229 5260

Vaccination: *see* British Airways
Immunisation Unit; and Thomas
Cook Vaccination Centre

Wales Tourist Board
Brunel House
Cardiff
CF2 1UY
Tel: (0222) 499909

Walking and rambling: *see* Comité
National de Sentiers de Grande
Randonée; Countryside
Commission; Countryside
Commission for Scotland; Ordnance
Survey; Ramblers' Association;
Scottish Youth Hostels Association;
Youth Hostels Association

Women's Corona Society
(Aid to families moving abroad or
returning home)
Commonwealth House
18 Northumberland Avenue
London
WC2N 5BJ
Tel: (071) 839 7908

Youth Hostels Association
(England and Wales)
Trevelyan House
8 St Stephen's Hill
St Albans
Herts
AL1 2DY
Tel: (0727) 55215
(*See also* Scottish Youth Hostels
Association)

Section 8

International SOS

Introduction

We assume that you will be taking a standard phrase book with you and will therefore have the basics of the language to hand (guide to grammar, pronunciation etc.). But there are times when you will probably need a more specifically child-orientated vocabulary and would not expect to find the Spanish for teat, French for dummy or Italian for bib in your average Berlitz!

We have chosen the words in this section seeing two main uses: one so you can go to the chemist for minor ailments, such as antiseptic for insect bites; the other helps you ask the local people for children's needs, such as a baby-sitter or a cot. Major medical terms have been omitted on the assumption that if your child is very ill you will go straight to the experts.

French, German, Italian, Portuguese and Spanish are the languages given here as they are the ones generally in use at the popular holiday destinations.

	French	German
accident	accident (*m*)	Unfall (*m*)
allergy	allergie (*f*)	Allergie (*f*)
antibiotic	antibiotique (*m*)	Antibiotikum (*n*)
appetite	appétit (*m*)	Appetit (*m*)
arm	bras (*m*)	Arm (*m*)
asthma	asthme (*m*)	Asthma (*n*)
baby	bébé (*m/f*)	baby (*n*)
baby-sitter	garde d'enfant (*f*)	Babysitter (*m*)
bib	bavette (*f*)	Latz (*m*)
bites	piqûres (*f*)	Stiche (*m*)
bleed	saigner (*v*)	Blutung (*f*)
blister	ampoule (*f*)	Blasen (*f*)
boil	clou (*m*) abcès (*m*)	Furunkel (*m*)
bone	os (*m*)	Knochen (*m*)
breathe	respirer (*v*)	atmen (*v*)
bronchitis	bronchite (*f*)	Bronchitis (*f*)
bruise	bleu (*m*) meurtrissure (*f*)	Bluterguss (*m*)
burn	brûlure (*f*)	Verbrennung (*f*)
child	enfant (*m/f*)	Kind (*n*)
choke	étouffer (*v*)	erstickung (*v*)
cold	rhume (*f*)	Erkältung (*f*)
colic	colique (*f*)	Kolik (*f*)
constipation	constipation (*f*)	Vestopfung (*f*)
cot	lit d'enfant (*m*)	Kinderbett (*n*)

Italian	Portuguese	Spanish
incidente (*m*)	acident (*m*)	accidente (m)
allergia (*f*)	alergia (*f*)	alergia (*f*)
antibiotico (*m*)	antibiótico (*m*)	antibiotico (*m*)
appetito (*m*)	apetite (*m*)	apetito (*m*)
braccio (*m*)	braço (*m*)	brazo (*m*)
asma (*f*)	asma (*f*)	asma (*f*)
bambino (*m*)	bebê (*m*)	bebé (*m*)
babysitter (*m/f*)	babá (*f*)	canguro (*m*) cuidar para los niños (*m*)
bavaglino (*m*)	babador (*m*)	babero (*m*)
puntura (*f*)	mordida/picada (*f*)	mordiscos (*m*)
sanguinare (*v*)	sangrar (*v*)	sangrar (*v*)
pustola (*f*)	bolha (*f*)	ampolla (*f*)
foruncolo (*m*)	furunculo (*m*)	tumor (*m*)
osso (*m*)	osso (*f*)	hueso (*m*)
respirare (*v*)	respirar (*v*)	respirar (*v*)
bronchite (*f*)	bronquite (*f*)	bronquitis (*f*)
contusione (*f*)	machucads (*m*)	cardenal (*m*)
scottare (*v*)	queimadura (*f*)	quemadura (*f*)
ragazzo (*m*)	crianca (*f*)	niño (*m*)
strozzare (*v*)	sufocada (*v*)	atragantarse (*v*)
raffreddore (*m*)	frio (*f*)	resfriado (*m*)
colica (*f*)	cólica (*f*)	colico (*m*)
constipazione intestinale (*f*)	prisão de ventre (*f*)	estreñimiento
lettino (*m*)	berco (*m*)	cuna (*f*)

	French	**German**
dehydration	déshydration (f)	Dehydierung (f)
dentist	dentiste (m/f)	Zahnarzt (m)
diarrhoea	diarrhée (f)	Durchfall (m)
doctor	médecin (m)	Arzt (m)
drug	médicament (m)	Medizin (f)
dummy	sucette (f)	Schnuller (m)
ear	oreille (f)	Ohr (n)
earache	mal à l'oreille (m)	Ohrenschmerz (m)
electric shock	secousse électrique (f)	Elektroschock (m)
emergency	urgence (f)	Not (f)
eye	oeil (m) yeux (pl)	Auge (n)
faeces	selles (f) fèces (f)	Stuhl (m)
fainting	s'évanouir (v) evanouissement (m)	ohnmächtig werden (v)
fever	fièvre (f)	Fieber (n)
finger	doigt (m)	Finger (m)
food poisoning	intoxication alimentaire (f)	Vergiftung (f)
foot	pied (m)	Fuss (m)
frost-bite	gelure (f)	Erfrierung (f)
genitals	organs sexuels (m)	Genitalien (pl)
graze	eraflure (f)	Kratzung (m)
hand	main (f)	Hand (f)
head	tête (f)	Kopf (m)

Italian	Portuguese	Spanish
disidratazione (*f*)	desidratação (*f*)	deshidratación (*f*)
dentista (*m*)	dentista (*m/f*)	dentista (*m*)
diarrea (*f*)	diarréia (*f*)	diarrea (*f*)
dottore (*m*)	médico (*m/f*)	médico (*m*)
medicina (*f*)	remédio (*m*)	droga (*f*)
ciucciotto (*m*)	chupeta (*f*)	chupete (*m*)
orecchio (*m*)	ouvido (*m*)	oido (*m*)
mal d'orrechio (*m*)	dor de ouvido (*f*)	dolor de oido (*m*)
scossa elettrica (*f*)	choque eléctrico (*m*)	calambre (*m*)
emergenza (*f*)	emergência (*f*)	emergencia (*f*)
occhio (*m*)	olho (*m*)	ojo (*m*)
feci (*f*)	fezes (*f*)	excrementos (*m*)
svenire (*v*)	desmaiar (*v*)	desmayar (*v*) desmayo (*m*)
febbre (*f*)	febre (*f*)	fiebre (*f*)
dita (*f*)	dedo (*m*)	dedo (*m*)
intossicazione alimentari (*f*)	comida estragada (*f*)	envenenamiento (*m*)
piede (*m*)	pé (*m*)	pie (*m*)
congelamento (*m*)	ulceração produzida pelo frio (*f*)	congelación (*f*)
genitali (*m*)	genitais (*m*)	genitales (*m*)
scalfire (*v*)	arranhar esfolar (*v*)	rozar (*v*) rozadura (*f*)
mano (*f*)	haõ (*f*)	mano (*m*)
testa (*f*)	cabeça (*f*)	cabeza (*f*)

	French	German
heat stroke	coup de chaleur (*m*)	Hitzschlag (*m*)
high chair	chaise d'enfant (*f*)	Stuhl für Kind (*m*)
hospital	hôpital (*m*)	Krankenanstalt (*f*)
ill	malade (*adj*)	krank (*adj*)
infection	infection (*f*)	Ansteckung (*f*)
injection	piqûre (*f*)	Einspritzung (*f*)
knee	genou (*m*)	Knie (*n*)
leg	jambe (*f*)	Bein (*n*)
medicine	médicament (*m*)	Arzneimittel (*n*)
mouth	bouche (*f*)	Mund (*m*)
nap	somme (*m*)	Schlaf (*m*)
nappy	couche (à jeter) (*f*)	Windel (*f*)
neck	cou (*m*)	Hals (*m*)
nightmare	cauchemar (*m*)	Alptraum (*m*)
nose	nez (*m*)	Nase (*f*)
nose-bleed	saignement de nez (*m*)	Nasenblutung (*f*)
pain	douleur (*f*)	Schmerz (*m*)
play	jouer (*v*)	spiel (*v*)
potty	pot de chambre (*m*)	Topf (*m*)
pregnant	enceinte (*adj*)	schwanger (*adj*)
prescription	ordonnance (*f*)	Verschreibung (*f*)
pram	landau (*m*)	Kinderwagen (*m*)

Italian	Portuguese	Spanish
colpo di sole (*m*)	insolação (*f*)	insolación (*f*)
sedia da bambino (*f*)	cadeirá alta (*f*)	sillita de niño (*f*)
ospedale (*m*)	hospital (*m*)	hospital (*m*)
ammalato (*m*)	doente (*m/f*)	enfermo (*m*)
infezione (*f*)	infecção (*f*)	infección (*f*)
iniezione (*f*)	injeção (*f*)	inyección (*f*)
ginocchio (*m*)	soelho (*f*)	rodilla (*f*)
gamba (*f*)	perna (*f*)	pierna (*f*)
medicina (*f*)	remédio (*m*)	medicina (*f*)
bocca (*f*)	boca (*f*)	boca (*f*)
sonnino (*m*)	cochilo (*m*) dormida (*f*)	siesta (*f*)
pannolino (*m*)	fralda (*f*)	pañal (*m*)
collo (*m*)	pescoço (*m*)	cuello (*m*)
incubo (*m*)	pesadelo (*m*)	pesadilla (*f*)
naso (*m*)	nariz (*m*)	nariz (*m*)
sanguinare dal naso (*v*)	nariz sangranda (*m*)	hemorragia nasal (*f*)
dolore (*m*)	dor (*f*)	dolor (*m*)
giocare (*v*)	brincar (*v*)	jugar (*v*)
orinale (*m*)	pinico (*m*)	orinal (*m*)
incinta (*adj*)	grávida (*adj*)	embarazada (*adj*)
ricetta (*f*)	receita médica (*f*)	receta (*f*)
carrozzina (per bambini) (*f*)	carrinho de bebé (*m*)	cochecito de niño (*m*)

	French	German
skin	peau (*f*)	Haut (*f*)
shiver	frissonner (*v*)	zittern (*v*)
shock	choque (*m*)	Schock (*m*)
sore	avoir mal (*v*)	Wunde (*f*)
sterilize	stériliser (*v*)	sterilisieren (*v*)
sting	piqûre (*f*)	Stich (*m*)
stomach	estomac (*m*)	Magen (*m*)
stitches	agrafes (*f*)	Stich (*m*)
sunburn	coup de soleil (*m*)	Sonnenbrand (*m*)
sweat	suer (*v*)	schwitzen (*v*)
swelling	enflure (*f*)	Schwellung (*m*)
teat	tétine (*f*)	Schnuller (*m*)
temperature	température (*f*)	Temperatur (f)
teeth	dents (*f*)	Zähne (*f*)
tired	fatigué (*adj*)	müde (*adj*)
throat	gorge (*f*)	Hals (*m*)
toe	orteil (*m*)	Zeh (*m*)
toothache	mal de dent (*m*)	Zahnschmerz (*m*)
toys	jouets (*m*)	Spielzeug (*n*)
urine	urine (*f*)	Urin (*m*)
vaccination	vaccination (*f*)	Impfung (*f*)
vomit	vomir (*v*)	brechen (*v*)

(*m*) = masculine   (*f*) = feminine   (*v*) = verb   (*adj*) = adjective

indefinite articles:	indefinite articles:
(*m*) un	(*m*) ein
(*f*) une	(*f*) eine (*n*) ein

Italian	Portuguese	Spanish
pelle (f)	pele (f)	piel (m)
tremare (v)	calafrio/tremedeira (v)	temblar (v)
schock (m)	choque (m)	susto (m)
piaga (f)	inflamação (f)	llaga (f)
sterilizare (v)	esterelizar (v)	esterilizar (v)
puntura (f)	picada (f)	picadura (f)
stomaco (m)	estômago (m)	estómago (m)
punti (m)	pontos (m)	puntos (m)
scottatura (f)	queimadura de sol (f)	quemadura de sol (f)
sudare (v)	suor (v)	sudar (v)
rigonfiamento (m)	inchação (f)	hinchazón (f)
ciuccio (m)	bico de seio (m)	tetina (f)
temperatura (f)	êle tem febre	temperatura (f)
denti (m)	dentes (m)	dientes (m)
stanco (adj)	cansado (adj)	cansado (adj)
gola (f)	garganta (f)	garganta (f)
dito (m)	dedo do pé (m)	dedo del pie (m)
mal di dente (m)	dor de dente (m)	dolor de muelas (m)
gioccattoli (m)	brinquedos (m)	juguetes (m)
orina (f)	urina (f)	orina (f)
vaccinazione (f)	vacina (f)	vacuna (f)
vomitaire (v)	vomitar (v)	vomitar (v)

(m) = masculine   **(f) = feminine**   **(v) = verb**   **(adj) = adjective**

indefinite articles:	indefinite articles:	indefinite articles:
(m) un, uno	**(m) um, umos**	**(m) un, unos**
(f) una, un	**(f) uma, umas**	**(f) una, unas**

Index

Index

Companies shown in CAPITAL LETTERS are featured in Section 2 of this book.

A COTTAGE IN THE COUNTRY, 145
A.A.T. KINGS AND AUSTRALIAN PACIFIC TOURS, 221
ABERCROMBIE & KENT TRAVEL, 221
Aberdeen Airport, 357
accidents, 339
ACTIVITY TRAVEL, 232
ADVENTURE CRUISERS, 129
AER LINGUS HOLIDAYS, 183
AFRICA BOUND HOLIDAYS, 221
AIDS, 342, 348, 349
Ainsworth's Homoeopathic Pharmacy, 357
air travel, 313–5, 318, 325, 340
Air Travel Advisory Bureau, 357
Air Traveller's Code, 315
airlines, 277–80
AIRLINK HOLIDAYS, 183
airports, 267–77
AIRTOURS PLC, 184
Albania, 4–5
ALBANY TRAVEL, 184
allergy, 340
ALLEZ FRANCE, 141
ALLSUN HOLIDAYS, 184
ALPINE TOURS, 232
AMARO COTTAGE HOLIDAYS, 141
animal bites, 340
antibiotic treatment, 346
antibiotics, 341
Antigua, 106–8
antihistamines, 341
antimalarial tablets, 350
AQUASUN HOLIDAYS, 184
ARCTIC EXPERIENCE LTD, 185
ARIES HOLIDAYS, 185
Association of Breastfeeding Mothers, 357

Association of British Travel Agents (ABTA), 357
Association of Pleasure Craft Operators, 357
Association Régionale de Tourisme Equestre (Riding in France), 357
ATLANTIC COAST CARAVAN PARK, 121
AULTBEA HIGHLAND LODGES, 141
Australia, 6–7
AUSTRAVEL, 185
Austria, 8–9
AUSTRIAN FEDERAL RAILWAYS, 212
AUTO PLAN HOLIDAYS LTD, 249
Automobile Association (AA), 357
AVIS, 134

baby wipes, 288
baby-listening, 317
baby-sitting, 317, 335
backpack, 288, 336
BALES TOURS LTD, 222
BALKAN HOLIDAYS, 185, 233
Barbados, 106–8
BARROWFIELD HOTEL, 171
BATH HOLIDAY HOMES, 142
BEACH CAMPER, 121
BEACH VILLAS, 249
BEARSPORTS OUTDOOR CENTRES, 243
BECKS HOLIDAYS, 121
bee stings, 341
Belfast Airport, 357
BELGIAN NATIONAL RAILWAYS, 213
BELGIAN TRAVEL SERVICE, 186
Belgium, 10–11
BELLE FRANCE, 163
BELL-INGRAM SELF-CATERING HOLIDAYS, 142

BEST HOLIDAYS, 186
BEVERLEY PARK HOLIDAYS, 171
BI LINE, 281
BI LINE UK LTD, 142
Birmingham International Airport, 357
BLADON LINES, 233
BLAKES COUNTRY COTTAGES, 142
BLAKES HOLIDAYS, 129
BLAKES VILLAS, 249
blisters, 342
BLISWORTH TUNNEL BOATS LTD, 130
blood transfusion, 342
bookclubs (children), 362
books, 288
books for children, 358
bookshops, 362, 363
boredom, 287, 295–300, 318–9
BOSHAM SAILING, 228
bottle-feeding, 314
Bournemouth Airport, 358
BOWHILL'S, 143
Brazil, 12–13
breastfeeding, 319–20, 322, 342, 357, 360
BRIDGEWATER BOATS, 130
BRIDGEWAY TRAVEL SERVICES LTD, 249
BRIGGS HOLIDAY HOMES, 171
Bristol Airport, 358
Britain, 13–17
British Airways Immunisation Unit, 358
BRITISH CHANNEL ISLAND FERRIES, 281
British Consulates, 309
BRITISH RAIL (BR), 213
British Rail (Motorail Reservations), 358
British Waterways Board, 358
BRITTANY CARAVAN HIRE, 121
BRITTANY DIRECT HOLIDAYS, 143
BRITTANY FERRIES, 281
BRITTANY FERRIES GITES HOLIDAYS, 143
BRITTANY FERRY HOLIDAYS, 186
BRITTANY VILLAS, 250
buggy, 293
Bulgaria, 17–18
BUTLINS HOLIDAY WORLDS AND HOTELS, 171
BUTTERFIELD'S INDIAN RAILWAY TOURS, 222

CAA, 353
CABERVANS, 122

Cadw Welsh Historic Monuments, 358
Camping and Caravanning Club, 358
camping, caravan sites and mobile homes, 119
Canada, 19–21
canal holidays, 128
Canaries, 85–6
CANVAS HOLIDAYS LTD, 122
CAPRICE HOLIDAYS LTD, 187
car rental, 133
Cardiff–Wales Airport, 358
CAREFREE CAMPING LTD, 122
CARIBBEAN CONNECTION, 187
CARIBBEAN VILLAS, 250
CARISMA HOLIDAYS LTD, 123
carrycots, 293, 313
CASAS CANTABRICAS, 143
CASTAWAYS, 187
CELEBRITY HOLIDAYS & TRAVEL, 187
CELTIK HOLIDAYS, 188
CENTER PARC, 172
CERBID'S QUALITY COTTAGES, 144
CHANDRIS LTD, 159
CHAPTER TRAVEL, 250
CHARACTER COTTAGES LTD, 144
CHATEAU WELCOME, 250
child-minding, 335
China, 21–3
CHINESE RAILWAYS, 214
C.I.E. TOURS INTERNATIONAL, 188
CITALIA, 188
Civil Aviation Authority (CAA), 358
CLANSMAN MONARCH HOLIDAYS, 137
CLAYMOORE NAVIGATION LTD, 130
clothes and clothing, 288, 320–21, 326
CLUB CANTABRICA, 189
CLUB MEDITERRANEE, 172, 189
Coach Transport and Coach Tours, 136
COAST AND COUNTRY HOLIDAYS, 144
COASTAL COTTAGES OF PEMBROKESHIRE, 144
cold climates, 321, 343
colds, 343
Comité National de Sentiers de Grande Randonée, 359
constipation, 343
Consumers' Association, 359
contraception, 343
CORFU A LA CARTE, 251
Cork Airport, 359
CORNISH TRADITIONAL COTTAGES LTD, 144
CORONA HOLIDAYS, 251

CORSAIR CRUISERS LTD, 131
CORTON BEACH HOLIDAY VILLAGE, 173
COSMOSAIR, 137
COSTA LINE CRUISES, 159
COTTAGE HOLIDAYS, 144
cottages, gîtes and farmhouses, 140
COTTER COACH LINE, 137
COUNTRY HOLIDAYS, 145
COUNTRY SERVICES, 145
Countryside Commission, 359
Countryside Commission for Scotland, 359
COUNTRYSIDE COTTAGES, 145
COUNTRYWIDE HOLIDAYS, 243
COURTLANDS CENTRE, 243
Coventry Airport, 359
creeping eruption, 344
cruises, 158
CTC LINES, 159
CUENDET ITALIA, 251
CUNARD, 160
CV TRAVEL, 251
Cycling, 162
CYCLING FOR SOFTIES, 163
Cyclists Touring Club, 359
CYCLORAMA HOLIDAYS, 163
CYPRAIR HOLIDAYS, 190
Cyprus, 24–5

DALES HOLIDAY COTTAGES, 145
DANISH STATE RAILWAYS (DSB), 214
DAVID NEWMAN'S EUROPEAN COLLECTION, 152, 196
DAVIES AND NEWMAN TRAVEL LTD, 190
dehydration, 322, 344
delays, 316
Denmark, 25–7
dental problems, 352
DER Travel Service, 359
DHSS, 353
diarrhoea, 343, 344, 346, 347
DIEPPE FERRIES HOLIDAYS, 146
disabled travellers, 202, 209, 224, 253, 307
DISCOVER BRITAIN HOLIDAYS, 145
dogs, 345
DOMINIQUE'S VILLAS, 252
drink, 288
driving abroad, 328
drugs, 345
Dublin Airport, 359

DUNAIRD CABINS, 146
dysentery, 346

earache, 346
ears, 346
East Midlands Airport, 359
ECOSAFARIS, 222
Edinburgh Airport, 359
Egypt, 27–9
EGYPTIAN ENCOUNTER, 223
Eire, 29–30
ENFANTS CORDIALES, 233
England, 13–17
ENGLISH COUNTRY COTTAGES LTD, 146
English Heritage, 359
English Tourist Board, 359
ENTERPRISE, 234, 252
ENTERPRISE SUMMERSUN, 190
EQUITY CRUISES, 160
EURO HOTEL, 173
EUROCAMP TRAVEL LTD, 123
EURODOLLAR RENT A CAR LTD, 135
EUROJET, 166
Europ Assistance, 360
EUROPCAR UK LTD, 134
EVAN EVANS TOURS, 137
Exeter Airport, 360
E111 (form), 326, 327, 349

FALCON FAMILY HOLIDAYS, 191
FARM AND COTTAGE HOLIDAYS, 147
FELINDRE, 147
FERMANAGH LAKELAND, 147
ferries, 280–84, 323
fever, 344, 346
FINLANDIA TRAVEL, 191
FINNCHALET HOLIDAYS LTD, 147
first-aid kits, 346
FLAMINGO LAND HOLIDAY VILLAGE, 173
FLORIDA HOME OWNERS' ASSOCIATION, 252
Fly/drive, 165
food, 287, 314
food safety, 347
FOREST HOLIDAYS, 148
FRAMES RICKARDS, 137
France, 31–4
FRANCOPHILE HOLIDAYS, 148
FRED OLSEN TRAVEL, 198
FREEDOM HOLIDAYS LTD, 148
FRENCH AFFAIR, 148

FRENCH COUNTRY CRUISES, 131
FRENCH COUNTY COTTAGES, 148
French Government Tourist Office, 34
FRENCH LIFE, 149
FRENCH RAILWAYS (SNCF), 214
FRENCH VILLA CENTRE, 253

GAER COTTAGES, 149
Gatwick Airport, 360
German National Tourist Office, 35
Germany, 34–5
Gingerbread, 360
Gingerbread Services Ltd., 360
GITES DE FRANCE LTD, 149
Glasgow Airport, 360
GLOBAL HOLIDAYS, 253
GLOBEPOST TRAVEL SERVICES, 223
Goa, 40
GOLDEN GATEWAYS, 192
GOODFELLOW HOLIDAYS LTD, 124
GORDON HOLIDAY COTTAGES, 149
GOZO HOLIDAYS LTD, 192
Greece, 36–7
GREEK ISLANDS CLUB, 253
GREEK ISLANDS SAILING CLUB, 228
GREYHOUND WORLD TRAVEL, 138
Guernsey Airport, 360

HALSEY VILLAS, 253
hand luggage, 292
HAVEN FRANCE AND SPAIN, 124
HAVEN HOLIDAYS, 124
HAYWOOD COTTAGE HOLIDAYS, 149
health care abroad, 326–7
heat rash, 322
heat stroke, 347
HEATHERWOOD PARK, 150
Heathrow Airport, 360
HELLENIC RAILWAYS ORGANIZATION
  (OSE), 214
hepatitis, 348, 353
hepatitis A, 348
hepatitis B, 348
HERTZ (UK) LTD, 135
HF HOLIDAYS LTD, 263
HIGHLIFE VALUE BREAKS, 192
Historic Scotland, 360
HIV, 342
HOBURNE HOLIDAYS, 174
Holiday Care Service, 360
holiday centres, 170
HOLIDAY CLUB PONTIN'S, 174
HOLIDAY COTTAGES, 150

HOLIDAY HOUSES DUMFRIES AND
  GALLOWAY, 150
HOLIDAY SCANDINAVIA LTD, 150
HOLIDAYS IN LAKELAND, 150
HOLIMARINE, 124
Holland, 69–71
HOME FROM HOME, 151
home-swapping, 180
homoeopathic medicine, 324, 357
Hong Kong, 38–9
Hong Kong Tourist Association, 39
HORIZON HOLIDAYS, 192, 234
HORIZON VILLAS AND APARTMENTS,
  254
HORNING PLEASURECRAFT LTD, 131
HOSEASONS HOLIDAYS LTD, 131, 151
hot climates, 322
HOTEL BOAT HOLIDAYS LTD, 132
hotel holidays, 182
HOVERSPEED, 281
Humberside Airport, 360

ice, 348
ILIOS ISLAND HOLIDAYS LTD, 254
immunisation, 341, 358, 363
India, 40–42
Indian Government Tourist Office, 41
INDIA RAIL, 215
in-flight entertainment, 314
INGHAMS TRAVEL, 193, 234
injections, 348
Inland Waterways Association, 361
insects and repellents, 322–3, 349
INSIDE TRACK, 244
insurance, 306–10, 349
INTASUN FLY/DRIVE, 166
INTASUN HOLIDAYS, 193
INTASUN SKISCENE, 235
INTERHOME, 235, 254
International Driving Permit, 328
INTERVAC INTERNATIONAL HOUSE
  EXCHANGE SERVICE, 181
INTOURIST TRAVEL LTD, 193
IRISH RAIL, 215
ISLAND HOLIDAYS, 194
ISLE OF MAN STEAM PACKET COMPANY
  LTD, 281
Israel, 42–4
Israel Government Tourist Offices, 43
ISRAEL RAILWAYS, 215
ITALIAN STATE RAILWAYS (CIT), 215
Italy, 44–8

JALTOUR, 223
Jamaica, 48–50
Japan, 50–52
JAPAN RAILWAYS (JR), 215
JASMIN TOURS LTD, 223
jellyfish, 350
JENNY MAY HOLIDAYS, 195
Jersey Airport, 361
JERSEY GATEWAY, 194
jet lag, 350
JET TOURS AND FRENCH TRAVEL
    SERVICE, 194
JETSAVE, 166
JETSAVE HOLIDAYS, 194
JETSET TOURS, 224
JOHN FOWLER HOLIDAYS, 174
Jordan, 52–4
JUBILEE HOLIDAYS, 195
JUST FRANCE, 151
JUST PEDALLING, 164

Kashmir, 40
Kent International Airport, 361
Kenya, 54–6
KILMINORTH FARM, 151
KOSMAR VILLA HOLIDAYS, 254
KUONI TRAVEL, 224

LA COLLINETTE HOTEL, 172
LA FRANCE DES VILLAGES, 152, 255
La Leche League, 361
LADBROKE HOLIDAYS, 175
LAKELAND EXPERIENCE HOLIDAYS,
    244
LANCASTER HOLIDAYS, 195
LANCASTER UNIVERSITY SUMMER
    PROGRAMME, 244
landing, 293
LANTEGLOS HOTEL AND VILLAS, 175
LASKARINA HOLIDAYS, 255
Leeds-Bradford Airport, 361
LES PROPRIETAIRES DE L'OUEST, 154
Liverpool Airport, 361
London City Airport, 361
long-haul travel, 325–6
LORNE LEADER, 228
LUNIGIANA HOLIDAYS, 255
Luton International Airport, 361

MACKAY/S AGENCY, 152
MADE TO MEASURE HOLIDAYS, 228,
    235
MAGIC OF ITALY, 166, 255

MAGIC OF SPAIN 256
Majorca, 86–8
malaria, 346, 350, 351
Malaria Reference Laboratory, 351
MALAYAN RAILWAYS (KTM), 216
Malaysia, 57–8
Malta, 58–60
Manchester Airport, 361
MANN/S HOLIDAYS, 152
MANOS HOLIDAYS, 195
MARK WARNER HOLIDAYS, 209
MATTHEWS HOLIDAYS, 125
Mauritius, 60–62
MEDALLION HOLIDAYS, 196
Medic-Alert Foundation, 361
medicines, 346
MELIA TRAVEL, 224
meningitis, 346
MEON VILLA HOLIDAYS, 256
MERIDIAN HOLIDAYS, 196
METAK HOLIDAYS, 196
Mexico, 62–5
MILKBERE HOLIDAYS, 152
MILL ON THE BRUE, 244
MILLFIELD VILLAGE OF EDUCATION,
    245
mineral waters, 353
MINORCA SAILING HOLIDAYS, 229
MOROCCAN RAILWAYS, 216
Morocco, 65–6
mosquitoes, 322, 349
mother and baby facilities, 291, 292, 294,
    316
Motorail, 327
Motorail Reservations, 358
motoring, 328–9
MOUNT HOLIDAY PARK, THE, 125
MULTITOURS, 196
MUNDI COLOR HOLIDAYS, 167

nappies, 315, 326, 329–30
National Caravan Council, 361
National Express, 362
NATIONAL EXPRESS LTD, 138
National Trust, 362
National Tourist Office of Greece, 37
NATIONAL TRUST FOR SCOTLAND, 152,
    362
NATURIST HOLIDAYS, 245
needles, 349
NEILSON SKI, 236
Nepal, 67–8
Netherlands, The, 69–71

NETHERLANDS RAILWAYS, 216
Nevis, 106–8
New Zealand, 71–3
NEW ZEALAND RAILWAYS
    CORPORATION, 217
Newcastle International Airport, 362
NIVERNAIS CRUISERS LTD, 132
NORTH NORFOLK HOLIDAY
    HOMES, 153
NORTH SEA FERRIES, 282
NORTH SEA FERRIES HOLIDAYS, 197
NORTH WALES HOLIDAY COTTAGES
    AND FARMHOUSES, 153
Northern Ireland, 29–30
NORTHUMBRIA HORSE HOLIDAYS, 245
NORTHWEST FLY/DRIVE USA, 167
Norway, 74–5
NORWAY LINE, 282
NORWEGIAN STATE RAILWAYS, 217
NORWEGIAN STATE RAILWAYS TRAVEL
    BUREAU, 197
Norwich Airport, 362

OLAU HOLIDAYS, 197
OLAU-LINE, 282
Olympic Airways, 37
OLYMPIC HOLIDAYS, 198
one-parent families, 196, 208, 359
Ordnance Survey, 336, 362
OWNERS HOLIDAY LETTING
    CONSORTIUM, 153

P & O CRUISES, 160
P & O EUROPEAN FERRIES 282
P & O SCOTTISH FERRIES, 283
P & O TRAVEL, 224
PAB TRAVEL, 199
PACIFIC CONNECTION, 199
PAGE & MOY, 199
PALMER & PARKER, 256
PAN AM HOLIDAYS, 167, 199
PANORAMA HOLIDAY GROUP LTD, 200
passports, 332
PEAK AND MOORLAND FARM
    HOLIDAYS, 153
PEEBLES HOTEL HYDRO, 176
PEREGOR TRAVEL, 167
PERRYMEAD PROPERTIES, 256
personal stereo, 288, 293
PERUVIAN RAILWAYS, 217
PGL FAMILY ADVENTURE, 245
PHILIPPINE RAILWAYS, 217
Philippines, The, 75–6

Pill, the, 343
P&O EUROPEAN FERRIES, 198
polio, 353
PONTINS, 176
PORTLAND HOLIDAYS, 200
Portugal, 77–8
PORTUGUESE PROPERTY BUREAU LTD,
    THE, 257
POUNDSTRETCHER FLIGHTS –
    WORDLWIDE, 200
POUNDSTRETCHER FLY/DRIVE, 168
POUNDSTRETCHER USA HOLIDAYS, 200
POWELL/S HOLIDAY COTTAGES, 154
pregnancy, 342
pre-sterilized, 349
PRESTON TRAVEL, 201
Prestwick Airport, 362
prickly heat, 351
PULLMAN HOLIDAYS, 201
pushchairs, 313

QUALITY COTTAGES, 154
QUO VADIS LTD, 201

rabies, 340, 351
RADFORDS COUNTRY HOTEL, 176
rail travel, 211
RAILWAYS OF AUSTRALIA, 212
Ramblers' Association, 362
RAMBLERS HOLIDAYS LTD, 263
reading, 291, 295–300
RECOMMENDED HOLIDAY COTTAGES,
    154
Red House, The, 362
REGENT HOLIDAYS (UK) LTD, 225
RENDEZVOUS FRANCE, 154
renting accommodation, 301–305
return home, 351
ROCKLEY POINT SAILING SCHOOL, 229
ROMANIAN RAILWAYS, 217
ROMANY CARAVAN HOLIDAYS, 125
Royal Automobile Club, 362
rubbish, 291, 292
RYAN TOURIST GROUP, THE, 201

safaris, treks and exotic tours, 220
sailing, 227
SALLY HOLIDAYS, 202, 257
SALLY LINE, 283
Saudi Arabia, 79–80
SAUNTON SANDS HOTEL, THE, 176
SAVOY COUNTRY CLUB, 177
SA35 (form), 353

SCANDINAVIAN SEAWAYS, 202, 283
SCANSCAPE HOLIDAYS, 200
SCILLONIA HOLIDAYS, 202
Scotland, 13–17
SCOTTISH SKIING, 236
Scottish Travel Centre, 363
Scottish Youth Hostels Association, 363
SEALINK, 283
SEALINK HOLIDAYS, 155, 178, 203
seasickness, 323
SEASUN HOLIDAYS LTD, 126
SECRET SPAIN, 155
sedatives, 315, 350
SELECT HOLIDAYS, 257
self-catering accommodation, 335
self-drive holidays, 328
SEYMOUR HOTELS AND HOLIDAYS, 203
S.F.V. HOLIDAYS, 155
SHAMROCK COTTAGES, 155
Shannon Airport, 363
SHAW'S HOLIDAYS, 156
Sicily, 46–7, 46–8
sightseeing, 334
SILK CUT FARAWAY HOLIDAYS, 225
SIMOLDA LTD, 132
SIMPLY SIMON HOLIDAYS, 203
SIMPLY TURKEY, 258
Singapore, 57–8
single parent familes, 202, 227, 253, 307, 360, 362
SKI CHAMOIS, 236
Ski Club of Great Britain, 363
SKI ESPRIT, 203, 237
SKI FALCON, 237
SKI RED GUIDE HOLIDAYS, 237
SKI SUPERTRAVEL, 237
SKI THOMSON, 238
SKI WEST, 238
SKI WHIZZ LTD, 239
SKIATHOS TRAVEL, 258
skiing, 231, 335
SKI-VAL LTD, 238
SKIWORLD, 239
skycots, 313
SKYTOURS LTD, 204
SLIPAWAY HOLIDAYS, 258
SOLAIRE INTERNATIONAL HOLIDAYS, 126
SONATA LEISURE LTD, 138
South Africa, 81–3
Southampton Airport, 363
Southend Airport, 363
Spain, 83–8

SPANISH RAILWAYS (RENFE), 218
special interest and activity holidays, 242
SPEEDBIRD HOLIDAYS, 225
SPLASH, 363
Stanfords, 363
Stansted, 277
Stansted Airport, 363
Stansted Airport Ltd, 277
STARVILLAS LTD, 258
STATE RAILWAY OF THAILAND, 219
STATTON CREBER, 156
STEEPWEST HOLIDAYS LTD., 204
stitches, 352
stories on tape, 362
SUMMER COTTAGES LTD, 156
sun, 352
SUN BLESSED HOLIDAYS, 204
SUN TOTAL, 259
sunburn, 352
SUNDOWN MARINE YACHT CHARTER LTD, 229
SUNMED, 239
SUNMED HOLIDAYS, 205
SUNSAIL, 229
sunscreen, 352
SUNSELECT VILLAS, 259
SUNSPOT TOURS LTD, 205
SUNVIL TRAVEL, 205
SUNVISTA HOLIDAYS LTD, 156
SUPERBREAK MINI-HOLIDAYS LTD, 205
SUPERTRAVEL LTD, 240
SUSSEX BEACH HOLIDAY VILLAGE, 178
SWANSEA CORK FERRIES, 283, 284
sweat rash, 351
Sweden, 88–9
SWEDISH STATE RAILWAYS (SJ), 218
SWISS FEDERAL RAILWAYS, 218
SWISS SKI, 240
Switzerland, 90–1
syringes, 349

TABER HOLIDAYS, 206
take-off, 293
tap water, 353
tapeworm, 363
TAUNTON SUMMER SCHOOL, 246
Teesside Airport, 363
teeth, 352
Thailand, 91–3
THOMAS COOK FARAWAY HOLIDAYS, 222
Thomas Cook Vaccination Centre, 363
THOMSON HOLIDAYS, 206, 259

TIME OFF LTD, 206
tissues, 288
TJAEREBORG LTD, 207
toys and games, 287, 289, 293
Travel Bookshop Ltd, 363
travel sickness, 290, 352
TRAVELBAG, 225
travel-cots, 335
travelling by air, 292
travelling by car, 290, 318, 321
travelling by coach, 294, 319
travelling by ferry, 293
travelling by train, 291, 319
TRAVELSCENE LTD, 207
TREBLE B HOLIDAY CENTRE, 126
TRUST HOUSE FORTE PLC, 207
Tunisia, 93–5
TUNISIAN RAILWAYS, 219
Turkey, 96–9
TWA FLY/DRIVE, 168
TWELVE ISLANDS, 208
TWICKERS WORLD, 226
typhoid, 353

UK airport facilities, 267–77
UK CHINA TRAVEL SERVICE, 226
UK EXPRESS, 208
ULEY CARRIAGE HIRE, 127
UNIJET, 168
United Kingdom, 13–17
United States, 100–4
US AIR FLY/DRIVE, 168
US RAIL (AMTRAK), 219
USSR, 104–6

VACANCES, 156
VACANCES EN CAMPAGNE/VACANZE IN
    ITALIA, 156
vaccinations, 353
VARMLAND HOLIDAYS, 246
VAUXHALL HOLIDAY PARK, 178

VFB HOLIDAYS, 246
VFB HOLIDAYS LTD, 157, 208
VIKING AFLOAT, 132
VIKKI OSBORNE, 198
VILLA MATCH, 260
villas and apartments, 248
VILLAS ITALIA, 260
VIRGIN HOLIDAYS LTD, 209
vomiting, 344, 353
VOYAGES JULES VERNE, 226

Wales, 13–17
Wales Tourist Board, 364
walking holidays, 262, 336
WALLACE ARNOLD, 139
WARNER HOLIDAYS, 179
water, 352, 353
WAVES HOLIDAYS, 209
WELCOME CARAVAN COMPANY, 127
WELSH HOLIDAYS, 157
WELSH WAYFARING HOLIDAYS, 263
West Indies, 106–8
WESTENTS LTD, 127
WINDERMERE LAKE DISTRICT
    HOLIDAYS, 157
WINTER-INN, INNTRAVEL, 210
WINTERWORLD, 240, 260
Women's Corona Society, 364
WORLDWIDE CARS LTD, 135
WORLDWIDE HOME EXCHANGE CLUB,
    181

YACHTCLUB CHARTER COMPANY LTD,
    230
YMCA NATIONAL CENTRE, 247
Youth Hostels Association, 364
YUGOSLAV RAILWAYS, 219
Yugoslavia, 108–10
YUGOTOURS LTD, 210

Zimbabwe, 110–12